an odd boy

Doc Togden

Aro Books WORLDWIDE

2017

Aro Books WORLDWIDE
PO Box 111, Aro Khalding Tsang,
5 Court Close, Cardiff,
CF14 1JR, Wales, UK

© 2017 by Doc Togden

All rights reserved. No part of this book may be reproduced in any form or by any means electronic or mechanical, including photocopying, recording, or by any information storage and retrieval system, without permission in writing from the publisher.

First Edition 2017

ISBN: 978-1-898185-42-0 (paperback)

ISBN: 978-1-898185-43-7 (hardback)

ISBN: 978-1-898185-44-4 (ePub)

http://aro-books-worldwide.org/

odd dedications

*To my wife Caroline Togden; to my son Robert E Lee Togden and my daughter Ræchel Renate Tresise Togden;
to my mother Renate, father Jesse, and brother Græham.*

To the lads: Steve Bruce; Ron Larkin; Jack Hackman.

Also to John and Pauline Trevelyan; Rodney Stillwell Love; Clive and Betty Bruce; Ernest Preece; Michael and Sandra Blenkinsopp; John Morris; Dereck and Susan Crowe; and all my marvellous mentors.

To Don and Hillie Young – and to all my comrades-in-arms and guitars; to the heroines of Art who have flittered—like fairies or valkyries— through my life, to show me the shine on the passing moment.

Contents

odd acknowledgements	*vii*
Introduction – *Don Young*	*ix*
the final curtain call: *an odd preface*	*xv*
part five – *kind-hearted women blues*	3
1 squirrel-toothed alice	5
2 bower ashton – you know the 60s are over don't you?	27
3 bower ashton – au'voir leonardo	49
4 bower ashton – apostate apostles in white	75
5 bower ashton – a room with a view	95
6 bower ashton – going to a funeral, dressed in white	127
7 bower ashton – hippie is dead	151
8 bower ashton – primal scream	169
9 bower ashton – almost a giraffe-hide greatcoat	195
10 bower ashton – heroines of art	211
11 bower ashton – the earl of groan	233
12 bower ashton – speaking with ravens	255
13 bower ashton – silk blancmange rottweiler	285
14 bower ashton – waterloo sunset	297
15 bower ashton – you 'girls' are quite the sensation	315
16 bower ashton – a woeful ballad made to his mistress' eyebrow	341
17 bower ashton – don't think twice . . . it's alright	357
18 ain't no djinn called alegbara	383
19 traintime's almost here	403
part six – *welcome home*	431
1 renate schubert	433
2 the rooms above nowhere	453
3 born under a glad sign	477

odd acknowledgements

I am lucky in having too many people to thank. In the past I have often made the mistake of trying to thank everyone – but that's no great service to anyone reading this book. I shall therefore keep it short and apologise to the myriad marvellous people I could have mentioned. I would like to thank:

My wonderful wife Caroline for unending patience with an *odd husband* who lived in a parallel reality whilst writing *an odd boy*.

My irreplaceable son Robert who enjoyed the stories of my life, He encouraged me to re-make the DEBIL – the bizarre imitation resonator guitar I made in 1967. It was crushed by an articulated lorry back in 1970 – and, when Robert heard that he said *"Dad! You've got to make another one! You can't just let that go!"* I remade it, thanks to Robert and to Miles Henderson-Smith, the luthier who made it possible. I wish Robert was alive to see, hear, and play it himself. Robert died of cancer at the age of 17 – in 2013. I have not re-written the final chapter of this book in the light of our loss – because I would rather leave Robert alive as he was when I wrote that chapter. No one ever dies as long as our love for them does not die. I can still see him now and enjoy my memories of the fun we had together. He was a better guitarist and musician than I will ever be.

When Marpa and Dag'mèdma's son Dar-ma Dodé *(dar ma mDo sDe)* died, they wept bitterly. Their disciples gathered and asked *"You told us that the world is only illusion – so … if that is the case, why are you crying brokenheartedly over your son's death?"* to which Marpa replied *"Yes—I did say that—everything is illusory … but the death of my son is a vast illusion – and, at the moment, I cannot bear the vastness of that illusion."*

My dear friend Don Young who did so much more for me than make my cherished NATIONAL RESOPHONIC 12-string guitars. Don's tragic death in 2016 left the world poorer. He was a genuinely good, kind and generous human being. Don was a man with vision – and a vision that made my teenage dreams of a 12-string NATIONAL a reality. It was a privilege to have known him.

gZa'tsal, who took a morass of riotously random information and turned it inside out. The original 170,000 word essay on the Arts—on which this book was based—was an idiosyncratic stream-of-consciousness informational harangue. It was peppered with hilarity, bizarre incidents, haphazard anecdotes, and whimsical personal accounts – and few would have had the patience to read it. gZa'tsal took this misbegotten mangrove of miscellanies and defined its narrative skeleton.

Dé-zér who contributed vastly to the musical references – as well as teaching me some mighty fine bass riffs.

Métsal for assiduous proofreading and valuable suggestions.

Nor'dzin and 'ö-Dzin for final proofing of the text and for pushing the extravaganza forward into the domain of published reality.

My old school friend Lindsay Berry née Goolding, who graciously provided suggestions, valuable insights into the historical odd boy, and information on events and dates pertaining to Netherfield School.

Græham and Jill Smith—last but not least—for hospitality, humanity, and hilarity in times of adversity. Græham is my brother and my friend.

introduction

Don Young

Co-founder of NATIONAL RESOPHONIC *Guitars*
transcribed and edited from tape

Let me tell you about Doc Togden. Really, this should be a movie where Doc rides in with his sun-bleached linen horse-coat flapping in the wind and his wide-brimmed hat pulled down low over his eyes. There'd be that slide guitar and harp like John Hammond plays in the *Little Big Man* – that movie with Dustin Hoffman. That's the first impression I had of Doc – that he'd walked out of a movie.

Anyhow, Doc was there, around pretty much from when I started NATIONAL RESOPHONIC GUITARS with McGregor Gaines in 1989. First I knew about him was, some Englishman wanted a 12-string RESOLECTRIC. We didn't make one at the time – that must have been about 1991. In fact, we didn't make any 12-string guitars at all at that time. So big thanks for that, Doc.

A year or so later another order came through for a 12 string TRICONE and I wondered if this was the same Englishman. I'd still not met Doc. Anyhow, with the first two 12-strings we made for him, we had to improvise tailpieces. Since then we make 12-string guitars as part of our line and have NATIONAL RESOPHONIC 12-string tailpieces for them. Now, I offered to exchange the improvised tailpieces on Doc's first two guitars with NATIONAL tailpieces – but he said he wanted to keep them exactly as we made them "… *because it's history, and history is important.*" That's one of the many things I like about Doc.

He's a kindly, soft-spoken, gentle-mannered eccentric. Now, I've met a lot of eccentrics. I've met a lot of egomaniacs too – and you can't often tell them apart. But Doc's never had anything to prove. He's a genuinely humble, sincere, and generous-spirited guy. I'll say more about that later. I'm not a writer so this thing isn't going to run in a straight line, alright. I'll just talk as the ideas come. I could talk for hours about Doc and his ideas and our collaborations on guitar design. Doc just has so many ideas; a lot of real good ones – and one or two plumb crazy ones. The craziest was putting a whammy bar[1] on a TRICONE – but he let me talk him out of that.

Doc's a real gentleman—and the politest man I've ever known—so he didn't mind me telling him it wouldn't work. He respects other people's knowledge and skill. I thought, when I first met him, that he was one of those English Dukes or Earls. He's so refined—and has that kind of aristocratic look—but then that 'poker face' of his often breaks out into a big smile and a huge laugh. Doc has a great sense of humour. He's always coming out of left-field with some kind of line that could have come from Monty Python. He has a rare kind of genius and a unique imagination. Doc's idea at the moment is to make a resonator version of the GIBSON ES355 and we're working on that at the moment – figuring out a way to shape the steel with an 'English Wheel'.[2] Doc's also thinking about an 8-string bass version of the RESOLECTRIC – set up like a 12-string with octave strings.

It's hard to remember just when Doc and I became friends – because there was never any clear point when he was no longer 'just a customer'.

---

1   Tremelo arm. There are tremelo arms for acoustic guitars but no one makes one for a 12 string – for good reason.
2   Device for shaping metal

I don't think Doc was ever 'just a customer' – and I don't think Doc ever saw NATIONAL as 'just a guitar company'. Doc always showed such interest in NATIONAL, that it was as if he had shares or something – but he just loves NATIONALS as much as I do. At first I thought Doc was a Country musician because of his Western hat and clothes – but he turned out to be a Bluesman on guitar – and a very fine harp player too. I asked Doc once how he planned to sing on top of a 12-string resonator – because 12-strings are louder than 6-strings and resonator guitars are loud anyway. So Doc said "*Like this.*"

And just sang '*Sitting on Top of the World*' for me—right there in the factory—and when he was done I had to peel people off the walls. I never imagined such a quietly spoken guy could boom like Big Bill Broonzy. It turned out that Big Bill Broonzy had been Doc's inspiration at the age of eight. That wasn't the last time I heard Doc sing either – because that happened whenever he came down to visit, which was twice a year and he always came to dinner with me and Hillie and we'd have the greatest time singing songs and telling stories and laughing. There'd always be a couple of students with Doc and they'd be musicians too – like Seng-gé who went on to order a cutaway TRICONE. Doc always had questions to ask about NATIONALS. He's real interested in the history and manufacturing techniques – stuff that otherwise doesn't interest people. That's when we got to talking about the DEBIL – the NATIONAL he tried to make as a 15-year-old in 1967. Doc never lets up on an idea – he's the most single-minded determined guy I've ever met – and that comes out in *an odd boy*. He explains how he made the DEBIL in Volume I and how he used these *ferrotype diaphragms* from WWII British Army field telephones. Wild stuff – and I could just see him playing that thing in pubs like a little white Son House singing '*Big leg mamma – get your big leg over me.*'

It's always surprising that his English accent disappears when he sings Blues.

But Doc's a dark horse. It was a few years before I found out he was Ngak'chang Rinpoche – a Buddhist Lama with students 'round the world. I thought he played gigs for a living – but he'd not done that since he was a teenager. He was the vocalist and harp player with the Savage Cabbage Blues Band – but he also played a low-tuned back up bass, which was his idea. I never heard of a two-bass band anywhere else – but I can see how that could work really well with a high-tuned bass playing lead-bass alongside a lead guitarist. Doc's ideas on music and musical instruments could fill a book on their own.

So anyhow, I found out Doc was a Buddhist Lama when he started making visits to NATIONAL with small groups of young people for tours of the NATIONAL Factory in San Louis Obsipo. They all treated Doc like the boss – but it was subtle and you could miss it. I only saw it because I'm curious. They obviously respected him – but he only ever acted like he was just one of them. I asked them how they knew each other and that's when it came out. Doc never tried to hide anything – he just wasn't out to blow any trumpet about it. After that I addressed my letters to Doc / Rinpoche – because I thought it was right to do that. A lot of things made sense after that – because I could see his love of *everything he loved* was spiritual in a way I don't have the words to describe. I could see that NATIONALS were sacred to him – and that everything he admired was sacred. It seems most things are sacred if you can see it. He's going to teach me about that and about meditation one day, when we both have more time.

As well as being a Buddhist Lama and musician, Doc's a poet, an artist, and a man who can ride a horse and shoot a .500 Linebaugh.

It takes a steady nerve to shoot a revolver like that. We share a love of Old West firearms and knives and Doc has a fine collection. Last year he brought me back a Gurkha kukri knife from Nepal.

So anyway, Doc's an interesting man. Knows a deal about unexpected subjects, like: American history and facts about Native American culture; and the Old West with all that history with Doc Holiday and the Earp brothers in Tombstone; and Old Delta Blues; and Papa Legba at the crossroads on Highway 61 – and how he rode his bike naked to the crossroads back in England when he was only 12 years old; and about how Blues got started in Chicago, and Shakespeare and English literature and poetry; and Indian Classical Music and instruments with sympathetic strings. And that's another idea Doc has: a quad-cone 18-string with sympathetic strings and a jiwari-bridge [3] that works as a mechanical effect that allows you to get that sitar sound when you want it. That'll take some believing when we make that monster.

I'll get down to Doc's books now – because that's what I'm supposed to be talking about. Doc's Buddhist books are pretty deep and make you think, but his memoirs are deep too – in a different way. Doc's memoirs are a great read but there's an awful lot of life packed between the covers. Doc's seen some things and lived through some crazy times that most people only ever hear about. He was there in the 60s and experienced all that scene – but it never made him crazy. He sometimes *had his foot to the floor* and he sometimes got in over his head – but he always kept his head and always came through.

---

3   A jiwari bridge is common to Hindustani classical musical instrument. It has a gradually sloping bone bridge that causes the string to buzz.

You have to admire that. How he wrote those psychedelic lyrics without ever doing the psychedelics is a mystery to me. I asked him about it and he just smiled and said "*I'm just psychedelic by nature.*" At Art School he was a surrealist painter and illustrator – and his paintings of ravens always hit me sideways. It seems he could have been a well-known artist—he could also have been a well-known poet—but being a Buddhist Lama turned out to be more important to him.

There's such honesty and integrity in *an odd boy* – and you feel as if you've been there yourself and seen every scene. Some parts of Doc's life were quite like mine – but some are the stuff of legends. Doc is legendary – a legend in his own time. No doubt about it.

No one's going to forget Doc Togden or Ngak'chang Rinpoche in any hurry. There's just too much of the guy in so many ways – but he's never been showy. I'd say you could pass him on the street and not notice him – but that's not true. He's the snappiest dresser you're likely to meet – but definitely not fashionable. Doc has a fashion all of his own. I once asked Doc if he ever dressed casually and he told me '… *that's something I tend to avoid even on holiday.*'

I could say a lot more about Doc and about his *odd boy* books – but it's better you read them. If you read Doc's books—all four volumes—you'll find a world you didn't expect to find. Doc's the real hero of a real story that tells you that you can be a real hero too. Doc's telling you that you can be an artist – that anyone can be an artist. Doc's telling you that life is art if you work at it – and that everything in your life can be art – all you have to do is plunge in. That's enough from me.

Don Young

the final curtain call: *an odd preface*

So … how does a story end? I'm still alive as I write these words in January 2017 – but my son Robert died of cancer in 2013 at the age of 17. It seemed then, that my story came to an end – but time has passed, and my life continues. The story of *life-and-lives* has no beginning or end.

Robert lives on in this book – and I speak of him as he was at the time I wrote the text. There's no need to change what was written in 2005. For those who are interested to know about Robert, there is THE BOOK OF ROBERT[1] – an anthology of images and fleeting impressions. One of these impressions came from his friend Jon, who recalls Robert calling back to his downhill-cycling companions *"Remember! No brakes! No Fear!"* And he never had any fear. He had no fear of life – and he had no fear of death. Being with him—with my wife Caroline—during his final six months, is one of the most profound experiences of my life. Robert's final words were *"Kèlpa Zang."* That is a Tibetan Buddhist phrase, which means 'we are happy.' It is a drinking toast a little like the Yiddish toast *'L'Chaim – Here's to life.'*

When Dar-ma Dodé[2] died, his parents Marpa[3] and Dag'mèd-ma wept bitterly. Their disciples gathered and asked *"You told us 'the world is illusion' – so why are you crying, broken-hearted over your son's death?"* Marpa replied *"Yes—I did say 'everything is illusory' … but the death of my son is a vast illusion – and, at the moment, I cannot bear the vastness of that illusion."*

---

1 The Book of Robert—ARO BOOKS Worldwide—2014
2 Dar-ma Dodé (*dar ma mDo sDe*)
3 Marpa was the teacher of the renowned Tibetan yogi, Milarépa.

Don Young—proprietor of NATIONAL RESOPHONIC GUITARS [4]—cried when he heard of Robert's death. He was a good friend. Robert was to have worked at NATIONAL in his Summer holiday between school and university – but that was not to be. I shed tears at Don's sudden death in June last year. Don lives on in the final chapter of this book – and in the 12-string guitars he made for me. He was a kind, generous, humorous, and brilliant man – and like so many I have known, he *was one of a kind*. The final 12-string guitar Don made for me is a steel bodied TRICONE with a '6-string width' electric neck. Don was keen that I had a signature model – and had DOC TOGDEN set in mother-of-pearl as each of the fret markers.

So, here's to the end – and to the beginning. Here's to the beginning of the end – and the end of the beginning. A good story has no end – or rather, its end is simply a reshuffled beginning: an open space into which we all move. I could have extended *an odd boy*. I could have written a fifth volume – but *an odd boy* ends where it ended when I finished writing the first draft, in 2005.

The first three volumes of *an odd boy* chronicle my life from the age of 5 to 20. During this period, my fascination with painting, poetry, and music, pirouetted against vignettes of romance that became increasingly creatively vital.

VOLUME ONE of *an odd boy* contains Part I—*the crossroads*—which takes me from the conservative '50s into the turbulently intriguing '60s. I lose my first love—a beautiful *færie of Art*—at the age of 7 – but she left me with a lifelong love of painting, music, and poetry.

---

4   NATIONAL RESOPHONIC was founded in 1989 by Don Young and McGregor Gaines, in a Californian garage. They measured old resonator guitars, and built new models under the 'NATIONAL RESOPHONIC' brand and trade mark, as used originally by the NATIONAL STRING INSTRUMENT CORPORATION for the resonator instruments. In 1990, the factory was moved to San Luis Obispo, California.

There'd been beatniks in Farnham in the '50s and early '60s but their culture was covert. I watched them avidly for signs of what I might become – but they were not exactly available for discussion with *an odd boy* who was little more than a child. By the time the iconic year 1967 arrived I'd been amorously abducted by a Swiss au pair girl—eight years my senior—and seriously seduced by Blues. I made the DEBIL – a home innovated resophonic guitar and taught myself lap-slide. My best friend from junior school, Steve Bruce, was a fine bass player and introduced me to Ron Larkin, a world-class guitarist at the age of 14. We formed a Blues band called Savage Cabbage and hit the road as often as we dared.

VOLUME TWO of *an odd boy* contains Part II and Part III. Part II—*hellhound on my trail*—chronicles my final two years of school as a mirage of amazement. I lose Lindie Dale, the second great love of my life. Savage Cabbage is gaining a serious reputation around Art Schools, Universities, and pub-clubs. We warm up for Rory Gallagher's Taste, the Groundhogs, and the Edgar Broughton Blues Band. We get the prime spot at Colonel Barefoot's Rock Garden [6] after a series of successful second acts – but, as the world is preparing to welcome the replacement for Cream,[7] life performs a somersault.

Part III of an odd boy—*living on solid air*—sees me alone, having lost Lindie Dale. Steve and Ron die, each under tragic circumstances – and I'm left to try to make my way as a solo Delta Bluesman playing the DEBIL. Without my friends however, I'm strictly mediocre. As a vocalist I'm a force to be reckoned with – but on guitar I'm little more than a goodtime chord-twanger.

---

6   *Colonel Barefoot's Rock Garden* was a Victorian-built concert hall on Eel Pie Island, Twickenham, London.

7   Cream—the Blues band comprised Jack Bruce, Eric Clapton, and Ginger Baker —disbanded in November 1968.

I give an acclaimed performance at the Farnham Blues Festival and warm up for Jo Ann Kelly, Ian Anderson's Country Blues Band, Brett Marvin and the Thunderbolts, and Mike Cooper. I spend an evening with John Martyn who is kind enough to offer encouragement. The British Blues Boom is over. It dies with Jimi Hendrix. Blues gives way to Progressive Rock – which eventually becomes Heavy Metal. To many, this shift is welcome – but not to *an odd boy*.

Volume Three of *an odd boy* contains Part IV—*when you got a good friend*—in which I find myself at Farnham Art School. Life spins the roulette wheel and I land next to the riotous Helen Mcgillvray whose passion for painting was matched by her passion for life – and, for a while, her passion for me. Poetry and painting oscillate with a welter of ideas and endless conversation. I meet Roger McGough and Adrian Henri who give valuable advice on poetry. I fail to understand the need to specialise in terms of Art. I grow in the belief that *the Arts* cannot be divided. Helen fails to appreciate why I cannot specialise – and, the end of the Foundation Year marks the parting of our ways. I take to the road again and experience a flurry of brief amorous liaisons. I flutter through a blizzard of chance encounters which end with the Debil being crushed under the wheels of an articulated lorry. I see *the writing on the road* – and realise my life as a public Blues performer is over.

Volume Four contains Part V and Part VI of *an odd boy*. Part V —*kind-hearted women*—chronicles my time at Bristol Art School under the inspired mentorship of Derek Crowe. I commence a romantic liaison with Claudette Gascoigne and share a house with her three friends. I embrace the gestalt of illustrator and produce the 'Speaking With Ravens' series of oil paintings in my spare time.

The lost time is over – and, one-by-one, old friends slip-slide away into compromised suburban safety. I become the weird werewolf of the past who still writes poetry – *still crazy after all these years*. After all these years? From 1966 to 1972 is a short span of time – but for me, it's an entire life. By 1973 I realise that *the lost time* was a fashion as much as a reality – and as the fashion fades the reality becomes increasingly rare. In September 1975 I leave for the Himalayas having made certain decisions that change my life irredeemably.

Part VI—*welcome home*—moves ahead thirty years to 2005 and sees me *more-or-less* as I am today: having understood enough about life to find delight in the sense fields as my raison d'être. The four volumes together are the story of a love affair with the Arts from 1957 to 1975 – from the age of 5 to 23. The lens of the narrative focuses on 1966 to 1972 but the lens is mounted on a time travel *camera-of-the-senses* built between 2005 and 2007. The love affair never ended however. It continues today as marvellously as it ever did. It includes my wife Caroline, my daughter Ræchel,[8] and our memories of Robert.

98.6% of the narrative reflects core events of the past – as I remember them. I chose this percentage because 98.6 Fahrenheit is *blood temperature* – and this adventure concerns the lifeblood of my appreciation. History speaks for itself—through each individual—so there's no need to objectify space and time, as if I'd alighted upon some principle Einstein missed. I have no way of giving an exact percentage as to historical accuracy – apart from 'a sliding scale from here-to-there'. The past and future are *what we make of them* – in the present. This is the only time we have.

I don't think the human mind can comprehend the past and the future. They are both just illusions that can manipulate you with thinking there's some kind of change. Bob Dylan

---

8   Ræchel Renate Tresise Togden was born in 2003.

Life is legendary. We only remember what is meaningful. What is meaningful is always poetic – and what is poetic is always *larger than life*. Historians seem bent on robbing the past of the poetry of its larger than life characters – but the quality of our humanity is the poorer without them. Some people wish to rob their own lives of *larger than life content*—the *poetry* of what they are—but whether the robbery is perpetrated in the name of psychotherapy, arithmetic, or iron-clad fact, there's no ecstasy in rational reductionist prose. As Shakespeare has Prospero exclaim in The Tempest '*We are such stuff as dreams are made of* …' So let us all be the heroes and heroines of our own stories and let us all admire the heroic in everyone we poetically encounter. I'd rather see individuals as glorious stars in the firmament; according to whatever life-theme they follow – and according to the enthusiasm of those for whom they shine.

The Artists I mention are those I've relished. The Arts mentioned are those that ignited my appreciation. Naturally, I compare and contrast – and when I do so, some people look finer than others. That's inevitable.

In the end it's meaningless to argue the relativity of subjective judgements. I'd have no one take *my* word that *Jill* was more talented than *Jack*. I have reasons for my qualitative judgements of the Arts – but they're entirely subjective. Let those who share my subjectivity rejoice in it. Let those whom it offends, forgive my foibles. To this end—to re-phrase *English Bob* from Clint Eastwood's movie 'The Unforgiven'—I shall *trust to the goodwill of humanity and the forbearance of reptiles*.

an odd boy

part five

september 1972 – september 1975

kind-hearted women blues

"Once I was checking into a hotel and a couple saw my ring with Blues on it. They said 'You play Blues – that music is so sad.' I gave them tickets to the show and they came up afterwards and said 'You didn't play—one—sad song.'" Buddy Guy

"I don't want to be in some big beautiful place that nobody wants me, because I play Blues" Luther Allison

1

the first year: september 1972

bower ashton – squirrel-toothed alice

Bristol—like Rome—is built on seven hills ... and in some ways I'd crossed the Rubicon.[1] Blues lay on one side and an illustration degree lay on the other. By the time I got to Bristol a fair few issues were resolved. I hadn't really chewed the fat with myself. The issues had simply resolved themselves—in my mind—in a similar manner to the way in which gossamer changes in colour: it drifts on the wind, taking on the colours of the landscape.

I hadn't struggled with feelings—although feelings there'd been in plenty—but decisions had made themselves. I simply let the shapes of my mind move – without attempting to control what happened. On the ride down, ideas came into an uncodified focus that felt slightly exciting – yet stable. Riding a motorcycle is marvellous for thought-free musing. The open roads of the early '70s inspired undirected lateral reflection – open-ended contemplation. They always availed me of formless certainty – if, I allowed it. I'd taken the country roads. I took them in order to have a leisurely ride, in which I could de-construe and dis-interpret my life as I'd known it.

I stopped off here and there to take refreshment in whatever small country towns seemed pleasant. No one was awaiting my arrival, so there was no hurry.

---

1 The Rubicon is a shallow river 50 miles in length – running from the Apennine Mountains to the Adriatic Sea through the southern Emilia-Romagna, between the Rimini and Cesena. 'Crossing the Rubicon' is an expression which means passing the point of no return. It refers to the army of Julius Caesar crossing the Rubicon River in 49 BC. This was considered an act of insurrection.

I'd ridden down two months earlier and found myself a bedsit[2] in Chesterfield, St Andrews. It wasn't where I *wanted* to be. It was a little too far away from where I imagined everything would be happening – but I couldn't afford Clifton and could find nowhere available in Redland.

Brawny tea fermented from the brine of science and walnut stockings; / From the antler hipped hurrah which divulges necessity according to salvaged piano heroism; / Garrulous garter-snake – the belt of graceful giddiness interrupting profusion of nascent elegance. / Naked plunge that shatters surface tension – eclectic pools of softly elastic personal eccentricity. / Brassier bravado—shimmering belly innuendo—impressible wit in diverse yet contiguous segments, / Improbability condensation yawns with insatiable sympathetic metaphors – courting spectacular synapses in Chesterfield Road. The Author—Chesterfield Road—1972

I arrived a fortnight[3] shy of the commencement of the Autumn term in order to explore Bristol on my own. I think the idea came from what Helen had done when she'd gone to Edinburgh. It was a good idea even though I hadn't enjoyed how the idea had affected me at the time. I had no regrets there at all – in fact, I was sure that Helen had made the right decision; on my behalf as well as hers.

So there I was … in Bristol. I wanted to acclimatise to the solitary quality that I thought would characterise my life 'til such time as I made good close friends within the Art School. I'd got used to being solitary in India and Nepal the previous year and felt that a fortnight alone would be useful in building a necessary sense of independence in the city.

---

2 Equivalent to a studio apartment in the USA.
3 A fortnight is two weeks in British English.

Knowing where the art supply shops were located was important – as was knowing where the interesting shops were lurking. I also needed to know where I could obtain good coffee. I'd set aside money to buy books, as I wanted to catch up on modern American literature – especially the material which had flooded out of the '60s.

I wondered what it would be like being in a 'single subject department' rather than being with students from every Art discipline. They were sure to be interesting people—dedicated people—effused with their various histories of creativity. They'd have landed in Bristol from all over the country. I wondered—off and on—if I'd meet someone like Juliet. Someone with the independence and freedom of Helen Mcgillvray – and the personality and intelligence of Lindie Dale. I was in no tearing hurry to plunge into a relationship – but it occurred to me that it would be wonderful—at some point—to find a partner who'd want to share my life as much as I wanted to share hers. 'til then however, I'd find like-minded friends.

I wanted to converse with as many people as possible and find out what was on everyone's minds. I wanted to find out whether an epoch actually *had* ended or not. The famous 'Hippie is dead' statement had been made in '67 – after the 'Summer of Love.' That was already in a previous decade – but five years had passed since then. 'Hippie' didn't look dead to me when I was with Savage Cabbage and it looked fairly lively during the academic year '70 – '71. From the middle of '71 and into '72 'Hippie' seemed to be ailing. Now at the waning of '72, I started hearing its death rattle. Mostly I tended to think that I was not grieving the demise of 'Hippie' – but that I was concerned about a more *generalised retraction* from the ambience of colourful creative excitement I'd enjoyed.

an odd boy

Something that ought to have been expanding, appeared to be shrinking. I wouldn't miss the bare feet, patchouli oil, and reek of sweet Indian incense. I'd miss the attendant attributes of vividness that were departing with them. I never wanted to be a hippie – but now that 'Hippie' was disappearing, I started to identify with what I'd never found attractive. I had a perverse sense of wanting to shout out *'I'm Spartacus! Please haul me off to gaol—anything—but don't let it all just die!'*

After such moments of gross sentimentality, I'd try to re-think the issue. Maybe the major truncation I sensed was simply the next evolution. Maybe it was a trend towards greater seriousness on the part of those who'd dedicated themselves to the Arts. There'd been so many ideas and I was eager to leap into the fray. I wanted to find out what was going on – and where everything was going. I knew that the pulse would be *right there* in the Art School. It would be in the conversation and the evenings shared with like-minded people.

After a day or two of sauntering—*here, there, and everywhere* 'round Clifton—I found myself having wandered down closer to the city centre. Park Street looked interesting. It boasted an unusual number of bookshops. *George's* was an old established bookshop that I'd frequent for the next three years – and just opposite was another book shop called *Chapter and Verse* which specialised in poetry, plays, and modern avant garde literature. I was delighted that such a shop existed. A book caught my eye immediately as I approached the window and I went in to enquire about it. The book was 'Trout Fishing in America.'[4]

---

4   Trout Fishing in America—published in 1967—by Richard Brautigan [1935 – 1984]

The cover photograph had no connection with any kind of fishing and I was amused by the surrealism of the word-image non sequitur.

Gazing from the cover, were a late 1960s couple looking vaguely late 1860s. The man—Richard Brautigan—was wearing almost what I wear today: waistcoat and western hat. He had a fine moustache. The woman—in bustle-free black Victoriana—was intriguing. I remember her to this day. The photograph was an image that spoke volumes—not informationally—but in terms of emotional texture. It purveyed some aspect of the gestalt that I'd felt was slipping away.

I was taken with the cover of the book – and the power of imagery. *This* – was Illustration. A book cover and an album sleeve were ways of speaking with the world that excited me. I'd just been personally addressed by Richard Brautigan's book. I felt I'd been told that a way of life I loved was still valid – and, that it still existed somewhere. I was going to buy that book and tumble into it. I entered the shop, strode right up to the counter – and there *she* was! The very lady from the book cover – right there in front of me! Maybe it wasn't her – but she looked as like her as I could've imagined. She had that Squirrel-toothed Alice [5] look about her. Was it her? I felt a little perplexed. In all likelihood it *wasn't* her – but the shock of seeing someone so much like her had momentarily stunned me. I must have been standing there gaping at her wide eyed, because she laughed – and, in what sounded like an American West Coast accent, asked "*Yes – and, can I help you?*"

In something of a daze, I replied "*Richard Brautigan—Trout Fishing in America—I'd like to buy a copy if I may.*"

---

5   Squirrel-toothed Alice was a Montana rodeo rider of the early 1900s.

an odd boy

She continued to grin at me "*Yes you may. You*—do—*know, it's*—*not*—*about trout fishing?*"

"*Yes*" I laughed "*I didn't realise I dressed*—quite—*so much like a trout fisher.*"

"*Well … where I come from …you just never*—can—*tell.*"

"*Must be an interesting place.*"

"*Yeah …*" she shrugged "*Like most I guess.*"

"*Bristol seems interesting – d'you like it here?*"

"*I like it well enough for now*" she smiled.

"*Maybe I could improve it …?*"

"*You're a character*" she giggled "*How would you propose to do that?*"

"*By asking whether you're doing anything this evening? I don't know restaurants in Bristol yet – but maybe you know somewhere … decorous?*" I'd never done a thing like that before – but the words were out of my mouth before I could think better of the insanity of it.

"*Well …y'know … that*—is—*very sweet of you – but I just don't think my husband would warm to the idea*—too—*much.*"

That *was* one of the possibilities when you launched in like that. "*Right … of course … Sorry.*" I apologised profusely.

"*No apology necessary*" she grinned in a kindly way "*Besides, I like your style …you're a charming man – and three years ago … well … but it's*—no—*problem … However … might I suggest his*—other—*book 'In Watermelon Sugar' – I think the two are something of a pair.*"

"*Well yes …*" I replied "*I imagine two of a wide variety of pleasant items would be*—something—*of a pair …*" I was still gazing at her in rapt wonder.

"*Touché*" she laughed "*I'll … wrap them then?*"

"*Yes—yes please—I'll take both.*"

"*Without looking at it first?*" she enquired.

"*Yes ... I'll go for most things ... apart from the querulous quotidianism* [6] *of quadrumvirates.*[7] *Besides ... I need some new reading.*"

"*You really are a—character*" she said, laughing at my horrendous alliteration. It served however, to establish my sense of dignity – having been so recently romantically declined. "*Have fun now – I think you'll enjoy 'In Watermelon Sugar'. The inBoil at iDeath scenario*[8] *is pretty crazy – but I think it's right up your street.*"

"*Think you're right – where d'you come from by the way?*"

"*Can't you tell?*" she asked and I hated to admit that beyond 'America' I had no idea.

"*California ...y'know I'm going to see the folks I dig I'll even kiss the sunset pig California I'm coming home.*"[9]

"*Joni Mitchell—nice song—I'll have to find the chords to that some time.*"

"*You play guitar? Whadya play?*"

"*Blues mainly. I play harp too – but mainly I was a vocalist.*"

"*Figures ...you talk like you were on stage one time.*"

"*One time ...*" I replied with a slight sigh "*Anyhow thanks for the books.*" I grinned and edged toward the door.

---

6 Quotidian – everyday-normal, or run of the mill.
7 Quadrumvirate – a union of four men.
8 'In Watermelon Sugar' tells of a group of people who meet at a house called iDeath. A bizarre character called inBoil leaves iDeath to live in the forbidden 'Forgotten Works' area – a vast rubbish tip where artefacts of a previous civilization lie haphazardly strewn. After various unlikely events inBoil returns to iDeath—with acolytes—and commits suicide by slashing himself to death with a knife yelling "I am iDeath!" and explaining that this is really what iDeath is all about.
9 Joni Mitchell—California—Blue—1971

"*You take care now*" she waved as I left.

"*Do my best*" I replied – and that was it. I never saw her again – even though I occasionally returned to *Chapter and Verse* to purchase other strange titles.

So there I was—out on the street again—with my back to the shop, feeling slightly dazed. I'd been in Bristol three days and fallen in love with an illusion metamorphosed from a book cover. This was new terrain. I walked up Park Street pondering the oddity of three recent sequential realities: the mysteriousness of Richard Brautigan gazing at me from a shop window; falling in love with Squirrel-toothed Alice and … and now – my post *Chapter and Verse* bemusement; having had my dinner invitation kindly declined. I had no particular philosophical conjecture about it – but I found myself surprised that three entirely different states of mind could occur in so short a period of time. What would happen in the next shop I entered? There were the two Richard Brautigan books under my arm – so it hadn't been a dream.

I wasn't disheartened by the lady's unavailability. Far from it – I felt vaguely amused with myself. Something had changed about me. This was *not* a thing I'd have attempted before – and, although nothing had come of it, I was now a person who could go out on a limb. I could spring sideways on a momentary romantic inclination. It occurred to me that she might not have had a husband – and that she might have worked on that line as a friendly way of turning away adventurous propositions. Whichever it *was* it was a remarkable moment. I'd left Farnham behind along with my teenage years. I looked back and felt somehow that I'd been younger than I thought I was as a 16 year old.

I'd felt so entirely adult then—so full of self assurance—but all based on supports that I'd deemed immutable.

All gone. I was still the same reckless romantic – but I was no longer as vulnerable and no longer brimming with naïve aplomb. There was still a sense of excitement though—I'd not grown cynical—but I'd become more resilient in terms of life being what it was. I no longer expected miracles to be my daily fare.

Muscular feasts of unruly discipline and wagers for walloping stockbrokers; / In antipathetical hindsight congratulations disclose stipulated accomplishments in order to repossess impressive gallantry; / Articulately garnished meanderings – girdle the charming volatility of suspended cornucopia – burgeoning with sophistication. / Vulnerable propulsion detonates façade of facile apprehension – miscellaneous amalgamation of delicately resilient private peculiarities. / Brandishing the audacity of iridescent abdomen implications, the impressionistic intelligence of sundry contiguous segments float in the moonlight / The condensation of improbability yawns with insatiable sympathetic metaphors – courting extravagant symposia in Chesterfield Road.
The Author—Chesterfield Road—1972

Having walked back up Park Street I swung right at the Oriental shop. I nosed in briefly but saw little of any interest. Before reaching the turn for Cotham—and thence St Andrews—I espied a shop called *Taro*. There were some shirts on a rack out front – and I absorbed their colours with delight: emerald green, a yet deeper emerald, a fabulous peacock blue, ultramarine, navy blue, and indigo. I was amazed by them and examined them carefully. They were the high collared Carnaby Street style that was in vogue back in '67 – but with a wide rounded collar style. I was intrigued by the fabric – I'd never seen such fabric before and didn't even know what it was called.

an odd boy

I went inside – and flew back in time to '67. Here was 'Hippie' – and *there* was a hippie lady behind the counter. She had extremely fine long back hair and reminded me ever-so-slightly of Morticia from the Addams Family [10] – although she was not possessed of quite the same ghoulishness. She wore a black satin dress trimmed with strange assemblages of beads—mainly jet and bloodstone—and I could see a great deal of work had gone into it. She noticed my interest and asked "*D'you like the dress?*"

"Yeah—it's really quite amazing—did you put it together?"

"Yeah man—all my own work—I don't think it would suit you though."

"Yeah …" I sighed in mock resignation "*Pity … but a jacket like that would be quite a thing.*"

She laughed but made no reply to my comment. She seemed friendly and took trouble to show me around the shop. I wasn't monstrously interested in any of her 'head-shop' wares—apart from the moss crêpe shirts—but I tried to show appropriate interest. There was the 'Book of Thoth' by Aleister Crowley and the deck of Tarot cards to accompany it. Alongside the 'Book of Thoth' was the 'Confessions of Aleister Crowley.' Then there were the usual hookah pipes, bongs,[11] cocaine spoons and mirrors, weights and scales for measuring narcotics, and ornate boxes for storing hashish. I started feeling that it wasn't such a tragedy that 'Hippie' was dead.

"*Where you—from—man? You're not from—here—are you?*"

---

10 The Addams Family was a cartoon series by cartoonist Charles Addams [1912 – 1988] which was published in The New Yorker magazine beginning in 1932. The dark humour satirised the image of the wealthy all-American family by substituting horror-comedy eccentrics with macabre interests as characters. The cartoon series expanded into an American television series in 1964 – and was screened in Britain a year or so later.

11 Bongs – marijuana water pipes.

"No. I'm from somewhere else" I laughed. "*Farnham, Surrey*" I continued in order not to be tricky. Someone had said that to me once on my interview day at Farnham Art School and I'd not appreciated it greatly – but it was a funny line, if augmented with fact.

"*Somewhere-else-Surrey – like your mind man.*"

"*Only one I've got*" I laughed "*Nice shop you have here*" I lied. "*D'you run it?*"

"*Yeah ... been here since '69.*" She took a long drag at her cigarette.

"*That's a while – I imagine it must have taken a while to get such a collection of things under one roof.*"

"*Yeah d'yer wanna buy any of it*" she laughed.

"*Absolutely – I'll take those shirts out there on the rack*" I grinned.

"*All of them?*"

"*Yeah—all of them—they're fabulous.*"

She giggled – blowing smoke on me. "*They're Carnaby Street throw-outs man. Didn't think—anyone—would want those. That's wild – I only put'em outside the shop this morning – I was desperate to get rid of them. You—really—want to buy them?*"

"*Absolutely. I love the colours*" I explained. "*I'm extremely fond of dark rich blues and greens.*"

"*You like colours—right—I can dig that. Colours man – like colours are just so ... far out.*"

"*Yeah that's what attracted me to your shop – the colours glowed at me from across the street.*"

"Groovy ...Y'know – I could take you 'round and about, y'know—show—you Bristol. We could have some—fun—yeah ...You up for a little—fun?" she smiled sensuously at me with smoke curling from her nostrils *"... but man—not—wearing one of those moss crêpe shirts ..."*

"That's really quite funny" I replied *"I mean – that you don't like those shirts."* I was attempting to avoid the issue of having fun. Fun with Morticia sounded ever-so-slightly dangerous to me. *"I sometimes feel the same about things—like polo neck sweaters; string vests; bum-freezer jackets; ties; button-down collars; and boxer shorts – hideous."* Pause *"Where did you find the shirts?"*

"Got them with the shop when I took it over – they've been here since I started and—y'know—no one's looked at them twice." She took another long pull on her cigarette *"But, like I said—we—could have some—fun."*

"Well y'know that's a—very—attractive offer indeed and ..." I faltered – realising I was going to have to address the proposal *"I'm about 99% up for fun – but ... I'm sorry to say ... I'm a strict long-term dyed-in-the-wool non-smoker ... and ... I just—love—those shirts."*

"You smoke dope though." She didn't make it sound like a question.

"Actually no. I don't use anything apart from the odd glass of red wine."

"Really!?" she almost choked *"Man, you're from the—Ark.*[12] *You're not a religious nut or something?"*

"... I'm more of a walnut – or maybe a wallflower" I obfuscated – observing her incredulity *"I just don't find the need. I was just born psychedelic – but I've got no moral angle on it or anything."* I lied. I did have some-sort-of-moral angle on it.

---

12 The Ark – Noah's Ark.

Düd'jom Rinpoche[13] the head of the Nyingma Tradition had written a booklet which described smoking as foul pestilence.[14]

"*You really—are—something else*" she intoned blandly shaking her head.

"*I'll take a trip 'round Bristol with you if you're inclined – but ... the cigarette thing isn't really workable for me beyond being friendly – unless that was the fun you had in mind.*"

"Hey man ...you make some heavy judgements y'know. What's wrong with bloody cigarettes!?"

"Nothing if you like them. I'm sorry – I didn't intend to sound judgemental or anything like that ... It's just my personal thing. I've never liked them – and I tend to choke on the smoke ..." I replied "*Anyhow ... I've been judged too much myself to want to judge anyone else. Everyone's free to make their own choices – far as I'm concerned.*"

"*Like really ...*" she intoned with an obvious disbelief that irked me.

"*Yes—really—I've suffered for choices I've made. I've been judged too— and pretty severely—but I suppose that's just how life is.*"

"Yeah ... that's how life is" she repeated in a vaguely mocking way.

"*Yes. The consequences of—me—looking like—me—have been pretty horrible – so I'm not about to lay any judgements on anyone else.*"

"No need to get—heavy—about it man – I was just commenting."

---

13 Kyabjé Düd'jom Rinpoche Jig'drèl Yeshé Dorje (*sKyab rJe bDud 'joms rin po che 'jigs bral ye shes rDo rJe*) – Head of the Nyingma Tradition during the latter part of the 20th Century.
14 Tobacco: 'The Guide That Leads the Blind on a False Path Which Ends in a Precipice' by Düd'jom Rinpoche, available as a booklet from ARO BOOKS worldwide, and at http://www.dudjom-on-smoking.org/.

"*Sorry—didn't mean to be touchy—but I'm really—not—judgemental ... I just don't smoke and I choke on it when other people do.*"

"*Yeah okay I guess I can handle that—it's cool with me—shame though eh?*"

"*Yeah*" I smiled "*it is a shame – because you're a highly interesting person.*" I needed to say something to change the atmosphere "*I like those Carnaby Street shirts though. Did you say ... moss crêpe?*"

"*Yeah ... moss crêpe*" she answered with a grin – having recovered her composure after my obviously entirely unexpected rejection. "*I guess they're nice colours – but that 'old lady's blouse' look, and those—frigging—high collars ... man they're something else.*" Pause "*Look why don't you take 'em all for a tenner*[15] *– and wear 'em in New Zealand or something.*"

"*It's a deal*" I laughed "*But I'm only taking them as far as Bower Ashton.*"

"*The Art School!?*"

"*Yeah. I'm just wandering around waiting for the term to start. Looking 'round the town – taking in the sights.*"

"*Good luck wearing those crazy shirts man*" she laughed "*You'll need it – 'cause you'll be the only dude there who doesn't toot.*"[16]

"*Yeah ... I believe you're probably right.*" I bid her goodbye. "*Thanks for the good deal on the moss crêpe.*"

"*See yer 'round.*"

"*That would be nice.*" I called back.

---

15 Tenner – £10.00.
16 Toot – to smoke cannabis.

"*You—really—gonna—wear—those shirts?*" she called out as if unwilling to let me go.

"*I'll try not to wear them around town too much*" I replied moving away from the shop. "*Y'know, just in case you ever want to take me on that tour.*" I heard her trailing laughter as I walked off toward Cotham.

Burly banquet of disorderly restraint fluttering against fractured stockpiles of stockings; / In anticipatory retrospection predetermined comings and goings divulge charred requisitions to recapture remarkable nerve; / Vociferously embellished consequences – are self-possessed in the captivating unpredictability of pendant profusion – mushrooming with erudition. / Impervious impulsion demolishes disguises of facetious consternation – heterogeneous fusion of dexterously pliant in clandestine eccentricity. / Flourishing the brashness of shimmering façade allusions, the indistinct acumen of miscellaneous neighbouring fragments hover in their moorings / The compression of implausibility yawning with voracious congenial similes – incite profligate conferences in Chesterfield Road.
The Author—Chesterfield Road—1972

Bristol seemed somehow miraculous. I'd fallen in love with Squirrel-toothed Alice and been partially seduced by Morticia. What miracle of human possibility would hit me next? I was sorry I'd had to say 'no.' It wasn't exactly like me – but I knew with certainty that we would have been entirely unsuited in almost all respects. The smoking was not the main issue – even though the idea of snuggling up to an ashtray was not my idea of heaven. Morticia was simply immersed in a codified counter-culture that I found almost as alien as the culture of Brigadier Dale – and there'd be incense and cannabis everywhere I turned … Damn it! I was judgemental. She was right. I was also a self-righteous prig. I *was* judgemental – without wanting to own it, or be caught out in that act of passing sentence on others.

But how could I just get on with *being myself* without it having to reflect adversely on other people? I reassured myself with the idea that I didn't judge her as unworthy – just too different from how *I felt myself to be*. I'd never smoked—and then I found out how Düd'jom Rinpoche considered smoking—so I had both scientific and religious reasons to avoid it. There were personal reasons too. Kissing someone who tasted like an ashtray was fairly nauseating – and it occurred to me that Morticia wouldn't be well pleased if I retched after one sampling of her lips. My father had smoked cigars and it turned my brother Græham and I into life-long non-smokers. We were always sick in the car on journeys and he'd always put it down to our being wimpish. My mother put it down to the cigars – but … that was not deemed possible.

It made me a little sad to realise that it was sometimes difficult to relate with people. They often inhabited narrowly formulated personæ that demanded you became like them purely in order to converse. It didn't seem to matter whether they were hippies or military dignitaries – they lived within trammelled margins. It was getting to feel as if it would take a miracle to make human contact with people as I once had done. I hoped Morticia wasn't correct about Art School. There'd been dope-smokers at Farnham Art School – but there'd never been any sense in which it was compulsory. Why did I have to be 'from the Ark' merely because of a personal predilection? It was as if I'd hoped for a miracle ….

Squirrel-toothed Alice was a miracle however, and one who lingered in my mind far longer than Morticia – even though I occasionally saw Morticia around town. Squirrel-toothed Alice was there—intangibly—as I ate my breakfast in a little café in Clifton.

I wondered how I'd suddenly felt so intensely attracted to a lady I'd never met before. The meeting had not been like my first vision of Lindie Dale – but there was *something* similar. I wondered whether I should distract myself in some way. Even though I'd never done that kind of thing before – I said to myself '*I might have to stop doing this kind of thing.*' Well yes… I either had to stop doing *that kind of thing* or I had to make sure that it was not a waste of time. Fiona Featheringstonehaugh had been an entirely improbable match – but we did have considerable fun together before her father caught sight of me. We both knew we were not suited and the end was entirely amicable and free even of the slightest melancholy.

Then I pondered the idea of a 'waste of time' over a second cup of coffee and a fine croissant. What was 'time wasted'? Was it possible to think of *any* association as a waste of time just because it didn't turn out to be permanent? Maybe not … Maybe not as long as it didn't cause you to miss meeting the love of your life. But, did such beings actually exist? Well… yes… they did – or at least they had. I'd had four such loves: Alice, Anelie, Lindie, and Juliet. It was vaguely mystifying that they were all still alive – somewhere. They all had lives that were not separate from mine. They still had ideas and talked about those ideas – and yet … they were all beyond my reach – for reasons that were vaporous. There was no cast-iron reason why I should not still be with any of them apart maybe from Anelie who was back in Switzerland. What if Alice Trevelyan turned out to be a second year Fine Art student at Bristol Art School? That would be strictly in the realm of novels. I wondered however, what Alice would make of me? Would she like me? What would she make of—me—as I'd turned out to be? Of course, I'd like—her—she was Alice. Then—after a vacuous interlude—somehow Squirrel-toothed Alice reassembled herself in my mind again.

I decided it'd be better to commit her image to poetry – so I set to work assembling word-juxtapositions to weave into a pastiche of my aimless wandering in Bristol. In order to equip myself with further images I returned to Park Street, not to revisit the bookshop—but absorb some of its day-to-day ambience. Walking up Park Street I passed *George's Music Shop*[17]—which I'd not noticed before—and lo and behold: a sitar. It's hard to describe just how unexpected that was. George Harrison had to get his in India – but here was mine sitting there ... just waiting for me.

"*Would you take a* 12 *string* Eko *for that* Bina *sitar?*"

"*Yes – if it's in good condition.*"

"*It's mint – although ... it has an interesting home-made case that you— may—not want.*"

"*We'd possibly take that too – you can never tell what someone might want.*"

"*Good – I'd hate not to find a home for it. I spent a long time making it and although it's heavy ... it's rather nice – and it's solid leather.*"

I went back to my room to fetch the Eko immediately. Within two hours I was the proud possessor of an instrument I couldn't play – and a handbook to change all that. They were impressed with the case and said that although it was unusual someone might well like it. "*We'll allow an extra ten pounds for the case. It*—is —*very unusual.*"

That was—I suppose—the final recognition that Frank Schubert had died. I'd built a nebulous tomb for him – created from atrophied phantasies.

---

17 There were two 'George's' shops in Park Street – one a book shop and the other a music shop.

I could no longer be any kind of public performance Bluesman – but I could be musical and experiment with this exotic assemblage of strings. I enjoyed the sitar immensely – and it enabled me to supplement my diet. I was intent on making my money last – and so when the proprietor of an Indian themed vegetarian restaurant called *Prashadam* offered me free meals on any evening I came to play, I accepted with alacrity. Of course I couldn't *play* sitar as sitar should be played. I could only engage in what I thought of as *free-form Jazz improvisation* – but no one seemed to mind. I was able to make it sound sufficiently pleasing to warrant meals.

As Blues was no longer part of my life as a public performer, I'd become increasingly interested in Avant Garde Jazz – especially where it seemed to segue with—or merge into—Romantic or Baroque music of the European tradition. I had listened to BBC Radio 3 since I was young and it had provided me with an extraordinary exposure to music. I knew what I appreciated most. It was chamber music – and of all the chamber music it was Bach who stood out. Jack Bruce considered Bach to be his preëminent bass teacher – and I could see why. Radio 3 also offered a weekly Jazz programme – and that simply underlined the fact that there was a huge divide between serious music and Pop. Classical, Blues, and Jazz were serious music. Other than serious music, I listened to the music I'd respected between 1966 and 1970.

I explored Hindustani Classical music – particularly music played on sitar, surbahar, and sarod.[18]

---

18 Surbahar and sarod – Indian instruments with sympathetic strings. The surbahar is a bass sitar. The sarod is a smaller fretless instrument with a metal covered neck.

an odd boy

I sought out music by Vilayat Khan, Asad Ali Khan—and a host of other inspired performers—and revelled in their flawless primæval Jazz.

Bubbles of pelluscent Palestrina are incidental to face-to-face conspiracy and impacts with luxuriously surreptitious ballerinas, / Evacuation of theatrical departure enables hermits to engender each nautical climax with scorching streams of darkness / The liquefying empathy of overweight crusades are tempted by diaphanous interrogation in the demography of unqualified craving. / Mud-slide banquet in seventh heaven—harassed by baroque bassinette bouquet—brunette basilisk in her barquentine bordello. / Merchant banker bathyscaphe filing cabinets lie purposeless and discarded in embezzled visas of vitality, / Impending quizzical consequences of elation shuffle the deck of speculative charisma / Faultless indulgence and perceptive injudicious proof of purchase leers at the firmament to remonstrate with unswerving hallucinations in Chesterfield Road. / Loops of Paganini in circumstantial head-on collusion collision with sumptuous clandestine mellotron, / Exodus of melodramatic flight of herons which generate oceanic crescendo and searing rivulet of night / Melted heart on butter crumpets – toasted under Dickensian grills in the dining-car of utter desire. / Muffin breakfast insidiously badgered by fragrances of coffee – smoked bacon bagarre bagatelle badinage. / Mephistophelean bathroom cabinet lying empty and abandoned in misappropriated September sunshine, imploding torrent, aftermath of joy. / Pristine peccadilloes and incisive indiscretions invoice the sky as a dalliance with direct dreaming in Chesterfield Road.
The Author—Chesterfield Road—1972

Having written 'Chesterfield Road' I concluded that poetry flowed more easily than lyrics ever would – at least 'til I'd got linguistic extravagance out of my system. I could craft poetry into a mirage minefield in which meaning and meaninglessness courted each other as an albatross and narwhal might court and spark.

One day I'd be able to turn it all around and write something simple and direct to a melody line like 'Sunshine of your Love' but 'til then I'd have to explore Art in whatever way it manifested in the moment.

I sat looking at my sitar—and all that it represented—as I sipped at a hot bowl of Lapsang Souchong.[19] The bowl was a very fine piece of Japanese porcelain that I bought on a wild impulse at the Clifton antiques market. It was decorated with three perfectly pale flying herons – and the whole ambience that surrounded drinking Lapsang Souchong from it, was beautifully eerie. The steam coiled upward from the cup and I perused my bedsit from the vantage point of *Colonel Greenhaugh* whom I had positioned in the rear bay of my room – overlooking the garden. *Colonel Greenhaugh* was a chair I'd rescued from the Sir Lindsay Parkinson's Scaffolding Yard. It was a 1920s wooden office chair – a swivelling recliner on castors that could be dangerous if you were not wary. It had a label on the back indicating that it was once a chair that was destined for the aforementioned military personage. As I peered through the steam a sense of gladness stole over me. This was my home at last. It was small – but I was the Lord and Master of this space. A new world was coming into being. It was a world in which I'd persevere through drinking Lapsang Souchong – even though it was an acquired taste that I'd not yet acquired. I'd bought the tea from a wholefood store down in the old city centre – I'd been talked into it by the proprietor. The store was situated in a covered market and had an impressive frontage made of old railway sleepers. They had sacks of rice and grains of various types and I was amazed at the sheer rustic extravagance of it.

---

19 Lapsang Souchong – tea from the Wü-yi region of China. It is distinctive in being smoke-dried over pinewood.

an odd boy

I bought three pounds of figs at the same time and the figs helped a great deal with making the Lapsang Souchong palatable. The coming of the wholefood store was something new—something that had evolved out of 'Hippie'—and although I never became a brown-rice convert, I was delighted to see that the world was actually changing for the better. There were all kinds of stores in that covered market: second-hand books; remodelled second-hand clothing; musical instruments; bric-a-brac; bicycle repairs; and some kind of tofu-burger emporium that I fastidiously avoided. This was *no* Farnham – and I was heartily glad of it.

The next cataclysm from the bestiary of beauty—riding on the ecstasy express—was due in on platform-infinity the following Monday at 10am. I thought back to my first morning at Hatch Mill and wondered if the experience would be in any way similar. I knew it would be different because I was no longer a school-leaver.[20] I'd lived in the Art School environment for two years and no one I'd meet would be fresh from secondary school. Most people I'd meet would be a year younger – and I wondered what difference that might make in terms of shared experience of music. It had made no difference in Farnham – so I was not troubled by the idea. I'd be associating with these people for three years – so meeting them for the first time would be slightly momentous. The only problem with Foundation had been the quick turnover – and the sense that friendships were almost necessarily transitory. Three years was a different prospect as we'd all be in for the long haul. I hoped they'd all be up for the high adventure of life as *artists*.

---

20 'School-leaver' – British parlance for a person who has left secondary schooling and either gone to work or on to higher education.

2

the first year: september 1972

bower ashton — you know the '60s are over don't you?

I'd chosen Bristol because it was the only Art School with a three year Illustration course — but no sooner had I arrived, than an unwelcome shift occurred. On the first day of term Dick Taylor—Head of Graphic Design—gave us an 'induction speech.' He'd recently decided that he'd rather be called Richard Taylor. Now the problem with changing your moniker from 'Dick' to 'Richard' is that everyone starts wandering why you— *don't*—want to be called 'Dick' ... and then 'dick' suddenly acquires the obvious double-entendre. You'd never think of 'Dick' as 'dick' if you were talking about Dick Heckstall-Smith [1] — but Dick Taylor ...

It was evident that some of the lecturers attended under slight duress — and that they were not *entirely* in tune with Dick. I realised with some sense of horror that Dick Taylor appeared to have the Übermensch [2] rôle for both Graphic Design and Illustration — and that he'd decreed sometime during the Summer that the first term should be a combined programme. I felt this was unethical as this was not the course for which I'd applied.

---

1   Dick Heckstall-Smith [1934 – 2004]. English jazz and blues saxophonist who played with some of the most important English Blues-Rock-Jazz fusion bands of the '60s and '70s.
2   The Übermensch (German 'Superman') is a concept in the philosophy of Friedrich Nietzsche. Nietzsche posited the Übermensch as a goal for humanity in his 1883 book 'Thus Spoke Zarathustra' (Also Sprach Zarathustra).

an odd boy

A joint first term with Fine Art would've been fine – but *this* was just the kind of thing I'd wanted to avoid.

We'd all had to read Dick's book '*A Basic Course in Graphic Design*' before we arrived in September and—although I'd dutifully read it—I was somewhat appalled by its 'industrial' feel. The book waged war on *rule of thumb empiricism* [3] – that is to say: anything that could be described as 'painterly.'

"*Graphic designers are*—not—*Artists*" Dick Taylor pronounced. "*If you want to be impressionistic or expressionistic you should have applied for Fine Art.*"

I thought that was an outrageously closed-minded view – but I was to be an illustrator, so I'd comforted myself with the idea that *this speech had*—nothing—*to do with me.*

"*I … am a committed philosophical rationalist*" Dick went on.

'*Well – good for you*' I thought. I wasn't exactly an 'irrationalist' – or anything as crude. I felt I was more of a *philosophical sensationalist* – but as a Buddhist, the *rational* and the sensational had never been at odds in my mind. I found it strange that he'd want to divide these perspectives – and stick like a limpet to rationality as if *that* represented truth.

"*Graphic design is a 'communication science' carried out by professionals …*" Dick proclaimed "*… and illustration is one of the tools of graphic design.*"

I had an entirely different view of the matter. I thought that Illustration could be what he was describing – but it could also be the *Art of image and text*.

---

3   Empiricism – **a.** any method ignorant of scientific practice **b.** knowledge derived from sense-experience.

bower ashton — you know the '60s are over don't you?

It struck me that Dick Taylor should really have had the Head of Department rôle in a technical college with Business Studies on the curriculum. He talked for an hour at least — traversing a list of numbered points beginning with 00 — after which came 01. I found the idea of 00 as the first item slightly amusing — but felt increasingly rankled as he continued. I could see the expressions on the faces of some of the lecturers — and it was clear that this man was not exactly popular.

This had almost nothing in common with Art School as I understood it. I started feeling that I should have applied for Fine Art — as the ladies in Exeter had queried. I'd been pinned by the Morton's Fork [4] I'd learned about in History lessons at Netherfield. I could either stand out against abstract expressionism as a Fine Artist — or stand out against graphic design as an Illustrator. I'd made my choice however — and change was not easily possible. It seemed purposeless to change in any case as there was no guarantee of anything being any better anywhere else.

At some point in his long speech, Dick Taylor must have become aware that an atmosphere of gloom had descended and decided to make a wise crack.

"However ... there is plenty of room for different approaches here — I don't want anyone to think of this as a dictatorship."

Suddenly—without thought—I blurted, albeit in a mild tone *"Sounds more of a Dick-Taylorship."*

---

4 Morton's Fork — a choice between two bad alternatives, originating from a tax collection policy devised by John Morton, Henry VII's Lord Chancellor. If King Henry was luxuriously hosted, sufficient income was deemed available to pay higher taxes. If King Henry was frugally hosted, it was an insult to the King and therefore high tax was demanded.

The room quivered slightly with uncomfortable repressed laughter. A few lecturers spluttered and had to control themselves rapidly. Dick Taylor eyed me sharply. I was *trouble*.

She gotta pearl handled pistol, a knife, and a razor too, / You can't ever tell her—she'll always tell you. BB King—Dynamite—1951

Nothing transpired however, and it seemed that things were not quite as brutally commercial as I feared. Poor Richard Taylor turned out to be a shrew who cast a giant shadow. He never bothered me – and I was no trouble to him either. I had a protector—and extremely kindly mentor—in the Head of Illustration, Derek Crowe. He championed not only the cause of keeping Illustration independent – but also of keeping me in my strange *Fine Art capsule* within the Illustration course. Fortunately for me I took to typography as it allowed me to produce my poetry and writing – and I was therefore able to look as if I was less of a renegade than I was. I became enthusiastic about word and image combinations – and, although I only ever illustrated my own words, that seemed sufficient to validate my situation in the general Graphics Department. I practically designed my own degree course – and, thanks to Derek Crowe, my initial fears proved entirely groundless.

I liked Derek Crowe on first sight. He had a natural goodness – written right through him like a stick of Brighton rock.[5] He reminded me of Mr Love in some ways. It was partially his dress and partially his delightful benevolence. He had an easy stylishness that he wore with taste and serenity.

---

5   Brighton rock refers to a stick of rod-shaped, hard-sugar confection traditionally sold in British seaside resorts. The name of the resort runs through the stick. It has some similarities to peppermint sticks sold in the USA.

bower ashton – you know the '60s are over don't you?

He dressed not so much like Evelyn Waugh – but Somerset Maugham: white shirts with widely spaced blue stripes; immaculate cravats; and, cavalry-twill trousers. He wore a straw boater in the Summer – and drove a vintage car that had to be started with a crank handle. He enjoyed Blues and had a collection of music that I enjoyed greatly. He liked the Blues ladies – Bessie Smith and others.[6] He had some quite obscure albums. His wife Susan Crowe was a lovely woman – wistful, serene, and other-worldly. It was strange being around them – because they reminded me so much of the Trevelyans. They were vegetarian and Derek had been a conscientious objector in WWII. He'd been with the medics running out with stretchers to fetch back the wounded. He never told me this himself. It was Roderick Peters—the other Illustration lecturer—who mentioned it. Derek Crowe was a man who was worthy of the deepest admiration. He had a clear sense of himself and wasn't about to demand that anyone was impressed with him. He wasn't a man to lord it over anyone or tell you that he had all the answers. He was genuinely accommodating – keen to ensure that students experienced their time as valuable. He was no Dick Taylor – and I felt that he'd not allow Illustration to become a penitentiary.

I was left to work in whatever way I wished. I have no idea how much Derek must have cleared the way for me. I was a fool in various respects. I had yet to learn circumspection. I worked hard however, and that probably gave me a great deal of licence. Derek never seemed concerned about where I was—or what I was producing—because I never stopped working.

---

6   Big Mamma Thornton, Memphis Minnie, Ida Cox, Ivie Anderson, Ma Rainey, Trixie Smith, and Adelaide Hall.

an odd boy

I would work every weekend. I would work through the holidays. I always had almost too much to show him.

My compatriots on the Illustration course seemed bland to my eye – but I decided it was unwise to judge by appearances. I'd been judged by appearances and had not enjoyed the experience. One fellow stood out in some way from the others – but mainly due to his slight edginess. I smiled at him and he reacted as if I'd done something unusual. After peering at me expressionless slightly longer than a second he turned his head. A few moments later he reorganised his chair in order to have his back to me. This was my first experience of Todd Whelcomb – all five and a half foot of him.

Ron Larkin had once told me "*Beware of short men – they want to rule the world. Hitler, Mussolini, Stalin, and your father – bloody dwarf fascists, the lot of 'em.*" That was after he'd met my father – and my father had corrected his speech. Dick Taylor was a short fellow too – so I wondered how it would turn out with this fellow student. Todd had the kind of deep black hair that really requires a person to have a beard. His face had the quality of co-respondent shoes [7] in contrasting shades of pink and blue. He possessed an assortment of outsize Fair Isle sweaters in musty hues that ranged between rotten egg and rancid kipper. He was fond of large Tattersall pattern winceyette shirts with button down collars; with which he'd wear casually-undone knitted ties.

---

7   Co-respondent shoes – a British slang term for two-tone shoes (usually brown and white, or black and white) which are said to be typically worn by the male co-respondent in a divorce case relating to adultery.

bower ashton – you know the '60s are over don't you?

He was evidently expensively dressed—I detected something of the Sloane Ranger[8] about him—but to me, he looked as if his parents had dressed him. His one deviation from the Sloane Ranger costume was a partiality for *Hush Puppies* suede boots and casual *corporate-executive business-lounge* shoes with buckles that served no purpose. He reminded me in some ways of Sidney the soldierman in his appearance – but I allowed him slightly better colour sense.

As I made my assessment of him – I realised I was being judgemental again and disapproved of myself. I therefore decided to take into account that he might have his own negative impression of my deep-emerald-green leather jacket.

It was second hand from *Granny Takes a Trip* and had obviously been tailor-made for *mister-someone-or-other famous*. It was severely waisted and flared with a fourteen inch vent at the back, double flap pockets on each side, and luxuriously expansive lapels. I'd bought the jacket with a pair of matching knee-length laced boots. I'd made an excellent deal with the lady in the shop as she wanted the trousers. She told me I could have the jacket and boots at a 60% reduction if I'd forgo the trousers. That was fine by me because the trousers were hipsters – and I never cared for low-waisted trousers. They also had some sort of diabolical 'crotch enhancing' lace-up fly that I considered grotesque. I wore the jacket and boots with any one of the high collared moss-crêpe shirts I'd bought at *Taro*.

---

8   Sloane Ranger – upper-middle class and upper class people in their twenties and thirties dwelling in and around 'Sloane Square' in South-west London. It is a word play on 'Lone Ranger', a television character from the 1950s Western of the same name. The US equivalents are 'Preppies.'

an odd boy

Together with a pair of velvet trousers of a lustrous Prussian blue that gave the impression of staring into the night sky – I felt as if I was dressed to live in two worlds: I was a Fine Art Illustrator. The old adage has it that *blue and green should never be seen*—and maybe Fine Art and Illustration were similar—but I loved that green and blue combination. It seemed to incense Todd however – especially as he was one of those 'don't speak to me before 11.00 am' people. I have never seen why people accept this affectation in others. Why should people have to tip-toe around 'bad-mood-in-the-morning' types as if it were a bona fide medical disorder? Todd looked as if he were continually on the verge of vituperative verbal disparagement. Eventually—after three weeks—he launched in.

"*D'you think you're trying to—*prove*—s*omething *by dressing like that?*"

"*No Todd—not far as I'm aware …*" I decided it was preferable not to take offence quite so early in the term – even though I'd been offered it first. I decided not to add '*I was wondering how long you could resist commenting – you've been eyeing me in a peculiar manner since you first saw me dressed this way.*' I smiled instead.

Todd looked bewildered.

"*Why d'you ask?*" I ventured in response to his immobility and vacuous gaze.

"*Why do I ask? What sort of question is that!?*" he spluttered – followed by a nervous giggle. He was evidently thrown by the question. He'd not anticipated lack of embarrassment on my part.

"*Just curious Todd … I don't*—need—*an answer …*" I grinned "*… but I imagine … these aren't the kind of clothes you'd like to wear.*"

"*Certainly not – I'm not a poseur.*"

"*Well ...*" I smiled warmly "*I can certainly see—that—Todd.*" He continued to stand gawping at me so I concluded our exchange by adopting a mock military mien "*Good for you—good for you—that's the spirit Todd, keep it up.*" I left him standing, staring into the air. After a while he mumbled something inaudible—in order to dissemble—and shuffled away. I went to my art desk and started work on the series of drawings I was to use as the basis of a collage.

I wasn't happy with how I'd handled the exchange with Todd – but couldn't see what I could have said that would have led to a friendlier outcome. '*Todd you're not being very nice to me and ...*' No ... I couldn't have pulled that off. No one had ever commented on my clothes at Farnham Art School and it had been a long time since anyone had taken such an exception to my appearance. The last *sartorial sarcastians* had been my father and the more boorish of the boys at Netherfield School. I'd thought that was a by-gone age. I thought I was now in the age where freedom of appearance could be taken for granted – especially at an Art School.

Maybe Todd was an anomaly – but whatever he was, I was going to have to find some way of coexisting in the Illustration studio with the fellow. I settled to the idea that he'd calm down when he realised I wasn't a threat. I'd make a point of being pleasant to him whenever I saw him.

Bower Ashton—the Art School buildings—were set in an area almost as countrified as Hatch Mill. They lay just below the grounds of Ashton Court, the fine old house whose orchards gave the name Bower Ashton to the Art School site. You could imagine you were in the countryside when you looked out of the windows because the Art School was surrounded by fields.

an odd boy

The Art School architecture was hideous—spawn of Moloch—but I decided to accommodate that. The Fine Art building was a single story extension of the main building. You could have walked directly onto its roof if you'd climbed out of the window of the Illustration Department. I took a small box tree in one day and stood it on the roof of the Fine Art building outside my window. It was being removed from the garden of the house where I rented a room – and I was not keen to see it discarded with the refuse.

Todd Whelcomb saw this as an eccentric act. "*Why*—on earth—*would anyone be concerned about saving a bush?*"

"*Why wouldn't anyone want to save anything that was alive?*" I replied. "*Wouldn't you wish to be saved if you were being thrown out?*" Damn – I'd done it again. I didn't know what else to say. I'd walked right into Todd's offensive again. I should simply have replied '*I don't know.*'

"*Dear me—dear me—still trying to prove something are we?*" Todd sneered.

"No Todd." I sighed "*I leave that to the scientists – they're far better placed to conduct experiments and … I was never any use with physics. They didn't even allow me to sit 'O' Level Maths. Said it would be a waste of the school's money … I'm a moron as you can probably guess.*"

"*What on—earth—are you talking about?*" Todd scoffed in an attempt at derision.

"*Nothing Todd—just gibbering as is my wont—but … I do think the box tree detracts from the unsightly architecture don't you?*"

"*Unsightly architecture?*" Todd snorted in contempt. "*You chose to come here – didn't you see the building when you came for your interview?*"

"*I did Todd – but I was more interested in the Illustration course and its tutors than I was with the building.*"

bower ashton – you know the '60s are over don't you?

"*There were no—other—illustration courses I suppose?*"

"*No Todd ... I thought you'd have known that ...? The only other Illustration course in Britain is Norwich – and that has a 1st year combined with graphics. I have no real interest in graphic design.*"

Todd made some garbled answer concerning graphic design and illustration being part of the same profession – but I had no great interest in that line of argument and didn't really follow the drift of what he'd said. I therefore decided not to comment. I burst into song instead. "*I had a little box tree and nothing would it bear / but a silver nutmeg and a golden pear, / the King of Spain's daughter came to visit me / and all for the sake of that little box tree.*"

"*The nursery rhyme—says—'nut tree', not 'box tree'.*" Todd pointed out condescendingly.

"*I do believe you're right, Todd*" I smiled. I made no reference to the fact that a nursery rhyme cannot 'say' anything.

I just smiled again and replied "*Still ... the King of Spain's daughter —may—wish to see it nonetheless. I shall therefore tend it with the greatest devotion in anticipation of her regal arrival.*"

"*Where did—you—come from? I don't get you – or your stupid sense of humour*" Todd snapped. "*If you expect anyone to talk to you in this studio you're going to have to drop these imbecile affectations.*"

I'd never come across anything as unlikely as this since Percy Gordon had raged at me with racialist invective and lavatorial expletives concerning my enjoyment of Blues. "*I don't think I'll drop them Todd – they'd make an awful mess on the floor.*"

Todd looked as if he was going to launch a nuclear offensive – and I wondered ... was Todd going to threaten physical violence as if he were in a school playground? That seemed unlikely – but how was I going to respond to this man? Remain blithe and cordial? What other option was there?

an odd boy

"Sing no more ditties, sing no more, of dumps so dull and heavy" I quoted merrily *"The fraud of men was ever so, since Summer first was leafy. Then sigh not so—but let them go—and be you blithe and bonny, Converting all your sounds of woe into: Hey—nonny—nonny."*[9]

Todd stared at me with incredulity *"You're—insane—I shan't speak to you again."*

"Well ... 'As You Like It' ... Todd."[10] I smiled and returned to my work – annoyed with myself for my failure to hold my tongue.

Why did I have to wander the face of the earth retaliating with manic quotations? Wouldn't it be easier to look stupid? Well yes, it would be easier to look stupid – but what would that accomplish? I was trapped with Todd for 3 years – but then he was trapped with me. Maybe he'd just run out of steam – and when he did, he'd suddenly find me pleasant. I'd act as if none of it had ever happened – but in the meanwhile, becoming the acquiescent butt of his curmudgeonliness was not a viable answer. I was no saint. I would have liked to have been a saint – but somehow it was difficult. I could go as far as not being unkind – but I was some-sort-of slave to wit. I tried my level best not to take wit too far and I would certainly avoid taking it as far as cruelty. I'd never set out to hurt someone with wit – but ... somehow I couldn't simply keep my mouth shut.

I'd initially been delighted that the majority of the Illustration year were female. Of eleven students [11] Todd and I alone were male – but the women were not exactly easy conversationalists and my exchanges with Todd didn't help.

---

9   Much Ado About Nothing—William Shakespeare—Act II—Scene iii—1599
10 As You Like It—William Shakespeare—1623
11 Todd Whelcomb and Veranda Peachornby, Normanda Riley, Silvia Winstaunleigh-Greaves, Gloria Mytholmroyd, Pamela Beauchamp, Janet Coleridge, Stephanie Lytton-Chatfield, Angela Grey, Linda Essex, and the author.

bower ashton — you know the '60s are over don't you?

I seemed to find myself defined as some sort of capricious verbal duellist — especially when others were not privy to the opening volleys from Todd. I was there for Art — not the architecture and it's too-frequently matching students. I'd come to learn as much as I could about everything that was difficult to arrange outside the Art School environment. This meant photography and print making. Print making was a remarkable experience in spite of the fact that it played dermatological havoc with my hands. I'd be bleeding after a week in the print making studio — but I was drawn back to it by the lure of the process. I was captivated by the elemental nature of eating into a zinc plate with hydrochloric acid.

Aside from the print making studio, I'd been fascinated by Albrecht Dürer's painting *The Great Turf* and wanted to produce something as timelessly beautiful. It astonished me that Albrecht Dürer painted a water colour that looks as if it could have been painted in the 20th Century. *The Great Turf* depicts a clump of grass and other forms of vegetation you'd find in any meadow. I thought it remarkable that he should have painted the commonplace in the 15th Century — because, at the time, ideas of what constituted beauty were fairly narrow. I kept coming back to that Albrecht Dürer image and trying to find a meadow that was as beautiful as that. I tramped across an assortment of fields — but never found a clump of grass accompanied by dandelions and burdock. I found a few sections of mixed plant life — but although I have noticed that *nature imitates Art*,[12] I never found it imitating Albrecht Dürer.

---

12 'Nature imitating art' derives from the Oscar Wilde aphorism: 'Life imitates art far more than art imitates Life.' Oscar Wilde refers to Ovid's 'Metamorphoses' in which 'Nature in her genius had imitated art.' This was a commonly understood idea in Art Schools at the time.

an odd boy

Eventually I dug up a suitably unkempt square of turf and took it into the photographic studio. I photographed it with a 12 by 16 plate camera under studio lighting conditions. The monochrome negative was half again as large as life and I used the negative to make a contact print. As there was no enlarger involved the image was almost painfully perfect. I green-toned the image, which was a tricky two part operation – and the final result looked eerie. That was the closest I ever got to Albrecht Dürer. The photograph was set with a stanza of poetry that I'd hand scripted in an old Italian typeface. I'd drawn the text four times as large as it would be printed in order to obtain a greater degree of crispness whilst maintaining the hand drawn quality of the lettering. I then photographed the text with a plate camera and made a line-negative which I used as a stencil. I placed the stencil below the grass image and projected the image of the grass through it.

The result was interesting as the text was constituted of grass. The piece won me some admiring comments from lecturers.

The ladies in the studio liked it and seemed to respond in a warm manner on seeing it. The piece wasn't weird in their eyes. Janet Coleridge went so far as to say "*It's very pretty – I'm surprised a man would make something as pretty as that.*"

"*Thank you Janet—I appreciate that—I don't think I'm much of an archetypal male.*"

Janet smiled and nodded "*That's unusual – but welcome to hear.*"

"*Take it home and show your boyfriend.*" Todd guffawed at the back of the room. Janet didn't catch his words and turned to look at Todd – but he merely shook his head. I concluded that he would rather not repeat himself. Todd was obviously homophobic as well as infantile.

"Todd doesn't seem to like your work" Janet shrugged.

"That's fine by me Janet ... I don't really do anything to gain anyone's approval. I'm glad you like it, however."

Getting a good audience response as a Blues performer was important – but it seemed somehow irrelevant with the visual Arts – as nothing depended on the outcome. I had no plans for exhibitions apart from the final degree show.

The first term moved to its close – and I was finally compelled to engage with the Graphic Design programme. It was Dick Taylor's pet project and there was no alternative. He'd split the illustrators for this project – each one with two or three graphic designers. In each project up to that point I'd been able to skew each one of the assignments in such a way as to take off in an unlikely direction. Now I was faced with team work – and I'd have to see what transpired.

I had no wish to be awkward or to subject others to my deranged inclination so I decided to go along with whatever happened and chalk it up to experience. It would not be courteous or cordial to act the psychedelic saboteur – so I'd have to knuckle down to mandatory mundanity.

I found myself with three graphic designers who looked friendly – two ladies and a fellow with extremely long hair. That looked promising. The sartorial appearance of the two ladies seemed not too far removed from the ladies I remembered from Hatch Mill and they were evidently bright minded.

Each group had to give a presentation using either video, tape-slide sequence, or overhead projection. The presentation task was to 'graphically depict the first term.'

an odd boy

I sat listening to the project being described and tried hard not to glaze over – this was nowhere close to anything that might remotely interest me – but I was curious to see what the three graphic design students would make of it. The group were pleasant and we got together in what seemed to be a mood of creative ebullience. This was good. I liked these three – and felt that something interesting could transpire.

"*Right. What's the first term been like then? Bunch of tedious crap I thought.*" Ralph Simons, the long haired fellow sighed forcibly. "*Started well enough when Dick wasn't calling the shots. I'm a photographer—not a Fine Artist—but I don't buy all this executive corporate image bullshit.*"

"*That's good to hear – couldn't agree more*" I ventured.

"*Yeah man really—and hey—that Dick-Taylorship thing you said at the start of term was—hysterical—bloody nearly wet myself. Thought I'd gone back to bloody school before you said that.*"

They all laughed remembering my witticism.

"*I took it as a sign …*" Ralph said "*… that things weren't going to be too locked into corporate image.*"

I laughed and looked over to the two ladies – Wendy Millhurst and Georgina Reynolds. They gave their impressions and I was surprised by the way they felt.

"*We've already talked about it*" Wendy offered "*We both started out quite excited but … it soon started feeling as if it was business studies or marketing or something.*"

"*Right*" Georgina added "*I became increasingly disinterested as the term proceeded. I applied for Graphics because I'm not a painter and my life drawing is—well, it's not great—but I never wanted to be some kind of slick image maker.*"

They all nodded and made more-or-less similar statements. They had no problem with having to be creative about the more commonplace aspects of graphic design work – but they'd all hoped it would be more illustrative.

"*Well … I'd hoped Illustration would have leant further towards Fine Art Print Making. I hope the next term's going to be more like that when I've escaped Old Dick.*"[13]

"*Yeah – all that stuff about 'the science of communication' that Dick Taylor went on about gave me the willies*" Ralph stated vehemently.

"*I really don't see why there has to be this big bloody division between the departments either. I mean – I don't paint but I like to see what the painters are up to.*"

"*Yeah—absolutely—that's what I liked about Foundation*" I said "*I find it inspiring to see people involved in other areas – y'know on a day to day basis. It used to spark me with ideas.*"

Ralph was keen to work with video and no one objected – so we collared the video technician and got a practical introduction to how we could proceed.

There were video clips available and amongst them was a clip from 'Gunfight at the OK Corral' in which a seemingly great number of people get shot in a matter of seconds.

I was intrigued by the clip and wondered if it could be used in some way. I kept replaying it because I was fascinated by what happened when the repetitions started to form a pattern. The others also became intrigued whilst they watched and jotted down notes.

"*So … *" I began "*… how was it for you?*"

---

13 Old Dick – a play on 'Old Nick', an epithet for the Devil.

an odd boy

This made them fall about laughing. "*You make it sound as if we'd just had a sexual encounter*" Ralph chuckled "*Glad you got a sense of humour ...you ... seemed a bit serious at the outset.*"

"*Well ...*" I replied "*this is not quite my area of expertise – so I suppose I was just wondering what we'll do together. I know I'm inclined to get loony when things are too tight – so I'm trying to be sensible.*"

"*No need to be sensible on our account*" Georgina said "*Any way of making this bloody project more interesting would be welcome.*"

I grinned. "*Right then – what about using this film-clip? Let's take it as a creative challenge to find a way to use it.*" Their faces lit up. It was agreed.

We turned the clip into a loop that kept repeating and sat there watching it. After three minutes had elapsed I said "*I think it needs music.*"

That seemed to meet general approval and so we looked through a pile of tapes that were lodged in the cupboard in the video room and busied ourselves reading what it carried in the way of recordings. "*What are we looking for?*" I asked.

"*Something with a Western theme*" one of the others suggested.

After a while I stumbled upon something. "*What about this?*" I asked "*Y'know – this might be just the thing ...*"

"*Whaddya found?*" asked Ralph

"*It's an orchestral version of a folk song—Shenandoah—it could make a bizarre juxtaposition because it's kind of Mantovani* [14] *meets Liberace.*"[15]

"*Really? That's grotesque*" Georgina laughed.

---

14 Annunzio Paulo Mantovani [1905 – 1980] was a popular conductor and light orchestra entertainer known for his use of the string section to replicate the sound one would experience in cavernous locations such as cathedrals.

bower ashton — you know the '60s are over don't you?

"*Yes—exactly—it's syrupy but incredibly smoooooth. What I have in mind is for the music to be as different as possible from the image of all the fellows dropping drown dead. It's like something out of Monty Python.*"

"*Riiiiight ... I get you now—very—funny*" Georgina chuckled. "*... but ... how d'you think Dick's going to react to it?*"

"*Don't worry about it — I'll take responsibility for that. If you three handle the graphics — I'll carry the can for the Monty Python sequence.*"

We rigged up a repeating cycle and recorded it along with the gunfight sequence and we had something to contemplate.

"*How's this going to say something about the first term?*" Ralph enquired – but in a friendly way.

"*Don't know yet*" I replied "*but I'm sure I'll think of something. This is too good to lose. Maybe if we sit and watch it for a while?*"

They nodded. "*Why not*" Ralph chuckled "*It's loony – but I guess you warned us about that.*"

We sat and watched the loop for ten minutes and an idea started to form. "*So you said that you started out feeling quite interested at the start of term*" I observed "*and then became a little jaded.*"

They nodded. "*So ... maybe that was like watching the loop?*" I'd piqued their curiosity.

"*That was what was so—weird—though*" Wendy said. "*It started out being quite interesting ... then I started feeling irritated by the loop and wondering what on earth we were doing watching it. Then— toward the end—when I'd accepted it was irritating ... it started getting interesting again.*"

---

15 Wladziu Valentino Liberace [1919 – 1987] was known as 'Mr Showmanship.' He was a Pop music pianist and joyfully glitzy entertainer, whose trademark was a lit candelabra and whose sartorial signature included tails and formal wear embellished with jewels, rhinestones, and sequins.

an odd boy

"*Yeah!*" burst in Georgina "*Just the way the action moved against the music and seeing the pattern of it – became kind of hypnotic.*"

"*So … the experience of the term …*" Ralph mused "*… has been a trough between two peaks.*"

"*Well that's not—so—surprising*" I commented – and Ralph immediately asked why. "*Well there are usually at least two peaks at a trough.*"

Ralph groaned "*Two pigs at a trough—jeeesus man—that was terrible.*" But then he and the ladies burst out laughing.

"*Well right – that was my experience*" Georgina piped up.

Wendy agreed and added "*I thought this project was going to be a drag – but I've started enjoying this. How did—that—happen?*"

We were enjoying the loony scenario with the film clip when it became clear to me that I had to get lateral with it. "*So … if it started out being interesting and ended up being interesting and had a trough in the middle … there—could—be a way of showing that. What if we show this clip to the others and get their reaction to it …*"

They were evidently excited about that idea – but thought it needed a little more graphic material if it were to work.

Wendy—the quietest of the three—suddenly chipped in "*Well if we were to take people's impressions with a survey … we could see how the entire group felt about the first term … and … if we made a graph of that which showed the trough we all experienced in the middle of the term – we could then get them to watch the video—provide them all with acetate—and get them to graph their individual responses to the film and … we could see if they matched with the graph of the term.*"

That was settled. It was a workable idea. It might *not* work – but it was worth a shot. The three were happy to handle the graphic side and the questionnaire.

bower ashton – you know the '60s are over don't you?

They decided I'd provided my share of the work with the film clip, the music and the whole loony notion – so I was free to go back to life drawing. I was slightly bemused by the easiness of my association with the graphic designers – because of my experience with Todd. It seemed to prove something to me – and that was that I was not quite the misfit that Todd wished to label me. That was reassuring somehow. I'd just been unlucky that Todd had applied for Illustration when he'd have been more at home in Graphic Design. He'd have liked Dick Taylor. I hoped I could find a way of making my interactions with Todd a little less ridiculous.

By the end of the day we all had to give our presentations. Dick Taylor sat and observed with obvious enthusiasm for the culmination of his project and one by one the presentations went by. They were mind-numbingly tedious – but my three graphic design colleagues became increasingly edgy. I sensed some feeling of apprehension in them as to what I'd perpetrated. We were last on. Overhead projection acetates were handed out for the gathered assembly to chart their impressions of our video.

Dick Taylor sat watching the many—many—*many*—repeats of the gun fight and I detected the beginnings of a twitch in his face. His irritation was palpable. Finally the acetates were gathered and an explanation was given. The acetates showed exactly what the survey of the first term had shown – interest at each end and a trough in the middle. Dick Taylor congratulated the group on the graphics portion and asked who had been responsible for the layout. Georgina, Wendy, and Ralph identified themselves.

"And whose—brainchild—was the video and soundtrack?"
He pronounced the word 'brainchild' with decided disdain. Ralph—with a broad grin—indicated me.

"*Yes ... I thought as much*" Dick commented with a deliberately wearied smile "*Well ...you three made the whole thing work well – in spite of Victor Simmerson's penchant for adolescent comedy.*" He gave a slight shake of the head. "*You—do—know that the '60s are over don't you?*"

I nodded "*Yes Dick—as a matter of fact—I do. Somehow ...*" Pause "*I worked that out on New Year's Eve 1969.*"

Muffled laughter from the lecturers ran round the room. Dick Taylor gave an icy glance and proceeded to sum up with regard to the presentations. I'd done it again. What *was* it about this man? He seemed to set himself up as the straight man – and I seemed unable to resist delivering a punch line. He obviously didn't like me—or what I seemed to represent—and I hoped it wasn't going to turn into some kind of interpersonal battle.

The thought that I might have to reap what I'd sown—in some way that would be damaging—hung in the air.

3

the first year: october 1972

bower ashton – au'voir leonardo

... words are flowing out like endless rain into a paper cup, they slither while they pass, they slip away across the universe.
Lennon/McCartney—Beatles—Across the Universe—Let It Be—1970

Claudette Gascoigne had a fabulously fruity voice. Her enunciation was the aural correlate of chocolate – or of sipping Brunello: the toffee nose ... the plummy tones ... the mellowed tannin ... the hints of oak ... Her voice reminded me of Farnham Grammar School girls in the Summer haze of '68. Before I heard her voice however, I was taken aback by her aristocratic presence. It was her strikingly elegant demeanour as she emerged from an unusually magnificent car. Was she a lecturer or an invited speaker? I remembered the Rolls Royce that John Lennon and Yoko Ono had sent to Hatch Mill with a picture of themselves on the back seat. I'd seen a Rolls Royce Silver Cloud before at a wedding and so I recognised the model *"They say every silver cloud has a leather lining – is that true of this one?"*

Claudette looked askance *"Indeed it is ..."* she replied imperiously *"... apart from the walnut veneer and carpeting."*

"Yes ... I suppose leather throughout would be a little kinky."

She laughed—evidently not what she had expected to do—and looked at me with curiosity. *"Who—are—you?"*

"I'm ... probably a figment of your imagination" I replied.

an odd boy

She laughed a second time and was evidently a little disconcerted that a complete stranger was causing her mirth. "*Undoubtedly ... but to what would I attribute such a figment?*"

"*Possibly an excess of stilton after last night's venison?*" I suggested with a chuckle. I imagined that her household must be awash with royal cheeses. "*Are you here to give a talk?*"

"*Good lord no! Perish the thought!*" she laughed "*Whatever gave you such an idea?*"

I was suddenly stuck for an answer that didn't sound gauche and stumbled into a direct reply "*Well ... I've not known many art students who drive such impressive vehicles.*"

"*I'm sorry*" she replied mischievously. "*My name's Claudette by the way.*"

"*Vic ... Vic Simmerson*" I replied slowly. "*Although I've been called other things.*"

"*I can well imagine*" she replied with a superior air "*Are you in Graphics?*"

"*No, not really*" I replied awkwardly.

"*Not really? What d'you mean by that?*"

"*I'm in Illustration. It's part of the Graphics Department — but I don't really see myself as having anything to do with Graphics.*" Pause "*I could as easily have applied for Fine Art — but I'm a figurative painter and that doesn't go down well in most Fine Art departments.*" Pause "*Where are you?*"

"*In the car park ... at the moment?*" she grinned.

"*Nice reply*" I laughed. "*I like that.*"

"*I'm in the first year of Fashion and Textile Design — but I have no interest in fashion.*" Pause "*I have no interest in commercialism either.*"

"*So you're ...?*" I prompted, as we took seats in the refectory.

"*... theatre wardrobe design.*"

"*Now—that—sounds interesting – that's a whole other field. I've always been interested in clothes – and I've always seen them as Art.*"

"*I can see you like to make your own choices – and, evidently, that applies to literature too.*" She replied indicating the book that was causing my jacket pocket flap to assume an inverted position.

"*Oh right ...yeah—Clouds—Aristo-faines. He's interesting ...*"

"*Who?*" she asked her eyes awash with tears "*You mean—Aristophanes—I think?*"

"*Yes ... I probably do mean Aris-stoff-a-nees ...*" I smiled slightly sheepishly "*... just never heard the name spoken out loud before ... so thank you for your—esteemed—correction. I am heartily obliged.*" Pause "*Anyhow ... Aris-stoff-a-nees interests me because he looks at the causes of corruption in education – and that's been something of a theme with me.*"

"*Aristo-faines is hysterically funny ...*" she resounded – evidently not intrigued to explore Aristophanes with me "*Sorry for laughing at you though.*"

"*No need to apologise*" I replied "*I enjoy being a jester – y'know ... like Wamba the Fool.*"

"*So you've read Sir Walter Scott's 'Ivanhoe' ...*"[1]

"*Indeed I have ... I was extremely keen on Vikings and Norse legends when I was young. I loved that period of history. Another book I enjoyed was Eric Brighteyes by Rider Haggard.*"[2]

---

1 Ivanhoe—written in 1819—is set in 12th century England. Its theme is that of the disquiet between the ruling Normans and the dwindling Saxon nobility.

an odd boy

"*Not—quite—in the same class of course ... but a ripping yarn nonetheless. Groa the witch and Swanhild are wonderful characters.*" Pause "*You know—of course—that 'the Fool' is often a wise man ...*"

"*Yes ... that—was—an intriguing aspect of Wamba in the book. Personally ... I just like making people laugh. I leave wisdom to those who've sat in caves for years.*"

"*Wisdom doesn't appeal to you then?*"

"*Well ...yes it does – but not 'wisdom' in the style of Groa and Swanhild – there's a little too much grief around them. I'd rather not deal in eerie fixed-fate enterprises – y'know the Norns*[3] *and all that – those two Norse gals needed to find something better to do with their time other than putting a Spaniard in the Works.*"

She laughed "*John Lennon's book ... didn't like it myself – but it's amusing to throw it into a conversation.*"

"*I mean*" I continued – letting her comment pass "*I wish Eric had come to a happier end.*"

"*An interesting point of view to be sure*" Claudette grinned with slightly raised eyebrows "*but you know ... It wasn't quite as simple as that. Beside the three Nornir, there were many other Norns – such as Norns who arrived when a person was born.*

---

2   The Saga of Eric Brighteyes—H Rider Haggard—published in 1890—is a Viking novel set in 10th Century Iceland.
3   The Nornir (norns) are three powerful Jotuns (giantesses) of the dísir class – female beings who decree fate. Their arrival from Jötunheimr ended the golden age of the Norse gods. The Völuspá describes the three most prominent nornir: Urðr (wyrd / weird), Verðandi, and Skuld. They draw water from the well of Urðr and pour it over the roots of the ash tree Yggdrasill—the life tree—in order that its branches will not rot.

"*They'd determine different fates – sometimes the direct opposite of the main Nornir. There were malevolent and benevolent Nornir you see. The malevolent Nornir caused the tragic events of the world whilst the benevolent Nornir were kind and protective – they ordered the positive possibilities and chances to overcome evil fates.*"

"*Well*—three cheers—*for them, then – I'm on*—their—*side.*"

"*You're not an enthusiastic tragedian then?*" Claudette cackled.

"*Certainly not. I like happy endings*" I chuckled "*y'know … being a working class lad …*"

"*Being a what?*" Claudette laughed riotously "*You don't*—sound—*working class – well, apart from the reference to Aristo-faines.*"

"*That*—is not—*working class*" I replied with slight seriousness "*that*—*is called*—*ignorance.*"

"*Not that there's anything wrong with being working class of course.*" Claudette's backtrack was the first example I'd witnessed of her feeling wrong-footed.

"*Indeed*" I smiled.

"*To reply 'indeed' is not typical though is it?*" she tittered "*I mean, you're not typically working class.*"

"*Perhaps not – but … I'm not sure I'd know a typical working class person if I met one.*" Pause "*I'm wary of stereotyping … I've been pigeon-holed a little too often to think that categories are helpful to people.*"

"*What of the middle classes then? What's your view of them, that you place yourself so*—decidedly—*as working class? I get the impression that you seem to want to distance yourself from any idea that you might be middle class. That does make me just a*—*little*—*suspicious …*"

Claudette had found her feet again.

"*Mmmm ... now ... there's a question. You've probably caught me out there. I suppose I do have something of a view of the middle classes — but ... it's ... mixed.*" Pause "*... best friends I ever had have been middle and upper-middle — but I've been treated fairly abominably by some middle class parents. I have observed —some— stereotypical middle class characteristics in people ... but they've all been in people over 35 — so it's hard to know what to make of them.*"

Claudette nodded — following my line of reasoning with quiet interest. "*Fair enough. You didn't mind my asking?*"

"*Not at all*" I replied "*It's an interesting subject.*" Pause "*But to take the thing further — I'd say I'm working class because my father's working class. His parents were from Lancashire. They were mill-workers ... My grandmother—on my father's side—choked to death on her false teeth.*"

"*Is that a—typical—working class demise then?*" Claudette grinned ever-so-slightly.

"*Yes?*" I replied with mock seriousness. "*It's responsible for the decline in the textile industry — so it should concern you quite closely in your field of study.*" I had no idea why I mentioned my grandmother's unfortunate death. She had died long before I was born and so there was no sense of personal loss in the story. "*She was a charming lady by all accounts — kept chickens in her back yard.*"

Claudette seemed to feel wrong-footed again and enquired after my maternal grandparents.

"*My mother's family was upper-middle class in Germany before WWII — but her family were quite badly reduced in circumstances ... having been opposed to Hitler.*" Pause "*I took Sociology 'O' level so I know that you drop a class or two by virtue of being foreign — so unless you're a 'Von Something-or-other' you take on the class of your spouse. I went to a working class school—a pretty bad one at that—so I'd say ... that defines me.*" Pause

"I had an excellent English teacher though—Mr Preece—who taught me all about poetry. He was brilliant!"

"*Ah!*" said Claudette – the light having dawned "*So—that's—where you got it from! I knew there had to be some answer to the conundrum.*"

"*Yes?*" I smiled at the idea of being a conundrum "*I learned a great deal from my friends as well. I'm more-or-less self-educated when it comes to culture.*" Pause "*So I take no offence at being*—mildly—*teased for my shortcomings … and*" I ventured with a wide grin "*I'm not about to vie with—you—with regard to literature.*"

"*That's fortunate*" Claudette answered—as if to reassure herself—with a slight tilt of her head.

"*Yes—I—thought so …*" I replied somewhat tongue-in-cheek. Claudette caught the irony of my reply and chuckled.

"*Y'know … about this happy ending thing … It's not merely a dislike of misery.*" Pause "*This may sound a little morally archaic – but I believe that literature should be uplifting to the human condition. I don't mind tragedy in terms of history – but when it comes to fiction I feel that the hero or heroine should win through. I don't like to see people coming to bad ends if they have shown courage and honour. I don't like to see people degenerate in terms of their integrity – unless they win it back again. Books that show good people being humiliated, thwarted, oppressed, and whatever else that have no positive conclusion … well they offer no hope. I feel it is not ethical for a novelist to deny hope to the reader.*"

"*My—my … but you are—quite—the Victorian in some respects … I can almost see you as a vicar.*"

"*Yes … so can I – but wouldn't exactly be qualified – or ever become qualified.*"

"*I believe you only have to attend a seminary.*"

an odd boy

"No … " I laughed "*That's not quite what I mean. I mean I'm the wrong religion to be Vic the Vicar. I think that at the very least you have to be a Christian.*"

Claudette gave me a quizzical look "*What would you happen to be then – Jewish?*"

"*No … a little further East … I'm a Buddhist.*"

"*Who isn't these days?*"

"*I'm not one of those 'Buddhists' … I mean I don't say that because I have a copy of the Tai Te Ching and the Evans Wentz edition of the 'Tibetan Book of the Dead' on my shelf. A fair few people who think they're Buddhist are actually Hindu in terms of their understanding – but maybe … we'd better not go too far down that road.*"

"*And why not … pray?*"

"*I don't pray.*" I grinned "*Buddhists are atheists – but—as to not going down that road—it's not for any reason beyond the fact that I don't like boring people. So many religious types will bore people into a state of catatonia with their religion – but … I really try to avoid that as far as possible. I'll answer questions if you're genuinely fascinated – but not if you're just being polite or … curious.*"

"*My—my … but you are a most … curious creature …you weren't even embarrassed when I suggested that you were slightly Victorian in your views with regard to literature …*"

"*Well … I have the outrageous advantage—you see—of being entirely immune to embarrassment.*"

"*Under—any—circumstances?*" she chortled.

"*More-or-less. I suppose if I was caught defæcating in the lecture theatre I'd be embarrassed – but I'm never tempted to do things that would prove embarrassing were I apprehended in the act.*"

Claudette—almost from the first—had the effect of encouraging me to speak like a thespian.

"*Now there's a thought. What made you think of*—that—*gross example may I ask?*"

"*You assuredly may. Nothing*—made—*me*—*as it were*—*the example arose spontaneously, of its own volition.*"

"*Let's hope that nothing gross descends of its own volition in the lecture theatre then.*" Claudette guffawed "*... but don't you feel embarrassed if you make mistakes or ...*"

"No ..." I interrupted "*Everyone makes mistakes. If I was worried about mistakes*—*or whatever*—*it'd feel as if I was under surveillance.*" There was something I thought I should make clear to Claudette – so I launched in "*Y'know ... I'm not actually*—ashamed—*of my lack of Classical education. It's just a fact-of-fate, as it were. The Nornir can feel ashamed if they like – but I had no hand in the matter.*" Pause "*I generally know all I need to know – and what I*—don't—*know, I'm always happy to learn ... as long as it interests me.*" Pause "*So ...*" I grinned "*... my education is vastly enhanced by the fact that I*—now—*know how to pronounce Aristophanes.*"

"*I must say ...you*—are—*unusual*" Claudette laughed. "*Men don't always take kindly to being corrected in anything.*"

"*Well ... if you can't be corrected ...you can't learn – but I think it depends on how the correction's delivered. And ... it depends on whether the correction's valid or not. Sometimes people just want to supplant your opinion with theirs and that can be tedious. I've got all kinds of opinions – but I don't feel the need to bludgeon people with them.*"

Claudette nodded. "*Yes ...you*—are—*unusual.*" She then peered at me as if I was hard to see across the table.

"*... about defæcating in the lecture theatre ...your question about 'embarrassment' brought up a weird memory ... I wasn't being gross for the sake of it.*" I told her about the possibly apocryphal tale of Aleister Crowley defæcating in public in San Francisco – followed by an account of Mister Monkey-beard.

"*My, my—what—an interesting life you—have—led.*"

"*Yes ... I have – but I wouldn't really count—that—as a high point.*"

Claudette naturally asked me what the high point was and I replied "*Couldn't name—one—there were ... many.*" I wasn't prepared to discuss ladies and so I talked about Mr Love and my history with Blues. I talked about Steve and Ron – and, to a lesser extent, Jack. She listened attentively – and ... I tried to keep it brief.

"*Sorry for being facetious earlier*" she offered quietly. "*You really—have—had an interesting life.*" Pause "*Talking to you is ... not the usual-kind-of-thing you know ... I keep expecting you to be the archetypical male – and you're not—or don't appear to be—and that keeps catching me by surprise. I think I have been a little ... combative ... I'm sorry.*"

"*My pleasure entirely – but y'know ... I don't really go in for being the archetypal—anything.*"

"*Not even the archetypal Art student?*"

"*Mmmm ... there you—might—have got me. Maybe I'll admit to that – but the definition is incredibly broad ... and I have the feeling that you'd have to go to Hatch Mill to see the kind of Art student I am or was. This place isn't exactly teeming with people I'd call archetypal Art students.*"

"*Well ...yes ... good point*" she sighed "*Things do seem to have changed a little – but then I didn't expect to find many Arty types in Fashion and Textiles. I'm only there because I want to go into theatre work.*

"That's ... why I buttonholed you ... I thought you looked as if you could converse – anyone who pays attention to their sense of dress can probably be counted on to provide a modicum of edifying conversation."

Claudette was tall – with luxurious dark wavy hair that trailed below her knees. She was possessed of searing pale blue eyes that gave her a pre-Raphaelite appearance. She had what I thought of as French physiognomy – especially in respect of her rather fine nose. She was quick to inform me that she had French ancestry – distantly descended from the Norman nobility. She was quick witted and curiously scholarly. She seemed to like to have *all-the-facts* at her disposal and to know an enormous number of facts relating to the Arts. There was not an artist, poet, playwright, or novelist of whom she knew nothing. I was radically impressed – and had no objection to being corrected on various false assumptions. I was intrigued by the way she had so much information at her finger tips. She must have done little other than read during the extent of her life. I thought *I'd* read a great deal – but Claudette was another Jasper Stanwell.

"Problem is ..." I confessed "That I read at the speed I speak and I don't speak that quickly ..."

"*Really!?*" she chuckled "*How did—that—come about?*"

"I don't know ... apart from the fact that I learned to read quite late due to having one childhood illness after another whilst I was at Infant school: mumps, whooping cough, chicken pox, turkey pox, goose pox, duck pox, pheasant pox, parrot pox, and every other pox."

"*How utterly fowl!*" she laughed. "*And ...you never caught up?*"

"It would appear not. It takes me a fortnight or more to read a book – unless it's quite short."

an odd boy

"*Really!?*" she replied with some degree of astonishment. "*I must say I'm quite surprised how easily you'll admit such things. Most people would hide such failings at all cost. It's really*—most—*unusual. Have you* —always—*been like this?*"

"Hard to say … I imagine I've always been more-or-less like this— whatever that is—*but, beyond that, I can't really comment. I see no point in trying to impress anyone. Pretending to be whatever it is that I imagine other people find impressive would be kind of tedious. It'd be like being some sort of monkey on a string.*"

"Isn't that 'puppet on a string'?"

"This time, no" I laughed "*I wasn't alluding to Sandy Shaw.*[4] *I actually* —meant—*monkey. I was thinking of being jerked around by a keeper of some sort and made to dance. My father told me about dancing monkeys in India and so I have a picture of that.*"

"*I am sorry to be trying to correct you so often – you must find it irritating.*"

"No. If you're right I'll learn something – and if you're not – then …*you might learn something.*"

"Point taken." She smiled sheepishly "*Tell me about monkeys in India then. I only know about dancing bears.*" Claudette noticed my smile and sailed in before I could comment – even though I had no intention of commenting. "*And I*—don't—*mean 'Simon Smith and his Amazing Dancing Bear*[5] *– I mean dancing bears in the Middle Ages.*"

---

4   Sandy Shaw was a 1960s Pop singer whose song 'Puppet on a String' won the Eurovision Song Contest in 1967. She is said to have hated the song even though it was an international hit.

5   Randy Newman—Alan Price Set—Simon Smith and His Amazing Dancing Bear —1967

I nodded with a grin. This lady was extremely keen on being on top – hyper aware of any possibility of jests being made at her expense. *"Y'know … I really—am—quite inoffensive. I can give as good as I get – but I'm not out to get the better of you or anything."*

"I'm sorry … it's just …" Pause *"Well I'm not used to good manners in people—in men—when it comes to discussion … and … I'm finding it a little difficult to stop being on my guard."*

"Don't worry about it. It's actually extremely hard to offend me – unless you're determined or something."

"Tell me about the dancing monkeys then."

"Well my father told me nothing of the actual dancing … he just told me how monkeys were caught, you see … it's an interesting account in various ways. This is how it goes. The monkey-catcher chains an iron pot to a tree and fills it with nuts. The lug—through which the chain passes—is up by the opening of the pot, so that it can't be turned over. The opening of the pot is fairly small – and so the monkey has to squeeze its hand inside to get the nuts. The problem—for the monkey—is that it can't get its hand out of the pot unless its hand is empty." Claudette was looking genuinely intrigued and I was glad that she'd decided to listen without making rejoinders. *"Anyhow … along comes the monkey-catcher."* Pause *"The monkey—aware of the danger—tries to free itself … but it's not possible unless it empties its hand."* Pause *"As the monkey catcher approaches the monkey struggles harder and harder to escape – but in the end the monkey's caught. Swift whack on the head and it's in the sack."*

"Most educational" Claudette tittered *"… but is it necessary to concuss the poor monkey?"*

"Don't know … never enquired. I was more interested from a philosophical perspective." Claudette raised an eyebrow in order to prompt me to elaborate.

"Well—put simply—it's a question of the price of liberation."

I paused for dramatic effect *"If you want to be free …you have to let go of your nuts."*

Claudette rocked backwards and forwards laughing *"That would make emancipation rather more difficult for women – don't you think?"*
I laughed with her – and when she recovered her composure she indicated the time. We needed to get back to our respective studios. I regretted the loss of the opportunity to discuss human nature – but decided there'd be other occasions.

The next time we met in the refectory, I asked about her amazing assemblage of costumes. I'd seen Claudette wafting round the Art School on a number of occasions and had been struck by the colours she wore. She was a marvellous tailor. She made many of her own clothes: capes, skirts, jackets, and items for which there is no ready description. Her cloaks were made of silk velvet in amazing shades of purple, violet, puce, and mauve. She had a large collection of flowing silk Pre-Raphaelite dresses in extraordinary shades of every colour imaginable – made by some haute couture establishments in Paris and London. Claudette was the first intriguing person I'd met for what seemed a long time. She opined—for no obvious reason—that people became disgusting and puerile when they drank. I agreed —to a certain extent—but said *"It depends on whether a person drinks for flavour or drinks for oblivion."*

"One has often led to the other in my experience – because so many people are irredeemably bestial. They too often revert to primitivism – and start finding themselves humorous, when they're actually merely infantile."

"Well … I couldn't afford to get drunk on the wine I prefer to drink – and even if I could I don't like being drunk. Did it once—thought it was insane—and never did it again."

Claudette nodded. *"So you do—really—just enjoy the odd glass of wine?"*

"*Yes.*" Then she enquired of beer. "*Never touch beer—vile stuff—if I'm thirsty I drink ginger beer.*"

"*The Famous Five!*" she cackled "*Lashings of ginger beer!*" she quoted. I evidently looked confused so she continued "*Enid Blyton—The Famous Five—the series of childrens' books?*"[6]

"*Oh right ... never read them. I hated anything written especially for children.*"

"*Well – you didn't miss much. They have some 1940s charm – but they are rather silly. All the villains have side burns and hair hanging over their collars.*" Pause "*Anyway the big treat as far as the famous five were concerned was lashings of ginger beer.*"

One of the Fine Art students overheard our conversation and laughed as she passed "*Famous—fucking—Five man—Jeeeeesus—you never read—that—stuff did you!? That crap rots children's brains.*"

Claudette stiffened. It was a slightly awe-inspiring sight. She stared at the offending party with unblinking eyes 'til she moved away.

Ralph Simons from Graphic Design was nearby at the time with Wendy Millhurst and Georgina Reynolds – and he looked at the Fine Art student, shook his head, and said "*Cretin.*"

I smiled at Ralph to let him know I'd appreciated his support for Claudette. Claudette hadn't noticed Ralph's remark and commented "*It's the mark of moronic vulgarians to use expletives.*" Claudette never swore – but not for the same reasons that I almost never swore.

---

6 Enid Blyton [1897 – 1968], British author of children's novels. Her most popular series was 'The Famous Five' [1943 – 1961] which extended to 21 novels. She also wrote 'The Secret Seven' [1949 – 1963] which extended to 15 novels.

"*Yes ... I'd not argue too much with that. Although ... I'd never refuse to use any usable word – it's simply a matter of time and place.*"

"*You think there's a time and place for vulgar expletives?*" she said rather crisply.

"*Yes – but one place where they're not appropriate is when butting into someone else's conversation. I'm not in favour of gratuitously expressed opinions. She didn't know what we were talking about in any case. She merely caught Enid Blyton or The Famous Five and decided to be pompous about it. I objected to the pomposity more than the language.*"

"*Well then – she was both vulgar and pompous and my opinion of her is even lower.*"

"*Well yes ... I'd say that extreme language is appropriate for extreme circumstances – and rarity of usage gives greater force to it. I'd throw out a 'fuck' if I really*—needed—*to ... but, it might only occur once a decade.*"

Claudette winced slightly at the word "*I'm afraid I just find it coarse and unnecessary ... even if it*—is—*Anglo Saxon.*"[7]

"*Well ...*" I grinned "*Never knew that ... however, it'll be a decade 'til I employ that archaic expletive again; so I'm not likely to re-offend.*"

"*Just as well*" Claudette tittered "*I'm happy to see you can employ restraint with language as much as with alcohol.*"

"*Restraint's my middle name*" I chuckled.

"*How*—marvellously—*Victorian ... Victor*—Restraint—*Simmerson ... like Lancelot*—Capability—*Brown.*[8] *How very droll.*"

---

7 King Offa of Mercia's charter granting land in Sussex mentions 'Fuccerham'—'the home of fuckers'—a village north of Hastings. Origins also as follows: Germanic—ficken; Dutch—fokken; Norse—fukka; and Swedish—fokka.
8 Lancelot Brown [1716 – 1783], commonly known as 'Capability Brown' – an English landscape architect remembered as England's greatest gardener.

Claudette had made an art of persiflage – that left me feeling a little slow. I was amazed by the way she'd pull arcane references out of thin air. I found her monumentally entertaining and informative – and for her part she seemed continually surprised anew that I was not offended by the rapier of her rapid badinage. Claudette—appearance-wise—would have fitted well at Hatch Mill. She *looked* like an Art student—albeit of the expensively dressed variety—and that was reassuring to me. I'd seen too many sartorially average persons at Bower Aston and was rather fearing that I was on my own.

The next time I met Claudette, I was sitting in the refectory eating lunch. It was a Friday. The canteen provided excellent fish and chips on Fridays. The fish was fresh—the batter always thin and crisp—and, they made their own tartare sauce. Claudette placed herself opposite me—in what seemed a deliberate manner—and engaged me in conversation.

"*What are—you—writing for your Related Studies essay?*" It was due in at the end of term. We both took Film as our Related Studies option with a man called Rick Frampton. He showed us films like *Ivan the Terrible – parts I and II*, *Battleship Potemkin*, and *October* by the Russian filmmaker Sergei Eisenstein – the pioneer of montage in film editing.

"*I'm not writing about the Eisenstein films. Rick Frampton didn't stipulate the subject matter of the essay. He said 'write an essay on an aspect of Filmmaking' – so that's what I am going to give him.*"

She laughed a *Horse and Hound* laugh,[9] and said—with a humorous flitter of her eyebrows "*That's a bold move.*"

---

9 Horse and Hound – a British magazine read mainly by those who ride and own their own horses.

an odd boy

"*I—thought so*" I replied with a slight irony that made her roar with laughter. Claudette had a way of using vocal intonation to suggest irony and seemed to appreciate that I was capable of the same ironic inflections. She employed a wide variety of extremely slight movements of facial expression to suggest quizzicality or light-hearted mockery. I found her entertaining – but I also found her pleasantly challenging. Conversation was obviously never going to be dull with Claudette.

"*So … what film have you chosen for your essay topic, may I ask?*"

"*'The Ruling Class' – with Peter O'Tool. Seen it four times now—taken a slew of notes—so he can't complain I've not researched it.*"[10]

She looked at me quizzically "*That's … a comedy isn't it?*" and I replied that it was – in part.

"*So … What d'you find that's interesting enough for an essay?*"

There was almost too much to say "*It fascinates me, the way 'The Ruling Class' moves seamlessly between different métiers.*" I detected the slightest of grins as I used the word 'métier.' "*It's not a 'musical' – but it becomes a musical—intermittently—and, in a way that's—nothing—like a musical. It's as if the musical sections are hallucinations suddenly injected into the flow of the narrative. They're kind-of out of place and perfectly positioned at the same time. It's as if the musical sequences are deliberately organised in the film to hit you as incongruous.*"

Claudette tilted her head as if to say '*Yes – but that doesn't add up to an essay.*'

I took her meaning—as if she'd spoken—and continued. "*And then … it shifts in form … between conventional reality and surrealism—between comedy and tragedy—horror and whimsicality.*

---

10 The Ruling Class—play and screen play by Peter Medak—1972

"It keeps you wondering what kind of a film it is – and what the major feeling is that it's going to portray. By the end you realise that it's some kind of nightmare that might be called 'Life in Britain.' Sometimes it looks like a political satire and sometimes it looks like a pastiche of reflections on the nature of sanity and insanity. I see it as a Surrealist film."

Claudette conceded *"Mmmm ... well ... if you approached 'The Ruling Class' as Surrealism that would give you a better basis for an essay."*

That was an interesting comment. *"So ..."* I grinned *"You're saying—that—would give it academic credibility?"*

"Yes."

"So ... why ... would I want that ... necessarily?"

"Why? Because an essay's an accepted academic mode ..." Claudette chuckled *"... I must admit to being somewhat surprised though ... that academic credibility isn't high on your list of attributes when it comes to—fascination."*

"No ..." I pondered *"... it isn't really."* Pause *"I'm not*—opposed —*to the academic approach ... it's merely not as fascinating as ... direct experience ... Academia rhymes with anæmia."*

"Very droll – but what does that mean?"

"Well ... academia seems more interested in numbers, dates, and facts than in ... the texture of life. I need to be fascinated and to follow my fascination wherever it leads."

"So you simply do whatever you like – merely because you're fascinated?"

"Certainly. What better reason?" Then I sang *"I'm not trying to cause a big sens-sation – I'm just—talking 'bout my fa—scin—ation."*[11]

---

11 Parody of 'My Generation'. Pete Townshend—The Who—My Generation—1965

Claudette shook her head "*You're incorrigible.*"

"Quite so, I can be—incorriged—*at the drop of a hat, just give it a try. I do whatever I want to do – and go my own way come hell or rogue waves – without causing unnecessary inconvenience or discomfiture to others, you understand.*" Pause "*You see … it's far more important to*—me—*to follow my enthusiasm than to get good marks for my essays.*"

"*You don't care what marks you get?*"

"Not—that—*much … no. What would I do with good marks anyway? I'm here to …*" Pause "*I'm here to explore … and to develop ideas … to the limit of whatever it is that I'm capable of creating.*"

"*That sounds a little vague though …*"

"*Well – let's call it open-ended rather than vague. My main interest*—I suppose—*is the interface between image and language.*"

Claudette seemed amused by my philosophical statement of intent. "*And you find the language in 'The Ruling Class' fascinating?*"

"*I do. It provides some fine linguistics in the* 14th Earl of Gurney's *speech.*"

She looked incredulous. "*In which scene?*" she asked – her face glowing with restrained mirth.

"*In the scene where he's recently left the lunatic asylum and arrived at his ancestral home to take his deceased father's place as Earl. Anyway – this is the scene: the* 14th Earl of Gurney—*believing himself to be Christ*—is *wearing a Lennonesque white suit.*"

"*He's taking his ease resting on a commodious living room cross*—almost *like some kind of vertical chaise longue*—when suddenly he wakes up.*"

Claudette was almost in tears in respect of the commodious living room cross likened unto a vertical chaise longue.

"*Anyhow*" I continued "*Then—he proceeds to give this magnificently outlandish speech.*" I rummaged through my shoulder bag and withdrew the speech as I'd copied it down. "*It's a surreal interweaving of ... the majestic and the absurd:*
'*For I am creator and ruler of the universe – Coda! The one Supreme Being! Infinite personal being! Yahweh; Shangri; Ti and El—the first immovable mover—Yay! I am the absolute, unknowable, righteous, eternal – the lord of hosts, king of kings, lord of lords—the father, son and holy ghost—the one true god, the god of love – the Christ! My heart rises with the sun. I'm purged of doubts and negative innuendos. Today, I want to bless everything. Bless the crawfish with its scuttling walk. Bless the trout, pilchard, and periwinkle. Bless Ted Smoothy of 22, East Hackney Road. Bless the mealy redpoll, the black-gloved wallaby, and WC Fields who's dead but lives on. Bless the snotty-nosed giraffe. Bless the buffalo. Bless the Society of Women Engineers. Bless the pygmy hippos. Bless the mighty cockroach. Bless me!*'—*Then—he leaps towards the camera and is suspended in mid air with the words: 'for today is my wedding day!'*
... *It's –* fabulous!"

Claudette found the speech hilarious – but asked, somewhat rhetorically "*I'm devilishly impressed that you can quote it – but ...you'd say these are—fine—linguistics?*"

"*Certainly I would. It's not—*just*—the words though.*" I tried to explain. "*If you look at them cold, you could argue that they're nothing in particular. It's in the—*delivery*—of the words. The words are Pythonesque—yes—but, there's also a quality of unbridled affirmation – without recourse to the criteria of conventional critical evaluation.*"

Claudette shrieked with laughter.

"*Maybe it's just the way I hear things*" I offered as an explanation of my particular eccentricity.

an odd boy

Claudette agreed "*Yes – it's definitely the way—you—hear things.*" Claudette appeared to enjoy my bizarre turn of mind – almost as if she'd alighted upon some rare zoological discovery. It was a peculiar conversation. Claudette seemed keen to talk with me – but also seemed to find me a curiously perplexing plebeian. "*You're surprisingly naïve for someone who appears to be unusually intellectually sophisticated.*"

Now it was my turn to laugh. "*I don't fit into a box you know … and I'm pretty much independent of approval and disapproval. I just like what I like. It doesn't matter a great deal if anyone else likes it or not. In that way … I'm always free to go with whatever moves me whether it's culturally sanctioned as high-brow or not.*"

Claudette pondered "*Doesn't that mean that your value judgements are entirely subjective?*"

The intriguing quality of our conversation was that I had no idea where it was going. "*Utterly …*" I replied "*… but 'objectivity' of any kind is often just subjectivity carrying the cudgel of authority.*"

Claudette raised her eyebrows to an unprecedented elevation "*Have you said that before?*"

"*No – not as far as I'm aware … Why d'you ask?*"

"*It's sounds very polished for an off-the-cuff remark.*"

"*Well … I may read slowly – but I read all the time … so I suppose it must impress itself into me or something.*"

"*Yes … that—is—the way it's supposed to work. I'm just a little surprised to see the theory being put into effect so … effectively.*" Pause "*So … what about criticism?*"

"*It's not that I won't listen to criticism—or learn from it—it's just that I demand the right to make my own final decisions*" I replied.

"*I don't respect authorities unless I have decided to accept them as authorities. Just because—the world out there—declares people to be authorities, doesn't force me to agree.*"

"*My, my – but you're passionate about this aren't you.*"

"*Yes*" I laughed "*But—y'know—I have known some excellent authority figures in my life, and when I've learnt to respect someone's experience – I pay serious attention to what they say.*"

Claudette's expression and body language spelt out '*fair enough*' – and we departed for our own departments. We seemed to keep meeting at lunch times and after a while I got the impression that she was looking out for me wherever I happened to be sitting.

"*My friends call me 'dette*" she said when she saw me next. She'd scanned the refectory for me and had walked across with her cup of tea and salad sandwich.

I made a token bow with my head "*I'm indebted*" – at which she pursed her lips slightly. It occurred to me that we were simply going to be slightly adversarial friends – amicable sparring partners in the fields of the Arts. "*So … 'dette—if you don't mind my asking—how d'you come to have a vintage Silver Cloud – aren't they kind of staggeringly expensive?*"

"*Yes—they are—but, mine …you see … was actually really quite reasonably priced. Probably no more than the average family saloon.*"[12]

My eyes widened with curiosity. "*So …?*" I asked without formulating the question.

"*So?*" she replied looking as if she was not sure as to whether to answer my question.

---

12 Saloon – sedan in the USA.

an odd boy

"*So my father's a bigwig at Rolls Royce—and—something of a scientist in terms of motor engineering. He got it through contacts – and I was very lucky to get it. It's a 1957 Silver Cloud and it was in—extremely—poor condition. I think it had been owned by some nouveau riche lunatic who seemed unable to avoid trees and dry stone walls. It needed considerable panel beating—you know the kind of thing—and replacement parts, not to mention attention to the engine.*" Pause "*Anyway my father lavished his fond attentions on it—and, as you see—it has become once more a thing of great beauty.*"

"*It's amazing*" I replied inanely – not knowing what to say.

"*Well, he had the time and resources to transform it for me – otherwise it would have been impossible. He had it re-sprayed at the Rolls Royce plant and had all the metalwork re-chromed.*"

"*It looks brand new. It looks as if Rolls Royce is your father's passion as well as his career.*"

"*Yes ... he likes nothing better than refurbishing a Rolls Royce that's seen better days.*" Claudette suddenly shifted the conversation as if she wished to confine my curiosity concerning her personal circumstances. "*So ... what would you—say—about the Earl of Gurney's speech?*" Pause "*We ran out of time and you never finished what you were saying.*"

"*Right ...*" a moment of reflection "*Well 'dette—as a poet—I'd say it was poetry. It's not critical to my appreciation that the speech was delivered by a delusional character who believed he was the first immovable mover – or that it's a string of absurdist non sequiturs. Poetry doesn't have to conform to logical linear anabasis.*"

Claudette shifted her expression somewhat on hearing the word 'anabasis' – so I explained "*Anabasis? It means a military advance.*"

I'd inadvertently scored a point with Claudette.

She seemed to change gear in relation to me, if only slightly. I might pronounce Aristophanes as 'Aristo-faines' – but I also threw out words like 'anabasis'. *"The speech wasn't presented as poetry – but in a poet's ears, poetry is what it is; whatever it may be termed by scriptwriters or film lecturers."*

"Interesting ... I've never come across—that—*idea before ..."* she pondered *"Definitely intriguing ... and*—*definitely*—*avant-garde."* Pause *"And all this ...you developed on your own?"*

"More or less ... although—*to be fair*—*I must have had several thousand hours of conversation with Steve and Ron. And then there was Mr Preece who gave me a lot of help – but not really with the avant-garde side of the business ... that just kind of evolved in tandem with writing lyrics."* Pause *"I did get some avant-garde influence from a maniac called Beowulf and later from Roger McGough and Adrian Henri."*

"You know Roger McGough and Adrian Henri!" she almost shrieked.

"No ... I don't 'know' them – or rather I no longer know them. I only met them once but I had some really interesting conversations with them about poetry."

"How did you come to meet them?"

"We were reading poetry together at Farnham Art School. All kinds of people came through Art School. We once had John Cage – and we sat at the piano together playing all kinds of weirdness."

"You play piano?"

"Not so you'd notice – but I love plinking around on a piano whenever I get the opportunity. I just play patterns – I find a pattern of notes that work and I ramble around on them."

"The true Renaissance man I see ..." she giggled. She had to be back in her department for a talk from a visiting clothing designer – so she bid me farewell "... *Au'voir Leonardo!"*

4

the first year: november – december 1972

bower ashton – apostate apostles in white

"So—*Leonardo* ..." the voice came from somewhere behind me before Claudette appeared sitting next to me "... *Mister Renaissance man ... how's your essay proceeding?*"

"Why hello, 'dette—I must say—that—was a finely executed approach; hardly knew you were there, before you were ... there."

"I like—everything—about me to be finely executed" Claudette giggled.

"Hung by the neck until grinning – or electrocuted 'til ... extremely pleased?"

"You're quick off the mark this morning—I must say—but what about your tour de force with The Ruling Class?"

"Well ... I've been dwelling upon the idea of the white suit."

"The—famous—white suit. Tell me more?"

"There's not—too—much to tell at the moment." Pause "It strikes me that it must have some kind of symbolism ..."

"I think it's probably Christian in influence. Christ was always shown in white – and this is probably a modern day version of the same thing."

"Really ... I wouldn't have thought of that ... I guess I'm not exactly big on Christian symbolism."

"Yes—of course—you're a Buddhist. I was forgetting."

"Well yes ... but it's not quite that – but it's not at the forefront of my mind. I've liked it since Alice told me that she wanted me to wear a white suit on our wedding day."

an odd boy

Then I had to explain about Alice Trevelyan.

"*I must say … that's highly romantic. I'm surprised though, that you'd remember such a thing.*"

"*I have a good memory for beauty, love, and laughter*" I grinned.

"*You—are—a continual surprise*" she chuckled "*You're always saying things I wouldn't have expected.*"

"*I trust is doesn't weird you out?*" I enquired.

"*Not at all – it's refreshing. People are generally so predictable.*" Pause "*So … what does a white suit mean to you … beyond your memory of Alice?*"

"*Mmmm … I'm not entirely certain*" I replied "*I've not yet put it into words for myself. It's a costume that … makes its own statement – and then you have to find out what that statement is … in your own case.*" Pause "*It's as if I'd have to find out what a white suit means … by wearing it.*" Pause "*Maybe—in view of the Messianic associations you mentioned—I could say that … in a white suit …you could become … one of the apostate apostles in white.*"

"*Apostate Apostles in White – that sounds … remarkably like something from a Leonard Cohen song.*" She laughed "*Are these apostles nameable or are they beyond the reach of mere mortals?*"

"*No—they're nameable—although this may—not—be the conclusive list … there's Sir Alec Guinness in 'The Man in the White Suit,*[1] *John Lennon on the album sleeve of 'Abbey Road,' Peter O'Toole in 'The Ruling Class,' and …*"

I slid to a halt wondering how I hadn't registered the Christian association of the white suit when it was utterly evident in the film. The Earl of Gurney thought he was the Messiah.

---

1   The Man in the White Suit – made in 1951 by Ealing Studios, London.

"And now—you—evidently" she dived in grinning. *"I can see—you—on the cover of—something—in a white suit."*

"Possibly ..." I replied with slight unaccustomed embarrassment *"although ..."* Pause *"... that image ... is just a ... space ... in my imagination."*

"A cat can look at a king" she commented.

"Y'know ..." I grinned *"I said—almost—the same thing once ... I said 'a bat can look at a bathroom' ..."*

"How did that come to pass – may I ask" she grinned.

I told her the story of the evening when Jack had talked about the possibility of Jimi Hendrix seeing us – if we happened to get booked up as a warm-up act. I failed to go into the deaths of Ron and Steve – but she sensed that a cloud had passed over me.

"It must be strange to have been so close to a ... marvellous future – and then to have had it snatched away."

"Yes ... it is strange – and the strangeness of it ... well ... I don't know what to say really."

"Yes ... I can imagine. So—you ... were saying ..." she injected in order to change a subject that was evidently difficult for me *"... the white suit ... makes its own statement?"*

"Yes ... as long as it's not one of those Mafia tuxedo jobs ..."

"Heaven forbid."

"Quite so – it's not a statement I can easily define though – because the definition can shift according to what's happening and where I might happen to be. The world's like some sort of story and I never know which way the plot's going to unravel. I like the unpredictable indeterminacy ... of how life might project me into weird and wonderful scenarios."

an odd boy

"*That sounds just a little ... unsettling – and, you ... feel happy with that?*"

"*Mostly ... it's ... the hand-of-cards I'm dealt, on the hoof—as it were—and ... I have to—be—whomever the situation suggests.*" Pause "*So ... I dress for a part that has no description. It's actually—in some sense—the closest thing to wearing nothing at all.*"

"*I'm not sure I understand ... but—you—obviously do*" Claudette laughed heartily. "*How long have you been talking like this; or have you —always—talked like this?*"

"*Well ... I've always—written—like this, in poetry ...*" I laughed "*... but I only started—talking—like this since ... the Foundation year at Hatch Mill. It was only there that people understood me. Well ... there were my old friends Steve and Ron—they always understood me—but then ... they were quite highly educated.*"

Claudette told me "*I've read a great deal – but I've never thought to speak as if I were living in a Jane Austen novel.*"

"*I've not read—that—much Jane Austen.*"

"*What have you read?*"

"*Pride and Prejudice.*"

"*You really are full of surprises ... I wouldn't have thought they were boys' books.*"

"*No indeed ... they're certainly not in the 'Biggles Flies Undone'[2] category ... I suppose.*"

---

2 Reference to the Biggles series of Boys' Adventure stories about Biggles (James Bigglesworth), a British airman character created by Captain W.E Johns [1893 – 1968]. Biggles was the hero of stories such as 'Biggles Flies Again' [1934]; 'Biggles Flies East' [1935]; 'Biggles Flies West' [1937]; 'Biggles Flies South' [1938]; 'Biggles Flies North' [1939]; 'Biggles Flies to Work' [1963].

Claudette shrieked "*Oh—now—that's just—too—funny* ... *Biggles Flies Undone – you are a card, and no mistake.*"

"*Ace of hearts at your service.*" I effected to doff my cap which provoked yet further laughter ."*However ... I never went in for reading what you might call boys' books. I might not have chosen to read Jane Austen—amongst all the other literature available—but a girlfriend —from Farnham Girls' Grammar—suggested her. They read all kinds of things there.*"

"*You should read 'Sense and Sensibility' – and 'Persuasion.' I'll loan you my copies.*"

"*Much obliged – although it'll take me a month. I find Jane Austen— slightly—slow-reading y'know ... I often have to re-read her longer sentences.*"

"*Yes ... Jane Austen ... she*—can—*be a little difficult at first*" she condoled.

"*Once I get through a chapter I usually find my feet with the style and then it becomes easier. It's always worthwhile though – because she's really quite witty when you fathom her sense of irony.*"

"*I had you down for a person who enjoyed irony*" she commented with a smile. "*It's always so much more pleasant to converse with someone who appreciates irony—conversation can all be so dull otherwise—don't you find?*"

"*Absolutely. Yes ... it can be a little like trying to make headway in a deluge of partially frozen slugs.*"

"*That's hysterical!*" she laughed.

"*Glad you find it so – it's a shame when a well-turned phrase slithers by unrecognised.*"

an odd boy

"A well-turned calf too. You know that in the 18th *Century a man's well-turned calf was the thing a woman admired. That's why they wore those silk stockings."*

"Really ... that's—most—*interesting. I must say I'm intrigued with history. It's fascinating to learn about the mind and how we see things differently at different times. The ideas about what's attractive and not attractive change all the time and people always seem to think their sense of æsthetics are personal. The reality of it, is that most people are almost entirely conditioned."*

"The Renaissance man and the—*philosopher*—*eh?"* she grinned.

"Well ..." I dissembled *"I'm just interested in everything – or almost everything. Arithmetic and mathematics leaves me cold ... as do Frank Sinatra, Liberace, Russ Conway,[3] Semprini,[4] beetroot, porridge, tripe, suet pudding and sport."*

"We obviously see eye-to-eye on—most—*things then"* she chuckled. *"How d'you feel about Andy Warhol?"*

"Andy Warhol looks a scream – hang him on my wall—*all*—*all*—*all"* I sang *"Andy Warhol, Silver Screen, can't tell 'em apart at a-all*—*a-all*—*a-all."*[5]

"D'you like David Bowie?" she smiled with amusement.

"I haven't listened to him enough to say."

"Enough to sing the chorus of that song though ..."

---

3   Russ Conway [Trevor Herbert Stanford, 1925 – 2000] was a popular music pianist. Conway recorded his first solo single in 1957, a novelty piano medley of Pop songs.
4   Alberto Fernando Riccardo Semprini [1908 – 1990], an English pianist famous for appearances on BBC radio in which he introduced with the words 'Old ones, new ones, loved ones, neglected ones.'
5   David Bowie—Andy Warhol—Hunky Dory—1971

"*Well ... I was a vocalist and I remember song lyrics – sometimes even from one hearing.*" Pause "*Anyhow – the words are quite fun in that song —and no—I don't care for Andy Warhol.*"

Claudette clapped her hands together with glee. "*What about ... Van Gogh?*"

"*I love his paintings—the man's a genius—the way he knows about movement and colour. His trees are phenomenal – the way you can see the effects of the wind.*"

"*There are trees like that in San Francisco – I went there once with my father on a business trip. It was fun.*"

"*I can imagine. I'd like to go there one day – and to Chicago—the South side—to hear some Blues.*"

I had the strange feeling that she might be homing in on me – but I wasn't as certain as usual, when such things happened. Our conversation had become increasingly pleasant and I couldn't deny that I enjoyed seeing her. She was witty, intelligent, vivacious, and ... unusually attractive. She wasn't attractive in any popular sense – she was more ... striking. General opinion would have considered her nose too hawk-like – but I found her face strong and statuesque. The cutesy button-nosed appearance of *common-concept-beauty* held no interest for me – that was strictly for television and the tabloids.

"*You were saying yesterday – that you wrote poetry ...*" she changed the subject "*d'you have ... any poems I could read?*"

I internally winced at the word 'poem' – I never used it to refer to anything I wrote. The word 'poem' sounded like some appalling assemblage of 'precious' lines scattered onto a page in cute shapes. I wrote poetry—not—poems. "*Certainly*" I said "*... but I don't have much to show. I threw most of my material away when I left Farnham.*"

an odd boy

"*I thought you weren't a renunciate?*"

"*Intriguing question …*" Pause "*No, I'm not … I suppose though, that that doesn't prevent me divesting myself of clutter.*" Pause "*Still – it's surprisingly observant of you to pick up on that.*"

"*It's my place in life …*" Claudette grinned "*… to be observant.*"

"*Happy to hear that – I look forward to your future observations.*" Pause "*Do you by any chance have an observatory at home?*"

"*Very droll*" she laughed "*Observatory indeed.*"

"*I've still got lyrics though—about* 30 *songs—and I've got poetry I wrote in Bristol before the term started – I'll bring it in tomorrow if you like.*"

"*I would*—like" she grinned.

With that I departed for the Illustration studio thinking how pleasant it had been talking with Claudette. She'd warmed up over the course of our chance encounters – and I began to wonder about her. Had they been chance meetings? Well maybe the first – but what of the 2nd, 3rd, 4th and now the 5th? I wasn't sure what to make of her. I had the curious notion that ambivalence had begun to oscillate between perceptual fascination and a more viscerally construed kind of curiosity. Was it possible that she was romantically interested—and if she was—what was I feeling on the subject? I didn't quite know. I'd never been in a situation where I was so unsure how I felt. When I'd first met her she'd been quite adversarial – albeit in a good natured kind of way. Now she was decidedly gracious in her demeanour. I remembered the scenario with Greg Ford's Beach Buggy – but that had turned out to be vaguely ridiculous, so I felt unsure as to whether I was going to allow myself to be … appropriated … without consulting with myself on the matter.

I'd allowed Helen to call the shots that inaugurated our relationship – and wondered whether *going along with things* was a pattern that I ought to examine. Claudette was definitely an intriguing lady – and I enjoyed her repartee, especially since she'd become less combative. It occurred to me that she had quite an incisive critique of most things – and it seemed that at the very least we'd be friends.

I came in the next day with a folder of lyrics. I felt somehow impelled to go to the fourth floor—to the Fashion and Textiles Department—in order to leave the folder on her desk. I'd written her name on the folder as I had no idea which of the desks belonged to her. Having done so ... I wondered about the act. Was it maybe taking things a step further than necessary – or was it merely friendly? It was ever-so-slightly unsettling not to understand my own intentions. I was in need of friends—of course—and so I concluded that I wasn't necessarily becoming seditiously enamoured. I skipped the mid-morning break in order to undermine any sense of acting on furtive-autopilot. Claudette however, sought me out in the lunch break.

"*And where were*—you—*this morning?*" she grinned.

I smiled at her. "*Sorry, were you looking for me?*"

"*Of course I was*" she giggled "*I wanted to talk about your ... mesmeric lyrics.*"

"*I was ... working and ... didn't notice the time—I don't always come down mid-morning, if I'm in the middle of something. Anyhow ... sorry to have misappropriated myself—as it were—but here we are.*"

"*Here we are indeed ...*" she laughed "*... an acute*—observation—*but I must say I*—am—*intrigued by these lyrics ... this really takes me back.*

an odd boy

"It's almost like a cross between ... 'I am the Walrus' and 'Hey Mr Tambourine Man' ... or ... 'Happiness is a Warm Gun' and 'All Along the Watch Tower.' It's ... almost as if I know them – as if they were songs I heard in '67 ... do these songs have melodies?"

"No. Only three have melodies – but I've never been able to play them myself because the chords were all-over-the-neck – insane barré chords."

"Who wrote the melodies then?"

"My friends Ron Larkin and Steve Bruce." Pause "They were brilliant musicians ... and ... they hadn't got round to composing any more than that before they died." Again—the eternal tragic tale—but I kept it brief.

"I—so—sorry. What a dreadful—dreadful—thing to have happened" she said without any hint of superiority. "*You wear it very—well— for such a recent bereavement ... it must have been terribly traumatising – truly horrendous.*"

"Yeah ... it was ... and ... it still is ... when I think about it – but ... I don't think about them all the time." Pause "But ... feeling grief has to have an end—some—time. Ron and Steve wouldn't want me crimping my style forever on their account – I know that ... I'd feel the same looking down on them from wherever. I'd want them to go out and take the world by storm."

"*Yes ...*" Pause "*They'd dedicate albums to you though ...*"

"Yes ... I imagine they would. So would I – and ... maybe I will." Pause "Or anthologies of poetry or whatever. I still think about working on lyrics."

She giggled "*Some of these are—really—quite funny too.*"

"I suppose they do have a certain naïveté – but I still enjoy the surrealism."

"*Sorry – I didn't mean it like that – I mean they're witty, I think that's important in lyrics like this. If they're not witty – psychedelic lyrics tend to be mushy, like 'Insipid Lucy in the Dreary Sky' and those kind of songs.*"

"*Ah yes … I know what you mean … 'Lucy in the Sky with Diamonds' could have been a little less cute in some lines … the 'rocking horse people eating marshmallow pies' … but … I think it was written as a song for children – and if so then it's fine.*"

"*You like to see the good in everything don't you …?*"

"*Yes … if I can … although … I have a hard time with fascist or communist dictators … and maybe the Eurovision Song Contest …* "[6] I grinned "*… but as to the songs … Maybe I'll revise them.*"

"*Not at all!*" she exclaimed in mock consternation. "*You dare touch them – and you'll have me to reckon with.*"

That convulsed me with laughter. It was good to hear – so I replied "*You have my word on it. You make me feel as if I'm not entirely antediluvian.*"

Claudette grinned "*So the flood gates haven't broken yet?*" She was *quoting* from my song *Before the Floodgates Break*.

In that twilight constellation rack – the barman makes a joke / He's counting down the seconds for the symphony of smoke, / The jolly japing jester tries but fails to mark the slate / But the smiling waitress checks the deal before the floodgates break. Larkin/Bruce/Schubert—Savage Cabbage—Before the Floodgates Break—Savoy Green—1970

---

6 The Eurovision Song Contest – an annual competition held among countries of the European Broadcasting Union. Each submits a song for performance on live television and each casts votes for the other countries' songs to determine the most popular. The Contest has been broadcast every year since its inauguration in 1956.

"*Some of them ...*" I continued "*... were written when I was at Hatch Mill.*"

"*So you kept writing even though you had no band ... that was ... brave of you.*"

"*Kind of you to say so – but I kept writing because ... that's what I do. If I get an idea for a song I just start jotting down ideas. There doesn't have to be a reason or the possibility of performing it. Lyrics seem to have their own ... volition I suppose. It's like that with poetry too – I have no sense of trying to get anything published – well, not as yet. I may look at that in the future though.*"

Claudette was shifting in her mien. I got the sense that she'd been continuously re-evaluating what sort of creature I might be – but that she'd come to a favourable conclusion. "*So ...*" she smiled "*... let's get back to the white suit and its 'unpredictable indeterminacy.' What would that mean then? You're going to have to be a —little—more explicit. It's a grand style ... and I—do—enjoy it ... but I'd like to get at the meaning behind it.*"

"*Well ... a person wearing a white suit is a person who could be expected to animate the audience in the theatre of life ... someone who could stand behind the facts of their creative imagination—as an Artist—and—be that—come what may.*"

"*The theatre of life, eh ... that's an intriguing concept.*"

"*Well ... it's intrigued me for some years*" I mused. "*I see people as being —or being capable of being—actors on the living stage.*"

"*Really ...? That sounds highly surreal – but then that—does—seem to be your forté.*"

"*Yes, it is ...you see ... I don't think that—life—has to be divided from Art.*"

"*Mmmm ... how do you ... deal with that in everyday situations?*"

"*Well ... I mean—you—make Art of life with the way you dress, for example. I can see that you've thought about it and ... there's no one else at Bower Ashton who dresses anything like you.*"

"*Why thank you. It's—always—good to be appreciated ...*" Pause "*... but—I must say—I'm intrigued by the notion that—you—see yourself as 'dressing for life' in the same way as an actor would dress for a part in a play. Is that—really—how you see yourself ... and your life?*"

"*Certainly. Anything else would seem like some kind of a living death.*"

"*Most—theatrically—put – if I may say so*" she grinned. "*You give everything such ... extreme importance ... I find it ... almost ...*" Pause "*You're not making all this up are you?*" she asked in a searching yet kindly way."

"*Certainly not. I suppose I've always been a little ... extreme. I suppose Steve and Ron got used to me being some kind of mild-mannered maniac ...*"

"*Lovely alliteration*" Claudette chuckled. "*But go on with the theatrical theory – I need a little more detail if I'm to understand what you mean.*"

"*Right ... well ... we're all simultaneously actors and audience. We create the play as we go along—or it creates us—or we write each other's parts. There's no rehearsal either – everything's a first time last time performance and the tickets cost you your life.*"

She gave this statement more consideration than she'd given my previous statements. "*I would normally have said this was—highly—outré ... but you articulate the idea a little too fluently to say that.*"

"*I've given it a lot of thought.*" Pause "*You see ... I've heard—so—much drivel ... and I don't go in for dope-dreams.*"

"*Yes ... I know what you mean. What you're saying could sound a little like the Magical Mystery Tour – or those who live as if they're on it.*"

an odd boy

"*Right.*" Pause "*But I've never smoked, sniffed, snorted, ingested, or injected anything. Anything weird about me is either congenital, or … assiduously evolved in response to the theatre of my senses.*"

"*And … how does this fit in with Buddhism may I ask?*"

"*I think … you are going to have to elaborate on that question a little – because … I'm not sure where you would see a disparity.*"

"*Well … aren't Buddhist supposed to blend into their surrounding and not be noticed?*"

"*Yes … if you're monastic or a renunciate – but I've not taken that tack. I'm a Vajrayana Buddhist – which means that …*" Pause "*D'you really want to hear about this?*"

"*Absolutely – I know you're not trying to convert me.*"

"*Well …*" I mused looking for a simple way to explain something that should take an hour "*… Vajrayana deals with transformation rather than renunciation … because it's not centred on emptiness. The more widely known form of Buddhism is based on recognising emptiness – but Vajrayana concerns 'that which arises from emptiness' and the recognition that emptiness and form are nondual.*"[7]

"*Ooooooh! I can see why you were reticent about explaining that … I think I'll just accept that Vajrayana has no problem with hedonism then?*"

"*You—could—say that …*" Pause "*… but … it would be … problematic.*" Pause "*I think if you said that it saw hedonism and asceticism as undivided – then that would be closer to the mark.*"

"*Like two sides of the same coin?*"

---

7 Nondual / nonduality (Tibetan: nyi'med – *gNyis 'med*) is propounded by Vajrayana Buddhism as the nature of reality in which substance and substancelessness / mind and the nature of Mind, are held to be indivisible.

"*Pretty much* … " I really didn't know what to say because nonduality was not a subject to be explained in conventional terms.

"*D'you ever go to the theatre?*" she asked.

"*Splendid non sequitur – and deeply appreciated. I went to the theatre once as a child. I enjoyed it immensely.*"

"*Once!*" she hooted with surprise "*Why did you never go again?*"

"*Y'know* … *I have no intelligent answer to that – apart from the fact that it just didn't happen.*"

"*Well …you absolutely—must—go to the theatre* …" Claudette smiled.

"*Yes … I'd be happy to go see a play.*" Then I surprised myself by adding "*Would you like to accompany me?*" Pause "*Y'know, just to make sure I didn't walk through the wrong door or something.*"

Claudette blushed scarlet—as if I'd said the most unexpected thing in the world—but I was discreet enough to act as if I'd not noticed.

"*Yes, of course, that would be fun*" she replied tentatively – with veiled pleasure.

"*Splendid* …" I replied "… *d'you know what's playing?*"

"*As a matter of fact I do*" she replied – regaining her composure "*There's … The Importance of Being Ernest' – Oscar Wilde; 'Uncle Vanya' – Chekhov; and 'Long Day's Journey into Night' – Eugene O'Neil.*"

"*Right … well the only play I—wouldn't—want to see is 'Long Day's Journey into Night.*'"

Claudette tittered at my reply "*Let me guess … it's because it's miserable.*"

an odd boy

"*Got it in one. It's like 'All-in Wrestling' for the emotionally deranged. I'd rather have ten in-growing toenails than sit through—that—again.*"

"*You're not saying—that's—the play you saw as a child!?*"

"*No*" I laughed "*I saw—that—on television … 'round someone's house one time. I decided it was one of the few occasions in my life that I could call a waste of time.*"

"*You—really—have it in for Eugene O'Neil.*"

"*Well … maybe not him personally …*" I laughed "*… but the play gives me no one with whom I can empathise. Watching people torture each other emotionally for three hours is little better than Roman gladiatorial fights or being entertained by Christians being thrown to the lions.*"

Claudette still laughing said "*Right then – I think I'll suggest 'The Importance of Being Ernest …' Uncle Vanya's not wonderfully cheerful either. 'The Importance of Being Ernest' is a comedy and I think you'll enjoy Oscar Wilde's language.*"

"*I think I will. I read his children's stories and found them quite touching.*"

"*You have interesting sensibilities …*" Claudette commented and I thanked her for the compliment.

I met Claudette at the theatre on the appointed evening. She looked quite radiant and wore an extraordinary 1920's dress. It shimmered in an astonishing variety of pale blues and silver. She wore a long matching jacket with pearls set into the collar. I wore my Uncle Charles' dark grey Edwardian suit with a deep-red tie I'd had to purchase for the occasion. She was quite surprised to see me dressed fairly conventionally and we talked of costume whilst waiting for the play to commence.

'The Importance of Being Ernest' was immensely enjoyable and I found myself utterly engrossed.

"*Theatre-going's been unforgivably absent in my life*" I told Claudette as we left the theatre. "*I'm sold—when shall we go again?*" Claudette was immensely pleased by my enthusiasm and pleased that I welcomed another evening with her. "*The costumes were amazing*" I volunteered. "*I can see why you'd want to be involved with theatre wardrobe.*"

Claudette lit up like a Christmas tree and told me about the projects she hoped to undertake. "*I'm interested in Shakespearian costume – in terms of producing garments that give the appearance of the period without having to replicate every detail. Costume is expensive and so it's a creative challenge to create impressions that are believable without enormous time and expense.*"

I'd never even considered such a problem and asked for further detail – which she was delighted to supply. I told her "*It's sartorial illustration—illustrating the play with the costumes—I'd love to be doing that as well! There's just not enough time is there …*"

That amused Claudette "*What would sartorial Fine Art be like then?*"

"*I wouldn't really make that kind of distinction – I only used 'Illustration' as an example because that's where I am at the moment*" I explained. "*I'm a Fine Artist really – it's just that I'm a figurative painter rather than an abstract expressionist.*" We talked about the way that people tended to divide everything into categories. "*That's what I loved about the Foundation Year …*" I continued "*… and it wasn't so much being able to experiment with every discipline – it was having people around who were involved in the different areas. That's what I miss.*"

"*Yes … that—was—a lovely aspect of Foundation – however …*" Claudette said with a slight flourish of her eyebrows "*… it looks as if we've become interdepartmental anyway – so … let's get back to the idea of this white suit. You'd like to get one?*"

"*Yes ... I'd like to get a white suit – but I've never seen one for sale other than extremely expensive Italian silk versions which aren't quite what I have in mind.*"

Claudette immediately volunteered "*I shall have to make you one in that case.*"

"*Really? That is—most—kind of you. I hope there's something I can do for you in exchange.*"

Claudette grinned "*We can discuss that perhaps ... over a nicely chilled Chablis?*"

"*Perfect. I'm not usually fond of white wine – but Chablis is dry and flavoursome. I'll get a bottle in and hope for a frost.*"

"*A frost?*" Claudette laughed.

"*Well ... I have no refrigerator ... I only have an abomination called an OsoKool[8] but you can't get a bottle inside it.*"

"*Maybe I'll bring one with me in a thermos bag, it—might—be easier.*"

"*Only on the condition that I pay ....*" I concluded and we seemed set up for a pleasant Saturday. We arranged to meet up in Bristol on the Saturday afternoon to buy the material – and I purchased some fancy hors-d'œvres from the local delicatessen. I was branching out – and found the whole situation quite interesting. I'd only drunk Chablis once before and that was with Lindie. I'd taken her out to dinner one evening and that's what she'd chosen. It cost an arm and a leg – but I was up for that kind of thing.

---

8   OsoKool – a food storage unit made of plaster with an aluminium lining and polystyrene-lined door. Water is occasionally tipped into a depression on the top of the container and this slightly cools the inside. These contraptions—invariably mouldy—were often found in bedsit accommodations in Britain in the '60s and '70s.

I was just glad I knew what Chablis was – after my ludicrous performance with Aristophanes.

Then it struck me that I was acting somehow out-of-character. Why should it concern me to know Chablis from Chateauneuf du Pape? The answer was obvious. I'd somehow become predisposed with respect to earning Claudette's good opinion. I had to concede that I'd unsuspectingly become interested in something more than friendship. It had been a strange beginning —but she'd mellowed—and seemed to have developed an open-ended acceptance of me as a human being. I was no longer an adversary to be contested – and that felt like such a relief that ... well, I had no idea. I was not utterly smitten – but I was hovering between known and unknown sensations.

I rolled up outside the John Lewis Department Store and was surprised to find Claudette already there. I'd made sure I was early ..."*Sorry I must have got the time wrong.*"

"*No, no, no – don't worry—it's just the parking—one usually has to leave a lot of time and I found a place far quicker than I expected.*"

The other thing that was surprising was the diaphanous green dress that looked as if it had been previously worn by Mæ West. Tout le monde sur le balcon.[9] I tried my best not to gawp. This was radically different from the Claudette at Art School or the theatre. "*You look surprised to see me?*"

"*No—or rather yes – but no*" I grinned with slight bemusement "*I'm just—pleased—to see you. I believe ... that is the appropriate answer*" I grinned.

She picked up the reference immediately.

---

9   Tout le monde sur le balcon – 'All the world on the balcony'. A phrase describing an ample bosom perched in a low cut dress.

"*And there was—I—thinking you had a gun in your pocket.*"[10]

"*My most profound compliments on both costume—and—contents*" I offered with a bow. "*I thought my ideas about the theatre of life were new to you. You were obviously—putting—me on.*"

"*Well ... I don't like to be—too—predictable ... and ... well I thought you might be the one person at the Art School who might appreciate this. I've never worn it before ... and it's been a bit weird standing here dressed like this. I'm just glad it's the afternoon rather than the evening.*"

I became aware that my grin must have become almost menacing so I changed the subject to alleviate any discomfort she might feel in being the object of determined scrutiny.

"*So let's go to the fabrics department then. I'm eager to sample the delights of John Lewis.*" For some reason I offered her my arm and she took it and we waltzed into John Lewis as if it were a royal visit. I bought a fair few yards of surgeon's cotton-drill. It was extremely white fabric—extremely dense—but not heavy. It seemed perfect for the purpose.

"*I will need to take measurements*" Claudette said with a grin once we'd settled down back at my bedsit. "*I've brought my tape measure.*" She unrolled it in what appeared to be a salacious manner and proceeded to measure a surprising array of dimensions – from here to there in every direction. The measurement became endearment – and endearment segued seamless blandishments and rapturous deportment.

Yes I dreamt I got married, I got married to a millionaire, / She took me down to the bank— "*Yeah,*" *she said,* "*Jack Dupree, all your money's in there!*" Champion Jack Dupree—I Had a Dream—The Tricks—1968

---

10 From the line attributed to Mae West: "Is that a gun in your pocket? Or are you just pleased to see me!"

5

the first year: january 1973 – february 1973

bower ashton – a room with a view

January exploded: snow flurries, multicoloured duffle coats, capes, cloaks, and boots. '*Big snow, little snow – little snow, big snow.*' That's what the Cherokees say – and I've generally found it to be true. Large flakes of snow mean the snow won't last. Small flakes of snow betoken a white-out. I watched the little flakes fall – and it filled me with an inexpressible sense of tranquillity: an unaccountable sense of joy and hopefulness. The world was happening. I was happening. Everything around me seemed festively exuberant. There was a big 'Yes' in the air and an icy wind that made me grin. It felt good to be alive on such a day.

At a quarter to ten Todd Whelcomb arrived – fifteen minutes late as usual.

"*Here since—dawn—again?*" he enquired.

"*At this time of year – yes.*" I replied.

Todd was trussed like a turkey in schoolboy duffle coat and college scarf – tied tight enough to garrotte himself. He'd entered the studio hunched—a little like some horror-movie Igor character—but failed to say '*You—rang—master?*'

What Art student would *buy* a college-scarf?[1] '*Utterly docile ...*' I thought – but said nothing. It wasn't for me to comment on what gave joy to others.

---

1   College scarves became available when the Art School became part of Bristol Polytechnic.

an odd boy

Todd trumpeted into his handkerchief and asked derisorily *"And why—d'you—look so happy?"*

"Enjoying the weather, not often we have snow. I find it … rather exhilarating."

"Fun for children perhaps. For—adults—it's an inconvenience" Todd grumbled, rolling his eyes to indicate I was a presence to be endured.

"I'm sure you're right, Todd." I resisted the urge to respond *'Care for a snowball fight?'* Instead I offered *"Glorious colours as the sun rose, though."* My comment seemed to incense him further – and he sidled off into a corner by the radiator as if he had arthritis, lumbago, or whatever.

Here we all are sitting in a rainbow "Hello Mrs Jones, How's your Bert's lumbago?" / I'll sing you a song, with no words and no tune, / To sing in your party while you suss-out the moon. Marriot/Lane—Small Faces—Lazy Sunday Afternoon—Ogden's Nut Gone Flake—1968

I could be guaranteed to say the wrong thing on most occasions as far as Todd was concerned. The fact that I remained cheerful and friendly didn't seem to help. The fact that my German grandfather's black ankle length 1920s evening coat and woven silk scarf were hanging behind me didn't help either – because my clothes seemed to cause him constant consternation. Occasionally Todd could be relatively civil – and when he was, I was. I'd converse as if there'd been no history of surliness on his part. I considered life a little short to take offence when it appeared senseless to do so. Todd had his perceptions of the world and they were entirely different from mine.

bower ashton – a room with a view

It was just unfortunate for him that his perceptions made him imperious and condescending to those he viewed as the hoi polloi.[2] It wasn't that Farnham Art School wasn't well represented by the upper-middle classes – but they weren't eager to be viewed as such. If anything, *everyone and his 'master-of-hounds uncle'* fancied himself as a born-again prole.[3] Ron Larkin was upper-middle class but adopted a working class London accent – so I was entirely unused to anyone of my own age group acting like a younger version of Brigadier Dale. Where had this fellow been in the '60s? Had he been closeted in some reserved conservative conservatoire for the clueless?

It was apparent that Todd found something about me 'threatening.' Unless it was that he was able to read my mind however – the nature of the threat I represented remained a mystery. I was as amiable as anyone could sensibly wish – so I concluded that it must have been the fact that I didn't know my place. I never challenged him on how *he was* and how *he dressed* – because he would have regarded that as offensive, and the others in the room would have noted my belligerence rather than his. I only ever made whimsical rejoinders when he was—*so*— entirely uncivil that he left me no choice but to respond. I was never rude in return—merely whimsical or bizarre—and he tended to act the impromptu straight man for me almost as if he'd planned it. He seemed to take it as fundamentally insulting to his person that I was different. It also irritated him that there was part of my life that I kept private. He knew it had something to do with the Himalayas, and that I was not exactly 'mainstream' concerning religion.

---

2   Hoi Polloi—Greek in origin—the many or the rabble.
3   Prole – abbreviation of 'proletarian'. From '1984' by George Orwell, referring to the working class of Oceania.

an odd boy

Derek Crowe had inadvertently let that slip when he announced that he'd found an article on Vajrayana Buddhism and Tibetan Art that he thought I might like to see.

Todd assumed his 'Primate of All England face'[4] and held forth *"Eastern religions belong in the East."*

"It's a point of view, certainly – but I believe, Todd ... that Christianity —was—*an Eastern religion at one time"* I pointed out mildly *"... or Middle-Eastern at least."*

Todd looked vexed and replied *"Always the clever answer."*

"I don't mind being predictable Todd." I replied in a dull matter-of-fact manner and turned my attention back to my drawing. Todd spluttered something but I didn't catch it and decided not to ask him to repeat himself.

After some ten minutes Todd enquired *"What made you turn to Buddhism then?"*

That threw me somewhat – as it was a reasonable question, from Todd at least *"Well ... it's a long story – but ... it started at junior school. I found two books on Tibet and the religious art was extremely impressive. I just took it from there."*

"Christian art wasn't impressive enough for you?"

"I wouldn't say that exactly. It wasn't a matter of comparison – and ... I wouldn't like it to be understood that I have a problem with Christianity.

"It's more that I didn't appreciate the way it was presented – or rather, the people who represented it. I realise now that I was unfortunate in the Christians I met – apart from my mother that is."

---

4   Primate of all England – title of the Archbishop of Canterbury, chief bishop of the Church of England, and diocesan bishop of Canterbury. The line of archbishops dates back to 597 AD.

"And how does she feel about it – I bet she's not impressed."

"Actually Todd … my mother is wonderfully tolerant and open minded."

Todd snorted at that *"What do you find so special about Buddhism then – apart from the art?"*

"I appreciate the logic of it, Todd – and the fact that it's not based on faith. I also appreciate its atheism."

"How can you have an atheist religion?" Todd spluttered. *"That's ridiculous."*

"Todd …" I sighed *"I didn't initiate this conversation … I'm simply answering your questions. I didn't ask you to ask me questions – and I don't want to have to defend anything, so—if you don't mind—I have nothing more to say on the subject."*

"Buddhist logic fails you does it …?"

"So it would appear, Todd."

"Neat evasion" Todd sneered – to which I replied *"Yes … I thought so."* And that was the end of our one and only religious discussion.

Derek apologised for breaching my privacy on the subject of Buddhism and I told him it wasn't a problem as I favoured the *school of no sword play*. I told him about Todd however, and he chuckled about the way in which I concluded the debate.

"The school of no sword play?" Derek enquired.

"It's from a collection of Zen stories. There's a boat crossing a lake and there are two samurai amongst the passengers. One of the samurai is standing and boasting about what a great swordsman he is. The other is lying in the back of the boat with his cloak covering his samurai insignia. The wind picks up at some point and blows the samurai's cloak so as to make him visible as a samurai.

"*The boastful samurai notices immediately and issues a challenge. 'I'm sorry but I must decline your invitation' the resting samurai responds. The standing samurai berates him for a coward but the resting samurai takes no offence. The standing samurai persists however demanding to know what school the other represents, and receives the reply 'The school of no sword play.' The standing samurai sneers and asks what kind of school that is. 'If we really must fight ...' the resting samurai yawns '... ask the boat man to put us down on that little island over there on the left — then I shall show you.' So that's how it works out. The boat reaches the island and immediately the boasting samurai leaps out and begins making his preparatory moves — oblivious to the boat, boatman, occupants, or the other samurai. He has no anxiety. He also fails to notice that the resting samurai has requested the boatman to cast off — and by the time the boasting samurai turns to face his opponent, the boat is fifty yards away. The resting samurai stands at that point and cupping his hands to amplify his voice, calls out 'That's the school of no sword play.' I've always loved that story.*"

"*Yes ... it's a good one — and I can see that it's stood you in good stead. As a pacifist, I can only applaud it.*" Pause "*However ... one thing I can tell you about the pacifist position, is that it often seems to promote violence in others.*"

"*Yes ... I can see that, Derek ... I've already seen it in fact ... I suppose there's nothing much to be done about that apart from taking it all with a sense of humour.*"

"*That's the spirit!*" Derek beamed "*Have an enjoyable evening — good to chat with you as always.*"

Later—talking to Claudette—I said "*I—had—to make—some—comment. What else could I have said?*

"I'd been tempted to say 'I'll provide a less erudite response next time' or 'No Todd the clever answer would have been to have asked you whether Fry's Turkish Delight[5] *belonged in the East as well.'"*

"Hysterical" she laughed. *"You should definitely have voiced either reply."*

"One bison in the room ..." I sighed *"... is quite enough."* Pause *"I really wish I'd told no one about my time in the Himalayas ... people almost always want to make something out of it or take me up on it or make it into a debate. I really dislike being put in a position where I seem to be defending Buddhism or my being a Buddhist. There are plenty of people out there who'll bore you insensible with their spiritual life – but I've never been like that and have no intention of becoming like that. If I had some sort of mission to preach Buddhism wherever I went I could understand people being irritated – but I never even allude to it."*

"Yes ... that must be tiresome." Pause *"You sound ... as if you're trying to walk a tightrope in relation to Toad."*[6] She laughed *"Why don't you just say whatever you like? I mean he—is—a puerile poltroon."*

"Well yes ..." I agreed *"... but I have no—need—to humiliate him any more than he already humiliates himself."*

"Very droll—of course—but wouldn't it be more—fun—to put him in his place?"

"In one way, yes – but I'm trying to curb my tendency to have fun in that way. I'd be happier to get him to realise I could be friendly. I'm sure he only makes himself look as silly as he does because he feels threatened. I'd rather avoid fuelling his need for enmity."

Claudette burst out laughing *"Yonder peasant, who—is—he?"*

---

5 Fry's Turkish Delight – a British confectionery item. A flavoured jelly coated with chocolate.
6 Claudette always referred to Todd as 'Toad'.

She'd found the microscopic reference to Good King Wenceslas too delicious to avoid.

"*Quite so ...*" I chuckled "*Where and what his dwelling ...
I sometimes wish he did live 'a good league hence underneath the adjectival mountain' ...*"

"*Yes ...*" groaned Claudette "*... he's an archetypal male. I'm just glad I'm in another department.*"

"*Archetypal males ...*" I mused "*Yes ... the need to lock horns is part of the personality ... trouble is ... it's not really part of mine. So ... I prefer to remain cheerfully detached.*"

There was a problem with that approach however, as Claudette saw quite clearly. "*But doesn't that defeat your stated purpose? Wouldn't that just make you appear smug?*"

It didn't take more than a moment's reflection to see that she was right. "*Yes ... and—I suppose—also, self-important. There's no winning is there? ... There's no tactical withdrawal either – let alone honourable retreat.*"

"*Toad probably makes sure the others in the studio are well aware of his opinion.*"

"*Yes ... he probably does – but there's no good alternative that I can find to smiling ... and occasionally responding as mildly as I can ... without—completely—selling out that is.*"

Claudette shrugged "*Yes ... I—think—I can see that. But why don't you just refuse to speak to the belligerent bovine bore? Why even—try—being friendly with the ... atrocious, asinine ape?*"

"*Fine alliteration, 'dette – but I'd rather not feel manœuvred into a hostile stance I never originated. His mind state has—nothing—to do with me. I have no interest in turning into the person he's fixed me as being.*

"*You see ... if I deliberately ignore him and refuse all communication, he'll achieve his aim.*" Pause "*He'll never learn anything from that and the others'll just think he's right.*" Pause "*... and ... I don't really want that. He needs to learn he can't control me.*"

"*Well yes – but that's—your—need not his.*" Claudette looked at me quizzically "*It seems—you—need him to learn that ...*" She'd made a good point. "*... but why bother?*"

"*Well ... because – the others—could—discover that I'm—not—the person he's presented me as being.*"

"*Yes ... it would be unfortunate to let Toad get away with pigeon-holing you in the style of his devising.*" Pause "*I'd guess that he just wants to rule the roost without owning the fact.*"

"*Yes ... I think you're right ...*"

"*Toad obviously wants to make you look as if you're the one who has the problem – but it seems that trying to deal with that would be a lot of work with possibly no good result. If it were me, I'd cold shoulder him. Life is too short to waste on the unworthy.*"

It always made me a little uncomfortable when Claudette assumed her Marie Antoinette air. "*That's as may be ... but, if I remain friendly—on the occasions he's reasonable—he'll not be able to make that work.*"

"*Dear me ... that would be—far—too much work for me!*" Claudette laughed. "*I'd put him in his place each and every time he was surly. You're good with words – I'm sure that wouldn't be difficult for you. You made your point with Dick Taylor after all. I don't see this is any different.*"

"*Yeah ... but Dick Taylor's the Head of Graphics and probably more than twice my age. I don't mind taking on the occasional Goliath – but Todd's just an overgrown schoolboy.*"

"*A Goliath beetle perhaps or maybe a dung beetle?*" Claudette quipped.

"*Yes ... but I don't see him as fair game*" I smiled making no comment on her insect jest. "*Anyhow ... being able to humiliate people verbally isn't really an aspect of myself that I admire.*"

"*I don't know why – when you could obviously accomplish it with such ease and aplomb?*"

"*Y'know ...*" I sighed "*Steve Bruce said something like that to me when I was 7 ... It was when I'd hit a boy on the nose and knocked him to the ground. He'd been bullying me for days – and it was really the last resort.*" Pause "*Steve admired me for that – but I told him I'd rather be admired for playing guitar than for being able to give someone a nose bleed.*"

"*Well certainly – fighting is repulsive, brutish behaviour.*"

"*Absolutely – but I don't see verbal pugilism as being—that—different. It reminds me of Netherfield Secondary School and all that bestial male horn-locking that went on there.*" Pause "*As I said ... with Dick Taylor it was different—he's in a position of power—and anyhow Todd's not conspiring to turn me into a graphic designer.*"

"*No he just wants to increase the size of the dung hill on which he crows.*"

"*Y'know 'dette ...*" I laughed "*...you should be on stage—that was almost Shakespearian—you'd make a fine Lady Macbeth.*"

"*Lady Macbeth indeed!*" Claudette snorted with mock indignation. "*I merely feel that 'the unworthy' should be firmly put in their place. Todd's a baboon and should live in a suitable enclosure along with his emaciated stick-insect paramour. She'd hardly make a serving for one, even—with—pommes frites and asparagus.*"

"*Well you're not exactly a porker*" I replied.

"*I shall ignore the vulgar terminology. No, I am not. I am perfectly proportioned as you know.*"

"Yes. I couldn't agree more – but isn't it equally as vulgar to describe Veranda as a stick insect?"

"Point taken – but they're still both unworthy specimens."

'The unworthy' again … I made no comment. I decided to take it as her sense of humour and that she'd not really advise the starving to eat cake. Claudette had some notion of an intellectual-cultural meritocracy in which social class was of far *less* consequence than high-brow acumen. Her idea was that with sufficient knowledge of the Arts one became an *Aristocrat of the Arts*. I found this idea problematic, as I had no interest in being part of any elite that looked down on others – unless it was to notice that they needed a helping hand. It occurred to me that I was—one day—going to have to express my own view. I never felt the need to challenge her ideas of cultural elitism however – as long as she didn't expect me to assume a place in *the order of things* as she saw it. I assumed that my occasional egalitarian preferences would—eventually—have a moderating effect on her theories.

"*Anyone can rise to regal status*" she replied when I informed her that I was more-or-less an anarchist, albeit with egalitarian leanings.

"That's a cheering point of view …" I replied "… *but I tend to be concerned about people who have no access to the Arts. I mean, where would —I—be, if it hadn't been for those who'd helped me. What if there'd been no Alice Trevelyan? What if there'd been no Mr Love, Steve Bruce, or Mr Preece? I've been lucky – but there must be many who have no opportunity at all. Do we have to see them as unworthy?*"

"*A well-presented case …*" Claudette grinned "… *in such cases I would recommend noblesse oblige on the part of the culturally privileged.*"

"What do you mean?"

"It's the obligation of the nobility to take care of those who need help. You see it often in the Jane Austen novels. Mr Knightley, Colonel Brandon, Mr Darcy, and so forth ... they were all respected for their kindness to the poor."

I wasn't keen on the idea of 'the poor' being a designated segment of society – but I took her point and suggested "*Maybe even poor old Todd is underprivileged in his own way. His parents might have been like Jack Hackman's parents.*"

Claudette burst out laughing "'*Ha! 'Poor old Todd'! You*—are—a complete—riot! *You can be so disarmingly and charmingly saintly sometimes. I can see you being canonised one day – can one be canonised in Buddhism?*"

"I doubt it ..." I laughed "... *but maybe the Pope would make an exception in my case and name me St Vic of Vicissitudes.*"

"Or St Vic the Evincible perhaps because *you could discuss any one under the table*—with—*utter charm of course.*"

"Glad I'm charming – but I don't think it quite deserves canonisation. Never heard of a Bluesman being canonised in any case – our lyrics tend to be a little too risqué. It's called 'the devils music,' y'know."

We both fell about in laughing at the whole insanity of the subject and enjoyed the rest of the evening sans reference to Todd.

Todd—along with sojourns in the Fine Art Department and my relationship with Claudette—contributed heavily to my increasing isolation within the Illustration studio. I saw Ralph Simons, Wendy Millhurst, and Georgina Reynolds from Graphic Design, occasionally – but our joint project in the first terms had not been sufficient to establish a lasting association.

I called into the Graphic Design studio from time to time – but I got the feeling that although they were cordial, they were not sure why I'd dropped by. They never returned the compliment so I let it drop. They always smiled and gave me a warm greeting if our paths happened to cross – but there was never any sense that we would get to know each other beyond that. Isolation became a sensation that tingled in the sense fields – but whatever isolation I experienced was offset by a sudden and unexpected change. I was soon to be moving home. I was to move closer to the Art School – to a house where I'd be living in a delightful environment with three marvellous new acquaintances.

Penelope Cholmoldeley, Rebecca Albemarle, and Meryl Stanhope attended the College of Music and Drama – and Claudette had attended Badminton [7] with them. They'd known each other for a decade and their jocularity was infectious – based as it was, on a great deal of shared experiences. Penelope, Rebecca, and Meryl had found a house for lease down by the river in Hotwells – and were looking for a fourth girl to share the house. They'd hoped in vain that Claudette would join them there – but she preferred home comforts in Bath where she lived with her widower father. That was how it came to pass that I became Victoria Hillary Simmerson ... as far as the agency was concerned. The house had become available due to a family having moved abroad for three years.

---

7   Badminton – a private (boarding and day) school for girls aged 3 to 18 years, situated in Westbury-on-Trym, Bristol, England. The school ranks third in the top 1,000 schools according to the 'Good Schools Guide'. Miriam Badock established the school in 1858 at Badminton House in Clifton. By 1898 it had become known as 'Miss Bartlett's School for Young Ladies'. The school grew in size, and in 1924 moved to the present site, under the headship of Beatrice May Baker [1876 – 1973].

an odd boy

The rental agency wanted 'girls only' – but Claudette had suggested me to her friends telling them *"He's astonishingly neat and tidy for a male—utterly charming—and he's neither vulgar nor loathsome in any respect. He's a Buddhist but you'd never know. He doesn't go in for talking about it – so he's in no way tiresome."* The three ladies were unsure about the idea—having only met me once—but they all felt that I was 'a pleasant fellow.' They couldn't afford to split the rent three ways without importuning their parents – and none seemed eager to do that. They had their allowances and felt it was proper to remain within bounds – particularly as their parents would have preferred them to have taken accommodation in the Halls of Residence provided – and encouraged for 1st year students. They couldn't find a fourth girl – so it was either the *odd boy* or lose the house. The house was deemed too good to lose and so it was that Claudette went to the agency in my place – and signed up as Victoria Hillary Simmerson.

Penelope, Rebecca, and Meryl treated me a little cautiously at first – and I wondered how to put them at their ease. I could find no obvious solution – so I decided I'd carry on as normal and hope I'd be judged worthy of house-sharing. I packed my belongings into Claudette's Silver Cloud and after two trips, I was installed. I spent all the next day arranging my books and albums. I also set up my stereo system – purchased on the proceeds of selling my MARSHALL PA system, bass amplifier, and microphone. It was a BANG AND OLUFSEN system with large black menacing SONAB speakers. I'd made a racking system for the stereo from salvaged scaffolding planks. I sanded them down in the Art School's Construction Department and applied a generous quantity of linseed oil and turpentine.

bower ashton – a room with a view

The treatment made the old Red Deal[8] boards darken to a deep lustrous colour that made it look like a hardwood.

I was delighted that a little work had transformed scrap wood into such luxurious shelving. I sat back and admired the sleek black stereo units with their light emitting diodes glimmering in the glorious subdued light of an early Winter evening. I placed Cream's 'Wheels of Fire' on the turntable and reclined to listen to 'Spoonful.' What better place in the world *could* there be? The room felt like a palace and I felt like … actually, I had no idea what I felt like – but there was a sense of rightness about it.

I purchased three bottles of Barolo.[9] and six wine glasses from a shop called Kitchens – and invited Penelope, Rebecca, and Meryl for an attic-warming drink. They'd had the same idea so we simply moved from room to room celebrating and listening to each other's music. My room was last on the list as we had decided to start at the bottom and work upward. Their music was either Classical or progressive Rock. I was relieved that the progressive Rock was music I also enjoyed. They were all a year younger than me and so—somehow—they'd missed Cream and Blues in general. It surprised me that a year could make so much difference – but it only extended to familiarity. They loved Cream and pressed me with questions about Blues. Eventually the story of Savage Cabbage came out. I'd moved into a different frame of mind and began to enjoy speaking of Savage Cabbage again. They noticed that the improvisation on Wheels of Fire was far superior to the improvisations with which they were familiar – and I was happy to speak of Jack Bruce in glowing terms as the master of bass who Steve had emulated.

---

8   Red Deal – Scots pine.
9   Barolo – Italian red wine made in the Piedmont region from the Nebbiolo grape.

I made a conscious point of not rambling on too long or getting too technical – but Penelope, Rebecca, and Meryl were replete with their own musical ideas and technicalities.

"*You're quite the bon vivant for a Buddhist*" Rebecca observed.

Somehow I often understood these French usages by guess work and so I was able to reply without seeming too gauche "*I'm maybe not quite the species of Buddhist you might imagine. I don't belong to a monastic tradition you see …*"

"*Ah … that's … a very welcome idea.*"

"*Yes … I thought so …*" I grinned "*… my teachers are all family people …*"

"*Really …?*" Meryl queried. "*So … it's not about austerity and abjuring pleasure?*"

"*No … especially not pleasure – it's more geared towards maximising pleasure through appreciation of the widest possible spectrum of phenomena – and, encouraging that in everyone and everything everywhere …*" Pause "*… but … I'm not usually in the habit of saying too much. I don't like to bore people any more than I can help.*"

"*Right … 'dette told us that …*" Pause "*… she also told us you were hygienic—and—tidy.*" Meryl giggled.

"*That's a bit mean …*" Penelope broke in "*… it's not fair to tease Vic – there are three of us you know.*"

"*Cheers Penelope*" I replied with a smile. "*It's not too frightening – and I'm fairly robust.*" Pause "*Being teased isn't such a big deal if people like you, it's when they don't like you that it's unpleasant – but then it's easier to ignore because it doesn't matter. It only matters to be disparaged by friends.*"

Meryl and Rebecca looked evidently a little shame-faced and said they could already tell I was a friend and that they hoped I was alright with what they'd said.

"*Absolutely.*" I replied and then all three said that they hoped I wouldn't be withheld on the subject of Buddhism because they'd all find it interesting to learn a little – if I was prepared to make it simple enough for them. I assured them that it was possible to be relatively simple – but that knowing 'this' often required familiarity with 'that' – and … so on. "*But basically I see Vajrayana as the essential nature of being an artist. Vajrayana explores the sense-fields as the ground of experience and perception.*"

"*That sounds almost more like science than religion*" commented Penelope – with evident interest.

"*Yes … in some ways. Maybe … like science and psychology – expressed through poetry and understood through all the Arts.*"

We had a lively evening and when Claudette arrived we were in full swing. She was happy to see that we'd made friends and they shared a few covert nods which seemed to indicate that I had been accepted as a bona fide human being.

The house in Hotwells was remarkable – all wood and white paint. The people who owned it had put a great deal of effort into stripping the paint off everything. The wooden floors were sanded. The doors, skirting boards, banisters, and picture rails were all stripped and waxed. I could see why the owners didn't want males of the species living there.

Penelope, Rebecca, and Meryl got over their initial apprehensions about sharing a house with me when they discovered that I had the greater propensity for tidiness. I was also more than willing to take my turn cooking – although I needed a little education in that field. I was amazed by the culinary Arts – it was entirely magical the way ingredients were combined and flavours were conjured out of herbs.

an odd boy

I bought an Italian cookbook in order that I could manage the adventure without unnecessary supervision and surprised the ladies with unexpected gourmet extravaganzas. Claudette and I had our assignations mainly on weekends so I began to spend more time than I had anticipated in the company of Penelope, Rebecca, and Meryl. Mysteriously and hilariously, I became one of the girls. "*What d'you girls want for dinner this evening?*" one of them would ask and I'd reply without any sense of incongruity at being thus included.

The rental agent visited once a term to make sure the house was being suitably maintained – and most times 'Victoria' was out. I'd been allocated the attic room – being furthest away from the front door and the room least likely to be viewed by the agent. He was usually satisfied by the first two floors and seemed more concerned with the kitchen and bathroom than the sleeping quarters. As I never left clothes lying around there was never any risk of obvious male clothing being observed. The agent's visits therefore, became increasingly perfunctory.

My attic room was a celestial realm. It had one large window in a dormer extension, a sky light, and a tiny window at floor level right next to my bed through which I could observe the river. The bed was a double bed—just a base and mattress—so I could lie and gaze through the window with relative ease. There was an old wardrobe and chest of drawers that lived on the landing outside my door. I had a card table and chair. Both could be folded away when I was not working in order to maintain the room as a floor-level space. I'd given *Colonel Greenhaugh* to the girls as it didn't fit with my arrangements.

I liked the emptiness of the room and arranged a few spot lamps on dimmer switches in different positions to create an amorphous ambience in which to listen to music.

Penelope, Rebecca, and Meryl—in any combination—would often come up to join me when I'd finished work for the evening. We'd sit—listen to music—and converse. There were never awkward lulls in conversation as each lady had creative notions aplenty. We'd sound each other out on ideas and found each other enormously encouraging and supportive. Sometimes I'd find myself vaguely wonderstruck by the situation. The world seemed curiously dreamlike and I occasionally wondered if I would wake up back in the cramped bedsit I'd initially inhabited.

Over the course of time Penelope, Rebecca, and Meryl appeared to forget my gender entirely and took to wandering in and out of the bathroom in various states of underwear and the absence thereof. I did my best to affect supreme nonchalance. I was a surrealist after all – so there seemed no problem with inhabiting such an unlikely setting.

Claudette's arrival—whenever she arrived—was a natural pirouette in the dance. Our disappearances to the attic were a segue that never seemed awkward or unnatural. There were sometimes the very slightest of grins when we reappeared – but otherwise we all inhabited an easy candour that defied description.

They all commented—during the first weeks—that it was hard to believe that I wasn't female, as they'd never experienced a male presence as having no effect on conversation. They could converse as if we were 'all girls together.' I told them on the first occasion it was mentioned *"I'll take that as a compliment."*

an odd boy

They apologised "*I hope that doesn't sound like ... well ...*" Penelope proffered with slight embarrassment "*... that we think you're a nancy-boy or something ...*"[10]

"*Never occurred to me ...*" I chuckled at the idea "*... my father used to worry about that though.*" Penelope asked why, and I replied "*Mainly because I wrote poetry, had no interest in sport, and preferred the company of girls. He never really saw the parts of my life that might have changed his mind about that idea ...*"

Penelope laughed "*We'll probably have to get your story one evening – 'dette tells us you've had an interesting life.*"

"Yeah ... it's been interesting ... sometimes it's been a little too interesting. Y'know the ancient Chinese curse?" She didn't. "*May you live in interesting times.*" Penelope tilted her head to suggest she didn't follow the logic of the curse. "*Well ... if you think of all the 'interesting times' in history ...you'd probably not want to find yourself in those situations.*"

"*Ah ... I see ... clever ... well, I wish you a slightly more tedious time ahead then.*"

Penelope was one of the kindest people I've ever met. She impressed me deeply inasmuch as she never had a bad word to say about anyone – yet she was never sanctimonious or supercilious when other people expressed criticality.

There were still 'love and peace' people around (*who were about as loving and peaceful as Heinrich Himmler*) and so it was good to find friendship with a person who shared my preference for amiable serenity. Rebecca was by far the most intense of the three friends – but in a genuine, well-considered way.

---

10 Nancy-boy – a British derisory slang term for an effete, effeminate male.

Rebecca was passionate about Early Music and loved all those insane old instruments like rackets, crumhorns, serpents, and sackbutts. I started out finding Early Music a little primitive – but it was impossible to talk with Rebecca on the subject without becoming enthused. She sat me down one day and played a variety of astonishing pieces—explaining the intricate aspects of their construction. I was sold. She talked about the rôle of music in the Early Music period in the 1500s and 1600s – and, like Blues, I could see that understanding this music was part of how you heard it. I explained Blues to Rebecca and the result was more-or-less the same. She came to enjoy Blues and saw various similarities with Early Music.

Penelope and Rebecca were music students. Meryl was a drama student. Meryl was a great entertainer and liked to recite. I could sit there entranced by her renditions. I'd seen acting before – but to have someone give life to a speech right in front of you was gripping. Meryl needed people to hear her recite and I was always willing. She'd sometimes ask *"Don't you find it tedious hearing me recite the same thing over and over?"*

"No ... I recite screeds up in the attic – and that's the same every day. Fortunately no one listens so it's not a problem."

"People often grow restless when hearing me rehearsing lines."

I was perplexed *"I could listen for hours. It's not just the recitation – it's the intonation and body language. It's as if I'm watching someone who's been possessed by Cymbeline."*

She was playing the part of Cymbeline at the time – and I was keen to see as much Shakespeare as I could.

Penelope, Rebecca, and Meryl were as keen on afternoon teas as Claudette – and so we spent rather genteel times together in accidentally exclusive soirées.

an odd boy

They shared an enjoyment of Jazz, so there was still a hearty link with *the previous age of the world where oddness was permitted.*

Bessie Smith, Big Mamma Thornton, and Memphis Minnie slotted in well with their tastes and so we enjoyed many musical tête-à-têtes with Earl Grey tea, and salmon and cucumber sandwiches. We lived in a secluded dimension mainly because no one was interested in joining us there. It was not that we didn't invite others – it was simply that anything other than the pub culture was seen as prissy – especially if sandwiches and tea were mentioned. Sandwiches and tea were not exactly a long standing part of my social repertoire – but these afternoons struck me as eminently civilised, especially as intelligent witty conversation was to be had.

My life outside the Illustration Department was of even less interest to the illustrators than my life within it. Todd Whelcomb did call round one day to borrow my palette knives. He wanted to lay a ground for a set of impressionistic watercolours. They were to be book cover illustrations for CS Lewis books. He'd never seen me at home – and appeared a little startled. I invited him in for a cup of tea and he sat awkwardly as I introduced him to my house mates. I told them about Todd's project. Todd was fond of CS Lewis.

"*Is he anything like Tolkien?*" Penelope asked in an attempt to be friendly – having heard that Tolkien was a favourite with Art students.

"*Not at all – CS Lewis was a far superior story teller.*"

"*Don't you … find him a little … derivative?*" Meryl exclaimed.

"*Don't know—what—you mean*" Todd replied with supercilious scorn.

"Derivative means imitative or plagiaristic" Meryl replied with a smile. I assumed she'd evidently taken an instant dislike to Todd – but learned later that her dislike had been pre-empted by Claudette.

"I know what 'derivative' means" Todd sputtered.

"Well then ..." continued Meryl *"... it shouldn't be too taxing to understand this is something that can more easily be said of CS Lewis than Tolkien."*

"I really don't see how you can make such an absurd statement" Todd threw back with a petulant toss of his head.

"Quite easily" Meryl replied. *"For example, there are distinct correlations with both Jonathan Swift and Lewis Carol – it's painfully obvious that he lifted from them both."*

I felt it was time I defended Todd, just a little *"Everyone takes their influences don't they ... I mean, it's hard to create anything without being influenced. I'm sure I'm influenced by a wide variety of poets – you know ... There's nothing you can do that can't be done, There's nothing you can sing that can't be sung."*[11]

Todd rolled his eyes *"I think we can do without the wretched—Beatles —in this discussion if you don't mind."* I was a little surprised that Todd hadn't understood I was trying to be supportive – but put it down to the fact that Meryl had launched into him with somewhat astonishing acerbity.

"Care for a cup of tea, Todd?" I asked – almost as if I hadn't heard his comment. Todd looked perplexed. *"I'll take that as a 'yes' ..."* I responded in relation to his confustication – and went to the kitchen to brew a pot of tea. When I came back Meryl was busy intellectually nailing Todd's hide to the wall.

---

11 Lennon/McCartney—Beatles—All You Need is Love—Magical Mystery Tour—1967

an odd boy

I was a little startled at the speed and sharpness of her wit. "*Tea, Todd*" I ventured. He took the cup with hardly a gesture of thanks as Meryl continued to lampoon his paucity of intellect.

Evidently taken aback by an intellectual onslaught from a woman, Todd dissembled. "*Would there be any chance of sugar?*"

"*Certainly.*"

"*Doesn't one usually have sugar with tea?*" Todd asked as if I'd deliberately denied him a cup from which to drink his tea – but I'd already moved in the direction of the kitchen and so Meryl answered in my stead.

"*No Todd – one doesn't. I'd be surprised if we have any sugar in the house – besides which, isn't it rather avant le déluge to have sugar in your tea?*"

I never heard Todd's reply – all I heard was something vaguely like the sudden onset of a strangulated hernia. I was gratified to have left the room.

Todd used the momentary hiatus to recommence with his views of Tolkien. "*Tolkien's Lord of the Rings' is horribly overwritten—grotesquely flowery—and those endless tiresome songs are so horribly self-indulgent.*"

Catching the words in passing Penelope said "*Well…yes… can't say they're my favourite aspect of Tolkien.*"

Todd ignored her and continued "*And all that dreary and unnecessarily—miserable—Mordor business is just so reminiscent of the trenches – it's clear he was merely obsessed with exorcising the ghost of the war.*"

"*Reminiscent of the trenches?*" Meryl burst out laughing "*You were—there—were you?*" Todd looked bewildered so Meryl clarified "*You were there—in—the trenches in WWII?*"

Todd still didn't understand so Meryl continued "... *in terms of finding Mordor reminiscent?*"

Todd looked distinctly sulky at that point "*You—know—what I mean.*" Pause "*In any case ...*" he added defiantly "*... CS Lewis' books are accepted classics.*"

Meryl laughed again admitting to being entirely surprised "*Accepted by whom? CS Lewis isn't exactly a—great—writer. His stories are poorly strung together – you can see him struggling to keep the narrative alive. His characters are wooden and stereotypical. And he's so utterly transparent in using them to express his naïve personal opinions – it's embarrassing.*"

Todd entirely disagreed "*What you're seeing—but are too immature to understand—is simply the charming approach he adopted to communicate with young people.*"

Meryl burst out laughing at that point – and I decided, in the way of the school of no sword play, to go upstairs in order to get the palette knives that Todd had come to borrow. When I returned however Rebecca had joined the fray "*... hideously unsophisticated – don't you find? Sickeningly Messianic – I mean, that infantile lion-baiting scene is frankly nauseating.*"

Todd looked extremely uneasy so I interrupted and said "*The palette knives Todd – hope you have fun with them.*"

He thanked me peremptorily and vanished. I accepted his sudden departure without demure. As soon as he was out of the door I said "*Well you savaged Todd and no mistake. I'm surprised I didn't have to call an ambulance – he barely got out alive.*"

Penelope, Rebecca, and Meryl burst out laughing. "*Are—all—the people on your course like that?*"

I considered the matter for a moment and replied "*Not entirely ... but they tend to see Todd as ... comprehensible – whereas ... I'm the weirdo in the studio. They're all a little like Todd in some ways – but they're not unpleasant. They just don't seem to know what to make of me and ... tend to accept Todd's version of reality. It's a pity. I'd hoped that loaning him my palette knives would show him I was ... normal in some respect.*"

"*Waste of time*" said Meryl. "*He couldn't even work out that you were offering him a little support. And Penelope too, y'know – when she said she didn't go for those Elven ditties too much.*"

"*Right ... I remember ... that was when you were intellectually wiping the floor with him, wasn't it ...*" I replied. "*I must say you were quite spectacular Meryl.*"

"*Didn't go too far did I?*"

"*Well ...*" I laughed "*... it depends what you wanted from the situation.*"

Meryl looked a little sheepish "*Well 'dette told us about him and ... well ... I decided I'd show him that you're a lot more amenable and affable than—we—can be ... when we're roused.*" Pause "*You just don't—get —roused ... do you?*"

I folded up laughing "*I can get roused—certainly—but ... that's probably not a subject I can discuss without offended decorum.*"

The girls fell about with mirth and Rebecca spluttered her tea across the room. Meryl still seemed a little anxious about having gone too far.

"*Maybe ...*" I chuckled "*... but he won't die of it – and, it probably did him good. I imagine he's used to ladies being like his girlfriend Veranda. She seems to hold him in awe.*"

"*She seems to 'hold him in.' Or, what?*" Meryl laughed.

"*Nice one Meryl! That was very quick!*" I laughed "*... I wish she would hold him in.*"

"*Think I'd rather hold him in a cage*" Rebecca opined "*...y'know like the geek in Dylan's song.*"

"*Ballad of a Thin Man.*" Pause "*... 'You hand in your ticket and you go watch the geek, Who immediately walks up to you when he hears you speak, Saying 'How does it feel to be such a freak?' And you say 'Impossible' as he hands you the bone ...*"

"*You should have taken drama – you have quite a memory for quotation – and it's useful with Todd. 'He's worse than a smoky house: I had rather live with cheese and garlic in a windmill, far, than feed on cates and have him talk to me in any summer-house in Christendom' ...*" Meryl chuckled.

"*Hotspur describing Owen Glendower*[12] *– Henry the* IV *Part One?*" I offered.

"*What a wonder—you—are!*" Meryl laughed. "*How did you come to know that – did you see it with 'dette?*"

"*No. Henry the* IV *Part One was the Shakespeare play we studied for 'O' Level ... but y'know ...'bout Todd ... I feel there—could—be a pleasant person lurking inside him somewhere. I offered to loan him my palette knives to give him the chance to show—that—side of himself.*"

"*You're very charitable*" Rebecca observed. "*Todd's a banal ... clod-buttock. Y'know ... I've met people like him before – overgrown, upper-middle class schoolboy. I'm surprised he didn't turn up in a Range Rover.*"

---

12   Owain Glyndŵr [1349 – 1416] – a Welsh ruler and the last native Welshman to hold the title 'Prince of Wales'. He instigated an ultimately unsuccessful, but long-running revolt against English rule of Wales.

an odd boy

"*Well—yes—I can see that ... maybe he'd be happier if he had a Range Rover. Given untold wealth I'd be happy to buy him one if it would help his state of mind.*" Pause "*He means no real harm y'know – he's just immature. And ... just a little too conventional. Everyone in the Illustration Department's headed for a profession in the publishing world or somewhere – and ... well ... they find me a little—too—bizarre.*"

"*We don't find you bizarre*" Penelope said. "*You may be—slightly—eccentric ... but I would have thought that was normal in an Art School. You're certainly interesting and fun – and ...you certainly have your own dress sense.*" The girls agreed on that.

"*Glad of your good opinion*" I grinned. "*You're like old friends already.*" Then I sang "*Lawd I'm going back down South – that's where the weather suits my clothes.*"

That made them laugh – and Rebecca said "*You'd have to time-travel to go where it suits your clothes.*"

"*You don't—particularly—dress like a freak though*" Penelope mused.

"*No ... indeed ... I don't see myself as a freak. I'm merely appreciative – without reference to the opinions of others. My tastes are simply coloured by the time when 'the unusual' was not unusual. The fashion just changed – and no one consulted me about it.*"

Meryl nodded "*Shakespeare had a few things to say about that – like What a deformed thief this fashion is' ... unless you're famous—that is —and then you can wear what you like.*"

"*Famous ...*" I mused "*... there's—that—word again ... I wanted to be famous at one point you know.*"

"*And now?*" Meryl enquired

"*Now ... it's more-or-less irrelevant.*"

"*You don't have to be famous to wear the laurels of fame*" Meryl proclaimed. "*You don't have to be a Paris fashion designer to design clothes – or to wear what you want to wear.*"

Claudette—who'd just walked in—opined "*The essence of haute couture is the enthusiasm of choice.*"

"*Quite right*" I agreed. Claudette could always turn a nice phrase. "*Anyone can be an artist of the streets. You just have to see your apparel as your canvas. Clothing can be the wardrobe of your personal theatre.*"

Rebecca nodded decisively "*Jean Cocteau said 'Art produces ugly things which become more beautiful with time. Fashion produces beautiful things which become ugly with time.'*"

Penelope—sitting in the window framed by strong Winter sun—volunteered "*We should all live the Art that we are – otherwise we're nothing at all.*"

"*Absolutely*" I exclaimed. "*None of us are enthusiasts of fawn, beige, taupe, or muesli-burger shades of nothing-in-particular. We all live in the existential wardrobe department of sartorial vivacity.*"

Meryl giggled at that point and said "*That sounds better than 'We All Live in a Yellow Submarine.'*"

There was no follow up to that – but ... I had a thing to say "*People labour under the illusion that they're free to make individual choices – but the choices are all given by societal mandate.*"

Penelope wondered why that was.

"*Well ...*" I replied "*... people only want what's societally sanctioned – and the many other possibilities hardly register on the screen of their perceptual faculties.*"

This was definitively Claudette's subject "*People's choices emerge in what appears to be great variety – but the choices are merely alternative versions of almost identical things.*

an odd boy

"*This is the range of colours for this season. These are the styles in vogue. These are the available shoes. This is the currently popular music. 'Fashion is a form of ugliness so intolerable that we have to alter it every six months' as Oscar Wilde pointed out.*"

"*Then there are the non-conformists of course ...*" Meryl said, taking another tack "*... they think they're harder to recognise – but they also wear a uniform.*"

"*Good point!*" Rebecca nodded. "*Not that there's anything wrong with uniforms per se – a uniform can be a splendid thing.*"

"*Yes*" I replied. "*I've always worn items of military uniform. I inherited various pieces from my father – a field jacket, dress jacket, coat, and cape.*"

Claudette turned to me and said "*Your living stage is the catwalk of celebrities – and those who don't count and don't care have turned to the Mao suits provided by the High Street shops.*"[13]

"*We can always count on 'dette for a regal pronouncement*" chuckled Meryl.

I noticed Claudette stiffen a little "'*dette's right though ...*"
I nodded "*... even though it doesn't affect me. I did dress for an audience —when I was on stage with Savage Cabbage—so I feel sad for those who've decided they're not celebrities and never will be. You don't have to be a celebrity to be a celebrity.*"

"*Ah—a koan*[14]*—I shall need to dwell upon it*" Claudette smiled wryly.

---

13 Mao suits – the drab, politically-imposed conformist dress of China during the latter part of the 20th Century.
14 Koan – a paradoxical adage or a riddle that has no common logical solution. Koans are employed in Zen Buddhism to transcend obsessive rationalisation. An example is 'What is the sound of one hand clapping?' This koan is attributed to Hakuin Ekaku [1686 – 1769].

Meryl decided to defend me "*It wasn't as arcane as—that— 'dette – Vic was just saying that everyone's a celebrity in their own right.*"

"*Yes ... or that you can be a celebrity for your friends – and they for you. Costume as Art can be an entirely private affair ...*" I commented "*... even if the outside world doesn't join you – you can be a theoretical thespian.*"

"*That could be a book title*" Claudette was convulsed. "*L'Homme de Théâtre Théorique.*"

"*Enough with theory already ...*" grinned Rebecca. "*Let's play!*" Out came the instruments. Claudette put her feet up and settled back to listen – as the three ladies and I improvised in **G**. The 'cello and oboe began to weave in and out of each other and I worked on insinuating fluttering glissandos on the sitar into the mix as the bassoon started to create an ominous wave that rose in dark sonic ellipses in the dimly lit room.

6

the first year: march 1973 – august 1973

bower ashton – going to a funeral, dressed in white

I was born by the river, just like this river, I've been moving ever since / Ain't got no body to call my own you know I've been moving since the day I was born. Rodgers/Fraser—Free—I'm a Mover—Tons of Sobs—1968

Claudette made a fair few items for the wardrobe of the *theoretical thespian*. I felt like 'The Phantom of the Opera' – a spectre on a living stage that only I could see. Claudette's costumes were all so finely crafted that you could have hung them on the wall as exhibits – and that never ceased to give me pleasure. She sometimes involved me in tacking[1] pieces together and I gradually learnt some aspects of needlecraft. It was fascinating watching her use a sewing machine. She had a splendid old Singer sewing machine – one which had been converted to electric. She was immensely proud of it and informed me that it was better than any modern electric machine – as it was far more powerful and had a 'good heavy foot'. She used the College sewing machines for button holes and certain complex manœuvres – but said that 'til she could afford such an industrial model, she'd stick with her Singer.

Claudette made me an item each term and I was always delighted with each prodigy she tailored: the white suit, the high waisted green leather trousers to accompany my green leather jacket and boots, and the green leather waistcoat to finish off the ensemble.

---
1   Tacking – basting in the USA.

an odd boy

It troubled me though – that I never seemed to be able to do anything for her. She was entirely self sufficient – and, if anything, she inhabited a more rarefied and insulated realm than the one in which I found myself. I was companionable and accompanied her on all the jaunts she had in mind.

Aside from our day trips Claudette was not the 'on the road' person that I was at that time. I'd read 'Dharma Bums,' 'On The Road,' and others by Jack Kerouac[2] when I was 16 and there was still a sense in which travelling somewhere was important *in and of itself*. There was a sense of importance to life when you were leaving – a person would say '*I gotta go*' and somehow that meant that they were bound for somewhere. They were not tied down. People who stayed in one place were seen as people who had *nowhere* to go – and when you had nowhere to go, your life was static. It was mysterious. I never really worked out why – but it seemed that people looked at you admiringly when you had to leave and go somewhere else. Living in transit was somehow seen to be ideal – and those who stayed in town over the weekend had no initiative. It made no sense – but it was unspoken and no one questioned it.

… for just a moment I had reached the point of ecstasy that I always wanted to reach, which was a complete step across chronological time into timeless shadows, and wonderment in the bleakness of the mortal realm, and the sensation of death kicking at my heels to move on, with a phantom dogging its own heels, and myself hurrying to a plank where all the angels dove off and flew into the holy void of uncreated emptiness, the potent and inconceivable radiance shining in bright Mind Essence, innumerable lotus-lands falling open in the magic mothswarm of heaven.

---

2   'Big Sur,' 'Visions of Cody,' and 'Desolation Angels.'

bower ashton – going to a funeral, dressed in white

I could hear an indescribable seething roar which wasn't in my ear but everywhere and had nothing to do with sounds. I realised that I had died and been reborn numberless times but didn't remember because the transitions from life to death and back are so ghostly easy, a magical action for naught, like falling asleep and waking up again a million times ...
Jack Kerouac—On The Road—1957

"It'd be nice to take a run up to Scotland, 'dette." Pause *"What d'you think?"* Claudette hummed – eyeing me warily. *"Have you ever been to Scotland?"*

"Good god no" she laughed. *"I agree with Flanders and Swann: 'The Scotsman is mean, as we're all well aware and bony and blotchy and covered with hair.'*[3] *I'd rather remain in civilisation."*

"It's really rather beautiful you know ... and I'm sure we—could—manage to avoid the more barbarous of the Picts."[4] Pause *"I think that Samyé Ling is south of Hadrian's Wall."*

"Well it's far too far to take the Rolls—I want it to last—who knows when my father might find another Silver Cloud to renovate."

Claudette was extremely careful with her car – which was never to be taken too far afield. Her father attended to every aspect of it other than its high mileage. I could see why she wanted to preserve it – it was a beautiful car.

"I can understand why you'd not want to run up the miles on the Rolls, 'dette – but there—is—the Pixie Chariot."

---

3   Flanders/Swann—A Song of Patriotic Prejudice—At The Drop of Another Hat —1964. Flanders and Swann were a British musical duo who wrote and performed comic songs. Michæl Flanders [1922 – 1975] was an actor, singer, and composer. Donald Swann [1923 – 1994] was a pianist and linguist.

4   Picts – the ancient Scottish tribal people who lived to the north of the Forth and Clyde rivers. They remained a distinct group up to the 10th century.

an odd boy

"*I wouldn't be caught dead on that*" Claudette winced in mock horror. "*It is a beautiful thing of course – but it's not my style at all … beside which my father would have apoplexy if he knew I was riding pillion.*"

Apparently her father had made her promise she'd never—under any circumstances—accept a ride on a motorcycle. I could accept that. I'd known a few young ladies whose parents had similar views – and even Steve Bruce's parents thought they were harbingers of death. I tried another tack.

"*Hitching's a workable system.*"

She shook her head "*Standing on the road in all weathers with a rucksack on my back … isn't—really—my idea of fun you know. I tried it once and it was utterly—utterly—vile. You have to have conversations with people you don't know and that's just—too—wearing for words. If there's one thing I can't stand it's making polite conversation with people I've never seen before – when I'd rather go to sleep.*"

"*Yes … I can see your point in some ways … the conversations aren't always riveting – but it's a two way deal isn't it? I usually find that I can find—some—area of common interest.*"

Claudette shrugged "*Yes – but why? And anyway it's more convenient by train if you absolutely—have—to travel.*"

'*If you absolutely have to travel …*' Now that was an idea I'd not anticipated. "*Right, 'dette. The farther one travels the less one knows …*"[5] Not that I really went for that 'quietist' approach – but it seemed courteous to volunteer a meaningful angle on Claudette's avoidance of long distance travel.

---

5   George Harrison—The Inner Light—The Beatles—B side to the single release of Lady Madonna—1968. The song is inspired by one of the many English translations of chapter 47 of Lao Tzu's 'Tao Te Ching.'

Without going out of your door, you can know all things on earth, / Without looking out of your window, You can know the ways of heaven. / Arrive without travelling, See all without looking, Do all without doing.
George Harrison—Beatles—The Inner Light—1968

"*Let's not get too spiritual about it*" Claudette laughed. "*I just have no great desire to sit on toilet seats that may have been sat on by—well ... let's not go into that—and ... there are a host of other loathsome inconveniences.*"

"*Like trees and grass and so forth?*" I asked, somewhat tongue-in-cheek.

"*Really!*" she exclaimed in affected Victorian disapproval. "*Besides which I like to get back to my own bed at night and wake up in pleasant surroundings. I'm happy for—*you—*to go off on adventures tramping all over creation ... if that makes you happy – but there's so much to see in the West Country that I'm really not tempted to go elsewhere – unless we went to Stratford that is.*"

I was happy she'd consider Stratford "*We'll have to do that one day when there's enough spare money to see a Shakespeare play there.*" I knew that she'd want to book into a hotel – and a hotel that was guaranteed to have rooms with *en suite* bathrooms that were the epitome of hygiene and commodiousness. *That* would push the price severely. She could run to such things on her extremely generous allowance – but I was invariably strapped for cash. Claudette's theatre-going appetite saw to that. I had no complaints – because money spent on Art never seemed prodigal. The theatre was new to me and I would have been happy to have gone every week had it been possible.

When Claudette and I weren't taking day trips in the Rolls to visit every quaint tearoom in Somerset, Wiltshire, and Gloucestershire, we'd travel to see a play – or, we'd go to Bath and have tea and scones at the Pump Rooms, or visit such places as the American Museum in Claverton near Bath.

Claudette and I also visited sundry Neolithic sites such as Avebury and Silbury Hill. Standing on top of Silbury Hill with Claudette I commented *"This would be a—grand—place to hear Hendrix perform."*

"But he's dead …"

"Well yes, 'dette" I smiled.

"But …" she commented in a kindly manner *"…you often speak of him as if he's alive?"*

"S'pose I do …" Pause *"… maybe … I've never accepted his loss in some way. I do miss him being in the world … and whenever I listen to him on record – he's there in the world with me."*

"You have a fine sense of tragedy – I thought you didn't like tragedy?"

"I don't … well not when it's fiction." Pause *"Well … I don't like it when it's fact either – but … I have no problem with missing people who were and are important to me."*

"Yes …" she mused *"… that's probably what I see in tragedy though. It's that poignancy … if you can dwell on that with Hendrix you could probably come to appreciate it in plays."* Pause *"Don't you think?"*

"Yes …" Pause *"That's an angle that's never occurred to me before. Alright – I'm convinced. I'll give it a go as long as it's—*not*—'Long Day's Journey into Night'. I think tragedy is one thing, but miserable futility's another."*

"And 'Othello', I imagine."

"*Thank you for remembering*" I laughed. "*But I wouldn't class 'Othello' along with the aforementioned. That would be monstrous. I think I could even take a good stab at 'Othello' if it was well acted. I can actually just enjoy Shakespeare's language for its own sake – whatever the play.*"

"*There's no Shakespeare this season – but you might enjoy Chekhov. 'The Cherry Orchard' is playing at the New Vic next week – maybe we could go and see it?*" Claudette replied.

"*Sure. Maybe I'll come out of the New Vic—as 'the new Vic'—the one who enjoys a good tragedy.*"

"*Very droll*" Claudette tittered. "*A finely delivered rejoinder.*"

"*Thank you – and speaking of Jimi Hendrix, I should tell you about Jennifer Morton – who we called Jennifer Eccles … even though … it wasn't her name.*"

Claudette had to sit down at that point because she couldn't stop laughing.

I used to carry her satchel – she used to walk by my side./ But when we got to her doorstep her dad wouldn't let me inside / I love Jennifer Eccles …
Nash/Clarke—The Hollies—Jennifer Eccles—1968

"*Jennifer Eccles?*" she asked after she'd caught her breath.

"*Yeah … she was inspired by Cynthia Albritton.*"

"*The famous 'Cynthia Plaster Caster'?*" Claudette chimed in.

"*The—very—same. Jimi Hendrix and Noel Redding were her first two subjects.*"

"*So Noel Redding was 'The First Noël!*" she giggled.

"*Indeed he was!*" I congratulated her on her wit. "*I'll have to remember that line. Frank Zappa also took part and encouraged Cynthia in her Art project.*"

"*Did he now …?*" Claudette said with a wry smile.

"The Art project involved plaster casting the genitalia of Rock musicians."

"I suppose Cynthia Albritton never contacted anyone in Savage Cabbage?" Claudette enquired mischievously.

"No – but I imagine that none of us would have proved unobliging." I was going to tell this story come what may – however many interruptions. *"Jennifer launched a similar project at Farnham Art School. The project was to make an ice-lolly mould. I remember her finding it hysterically funny the way that most of the male students found it slightly unnerving to lick her frozen fruit juice desserts."*

"And how did you—enjoy—your priapic ice-lolly?" Claudette asked with mirth.

"Said I wasn't fond of raspberry – and passed mine on."

This—for some reason—caused Claudette tears of laughter again. *"I just—cannot—imagine having this conversation with anyone else. Who apart from—you—would be talking about penis ice-lollies on Silbury Hill?"*

"I see no penises" I replied in the style of Lord Admiral Nelson – holding an invisible telescope to my right eye.

"Nor do I as yet ..." she laughed *"... more's the pity, I say."*

"D'you have a more appropriate place in mind for the discussion?" I ventured – when her mirth had subsided.

"Speaking as an historical couturier ... I would recommend ... West Kennet Long Barrow" she replied with a grin. *"I've got ... a ground sheet and blankets in the boot of the car.*[6] *I believe a pleasant hour could be spent there discussing that subject. Provided there are practical examples to hand."*

---

6   Boot – trunk in the USA.

Claudette could always be relied upon to conjure wit out of any situation and occasionally it was hard to keep up with her.

"*Did you know ...*" Claudette said out of the blue "*... that werewolves have a genuine basis in fact?*" I admitted that I didn't know anything about werewolves. "*They were once witches and warlocks you know. People call such people shamans now – but 'shaman' is a Siberian word.*" That, I did know. "*So ...*" she continued "*... these were people who became possessed by the wolf spirit and probably wore wolf skins and wolf masks in their dances.*"

"*Right ... like the American Indians with their power-animals?*"

"*I can't say ... I've never read anything about that – but I'd imagine it's similar.*"

"*Christianity wiped all that out!*" Claudette sneered. "*They reinterpreted everything in a negative way. Even the devil ...*"

"*So the devil's a good guy then?*"

"*Well maybe not the devil as such – but the image of the devil is simply a pre-Christian fertility god – who's more-or-less like Pan of the Greeks.*"

"*So that whole cloven-hoof—hornèd—thing has nothing to do with the devil in the Bible?*"

"*Nothing at all. Lucifer means 'the bringer of light' and was being punished for bringing light to human beings. It's a direct parallel with Greek myth.*"

"*That's amazing! Thank you very much indeed for the history lesson – this stuff's important to know.*" I told her about Santa Claus and the whole reindeer urine story. I was delighted to find that I knew something that I could add to the conversation in similar vein.

"*Fascinating. I had no idea that you were interested in this kind of thing.*"

"*I'm interested in almost everything – the only problem is that there's not enough time to read about everything that grabs my attention.*"

I then told her about the way that Legba had been converted into 'the devil' as well. Claudette's reading hadn't taken her to Africa either – so she was intrigued to hear what I had to say on the subject.

Claudette liked antiques and took me to antique markets and shops. The world of antiques was fascinating. A quality of craftsmanship existed that was hard to find in the modern world – and I found it uplifting. I started wanting to fill my environment with antique *anything*. Claudette was *the thaumaturge*[7] *of tchotchkes*.[8] She collected eggs of all kinds: cloisonné, boxwood filigree, soapstone, agate, marble, silver, too many to think about. She'd make egg boxes for them out of antique boxes and line them with satin or velvet. She worked at her collections with the most fantastical unremitting care – as if she were a museum curator. Everything she made was extraordinary – and I was impressed. You could go ahead and assemble an astonishing variety of anything – *and* house it magnificently. I was happy to go exploring antique shops. I could see that there need be no reason whatsoever not to collect anything. I acquired an old Tibetan tea bowl and used it for coffee. I liked things I could use rather than ornaments.

Claudette—according to Meryl—maintained a state of pristine order. She lived in an astonishing world of miniature objects – but I'd never seen her home environment due to her father having a variety of ungainly predilections that sounded vaguely like misanthropy. He wasn't keen on visitors and somehow it was always inconvenient for me to drop by.

---

7   Thaumaturge – from the Greek, Thaumatourgós, meaning 'magician'.
8   Tchotchkes – Yiddish, meaning bits and bobs, or knick-knacks.

I made nothing too much of it as I was not a great enthusiast when it came to parents. I held most of them to be inane, insane, and far from urbane. Claudette was more than happy to visit me in Hotwells and I was content to go along with the situation as it was presented.

"*Don't you ever ask 'dette if her comfort parameters are a little confining?*" asked Meryl when I'd told her that Claudette wasn't going to go to Scotland with me.

"*No ... I wouldn't feel it courteous.*" Meryl screwed up her nose at the word 'courteous' and asked me what I meant. "*Well I feel that people are ... as they are ... and shouldn't go round trying to change each other — as if one way of living was better than another.*"

Meryl thought that was highly accepting on my part. "*I think 'dette really*—ought—*to try a little travel you know. It can't be good to put such tight limits on life. I know it's her style — but ...*" Meryl ran out of words or out of impetus — I wasn't sure which.

"Yes ... it's her style — and in some ways, I like it. I can't say I blame her either. I've seen some pretty grim situations travelling and I wouldn't like to pretend it was all fun."

Meryl gazed at me intently for a moment and I wondered what it portended — but she seemed to decide on something internally and changed subject without having broached what was on her mind. "*Where are you off to then?*"

"*I'm keeping a promise to myself. I'm going to Scotland — to Eskdalemuir*" I replied — happy to change subject. I didn't feel comfortable discussing Claudette with her friends.

"There's a Tibetan centre there and I've always wanted to go, and spend some time there since I came back from India."⁹

"That sounds intriguing ..." Meryl responded. "I'd fancy coming with you – but ... well, anyway – I'm sorry that 'dette's not going with you."

"Well ... It's not her bag y'know ... and she hates travelling."

Meryl had her eye on the window and spoke almost as if in a dream "Yeah ... she does. That's a pity though ... I think it'd be good for her to be open ... I mean to learn a little about Buddhism as it's so important to you."

"Well, yes ... but it's not one of those evangelical numbers – I'm not out to convert anyone and proselytising is something that's alien to me."

"I know that, Vic – but it's good to share things with a partner – but ... it's none of my business really. Sorry, I shouldn't have said anything,"

"That's fine, Meryl – not a problem. I don't mind what you say – I know you have my best interests at heart."

"I heard they've got two yaks there" Meryl observed, to change the subject.

"Yes ... a yak and a dri – the females are called dris." I accepted the change in subject without comment.

"You're an expert on livestock too!" Meryl laughed. "There's no end to your vaults of information."

"Well ...you just pick things up on the road you know – and I went to the Himalayas in my year out."

---

9   Samyé Ling in Eskdalemuir, near Langholm, Dumfries and Galloway, Scotland. It was originally a hunting lodge called 'Johnstone House'. In 1965 the Johnstone House Trust was formed to make available Buddhist facilities for study and meditation. In 1967 the Johnstone House trustees invited the Tibetan Lamas Chögyam Trungpa Rinpoche and Akong Rinpoche to assume leadership.

"*Right ... wish I'd have taken a year out now.*"

"*Well ... maybe ... maybe not. I sometimes wonder whether it wasn't such a great idea. Times seem to have changed at Art School.*"

"*In a year?*"

"*Even a year. I've been amazed by the way things can change.*"

"*Yes ... I can see what you mean. But ... if you hadn't taken a year out we might not all be here in this house together – and that would have been a pity. What you've told me about your experience of 1966 to 1970 seems close to what we have here.*"

"*Absolutely*" I chuckled. "*I wouldn't be anywhere else in the world right now – even if I have to hit the road from time to time.*"

"*On the Road eh, like Jack Kerouac?*" Meryl chuckled. "*A hero headed for an adventure.*"

"*Or a heroine ...*" I nodded. "*I think that must be the idea behind it all. I think the idea is that people who stay in one place are seen as the sheep who crowd into domestic fields to be safe from the wolves of weirdness.*"

"*The wolves of weirdness ... I like that. I'd like to be one of those.*"

"*You already are Meryl – watching you recite your lines is like watching a wolf high up on a rock somewhere.*"

"*Great image ... I'll keep that one at hand when I feel nervous. It's a good picture. Y'know ... if you have nowhere to go, your life's static by default.*"

"*From one point of view*" I replied.

"*Yeah ... I'm not saying it's entirely my point of view – but I can empathise with it, at times at least.*"

"*Maybe you're changing ... becoming – a weird wolf.*"

"*Yeah ...*" Meryl laughed "*... or a werewolf*".

We sat in silence for a while and I mused on the words of the Steppenwolf song 'Born to be Wild' ... *head out on the highway* ... and it occurred to me that there was a part of me that was like that. "*Y'know ... the Open Road thing ... that's possibly the last vestige of the '60s ... I wonder how long it'll be there.*"

"*As long as there's somewhere to go I suppose*" Meryl replied. "*The roads aren't going to go away and so there's nothing to stop you taking off whenever it grabs you.*"

"*Yes ... it does grab me from time to time ... especially when there are old friends I'd like to see again – people from Foundation. There's no telling where you'll end up each night or whether you'll ever reach your destination. It's an amazing feeling.*"

Meryl looked at me curiously "*You really sound as if you're itching to get moving.*"

"*In some ways ...*" I replied "*... but really only when I think about it – and I don't think about it*—that—*much. It's a push-and-pull thing anyhow – because I'm extremely happy just being here in Hotwells and at the College. Going to Eskdalemuir is just something I've been storing up.*"

During the second year at Bristol I finally put my thumb to rest. Claudette never took long trips with me. The Pixie Chariot was no longer fit for long distance – and Jack Kerouac ceased to whisper in my ear '*You should be leaving for somewhere.*'

The old friends I visited were shifting perceptually, away from *the lost time*. They were developing career concerns – matrimonial concerns. They were getting married to people who had no interest in Art. They'd married vets, dentists, civil servants, taxidermists, school teachers ... and these partners looked at me with a wary eye – as if I were a wicked weird-wolf— a wild wayward wastrel drunk on wanderlust—a wily wild card on the loose.

Left Chicago in the summer, New York in the fall, / Detroit in the winter didn't prove a thing at all / I got those roaming blues yes I got those roaming blues, / Can't find no place to settle, woo I got those roaming blues. Louis Jordan—Roaming Blues—1947

It had been a delight to visit Pete Bridgewater but other than that, I'd made one too many decisions that hadn't worked out well. I'd gone to Guildford to see Richard Oliver, an old friend from Farnham Art School. He was getting engaged to a trainee vet[1] named Jemima who appeared to be a pre-packaged consignment from the department of terminal ordinariness.

She reminded me of Steve Bruce's description of Synthetic Cynthia and I wondered what she was going to make of me. She had that look of anxious hostility on her face, reminiscent of Lindie Dale's parents when they beheld the monster their daughter had brought home. Richard and I were to pick up the engagement ring from a jewellers' shop – and in my mind, that item had evolved a certain symbolism. It would be worn on her finger but it was the controlling device for a large iron band that was about to close round Richard's neck. There'd be a long chain attached to it in order that Jemima could jerk him back if he ever looked like he was about to engage in anything interesting. Jemima decided to accompany us into Guildford – which was slightly less desirable, because it crimped the conversation. I was accustomed to ladies who were capable of banter and quick repartee – but Jemima was like a time-traveller from the 1950s. It was evident that she understood so little of what I said that I had to trim my vocabulary and constrain the conceptual acrobatics for fear of excluding her.

---

1   Vet – an abbreviation for veterinarian in Britain, rather than 'veteran' in the USA.

an odd boy

It was not that she was unintelligent – but her intelligence had been channelled into terminal everyday consumerist pragmatism.

"*No … I don't really watch television – so I don't know the series …*"

"*Why have one then?*" she countered – as if she were a parent.

"*I don't.*"

"*They're not—that—expensive.*" She found it incomprehensible that I didn't own a television.

"*Yes … I believe you're right – but I don't think I'd watch enough to make it worth the licence.*" I thought that was polite as I wouldn't have watched it at all – but she seemed offended nonetheless.

"*What do you—do—with your time then?*"

"*Well … I either work, or listen to music.*"

She looked flabbergasted, as if I'd told her I inhaled decomposing slugs whilst sitting in a vat of rancid offal. "*You just sit and listen to music?*"

"*Yes – I also read … sometimes I talk with friends. I live in a shared house and we often spend evenings talking and listening to music.*"

The fact that we spent whole evenings talking was as foreign to her as if I'd told her we hung upside down in laundry bags.

"*What do you find to talk about all evening?*"

"*Painting, poetry, literature, film making, theatre, and music – especially music.*"

"*What's there to say about music apart from liking it or not liking it?*"

Richard came to my aid "*Vic was a vocalist and bassist with a Blues band.*"

"*Were you famous?*" she asked with a sneer "*Would I have—heard —of you?*"

bower ashton — going to a funeral, dressed in white

"*Probably not ... it was back in '68 ... and we only played 'til early '70.*"

Richard looked a little edgy "*Two of the band members died before they had a chance to get anywhere.*"

"*What did they die of?*" she enquired disdainfully "*Drugs?*"

I was silent for a moment. Jemima had been discourteous and invasive — but I chose to be diplomatic in my response.

"*No ... none of us used the stuff.*" Pause "*Ron died of a heart attack — he had a weak heart from birth. Steve died in a car crash along with his father—his father was driving—it was a multiple collision.*"

Jemima went silent.

"*They were fine musicians and ... the best friends I ever had.*"

Jemima remained silent. Richard kept his attention on the road and the car made its inexorable way to the abattoir of Art—the jewelled gallows—where Richard would sacrifice his individuality on the altar of average expectations. I contented myself with watching the trees on the delightful country roads. I decided not to speak again as I didn't find myself in the right frame of mind for a diplomatic switch in subject matter — merely to make Jemima comfortable. That was Richard's task — and one that might occupy him for life. Finally Richard asked me about Pete Bridgewater.

"*He's doing well at Brighton Art School and he's got prospects of working at Thames and Hudson publishers when he's through.*"

"*Remember that 'hot hand' warm water bottle he made on Foundation?*" asked Richard. "*That was a gas.*"

"*Yeah*" I replied. "*The perspex presentation case was a beautiful touch — especially the red velvet lining.*" Richard described the project to Jemima but she was unimpressed. Our 'school boy pranks' were of no great interest to her.

He explained that it wasn't a prank and that the piece had been appreciated by the Head of Foundation for both its craftsmanship and humour – but she shrugged "*Well I never went to Art School – so I wouldn't understand what goes on there. I'm training to be a vet.*"

Jemima was hard work – and I wondered why Richard was considering engagement to such a person.

I made some comment about what a beautiful Autumn it was and Jemima said "*I don't like the Autumn – everything's dying.*"

I resisted the urge to say 'Yeah … *we're all dying – just very slowly.*'

We eventually entered the jewellers'.

Richard looked a little sheepish and as an awkward greeting said "*I've come to pay for the ring. I put a deposit on it.*"

The shop assistant smiled—took his ticket—and bent down to open a drawer beneath the counter. I took the opportunity for a jest—leant over—and said in a mock whisper "*Don't worry they've probably cleaned it off by now.*" Jemima looked daggers at me and Richard looked wearied – as if he was going to have to explain me away later. I apologised and said I meant nothing by it. "*I just like to make people laugh – and … it's not always appropriate.*" I'd desist from such ribaldry in the future.

The worst was somehow that I was the one who'd been to the Himalayas for months on end; on an adventure no one understood – and if they did understand it, it was alien to those who'd suddenly decided they were Christian. Jemima was an avowed Christian and it had seemed that this was her major objection to me – albeit couched in other terms and other modes of disapproval. It seemed that people had a curious way of aligning everything they disliked to Buddhism.

I didn't watch television and that was obviously a perversion of which Buddhists were guilty. I had conversations about the Arts – another vile indulgence of Buddhists. I rarely mentioned Buddhism – but it often filtered back to me that my 'Buddhist ideas' were not appreciated. Richard had whispered that to me as a reason for Jemima's manner.

"Richard ..." I replied – somewhat bewildered "... *I never mentioned a word about Buddhism ... so ...*"

"*Well ... she asked why you went to India ... and so I told her you were a Buddhist and had gone to get some instruction or whatever.*"

"*Ah ... but ... what has that got to do with not watching television? There's no Buddhist edict about abjuring television or compulsorily talking about the Arts ...*"

"*Yeah ... right ... I can understand about the Arts – but I thought not watching television was part of the ascetic thing to do if you were a Buddhist – y'know, giving up the world.*"

"*Richard ... do I look as if I've given up the world?*"

"*Errrm ... well, no – not too much ... but ...you're not exactly aiming at the high life or anything like that.*"

"*And ... that's what you and Jemima are doing?*"

"*Not exactly ... I just want to earn a decent income.*"

"*Well ... that's no different from my plan ... if I can – but I also want my life to be centred around the Arts as much as possible.*" Pause "*And ...that's not particularly a Buddhist thing. It could as easily be Jewish, Christian, Agnostic, or Atheist.*"[3] Pause "*I'm not a renunciate ...*

---

3   The author had taken gö kar chang lo (*gos dKar lCang lo*) vows. He was thus a ngakpa (*sNgags pa*) – a non-celibate yogi of the Nyingma Tradition of Tibetan Buddhism. Members of this order are not required to be renunciates and can live ordinary family lives.

an odd boy

"*I could explain – but it would take too long and ... it's only interesting to people who're interested – if you see what I mean.*"

Richard said he'd try to explain that to Jemima – but that it wouldn't be easy because she had strong feelings about heathens and such like. She was also somewhat anti-Semitic so he'd have to leave out the Jewish part of the list. I then had to constrain myself quite ruthlessly from asking '*Why in hell are you so dead set on marrying this ... this ... this ... person?*' I simply raised my eyebrows and sighed, which—I suppose—was the same as saying what I had left unsaid. Sometimes you just can't win.

I inadvertently held to my promise to Richard to desist from ribaldry in the future – because I never saw Jemima again. I never saw Richard again either. I wrote a letter thanking him for his hospitality but never heard back. I sent Richard and Jemima a Yuletide card—as normally worded as possible—but it probably looked as if it had been posted from Desolation Row. I was one of those people who lived in the margins—in the twilight zone—in the depths of weird. The card vanished into purple haze.[2] I took the hint and somehow failed ever to write again.

Old friends were disappearing fast. The new partners of my friends saw their spouses as having 'settled down'. They'd left all that craziness behind. Then I'd turn up on the doorstep and I could see the horrible reflection of myself in their eyes: fifth ace up my sleeve, derringer in my waistband, Bowie knife in my boot.

---

2   A common saying at the time – referencing the song 'Purple Haze,' written by Jimi Hendrix in 1966, and released as a single by The Jimi Hendrix Experience in 1967.

I was a dangerous lunatic who was going to lure their husband or wife back into the grotesque Gomorrah of the Arts – or worse.

Over the green hills and into the sun that's where I feel I ought to be go'n' / Blue sky above me and green earth below / Don't even matter which way I go. Rodgers—Free—Over the Green Hills, Part I—Tons of Sobs—1968

Then even the old friends started looking at me as if I were a werewolf. It was hard to focus on what was happening – because I was charming enough. I was cordial and polite. I always have been. I was not the depraved drug dealer, dissolute dope fiend my father had feared I'd become. I was not a lieutenant of larceny or combustible caricature Casanova either. I wasn't even born to be wild. I was about as wild as a salmon and cucumber sandwich. I just liked to converse with friends about perception and the nature of reality. I liked to talk about music and poetry – but they seemed to have lost interest in these topics.

"No. I've not written poetry since the Foundation Year … don't know why." Giles Gordon seemed embarrassed by the question – and so the idea of pulling a sheaf of poetry from my satchel seemed inappropriate. It would have been fine a year and a half before. Then in 1973 I had the sense that *only poets wrote poetry*. Poets were people who'd had books published—poets laureate and the like—and *'who d'you think you are to be writing poetry.'* The words were not direct but the looks said *'Nobody wants to hear your poetry anyway – it's just a lot of words that don't make sense.'* I have always had the ability to mind-read faces. It's *all* in the face. You can see an attitude fully formed – immediately. No need for a word to be uttered. So … I had no interest in forcing anything on anyone.

Giles' societally-sanctioned government-issue wife Delia looked at me with disdain and asked "*Why do you have to wear a white suit?*"

an odd boy

I thought of saying '*I am not impelled — I wear it of my own free will,*' but decided against being witty. I wore the white suit quite often at that time and the first whom it incensed was Todd. He seemed to have forgotten his failure to embarrass me concerning my green leather jacket and boots. "*See you're still trying to create the illusion that you're out of the ordinary*" he'd sneered on the first occasion he saw the white suit. I'd replied "*Vestio ergo sum, Todd.*" Claudette had taught me the Latin phrase. I'd enquired of her as to what it might be — on the basis of Descartes' *Cogito ergo sum*.[4]

"*I like it ...*" I replied meekly to Giles' wife. "*I like how it looked on John Lennon — y'know, on the cover of Abbey Road.*"

"*Don't you feel self-conscious in it?*"

"*Well no ...*" I replied seconds before I put my foot in my mouth "*... or at least not 'til you started asking me about it ... but I don't think it'll be a long lasting sensation.*"

I smiled to show her all was well — but she stood up with alarming rapidity and left the room. My friend looked uncomfortable. "*Vic ... mmmm ... I think you might need to say sorry to my wife.*"

"*Yes ... right ... certainly Giles ... I'll do whatever you think — but ... don't you think she ... opened fire first?*"

"*Well, Vic ...*" he said "*... but you didn't have to come back at her with Buddhism.*"

That threw me slightly "*Giles ... what I said was just the mildest thing I could think to say — and it had nothing to do with Buddhism.*"

"*No ...? Aren't they always banging on about impermanence?*"

---

4   Cogito ergo sum — I think therefore I am. Vestio ergo sum — I dress therefore I am.

"Yes, Giles … they are – but y'know … that idea isn't exactly exclusive to Buddhism."

"Alright, point taken – but … if you—will—go round wearing a white suit like that …you—have—to expect people to ask you why you're wearing it. I mean – it's a bit of a statement isn't it."

"Right—I'm sorry—hadn't realised times had changed quite so much …" Pause "… I suppose I'm probably living as if we're still at Hatch Mill and it's still 1970 …" Pause "… but … maybe that's a thousand years ago now."

Giles looked as if he'd not understood what I'd said – or maybe that he didn't feel like understanding. I never knew. I decided it was not opportune to open a discussion on the matter.

"Anyhow … I'll certainly apologise without further delay. I didn't intend to offend her. I was just kind of thrown by the question."

I apologised to Delia. My apology was kindly stated – but received with cold, silent indifference.

You're the kind of woman, would feel right at home in hell, / Ya stick me with a pitchfork, just to hear me yell.
Johnny Winter—Serious as a Heart Attack—1965

Right … what next? Delia remained in the kitchen – stiffly attending to things that needed no attention. I returned to the living room. "Giles …y'know … I think … it might be better if I left now. You and Delia …you might want to talk or something."

"Right—yeah—I think that's probably best … under the circumstances."

I moved rapidly and was on the doorstep almost as his sentence ended.

"So, Vic … right … I'll be in touch then."

an odd boy

His voice echoed from the living room. I smiled and nodded. I decided not to say anything. Giles could say something he didn't mean – but there was no reason I should play along with the fiasco to the bitter end. I knew as well as he did that he'd not be in contact again. I was right. I sent no 'thank you' letter – not because I was annoyed – but simply because I was sad.

There was no purpose in communication. I had nothing to say. He had nothing to reply. Our friendship was a phenomenon that had existed in the past when it was the convention to be weird. Now it was becoming the convention to be ... something else.

I'm going to a funeral dressed in white, / I'm going to a nightclub, to sleep with night, / And I'm not going with you—no. Jack Bruce/Pete Brown—The Weird of Hermiston—Songs For a Tailor—1969

It was like that—or getting like that—everywhere. Friends started saying *sensible things* about life insurance and investments. I'd look at their mantelpieces and chimney breasts – and there'd be portraits of Moloch there. Moloch rosettes. Moloch medals. Moloch golf statuettes. They'd show me their Moloch lawnmower, Moloch washing machine, Moloch rotisserie, Moloch dishwasher, Moloch kitchen clock, Moloch holiday photographs, Moloch lawn furniture, Moloch wristwatches, and I'd start feeling a message coming through. *Mene, mene, tekel, upharsin.*[5] The writing was on the wall. Moloch had weighed me in the scales and found me wanting.

---

5   Mene, mene, tekel, upharsin – idiomatic for impending doom that originates from the story of King Balshazzar of Babylon in the Bible, Daniel V: 25.

7

the second year: september 1973 – december 1973

bower ashton – hippie is dead

I ceased to understand being *on the road*. I'd return to Bristol after these visits feeling more estranged from society than when I'd left. I started to prefer conventional high street society, to what was left of *the lost time*. A ghostly hand inscribed psychedelic word-colours in the air: '*Stay in Bristol and paint.*' There was too much work with my painting to be *on the road*. I was going to stay where I was – with my canvasses, oil paints, and my many illustration projects.

"*Y'know, 'dette ... the illustrators seem to treat the Art School as if the facilities will always be available – as if they'll all have access to an etching press or a photographic studio when they've left here.*"

Claudette pondered my statement for a moment and replied "*Maybe they're just not quite as ... dedicated to Art – as you are ... You do work very hard you know.*"

"*Well, that's how everyone used to be at Hatch Mill – apart from a few idiots ...*" I sighed. "*I suppose that I must have been a fluke of nature. I suppose enthusiasm will be illegal one day ... I suppose Dick Taylor was right ...*" I sighed "*... and the '60s are over. They did say 'Hippie is dead' after* 1967."

"*Oh come on!*" Claudette harrumphed amusedly. "*You—never— really—saw—yourself that way. You're—always—saying that you were never a real hippie.*"

"*True enough, 'dette – but I can still be nostalgic about it. It's easier to like 'Hippie' now it's gone. Y'know ... even though I never was a hippie – I was damn glad to see people—being—hippies.*"

"*Why—on earth—would—that—be?*" she chuckled.

"*Well ... they made me feel ... conservative.*" Pause "*I think I—liked —feeling just a little conservative.*"

Claudette clucked "*You are—definitely—the most contradictory creature I've ever met.*" Pause "*You're the mister-freedom-anarchist who conforms to the system by working non-stop.*"

"*Yeah ... but I don't think I ever planned it that way ... just because I'm the only one who arrives early and puts in a full day's work?*"

"*Yes – but you—have—to admit you're a slave to your creative impulses.*"

"*You being one of them, 'dette ...*"

"*I'm jolly glad to hear it*" she laughed.

"*But seriously ... no one—owns—this slave ...*" Pause "*... anyhow, I think you'd have to call me a share-cropper – as slavery was more-or-less abolished by the time I was born ...*"

"*Very droll.*"

"*Anyway, the music I love most comes from the descendants of slaves ... so ... maybe it's entirely appropriate. Why shouldn't a Bluesman work like a slave if he's his own master?*"

"*You're just obsessed!*" Claudette laughed. "*And making fanciful allusions to the Mississippi Delta won't let you off the hook*" she said giggling and wagging her finger at me in the manner of a scolding mother.

"Hook ... ?" I laughed "Well I wish I – was a catfish – swimming i-i – in the deep blue sea – but there ain't no pretty woman ever gonna get a – hook in me; lord got no hook in me."[6]

Claudette harrumphed with mock consternation.

"Alright ... I'll take your question seriously ..." I pondered "... well, I —do—work hard ... but then we only have three years here and I want to go on to an MA and I'll need a 1st for that."

"Or an upper 2nd" she responded with swift legal exactitude. "You don't—have—to have a 1st."

"True ... I know ... but if you want to—guarantee—a place ... it's as well to be the best candidate you can be. I could get a 1st with the standard of my work—that's what Derek told me—and I have no reason to disbelieve him."

"But you said you didn't care about results in the 1st year – you know, when we first talked about your Film essay for Rick Frampton."

"You have a good memory, 'dette. I did say that." Pause "Although ..." I laughed "... I—did—get 87% for that thing I wrote on 'The Ruling Class'."

"Most fortuitous" Claudette chuckled. "So—now—academic brilliance is the latest fashion?"

"If it gets me into the London School of Printmaking or the RCA."

"This is quite a turnabout I must say."

"No ... at that time I didn't care about essay results – because I hadn't really started thinking about the end of this course ... I was just at the beginning. Since then, of course, Derek's been talking to me about my future plans."

---

6   Jim Jackson—Kansas City Blues, Part 3—1927; later it became known as 'Catfish Blues' and was performed by many Blues musicians.

an odd boy

"*Mmmm ...*" Claudette looked thoughtful. "*I suppose there is no MA course available here is there ...*"

"*No ... I wish there was. I'm not wild about living in London – but there seems to be no choice*" I replied.

"*So it's nose to the grindstone until you leave, is it?*"

"*Yes ... more-or-less ...*"

"*Hmmm ...*" Claudette ruminated. "*Well ... I have no penchant for staying late. I work hard – but I see no need to reach Olympic standards.*"

"*Well ... I never stay as late as I stayed in Farnham because I like to spend the early evening with you.*" Claudette liked coming round to the Hotwells house each day before heading home for dinner. Her father was something of a chef and she liked to keep him company on the week days.

"*And you work after I've gone!?*" She almost shrieked with incredulity.

"*Certainly. And then – I have the rest of the evening with 'the girls' when they've got through with whatever projects they're working on.*"

"*Proper little bevy of bees you are to be sure – are you the Queen bee though or one of the drones of the hive?*"

"*Queen Bee—Queen Bee—come on back to me. Said, Queen Bee—Queen Bee—come on back to me 'cause you got the best darn stinger – I most ever see'd*" I sang.

"*Blues ...*" she remarked wagging her head as if to call me incorrigible.

"*Yes, Bumble Bee Blues ... John Lee Hooker.*"

"*These quotations aren't—exactly—the acme of English ...*"

"*They're a genre that doesn't need to be compared with anything else ... You can't compare Beat Poetry and Byron either ...*"

"Point taken ... that was rather judgemental of me."

"Well ... I can see how it becomes tiring to hear Blues quotes too often ..." Pause *"... but ... can I ask you ... why—and don't take this amiss— you're ... critical ... about time I spend working ... when you're not exactly inconvenienced by it?"*

"Well ... it just seems ...you don't have any social life apart from me."

"There's Rebecca, Meryl, and Penelope ... I have some fine social time with them – and ... actually that fits the bill pretty well. I don't need any more society than you and your friends."

"You do seem to have hit it off very well with my friends. They see more of you than I do."

"Well ... I've not made a study of the time – so I wouldn't know ... I guess, living in house with them, I'm bound to spend a lot of time with them – but what percentage is social time is impossible to calculate. I do get on well with them – but there's no reason they should see more of me socially." Pause *"I don't quite know how to put this without sounding ever-so-slightly curmudgeonly ... but you do ... call the shots on that. You only come 'round on weekends – and ... I can't go to your place because your father won't have visitors ..."*

Claudette looked slightly miffed that I'd underlined the obvious – but smiled sheepishly *"I suppose so – if you put it that way."*

It occurred to me that Mrs Bennet had made a similar statement in 'Pride and Prejudice' but decided it would not be conducive to good feelings to draw a comparison. I wasn't sure what I should say next – so I took a slightly divergent angle *"Life with Rebecca, Meryl, and Penelope is infinitely more congenial than being peered at by Todd – in that way that he has ...Y'know I never really know what he's expecting when I enter the room. He sometimes looks as if he needs to defend himself from some unlikely act I might perpetrate."*

"Like ...?" she asked.

an odd boy

"*Let's see ... like regurgitating nine live black mambas; like, announcing I was the incarnation of a Playtex Living Bra*[7] *and devoutly intending to keep abreast of the times; like, suddenly filling the studio with shrimp-shaped dirigibles; like, summoning apparitions of Reginald Bosanquette*[8] *from the vasty deeps ; like ... well ... probably like being myself.*"

Claudette found the list amusing – but shook her head "*Very droll.*"

"*He—and Veranda, who never addresses a word to me—seem to view me as a creature from the past ... a denizen of the disturbing and dangerous '60s where insanity was the accepted norm. It's as if I have a contagious disease called unpredictability and they don't want to be infected by it.*"

"*Methinks you overplay your part somewhat. You just might not be quite as outlandish as you like to think you are in spite of your predilection for Monty Python.*"

"*You may well be right ...*" I grinned "*... but however it is ... I seem to have nothing in common with Todd and Veranda – or with most of my peers in the Illustration Department. I feel like Albert Camus' Outsider.*"

"*That adds such dignity to your dilemma.*" Claudette whooped with mirth "*... but I doubt that you'll be executed for it.*"

"*Quite so.*" Pause "*It saddened me a little at first – but ... I suppose ... I've grown accustomed to insularity – and ... I could almost begin to enjoy its self-contained quality.*"

"*My father certainly does.*"

---

7   Playtex is a manufacturer of brassieres and women's undergarments. The name is derived from 'perforated latex'. Latex—sandwiched between cotton—gave the underwear an elastic character that shaped to the body. Playtex was founded in 1932 by Abram Nathaniel Spanel—inventor and philanthropist—who was a Russian immigrant to the USA.

8   Reginald Bosanquet [1932 – 1984]. British journalist and television news presenter in the 1970s – known for his slightly dour expression.

"*Yes ...*" I mused "*... maybe there's something to be said for anchoritic existence – and maybe I could view it as a preliminary to the cave dwelling that lies ahead of me, when I'm in my dotage.*"

"*Ah yes ... the romantic plan to spend your final days immured in a dark noisome hole in the Himalayas.*"

"*I'd envisioned it as light and airy actually, 'dette ...*"

"*That would be preferable – but don't you think your romance with the esoteric East might wane over the years?*"

"*No ... anything is possible I suppose ... but I wouldn't describe it as 'romance' – well ... not entirely ... but—in the realm of anything being possible—you might tire of Bath and the theatre ... and end your days as a Jesuit nun.*"

"*I think that might be taking things a little far*" Claudette harrumphed. I noticed that Claudette was never keen on having a point of argument floored – even when she'd initiated the duel.

And yes ... it was often a duel – and she'd often say 'touché' ... and I wondered why ... It was mainly light hearted – but sometimes there was an edge to it that didn't feel entirely friendly. At those times it felt a little like our first meeting when she'd been adversarial. I wondered if she was drifting back in that direction and why ... I decided to shelve that idea on the basis that it wasn't conducive to an open state of mind. I decided to wax positive instead and refer to my conversation with Janet.

"*Still ...*" I resumed "*... Janet Coleridge has started talking to me.*"

"*Wonders will never cease*" Claudette chuckled. "*Did she have anything amusing to say?*"

an odd boy

"No – it wasn't that kind of conversation. We talked about Todd and she expressed how she felt about his antagonism. She seemed to have come to a reappraisal of me – and … seems to feel that the others in the department have begun to grow distrustful of Todd and Veranda."

"They certainly took their time about it, if you ask me."

"Yes … but then … they had to overcome some degree of conditioning – both from Todd and from society."

"It's up to them what kind of conditioning they accept isn't it?"

"Yes … that's true of us all – but you had some conditioning to overcome too when we first met."

"Such as?" Claudette threw out imperiously with a slight flick of her head.

"Well only what you told me at the time – that you'd expected me to be the average male with all the vices that you would attribute to such a creature."

"Oh—I see—well yes … but I wouldn't call that conditioning. I was simply speaking from experience."

"Fair enough, 'dette – but maybe the ladies in the Illustration Department all had bad experiences with eccentrics – or with weirdoes, hippies, freaks, heads – or whatever people call people like me."

"Well … if you put it like that …" Pause "… but as you well know – you bear very little resemblance to what anyone would ordinarily think of in that way."

"Apart from being a Buddhist …"

"Yes … pity they had to find out about that."

"It's not some kind of dark secret, 'dette."

"No … I suppose not."

"Anyhow … my time at Bower Ashton feels like a sealed envelope of time – which is … quite good in a way … in fact, in many ways."

Claudette—her eyes flashing quickly to her tastefully diamond-accented watch—laughed *"I'd better lick the envelope and dispatch myself haste-post-haste. It's time for me to go home."*

Claudette never liked to leave on a dour note – and I was always happy to let her change the atmosphere. *"Off to the cotton fields with you then my dear – or you'll be in trouble with the plantation owner."* She chuckled as she rolled up the window of the Rolls and purred off into the dark.

I stood for a while in the very finest drizzle. It was cold but I rubbed my face with it and felt refreshed. I looked up at the stars which were visible in spite of the big city halo of dull red. As I stood there I became aware of something I'd begun to recognise—so slowly—that it had remained un-worded. Then suddenly there were words – or at least, perceptions. I recognised that something had changed in my relationship with Claudette. I felt uncomfortable about the recognition – because what I recognised didn't sit easily with how I felt—*I*—should be.

It seemed that Claudette's respect for me had ebbed somewhat … I was no longer 'Mr Renaissance Man' – and my ideas weren't quite as intriguing as they were at the beginning of our relationship. My ideas had become subject to a vaguely censorious imperative on Claudette's part – and although it was not marvellous, I didn't see what complaint I could reasonably make. How could I phrase such a complaint without sounding like some hypersensitive narcissistic cretin? I had no staggeringly huge vanity that needed feeding—as far as I could see—and I had no need to be admired in any worshipful manner. So … what was it that I didn't enjoy about Claudette's shift in mien? It occurred to me that it had something to do with the disparity in the ways we regarded each other. Claudette had become somewhat more critical … and I had not.

Well, that wasn't entirely true … I was critical to a slight degree, in response to her judgemental initiatives – but I never instigated them with her. Still … it wasn't as if I didn't like her quickness of rapier repartee and brilliant badinage. That was something I'd liked from the start – but somehow, it didn't always seem kindly.

Eventually I went inside – still slightly bewildered by what had passed through my mind on the doorstep. The words vanished – as if they'd been too tenuous to trap as a logical conclusion. I was sure I'd been deep in thought but once I crossed the threshold my thought structure collapsed in on itself. Meryl was sitting in the living room when I came in. She was listening to the Bach French Suites and so I went to sit with her.

"*How're things?*" Meryl asked.

"Fine …" I said vaguely. "*I'm spending more time in the Fine Art department than the Illustration studio now … but … I'm mostly ignored there as well.*"

"*I'd have thought you'd have got on well with the Fine Art students*" Meryl replied.

"Yes … I thought the same." Pause "In Fine Art I'm 'the Graphic Designer' who wants to draw pretty pictures." Pause "In Illustration I'm 'the Illustrator with Fine Art pretensions' who thinks himself superior. No one ever says it outright—apart from Todd—but it hangs in the air like rancid rhinoceros flatulence."

Meryl laughed "*And so what's wrong with being superior to Trophy-head?*"

"*Well … whether I am or not … I don't enjoy the idea of relative status. I certainly say nothing to indicate that I feel those around me are inferior. That concept wouldn't actually mean anything to me.*" Pause "*I just do what I do … and they make of it what they will.*"

"*And what could—Trophy-head—make of it anyway ...*" Meryl said indignantly on my behalf. "*He's a facile Philistine who can't even follow your sentence construction from what I've heard.*"

"*Maybe ... but I'm not—that—convoluted. It can't be that intellectually taxing to talk about music ... can it?*"

Penelope and Rebecca appeared through the front door at that point and regaled us—in a gale of mirth—about bumping into Todd in town.

"*Trophy-head*[10] *didn't notice us at first ...*" Rebecca laughed "*... so he had no idea we were watching him walking towards us. We just couldn't believe it. He was pulling faces as if he was having an argument with someone – and talking to himself. He nearly jumped out of his skin when he recognised us. Then he just turned on his heel and rushed off.*"

"*It was strange ...*" Penelope giggled "*... maybe he's going mad. Talking to yourself is one of the signs isn't it?*"

"*I don't know ...*" I mused "*... I talk to myself.*"

"*You do?*" Rebecca asked incredulously.

"*Yeah ... I think a lot of people do – they just don't like to admit it.*"

"*Yeah ...*" laughed Rebecca "*... but they don't have—arguments—with themselves like Todd was having. He looked as if he was having some sort of debate.*"

"*Maybe he's taking part in a play or something?*" I suggested – because I was always wary of labelling unusual behaviour as problematic.

"*You're just too much sometimes ... maybe he was practising having a witty exchange with you where he comes out on top for once.*"

---

10 Rebecca and Meryl often referred to Todd as 'Trophy-head' on account of his protruding ears.

an odd boy

I had to admit that this was more likely than his practising for a play. "*Yeah ... I suppose that's quite funny. Good luck to him.*"

Penelope nodded "*Still – I like it ... the way you don't like laughing at him.*"

"*No ...*" I sighed. "*I don't get much out of it ... because I have to see him every day and if I invested too much in ridiculing him I'd become too much like him – and ... I'm still trying to establish a better atmosphere in the studio.*"

"*I can see the sense of that ...*" Penelope replied "*... but I'm glad you found it a little funny too.*"

"*Yeah ... I'm sorry for being stodgy about it. It is funny – I just hope he's got some good lines to throw at me. It would be fun if he said something witty ... then I could congratulate him or something.*"

Meryl laughed again. "*You—say—you don't say anything to Todd and Veranda to make them feel inferior – but I don't suppose you drop in the occasional Shakespeare quote?*"

"*Indeed. 'Give me some music; music, moody food of us that trade in love.'[9] However ... I haven't dropped a quote since the first term. I don't really try to have that kind of conversation anymore.*"

"*Even if you don't quote – you make them feel inferior quite naturally*" Meryl commented.

"*You work far harder than Trophy-head—from what 'dette says—and your work is better, more imaginative, and more prolific.*"

"*Yeah ... well ... I'm certainly more prolific – but the others are quite talented. Todd's a good designer and some of Janet's etchings are brilliant. Janet produced this etching of a bull rush – that's so ... pure ... it's simple yet incredibly subtle. It's also powerful in a way that's hard to describe.*"

---

9   William Shakespeare—Antony and Cleopatra—Act II—Scene v—1607

"*I try to be friendly to everyone – but ... I suppose, not—utterly—at the expense of integrity. I have to make some sort of reply to Todd when he tries to lock horns with me ... but ... no matter how mild I make it, Todd ends up with his nose pressed into his own ridiculousness.*" Pause "*Sometimes it's as if he was a hired straight man who'd been employed to set himself up to be humiliated. He keeps giving me the perfect cues. I try to avoid responding to cues when I can – but sometimes it seems impossible. Sometimes it even happens by accident – like the time he said 'Always something clever to say' and I answered 'Sorry to be so predictable, Todd'.*"

Penelope rocked backwards and forward laughing at that "*And your answering that was an accident!?*"

"*Yes ... it was – I realised how it sounded as soon as the words were out of my mouth. I'd not intended to humiliate him – but it just happened by itself. It's as if he was born to be humiliated ... I just wish it wasn't my rôle.*"

Meryl nodded "*It sounds rather grim for you – but it's also quite funny, from a distance that is.*" Pause "*But y'know – Todd was the same with me, and I had no compunction about humiliating him. As you said – he was born to be humiliated.*"

That had the ladies in hysterics – which, when the laughter subsided, gave way to the question of dinner. "*I've got that in hand*" I grinned. "*It's a vegetarian lasagne.*" The ladies nodded with interest and a slight hint of caution."*Well that idea put a crimp in the evening*" I laughed. "*It's a killer recipe really. It's got enough garlic to polish off a legion of vampires – mushrooms, onions, leeks, lasagne verdi, spinach, broccoli, mozzarella, cheddar, and dolcellate ...*" Dramatic pause "*And ... the slurry's made of grated courgettes* [11] *and pesto!*"

---

11 Courgette – zucchini in the USA.

"The slurry?" Meryl laughed.

"Yeah—wrong word I know—but I don't know what else to call it."

"Sauce?" Meryl suggested.

"Exactly" I replied. *"It's sitting in the oven—even as we speak—and if I turn up the gas now – it'll be fixed in an hour."*

Meryl was in tears of laughter at this point. *"Sorry – I'm not laughing about the lasagne – I'm laughing about the idea of the romance of the open-road we were talking about earlier – and here you are: the acme of domesticity."*

"Whatever made you think I wasn't riddled with paradoxes?"
I guffawed.

"You're a weird wolf alright, Vic."

"Thank you – let's howl at the moon a little. I'm in the mood for a little music before dinner."

On that note we changed the scene and the instruments came out. I tuned my sitar to the scale suggested and we began one of our journeys across time and space. The limit of the piece became evident only when the lasagne started making itself obvious.

Next morning Rebecca continued the conversation about Todd asking *"What does 'dette say? I bet she has some amusing angles on it"*.

"Yes … she does."

"I suppose 'dette enjoys revelling in her aristocratic mien. Her answer to most things is 'Let them eat cake.' isn't it?"

"Yes …" I replied, although discussing Claudette in this way made me a little uncomfortable *"… right … 'dette's really amusing on that subject … within limits …"* Pause

"*I suppose I don't quite share her penchant for Marie Antoinette – and … she can't quite understand my 'unnecessary egalitarianism'*" I laughed, hoping to change the subject with a jest. "*I guess she's less afraid of the guillotine than I am.*"

I failed in my jest – because Meryl continued "*Yes … she wants us all to distance ourselves from the culturally-ignorant-proletariat – because there's a cultural nobility of theatre goers to which we're all supposed to belong.*"

Penelope saved me by coming to Claudette's defence "*Oh she just likes to give that impression – I'm sure it's all tongue-in-cheek.*"

"*I usually take it like that – and it mainly comes up in response to things I say about the atmosphere in the Illustration Department.*" Pause "*Which reminds me …*" I offered in excuse for absenting myself from the conversation "*… I need to draw up a few layouts for tomorrow – I'm meeting with the silk-screen printer.*"

When Claudette visited the next afternoon something caught her eye and she cackled "*Crucifixion suits you.*" Claudette picked up a diptych collage from the first term at Bower Ashton that had been lying on my bed en route to the rubbish bin. "*So—if I may make so bold—what moved you to die for the sins of the world?*"

"*Right …yes … I was going to throw that out. That project wasn't such a great idea. It's on its way to the bin.*"

Claudette looked quizzical and seemed to want to make a point. "*Have you read anything about persecution complexes and paranoid delusions?*" she giggled.

I almost choked on blackcurrant juice. Once I'd recovered I gave my usual line on that subject "*I'm a-Freud I'm too Jung to know about that. I've not read a great deal of psychology – but I know enough to know that—whatever I am—I'm not paranoid.*

an odd boy

"*Apart from Sweeney Todd,*[10] *I suspect no one of harbouring ill will toward me – and even he hasn't tried to convert me into a pork pie as yet.*"

Claudette laughed – but persisted with her questions. "*Well—this—is spooky – in an interesting kind of way. If it was such a bad idea, why did you do it?*"

I gave Claudette the background. "*I had a series of strange dreams in the first term—weird dreams in which there was all this antagonism toward me. I saw faces I'd never seen before – and they had hateful expressions.*" I laughed because it seemed so ridiculous. "*Christ you know it ain't easy—you know how hard it can be. The way things are going—they're gonna crucify me.*"[11]

"*Very droll*" Claudette chuckled – but she wanted to know more.

"*Yeah ... anyway ... they were all talking at once – and I couldn't make out what they were saying. It was some intellectually deranged version of the Tower of Babel.*"

"*That all seems ... quite unlike you.*"

"*Yes ... I don't really have dreams like that. I've never experienced social antagonism apart from a few incidents at Netherfield – and so I couldn't work out where these ideas were coming from.*

"*So ... I decided to treat it as one of my first term Art projects. Being an Artist ... means exploring ideas – and this is just an idea I had at one time.*"

---

10 Sweeney Todd is a character from 'The String of Pearls', 1846 – 1847. He is a barber in Fleet Street, London, who murders his customers by heaving a lever whilst they sit in his barber's chair. The lever flips a trap door and the customers spin head-over-heels into the cellar where the impact of the fall breaks their necks. Sweeny Todd then slits their throats with his razor to make sure they are dead. Then with his assistant—Tobias Ragg—he converts their remains into pork pies.

11 Lennon/McCartney—Beatles—Ballad of John and Yoko—1969

bower ashton – hippie is dead

"*So ... if you're throwing it out ...*" 'dette asked "*... could I have it?*"

"*You're welcome to it.*"

"*Tell me about it though*" she asked. "*How did you make it?*"

I propped it up in order to talk about it. "*It's a collage composed of my own drawings. These are faces taken from newspapers and some historical photographs. Then I worked on a photograph of myself standing leisurely on the kind of living room cross on which Peter O'Toole posed in 'The Ruling Class'. I wore white plimsolls and the white suit the Earl of Gurney wore.*"

Claudette seemed to settle to the idea that I hadn't had a psychotic paranoid interlude. "*So all these angry or troubled faces around you came from newspapers ... they weren't invented ...*"

"*Certainly not. They're bank managers, chartered accountants, football players, criminals, politicians. There are the famous human horror stories too: Joseph Stalin, Adolf Hitler, Maximilien Robespierre, Tomás de Torquemada – Grand Inquisitor of the Spanish Inquisition, King Leopold of Belgium, Charles Manson, Benito Mussolini ...*"

Claudette explored the faces for a while and asked "*Who's this?*"

It was Phil Silvers.[12] "*He played Sergeant Bilko in an American comedy series I used to watch as a child. I just placed him there for light relief – like Evel Knievel, Tiny Tim, and Screaming Lord Sutch.*"

Claudette looked curious and asked "*I didn't think Phil Silvers was oriental?*"

"*No he's American – but in the photograph I found, he was wearing a military hat. I decided to remove the hat to balance the composition.*

12　The Phil Silvers Show, starring Phil Silvers as Sergeant Ernest Bilko of the US Army—was a comedy television series which ran on CBS from 1955 to 1959.

an odd boy

"*As I had no idea how his hair grew or where his hairline began I decided to leave him bald – and yes ... it does make him look strangely oriental.*" I'd also added Frank Sinatra on the basis that I really didn't enjoy his singing. "*There's 'Taxman Mr Wilson' and 'Taxman Mr Heath' because of George Harrison's song on Revolver. I've always loved that song.*"

Claudette was busy finding faces to recognise. "*Here's Richard Nixon – that's hysterical.*" Pause "*And Mao Tse Tung ...*" she continued. "*Why Mao Tse Tung?*"

This was an opportunity too good to miss – so I sang "*Because ... If you go carrying pictures of Chairman Mao—you ain't gonna make it with anyone anyhow.*"[13]

Claudette laughed "*You can get a musical quote out of anything.*" Then she returned to the subject. "*So ... how do you feel about these people?*"

That was the first question that drew me in. "*The fascinating thing ... about drawing all these people ... was that I came to feel—kindly—toward them all ... in a strange way. The act of replicating the areas of shadow on their faces provided a surreal intimacy – even with the most horrific dictators. I ended up feeling that although some of these people were the worst examples of humanity – I could still endeavour not to hate them.*"

Claudette grinned mischievously and replied "*Even the evil Frank Sinatra!?*"

I was glad that Claudette and I could be on the same grid with humour. Once I'd stopped laughing I handed her the image and said "*Right – now you need to take it somewhere—anywhere—that I'll never see it again.*" So she took it home. I never saw it again.

---

13   Lennon/McCartney—Beatles—Revolution—The White Album—1968

8

the second year: december 1973 – march 1974

bower ashton – primal scream

The *Art of Illustration*—word and image—had taken hold of me. As soon as I set foot in the illustration studio in the Spring term of 1973, I knew I'd made the right decision. Derek Crowe was practically a father to me – supportive of everything I had in mind. That atmosphere of work rolled on into the second year. Dick Taylor was nowhere in sight – and it was almost as if he never existed. Derek was the final arbiter of all decisions that concerned my working life within the Art School – and, with his support, I more-or-less devised my own degree course. By the January of '74 he said *"I know that wherever you are – you're working. There is no need to have tutorials apart from the fact that I like to hear about your latest endeavours ... and, of course, simply to converse."* How delightful. What a kind and generous man he was.

"I enjoy my tutorials Derek ... I'd not want to forgo them" I replied. *"They remind me of Hatch Mill where this kind of conversation happened all the time and where creativity was important ... of itself."*

"Good – I enjoy talking with you personally" Derek smiled *"and of course – no one else seems to enjoy my puns."* He enjoyed my puns and I enjoyed his. Derek—if not the person who started it all off—was the one responsible for my penchant for puns. I'd always made the occasional pun – but he was the past-master of punning. If there was a Nobel Prize for punning – he would've got the award. Our tutorials were awash with puns to the extent that Roderick Peters took to absenting himself at the slightest opportunity. In the end he stopped attending altogether.

an odd boy

Roderick was an avowed 'pun groaner' and seemed to regard puns as subordinate to sarcasm as the lowest form of wit. I have always found 'pun groaners' difficult to relate with because they almost seemed to object to laughter.

On one occasion—when the laburnum trees in Ashton Park were mentioned—I asked Roderick "*Did you know they were named after the famous French arsonist?*"[1]

Roderick remained impassive whilst Derek laughed and proceeded to ask "*He must have been the very same hooligan who vandalised that Parisian restaurant kitchen.*" Pause "*That atrocity was described in 'Le Monde'*[2] *as 'Linoleum Blown Apart'.*" That almost had me in tears.

On another occasion—when Ivor Emanuel's name came up—I said "*I thought that was an Elephant hunter's guidebook.*"[3] Roderick grimaced. Then there was the anthem of Northern Ireland 'Londonderry Aire'. "*Ah yes—the London Derriere—a lovely ditty concerning ample buttocks in the nation's capital, I believe.*"

Derek roared with laughter. Roderick rolled his eyes heavenward and pronounced "*On that note I think I will leave you two to your ... banter. I need to see how work proceeds with the other second years.*"

Roderick didn't dislike me. He was never unfriendly – but he made it plain that he regarded me as *a space oddity* – a lad insane.[4] Roderick was significantly younger than Derek Crowe – but had a face that bore no signs of mirth.

---

1 Laburnum – Le Burn'em.
2 Le Monde—the world—is a French national newspaper.
3 A pun: Ivor Emmanuel – Ivory Manual. Ivor Emmanuel [1927 – 2007], an actor.
4 'Space Oddity' and 'Aladdin Sane' were albums by David Bowie. Space Oddity was also a single released in 1969. Aladdin Sane was released in 1973.

He was a devout Christian—a good and sincere man—but he saw me as a person who was wasting his life in almost every respect. I was not advancing myself toward a career and I had a head full of ideas which were likely to doom me to grief of one sort or another – such as being a Buddhist and therefore an apostate. He never made comment – but I always detected an expression on his face that betokened his pity for me in my benighted state.

Roderick Peters was friendly with Todd Whelcomb and Veranda Nugent – and they socialised to a certain extent. When Todd and Veranda had somehow become a couple during the first year, I was naturally pleased that romance still sprang eternal. I was slightly less pleased by the way Todd and Veranda seemed to employ their liaison to foster an impression that they were the feudal dignitaries of the Illustration Studio – as if ostensible marriage had advanced them on the social ladder. I decided it was preferable to be amused by their hauteur and made no comment when Todd would hold forth with "*Veranda and I feel that ...*"

It was usually some idea about how the studio should be arranged – and I'd usually either fall in with their ideas or say "*Somehow Todd ... I think I prefer my table where it is – but please do feel free to re-arrange the rest of the room any way you like – I'm sure it'll be just fine.*"

Todd and Veranda seemed to want to evoke group cohesion and discussion. It was their idea of a professional design studio. They wanted to operate as if we were out in the real world with assignments. I felt that the time for creative discussion had passed by a year at least. I'd been utterly open in the first year to talk and exchange ideas – but they'd shown little interest in conversing with me then.

an odd boy

I was—anyway—far too weird and was only likely to cause consternation and irritation. My Artistic interests were unwelcome. Painters were once raised by Derek Crowe as a group discussion.

"*Favourite painters?*" Derek asked.

"*Rene Magritte, Max Ernst, Simone Breton, Gala Éluard, Salvador Dalí – and … Arcimboldo*"[5] I listed when my turn came.

"*Well we all could have guessed that*" Todd replied "*Renoir's paintings would be too pedestrian for you.*"

"*Never seen an ambulant Renoir, Todd – didn't know he was a Surrealist …*" I regretted it—slightly—as soon as I'd said it. I was *trying* to avoid sparring with Todd. It always felt as if he'd dragged me into his world whenever I gave way to rejoinders. Badinage between friends was fun – but this was just silly. Derek Crowe chuckled however – so I decided that the occasional humorous response to Todd was feasible.

By the second term of the second year it seemed vaguely purposeless to act as if we had something in common – especially if it meant my having to explain my work in the context of becoming a professional illustrator.

I wanted to be a Foundation Year lecturer where I could work with the kind of students I used to know. I did sit in on a few of their group discussions but Todd and Veranda had covert agendas and I began to wonder whether some of their ideas about professionalism were coming from Roderick Peters.

---

5   All Surrealists apart from Giuseppe Arcimboldo [1527 – 1593]. Other Surrealists who interested the author were: Paul Éluard, René Crevel, Jacques Baron, Michel Leiris, Georges Limbour, Antonin Artaud, Raymond Queneau, André Masson, Joan Miró, Jacques Prévert, and Yves Tanguy.

In the end I had to say *"Y'know ... I think this is all really valuable for those of you who want to be professional freelance illustrators or work in graphic design studios – but that's never been my direction. It's not why I came here. There's nothing I can contribute—apart from surrealism—and that would just distract from the idea of these meetings. I don't want to appear unfriendly or anything – but I'd really rather be working."*

Todd and Veranda said that they found my attitude dismissive and arrogant. *"You just want to be seen as special with different rules that only apply to you. Why didn't you apply for a Fine Art course if that's what you wanted?"*

I sat gazing at them for a while attempting to compose a response that wouldn't merely sound like verbal retaliation. *"Sorry you feel that way – I've no intention of being dismissive. I simply want to be a Foundation Year lecturer – so ... there's just no connection for me as far as professional illustration goes. As far as I'm concerned I'm still a painter. I'm a figurative Fine Artist working in an Illustration studio – so ... print making's my major interest."*

"Why didn't you take a Fine Art Printmaking course then?" Todd's smirk betrayed the fact that he considered himself to have utterly undermined my explanation and exposed me as whatever he thought I was.

"Fine Art Printmaking—is—part of the Illustration course" Janet interjected. Janet Ferris was usually the quiet one in our group. I nodded to her in thanks for her comment.

*"However Todd—maybe you're right—maybe I shouldn't be in this department ... maybe I should have applied for Fine Art Printmaking but etching wasn't available on my Foundation course and I had no work to show in that area. And ... now I'm here ... I—*am*—enjoying it here – especially with Derek Crowe overseeing me. I wouldn't fit in – in the Fine Art Department ... because I'm not an abstract expressionist. So ...Todd, that's my story ... I trust it makes sense to you."*

The others apart from Todd and Veranda seemed to take my point quite well. Said they were glad I'd explained. Janet came over looking as if she wanted to continue the conversation so I said *"I'm glad you don't think I'm being unfriendly. I'd always rather be friendly. It's just that ... sometimes ... I wish it was still 1968 ..."*

Janet took that opportunity to ask me *"Isn't it sad to wish you were living in some other time."*

"Yes ... in some ways ... it is ... although ... I wouldn't say I let it get me down."

She found this poignant *"Don't you worry about becoming isolated?"*

"Well yes ... and no ... there're still parts of that time left – and ... I hope there always will be. I share a house with musicians at the moment and we have a really splendid creative environment." I caught Todd in my peripheral vision. He was pulling 'ga-ga' faces as a child might at school behind the teacher's back as we talked. I affected not to be aware.

Janet had obviously also noticed. She raised her eyebrows *"I sometimes wonder if there's something wrong with Todd you know ..."*

I tilted my head slightly in response. *"I've wondered that myself. It's as if he was ... I don't know how to say this – but it's as if he was a 12-year-old in a 20 year old body. He's obviously bright and well informed. He's talented too – but ... he's emotionally in the school playground."*

Todd kept his eye on us as we chatted. *"Still ... in terms of time travel ... it could ... almost be 1968 – from one perspective"* I continued on my previous thread. *"I get to play some interesting music back in Hotwells. I share a house with three ladies from the College of Music and Drama and it's really rather wonderful—bassoon, oboe, and 'cello—and I play sitar."*

"That's amazing I'd like to hear you play one day. Todd's been saying that you wanted to be in the College band but they wouldn't have you."

"That's partially true. They asked me if I'd be interested – and it turned out that we weren't suited musically. It was a mutual decision ... I'm a Blues vocalist and have no interest in ... well ... fast music. Gravy Train play for dances and so they need to make everything up-tempo."

Janet nodded thoughtfully. "That's a completely different story from the one Todd tells."

"I bet it is" I laughed "but if it makes Todd happy to see me as a reject ... I have no problems with it. I have nothing to prove to him or anyone else about it. I played on stage once and played with musicians I admired. I've got no regrets and if I wanted to be proud of it – I certainly could be ... so Todd's opinions are kind of meaningless to me."

"To listen to Todd you'd think you had no friends and lived in a cave or something" Janet chuckled.

"Yeah ... that's kind of amusing. Penelope, Rebecca, and Meryl have become really good friends. We spend a lot of time together."

"I thought you were going out with that beautiful, tall, dark haired girl from Fashion and Textiles."

"Claudette, yes – I got to know Penelope, Rebecca, and Meryl through her. They're her friends ...They wanted a fourth person to share the house."

Janet giggled "What's it like living with three girls?"

"It's ..." I was somewhat stuck for words "This might sound stupid – but it's like it is. I don't really notice gender that much when I'm in conversation."

"Really?" Janet seemed entirely surprised "So you don't notice I'm female?"

"Certainly ... now that you mention it" I laughed. "But it's not at the forefront of my mind—all—the time. We're just—here—having a conversation ... and 'gender' doesn't play much part in that."

"*It's refreshing to hear that. I've never liked it when men have talked to me as if my gender was part of the discussion – y'know, making out that 'girls see things this way' and 'they see things in other ways'.*"

"*Well ... there—may—be differences ... I don't know ... I won't say there's no judgement involved – but apart from—a few—fellows I've known, I—far—prefer talking with ladies.*"

Janet looked a little confused. "*And yet ...you say you don't really notice gender ...*"

"*What I mean*" I replied "*is that I don't—key in—on physical difference, in the sense that I don't see myself as different. I mean we're just here together talking. The fact that we're different genders doesn't really come into it. There may be differences in the way that we look at things but that may have—nothing—to do with the contrasting nature of our genitalia.*"

The mention of the word 'genitalia' caused great mirth for Janet. "*You really are—very—funny. I can imagine you'd get on very well with the girls in your house.*"

Todd was doing his best to overhear our conversation and—at the same time—confounding his efforts with his own commentary to Veranda. I caught the words '*... arrogant self-obsessed misfit.*'

Janet heard the words too and shook her head in disbelief. "*Todd's really worked himself into a lather this time. Strange to think there was a time when I accepted the way he saw you. I suppose he must be annoyed that we're talking to each other – especially after the horrible discussion he and Veranda started.*"

"*What I find bizarre*" I sighed "*is that I have such an effect on Todd – when I don't do anything apart from get on with my life. Anyone would think I set out to impinge on him.*

"*I fail to understand why he doesn't ignore me if he doesn't like me – but he always wants to take me on in some way.*"

"*And you always find a way of replying that makes him look stupid.*"

"*I do try—not—to do that ... but it always seems to end up like that. Sometimes he can be relatively human and then I try to act as if there was no problem.*"

Janet smiled "*I admire your composure.*" This final remark seemed more for Todd's benefit than a remark she'd have otherwise made.

"*Well ... I'm always happy when I'm working, y'know.*"

"*I'm not sure how to ask this ... but has your composure got anything to do with Buddhism?*"

The dreaded 'B' word ..."*If I—have—any composure ... I guess it must be due to the effect that it's had on me – but ... I'm pretty sure Christians and Jews can be composed. I think that anyone who is basically humanitarian is going to have some sense of composure and self-restraint.*"

Janet looked puzzled for a moment "*...you sound ... as if you want to play it down ... Buddhism, I mean.*"

"*Well yes ... I do ...*" Pause "*... because I have a dread of coming across like an evangelist. I've met people who do that.*"

Janet laughed "*I've never heard you say a word! The only reason I know about it is from the time Derek mentioned it and Todd decided to give you a hard time about it. So, the last thing I'd ever accuse you of is preaching.*" Pause "*I'd like to ask you about it – if you wouldn't mind ... telling me something. I'd find it really interesting.*"

"*Sure ... Maybe tomorrow ... before Todd arrives?*"

"*Thank you – yes that would be better.*" Janet mused. "*Todd's got this thing about Buddhism or any Eastern religion – he thinks they're primitive superstitions.*

an odd boy

"He says it's just more of your posing and that '… only dropouts, misfits, cranks, and marginal types take to eastern religions' …"

"That's quite funny really … when the moral majority seem to think that Art Schools are full of people they'd describe in that way. At school we were advised not to apply to Art School because we'd never get jobs."

"Yes … they said the same at my school and my parents warned me about the weirdoes I'd meet here."

"Well, that would be me" I chuckled. "Maybe I'm the last one – y'know, like 'The Last of the Mohicans' …"

"You're actually fairly … non-weird in most ways—to talk to—that is."

"In the safe environs of the Art School rather than back at the Bat Cave …"

"No …" Janet giggled. "I mean you're not emotionally weird or anything – you're funny and a little eccentric, but not weird in the sense of being … peculiar or … creepy. You're not hard to get on with and you don't play games with people – even Todd. You sometimes shut him down with humour – but only when he becomes too verbally aggressive and ridiculous with you."

"I'm glad I come across like that – because I never try to be weird … I'm just … well this is just how I am."

"I'll come in half an hour early …" Janet said as she turned to her work "… and that'll give us plenty of time as Todd's always late. Nice to talk to you."

The next morning Janet arrived shortly after me – and I was surprised she'd come so early. We had an interesting conversation. She asked a lot of questions and I did my best to answer as simply as I could. That wasn't always easy because she'd ask fairly profound questions. I could answer them – but not without recourse to a great deal of terminology.

I realised that trying to explain anything beyond a certain point without Vajrayana terminology was immensely difficult. I tried to use as many analogies as I could – but sometimes got entirely out of my own depth, especially in terms of physics. I tried ways of explaining emptiness as being the space in which the neutrons and electrons existed – the space where there was nothing at all. It was that space that allowed the neutrons and electrons to come into being. *"If you can imagine that mind is like that space and that the thoughts in mind come into being in the same way ..."* but that just sounded baffling.

"Yes ..." Janet mused. *"It's like ... having to understand this as if it was poetry ..."*

"Yes!" I grinned broadly. *"That's exactly it!"*

This was more or less the end of our conversation as Todd and Veranda had sashayed into the room. They noticed us and looked put out that we should be engaged in conversation.

"Good morning Veranda – good morning Todd" I called from the midst of the final flourishes of our conversation. Janet called out the same. Todd wheezed a few indecipherable polysyllabics and Veranda echoed in a higher register.

"So ..." I concluded with Janet. *"It's mainly a question of pragmatics – and being able to experience it first-hand. That's why it's not a belief or a faith. There's no creator deity and so there's no unfathomable mystery. It's all there for anyone to discover."*

As Janet and I moved back to our tables to commence work, I noticed Todd muttering at Veranda. His face had tightened into something resembling a walnut and he was obviously agitated. I wondered slightly whether Todd was mentally unstable because I'd never come across behaviour—*that*—peculiar since Percy Gordon had vituperated about music when I was 12.

an odd boy

Be that as it may – I felt lighter in knowing that someone was willing to engage me in conversation. Todd and Veranda fumed privately like kippers left too long under the grill whilst I returned to my *hand colour separations*: an image of three carp swimming through a reed-bed. They were to accompany a recent poetic exploration of fish eye vision.

Usually I illustrated my own writing but a project came up that caught my attention. Derek had arrived with a box of cards and suggested we all pick one. Each card had something written on it and we each announced what chance had given us.

"*Primal Scream*" I read with relish.

"*Glad—I—didn't get—*that*—card*" Todd cried out in feigned horror. "*What on earth could anyone do with that!*" Janet shot me a quick glance that spoke volumes in terms of our previous conversation—and suddenly, I knew—*this*—was the one card in the box that had my name on it.

"*Naturally* ..." Derek smiled "...*you're not stuck with the card you've picked – I just wanted to see if I could spark you all in unexpected directions.*"

"I'm happy to go with 'Primal Scream', Derek – I've got an idea already."

"*That's the spirit! Glad you're up for the challenge!*" Derek chuckled – with one eye on the curmudgeonly grimace that Todd was encouraging to settle into his face.

I decided to work in silkscreen using hand colour separations – but using one layer as a monochrome photographic transparency to tie the layers together crisply. The other layers would all be wax crayon on acetates. I'd evolved a way of waxing areas and then scratching back into them with different kinds of handmade styli.

The image was to be a photograph taken by Claudette. "*What I want for this 'Primal Scream' project, 'dette, is a naked photograph of me amongst trees – with my mouth wide open, looking as if I'm screaming.*"

Claudette chortled "*What a hoot. That'll make a change from you painting me.*"

"*That's what I thought.*"

"*Will I be required to provoke a primal response from you?*" she grinned.

"*I think there'll be a more suitable opportunity for that later on.*"

"*The sans culottes photograph ...*" Claudette enquired "*... that's also a John Lennon thing isn't it? Like the hair, the white suit, and National Health glasses?*"[6]

"*True enough ... I'm not—shy—of admitting emulation ...*" I grinned "*... and ... in a year or so ... I'll probably find myself a Japanese wife.*"

Claudette frowned "*Yes ... that—would—be like you.*"

"*No, 'dette ... I don't think it would – besides which, I was joking. I'm not offended by the mention of emulation. I probably emulate—everyone—I admire ... in one way or another. It's just fortunate for me ... that I admire too many people to have it typecast me in any obvious way.*"

"*Good plan as long as you don't end up looking like Frankenstein's monster*" Claudette chuckled—having returned to good humour—and enquired about the posture I'd adopt. "*So ... is it to be à derrière ... or de face?*"[7]

---

6   Arthur Janov—originator of Primal Therapy—wrote the book 'The Primal Scream' in 1970. The book was subtitled 'Primal Therapy – The Cure for Neurosis'. The book's cover was a section from the Edvard Munch painting 'The Scream'. Janov's patients included John Lennon and Yoko Ono. John Lennon featured a 'primal scream' on his Plastic Ono Band album.

7   À derrière – from the rear. De face – full-frontal.

an odd boy

"*Well* ..." I smiled guessing at the meaning of the French "*... being as I haven't taught my buttocks to scream, it'll have to be de face. I haven't got it quite fixed yet—it'll depend on how it works out—but what I have in mind is this. I'll be kneeling—kind of arched backward— and appearing to be tearing my hair out by the roots. I'll have my mouth wrenched into a scream.*"

"*I can see the theatre has had quite an effect on you*" Claudette chuckled. "*That—will—look suitably dramatic ... well, if it wasn't so ... cold ... that is.*"

"*Valid point – but I'm not violently concerned about impressing the world or anything.*"

Claudette laughed "*Well you impressed me with your understanding of my French.*"

"*It was just a guess, 'dette. I guessed that de face would have to be the opposite of derrière.*" Pause "*However—speaking of French—there's a saying in French which means something to the effect of 'That's the way it goes.' I only remember the English translation and would be keen to learn the French.*" Pause "*Could you oblige me?*"

Claudette nodded and so I held forth "*To the water, it is the hour.*"

Claudette looked puzzled – but replied "*À l'eau ... c'est l'heure.*" Pause "*... but that's meaningless in French ... and I've never heard the saying – are you sure you have the correct translation?*"

"*Absolutely – could you repeat it just one more time?*"

"*À l'eau c'est l'heure.*"

"*Just—one—more time?*"

"*À l'eau c'est l'heure.*" Then suddenly Claudette understood the jest. "*...'ello sailor indeed – that's absolutely disgraceful!*"

Claudette laughed with good grace at having been unwitting in respect of the joke.

"I shall have to be on guard for your linguistic tricks in future – that really was too—too—bad."

By this point in the conversation we'd arrived in the grounds of Ashton Court and I saw the lane of wonderfully gnarled trees I'd seen from the roof of the Art School. *"Perfect!"*

"It's lovely—I wouldn't argue about that—but what's 'perfect' about it for a primal scream may I ask?"

That was simple to explain. *"The branches of these trees look like the interior of a skull – you see ... the patterns made by blood vessels."* Claudette still looked quizzical – so I continued. *"My idea of a primal scream is that it's launched from the head – out of some tortured concept. So ... my kneeling in this environment will be a little like a play between inside-out and outside-in. The scream—coming out of me—will explode inside a projection of my head – from the inside. It'll be like some kind of psychological hall of mirrors."*

"Quite an elaborate composition" Claudette nodded. And then in a strange approximation of a London accent growled *"But now ... it's time ... to ... get 'em off!"* She cackled ferociously and I found it monstrously amusing. Claudette—humming the melody to 'The Stripper'[8]—set up the Rolleiflex[9] on the tripod and bundled my clothes carefully into the large camera bag we'd brought with us. It was indeed colder than I'd expected – but I assumed the position *"How's this, 'dette?"*

"Well ... mmmm ... I think it works quite well for what you have in mind. Your head's a little too far back though. I think we need to see a little more of your face."

---

8   David Rose—The Stripper—1962—an instrumental Jazz influence piece with prominent trombone phrasing employed to evoke the ambience of a striptease performance.
9   Rolleiflex – a 2¼" square format twin-lens reflex camera.

I angled my head 'til the required elevation met with Claudette's approval and she worked her way through 12 shots. It took a little longer than I expected because of alterations she appeared to be making to the tripod. When I released the grasp on my hair and opened my eyes the sight that greeted me was … an elderly lady walking her Irish Wolfhound.

"*How charming to witness the situation reversed for a change*" she commented – and walked on without looking back.

I dressed hurriedly. "*So … why—exactly—didn't you tell me that the elderly lady and her dog were sauntering by?*" Claudette—with tears of laughter trickling down her face—was not immediately able to answer my question. I found it quite funny too—after a while—especially as the lady had made no mention of the police or indecent exposure.

"Well …" Claudette began, still laughing "… *she appeared quite suddenly you know … and by the time she appeared she could see you quite … entirely – as it were. So … I thought it was better to act as if this kind of thing happened all the time and we weren't especially concerned by her walking past. Anyway I had the feeling that she was the kind of person who'd be good-humoured about it.*"

"*I'm highly gratified …*" I observed "*… that you seem to have been correct in your assumption.*"

Claudette continued to laugh "*I thought you said you—never—got embarrassed?*"

"First time for everything …" I laughed "… *maybe I'm wrong – but I think it was probably anxiety rather than embarrassment. I mean … the police don't look favourably on this kind of thing do they?*"

"*No, I suppose not.*" Claudette—satisfied with my response—simply continued laughing.

I printed a photograph onto transparent film and used it as the basis of further textured work. The final print was a composite of five layers of gradated green. I decided it was an album sleeve: 'Primal Scream' by Savage Cabbage. I produced the cover complete with song titles and sleeve notes. Todd and Veranda made their comments in the group tutorial afterwards. They seemed personally enraged by my work.

"*You don't appear to take anything seriously ...*" Todd announced – impersonating adult tenor "*or to produce anything representative of a professional assignment.*"

Derek Crowe shifted his gaze to me – curious to see what I would say. I'd had it with Todd by this time and decided that he'd have to hear me in unguarded mode. "*Au contraire dear Todd*" I'd learnt that phrase from Claudette "*I take everything seriously – especially humour. But this album sleeve is not particularly humorous – unless you're referring to effects of the chill.*" Derek chuckled at my remark. "*There—was—humour in it however ...*" I added "*... when the elderly lady and adjectival wolfhound sauntered past.*"

"*She would appear to be out of shot*" said Derek, laughing heartily and slapping his leg. "*I can imagine that she and her Irish Wolfhound would have added considerably to the composition. I can see it as a large oil painting after Manet's 'Le déjeuner sur l'herbe' ...*"

"*I sat for that one at Hatch Mill for a group of the female Foundation students, Derek – I'll tell you about it some time if you like – it was quite an intriguing experience.*"

"*I can imagine – and yes, you must – Susan, I'm sure, would be tickled to hear about it*" Derek chuckled. "*Good for you—good for you!*"

Todd and Veranda seemed appalled that Derek appeared to support me in my 'anarchic childishness'. Their words reached me later and I felt sorry for them.

"It's as if they're afraid of not being adult …" I said to Claudette that evening. "I used to see people like that after I left the sixth year … they'd left school and were working in offices or whatever and looked as if they were trying to be middle aged."

"Yes." Claudette nodded "I've seen a few girls from Badminton who had that affectation – and who lacked the intelligence to carry it off."

"It's a shame …" I ventured with some sense of sadness. "What a life they'll have …"

"Indeed. They're emotional troglodytes – but they'll probably be happy enough in their suburban tepidarium."

Tepidarium – now *that* was a word. Claudette had to explain – and the idea of a transitional room between the sauna and the cold plunge caused me much mirth.

"*Still*" I replied "*I wish better for them – I don't think they really understand that life is far more spacious than they imagine. They're just not conversant with the idea of education as something expansive and open-ended. Derek Crowe believes in education for its own sake. Unlike Dick Taylor, Derek believes it's irrelevant whether a person becomes a professional illustrator or not. What's important to him, is that students make the best use of the time and facilities of the department.*"

"*He's an enlightened man*" Claudette responded. I sat back with the glowing sense of that – and how fortunate I was to have ended up at Bower Ashton on his Illustration degree course – in spite of the emotional gargoyles who dwelt there.

I was sitting with Derek some days later and he said "*Education doesn't appear to be moving in a healthy direction as far as I can see. There is too much emphasis on specific careers at the expense of a more rounded education. I would not want to revive classical education – but I do see it is as having many advantages over the increasing specialisation that's becoming the rage.*"

I was glad to hear him say that and replied "*Yes – apart from the fact that I'm really very happy to be here doing what I'm doing – I'd have opted for another three years on a Foundation Course.*"

Derek grinned "*Yes, I suspected as much – but do you feel that the scope you want is still available here?*"

"*Yes. No doubt about that – and I am tremendously thankful to you for making it possible. I can't really imagine where else I could have gone to have been able to do what I've been able to do here. My only regret is that I have no real peer group.*"

Derek laughed "*That's not what I've heard.*" Noticing my confusion he continued "*I hear you have quite an array of peers down in the docks.*"

That made me laugh. Derek could find puns in almost anything. He intended the three ladies with whom I lived in Hotwells. I agreed that they were indeed a peer group – along with Claudette and a few others in the Fine Art Department.

"*Yes. I suppose it's a little churlish to bemoan the lack of peers in the Illustration Studio when it's so far from the river – but the odd wharf wouldn't go amiss.*"

"*Yes …Todd and Veranda do seem unusually antagonistic towards you. I've mentioned it to Roderick – but he tells me it's simply the cut-and-thrust of the thing and that you give as good as you get.*"

"*Cut and thrust …*" I pondered "*… well yes … I can see myself in a fencing costume – but I'd prefer to be cordial and I've only recently started being more unwithheld in my replies to Todd. I started out trying to be as ameliorative as seemed feasible.*"

"*I can well believe it – but what's this about your fancying yourself in overalls?! I wouldn't have thought that was your style at all …*"

Derek asked with a grin – deliberately misunderstanding fencing costume for the outfit worn by a builder of fences.

"*Well if I had a hammer and a stake …*"

But Derek was there before me "*I'd prefer eating a steak with a knife and fork – if I were to eat a steak that is.*"[10]

"*I'm fairly content …*" I continued, once I finished laughing "*… to be a loner in the studio. It's not entirely Todd's fault … I'm an odd ball in his world – and he's … well he just doesn't inhabit a sufficiently loose framework to see that I'm not a threat to him. I don't know what they've told Roderick – but I've never instigated any 'cut-and-thrust' with Todd. All I've ever done is respond. As I said … in the past I used to make my responses fairly bland – but now I've given up.*" Derek raised his eyebrows. "*Janet's idea. She thought it was purposeless to be withheld when Todd so evidently attempts to bait me whenever it suits him.*"

"*So you haven't always replied in the way you did when he remarked on your Primal Scream piece?*"

"*No, not at all.*" Derek looked a little troubled so I continued "*Of course I had to say—something—but I avoided being sarcastic – let alone acerbic or caustic.*"

"*Well your wit did you credit at any rate. I gather you wouldn't wish me to … say anything to Todd?*"

"*No—not at all—I really don't mind.*" Pause "*It would be better if … well if there was a better atmosphere – but I wouldn't want Todd to think I'd complained. And … I wouldn't want him to feel constrained … I think he'd just resent me even more then – and … I don't think that would be good for him.*"

"*That is unusually circumspect … for someone in their 20s – if you don't mind my saying.*"

"*Well Derek … I've been in my 20s since I was 14 …*"

---

10 Derek Crowe was vegetarian.

I told him there was a story I could tell which would make sense of that statement and he said he'd like to hear it. I told him about Anelie my Swiss au pair girlfriend.

"*Well, well, well ... there's a thing and no mistake. It's not everyone who can give such an account of themselves. That would certainly throw you into the adult world quite rapidly.*"

Derek—genuinely interested in my well-being—asked "*Your friends in Hotwells ... they're not from the Art School – but they're students in Bristol?*"

"*Yes – they're at the College of Music and Drama. Meryl's taking theatre – Penelope and Rebecca are taking music. They were friends of Claudette at Badminton.*"

Derek nodded in appreciative enthusiasm. "*So you're able to pursue your musical interests with them?*"

"*Absolutely – and they're somehow more like artists than the students I meet in the Fine Art Department.*"

"*Really ... ?*"

"*Yes, the Fine Art students seem to see me as some sort of interloper to a certain extent ... Penelope, Rebecca, and Meryl—on the other hand—have no problems relating to me as a musician.*"

"*I'm glad of that ... and your ... lady friend—in Textile Design and Fashion—what's her name?*"

"*Claudette, Claudette Gascoigne – she's interested in theatre.*"

"*Fine old name – fine old name*" he exclaimed. "*You must come for dinner one evening – my wife Susan would be pleased to meet you both.*"

"*I'd be delighted. I'm sure Claudette will also.*"

an odd boy

"*Claudette's in the right town for theatre. Susan is a great theatre enthusiast you know. I'm certain they will have a lot in common*" Derek opined. "*What aspect of theatre interests her?*"

"*She's interested in the wardrobe department. She enjoys designing and making clothes. Especially revamping period costume – she's really good at that.*"

"*And I can see that you're taking full advantage of her skills*" Derek chuckled.

"*Yes ... I wish I could sew myself—as it were—because she doesn't have time now to make clothes for me. It was alright in the first year – but now she has too much course work.*"

"*We'll have to see about getting you some time up in her department then – I'm sure you could manage to dream up something as an illustration project.*"

"*Now—that—is—very—interesting*" I exclaimed. "*That really opens up a whole realm of ideas ...*"

"*If we're not careful ...*" Derek laughed "*... we'll have the five of you down in Hotwells staging your own theatre productions – maybe your talents could find a niche in set design?*"

What an idea. "*I'd be interested to try anything – with enough time I'd like to look at film too.*" There was no end to my fascination with the Arts.

"*I'm afraid the Art School hasn't been built that will accommodate—all —your interests ...*" Derek admitted with a chuckle "*... although ... maybe a joint project might be possible with the College of Music and Drama – if you would like me to look into it.*"

"*Absolutely – that would be brilliant!*" Unfortunately it turned out to be too complicated to arrange and I had to settle with being an observer of theatre.

Sunrise meadows they're a-moaning – somewhere morning's coming through, / Rising through the circuitry –of all the systems that we knew, / There is no real beginning – and maybe there's no end, / Beyond where we find ourselves – either then, or way back when. / There's a moon slipping sideways – out on the midnight trail / But the ravens will be with me – when the night-sky sets its sail. Frank Schubert—Ravens—1973

I told Claudette about the invitation and although at first she was a little reluctant about spending an evening with the Crowes – she came round to the idea and we had a marvellous evening together. She enjoyed talking with Susan Crowe and found the evening to be just the kind of pleasure she'd be eager to sample on future occasions. We drove back to Hotwells – and as we whisked—at a sedate pace—through the elaborate patterns of tree branches in dark country lanes Claudette and I fell to further discussion of theatre.

"*I loved talking with Susan Crowe. She knows such a lot about theatre.*"

"*Yes – they're a lovely couple. I really admire them both – they're an inspiration as human beings. And y'know, 'dette ...you've really inspired me with a great interest for theatre. I consider that an immense gift.*"

"*My pleasure entirely. Don't know why you never went before – it's a mystery to me.*"

"*To me too – but you have to remember that it's not an obvious direction for someone who went to secondary school. Most of the teachers at that place wouldn't have been able to distinguish culture from bacteria.*"

"*Very droll ...*" Claudette chuckled "*... I remember you saying that your parents never took you to the theatre.*"

"*Well ... I went to Farnham theatre once—when I was still at junior school—but my father saw some play there to which he took great moral objection – and that was the end of it.*"

"*What play was that?*"

an odd boy

"*No idea – my father never let us in on that spectre-of-outrage against public decency.*" Pause "*I performed there once too … it was at a Christmas thing the Art School students and lecturers put on. It was a lovely old Theatre … in Castle Street. I sang a few Blues numbers. It was a good evening and it ended with a duo … Rosalind Price and me. She played her 12 string* Eko *and I sang.*"

"*Like the one you used to have?*"

"*Yes – but hers was older than mine—had a much better tone—and the wood had darkened. Fine—fine—low action … couldn't play slide on it though. I played washboard, kazoos—two of them—and vocals on my parody of 'Mamma Don't Allow No Guitar Playing in Here'. If anyone ever tells me that you can't finger pick a 12 string – I remember Rosalind Price. She was supremely nimble fingered.*"

"*Girlfriend was she?*" Claudette asked in an amused tone.

"*No … she was at Farnham Art School – but we've lost contact. We weren't that close, y'know.*"

"*So …*" Claudette changed gear – evidently a little embarrassed by having betrayed her momentary jealousy "*… can you still sing that song?*"

I obliged. "*Well Papa don't allow no long haired freaks in here, Said papa don't allow no long haired freaks in here, Well I don't care—gonna do what I please—grow my hair to the antipodes – yeah papa don't 'llow no long haired freaks in here.*"[11]

Claudette—surprised at my volume—chortled "*How did—that—go down at Farnham theatre?*"

"*Went down a storm. I remember being extremely gravel-voiced and unprecedentedly loud.*"

---

11 Author's parody— Papa Don't Allow No Long Haired Freaks in Here—1971

"*You brought the house down then?*" she said – smiling at me.

"*Yes ... I was utterly surprised too ...*" Pause "*My brother Græham came to the concert and was almost startled to see me looking like someone who looked as if he did-what-he-did professionally. We had quite a conversation about it afterwards. Said he was sad not to have seen Savage Cabbage.*" Pause "*I almost decided to hit the road again – but ... anyway ...*"

"*It still haunted you ... of course ... it must have been difficult with your friends so recently dead.*"

"*Yeah ... it haunted me then. It still haunts me a little now – but only when I talk about it. Haven't thought about being on stage for a year at least. I'm happy to have been on stage as a Bluesman in the past ... and now ... it's just part of my history ... like a lot of other things. Anyhow, 'dette – I've got all—sorts—of fish to fry! I'm on a roll most of the time ... with one thing or another.*"

"*I like the way you can be so positive in spite of everything that's happened.*"

"*Well—y'know—there doesn't seem to be any other choice, not if I want to—live—life. You have to move on or you can't enjoy the moment.*"

I watched the silhouettes of trees fleeing into the distance as we made of our silent way through the countryside. The Silver Cloud was insulated from the world and insulated from its own mechanics. It was an eerily quiet car and apart from the occasional gear change I was watching a movie of the night. I caught glimpses of twisted branches and briefly thought of Helen Mcgillvray's paintings.

It was curious how life moved and how patterns were created.

9

the second year: january 1974 – march 1974

bower ashton – almost a giraffe-hide greatcoat

Apart from the Savage Cabbage years and the Foundation years at Farnham I was never quite on the same grid as other people. '66 to '71 was the peak of *the lost time* – and during those seven years I was surfing the moment without any sense that I was alone. Life was not always wonderful – but life was always congruous with what I felt myself to be.

After '71 the ethos of *the lost time* was still performing itself here-and-there – but it wasn't the pervasive trend it had been. Attitudes were shifting. Everything was moving slowly but inexorably toward fashionable mundanity and popularist mediocrity. Boundaries were being erected between subjects and areas of interest. The opposite was unfortunately also true in terms of agglomeration. Illustration was in danger of being eaten by Graphic Design. Art Schools were becoming Colleges and the Colleges were being eaten by Polytechnics. Even in the Fine Art Departments of Art Schools there was a lessening sense of freedom. Students were free to paint whatever they wanted as long as it was Abstract Expressionism.

The sense of wonder communicated through Art was withering and being replaced by pedestrianism. Gone were the days when Cream installed stuffed bears and bison on stage – and left them utterly unexplained. It had made perfect sense to me. I'd have worn a giraffe-hide greatcoat with Savage Cabbage, had one been available.

Such a garment almost did become available through the auspices of Clifton antiques market – I walked in, and there it was: a huge giraffe hide replete with tail! I was transfixed when I saw it. The hide was in good condition. It was lightweight and extremely supple. It occurred to me immediately that it could be made into a floor length single-breasted greatcoat! Perfect for a maniac vocalist and rhythm-bass player! The tail could remain attached hanging down the back. That *would* be wild.

I mentioned the idea—extremely tentatively—to Claudette – but she made it fairly plain "*Those days are over I'm afraid. I have—far—too much work to make clothes for you now, especially something as loony as a giraffe-hide coat.*"

"Right ...yes ... I understand, 'dette ..." Pause "I—do—realise that I already owe you a great deal clothing-wise. It's been really generous of you to make clothes for me. The white suit – let alone my green leather trousers and waistcoat took a lot of your time."

"*Well ... I was happy to do it at the time – but now it's a little much. Unless you write a play for it that Meryl can stage in the Drama College in which case I'd be able to count it as a project.*"

"Well that's an idea – but I don't think I could buy the giraffe-hide on the off-chance that I could swing a deal like that. I wish I could have compensated you adequately ..." Pause "... if I ever get to sell any of my work I'll take you to Stratford."

"*That would be nice ...*" Pause "*I'm sorry if I sounded a little abrupt about your giraffe idea – but ... the idea of a coat with a real tail ... but you must admit it's a bit ... outré ... a bit Magical Mystery Tour ... as in I am the egg man, they are the egg men, I am the Giraffe or whatever. It's ... the kind of thing you could only wear theatrically. I mean ...you—couldn't—wear it on the street—could—you; so it would be a frightful lot of work for an item that would be worn so rarely.*"

"*Well now ...*" I grinned "*... I'm not trying to persuade you into anything* – *but I'd wear a giraffe-hide greatcoat—any time—any place—anywhere; as long as it was cold enough of course.*"

"*With a tail on the back!*" she shrieked with mixed mirth and horror.

"*Yeah ... especially with a tail on the back!*" I exclaimed with delight. "*I'm sure it would swish around with fabulous aplomb.*"

"*Not in—my—company it wouldn't!*" she responded slightly irritably – as if I were some kind of liability. "*You can swish your giraffe-tail to your heart's content when I'm not around – but dressing up in animal skins is strictly for the Wildman of Borneo* [1] *– unless, of course, it's mink we're discussing.*"

"*Well, 'dette ... I'm the wildman of somewhere-or-other – but ... I see no profound ontological difference between giraffe and mink.*"

"*Except that people—wear—mink, and people—don't wear—giraffe.*"

"*Well yes ... but I'm not 'people' ...*" I grinned. "*You must know that ideas like that have—never—impressed me. What's done and what isn't done has always seemed ... kind of ... militaristic. I like to like what I like – without reference to what other people like or don't like.*" Pause "*Anyhow, 'dette—I really shouldn't have asked—I should've realised that you're as busy as I am with your course work.*" Pause "*I trust you'll forgive my importuning you.*"

---

[1] Wildman of Borneo – a common term in Britain in the '60s and '70s for hair that extended over the shirt collar. The abusive term was used of Jimi Hendrix in the British press. In the early 1800s Hiram and Barney Davis, two mentally disabled farm boys from Connecticut, were named the Wild Men of Borneo. They were approximately 3½ feet tall and weighed just over three stones. They could however perform amazing feats of great strength. A deserter from the German Army was billed as the 'Wild Man of Borneo' at a San Francisco freak show during the Gold Rush. He covered his body with a mixture of tar and horsehair, and was placed in a cage and fed raw meat by an assistant.

an odd boy

"*Think nothing of it—I certainly shan't—in fact I shall banish the very thought of giraffes from my mind this instant.*"

A few minutes afterwards I said "*Don't think about a giraffe.*"[2] and Claudette had the courtesy to grin.

I made no further mention of the giraffe-hide greatcoat idea – but I did wonder what sort of play could centre around such an item. The girls thought the coat was a marvellous idea—especially Meryl—and they said they'd like to help me with it. None of them however, were skilled in that way and they feared they'd ruin the hide. I regretfully agreed that it would be a risk and let the idea evaporate.

"*Well … it—would—be a shame to waste the hide if we couldn't get it to work*" Meryl sighed.

"*True … maybe it's just as well … it wouldn't go down a storm with 'dette …*"

"*I think that 'dette needs to lighten up a little …*" Meryl chipped in rather briskly "*… she really should be—glad—you're so inventive. She's complained in the past that everyone's too conventional – and now she's getting conservative on giraffes.*"

"*Maybe the giraffe voted Tory*" I said in order to deflect the conversation away from Claudette. "*And anyway … Todd might require medical help if he caught sight of it.*"

"*Thought you didn't care how people saw you?*" Rebecca asked. "*Why should you worry what Trophy-head has to say about it?*"

"*I don't – but I don't like to provoke people either. Janet and some of the others seem to have warmed to me recently – so I'd not like to weird them out …*" Pause "*… well – not too much.*"

---

2   This refers to a Zen koan 'Don't think about a monkey.'

"*Right ... well ...*" Meryl nodded as if she were unsure of what to say "*I still think it's a pity that 'dette's not up for making the coat for you. I think life would be a lot more interesting if people dressed with a little more imagination. A floor length giraffe-hide coat would look fabulous on you.*"

"*Thank you Meryl!*" I replied. "*I appreciate your saying that – but 'dette does have a point about her degree work. She can't be sewing all the time and leather work is difficult. She had quite a time of it with my leather waistcoat and trousers y'know and ... even though I don't see eye-to-eye with her on mink being acceptable—for a coat—and giraffe unacceptable I can see that it would be a lot of hard work.*"

Meryl gave a mixed nod and shrug to suggest that she was not pleased with 'dette's attitude – *whatever* I said in her defence. Penelope seemed to notice Meryl's irritation with 'dette – and remarked regretfully, seemingly to change the subject "*It must be sad to be in an Art School that's so unlike Hatch Mill.*"

"*Yes ... in some ways – but I've got used to it now*" I replied, relieved to have moved away from group censure of 'dette's refusal to make the coat. "*Anyhow I like it for the facilities and for Derek Crowe.*

He's an amazing man, y'know – he just makes everything possible. He's practically let me design my own course – and I really can't imagine a better situation."

"*Even with the lack of a Folk and Poetry Club?*" Penelope asked.

"*I'd overlooked that ... yes, that—is—a shame*" I replied. "*There's not even interest in the possibility of inaugurating anything – I did ask around but no one's interested in poetry readings – so it looks as if I'm on my own with that. It would be good to hear poets reading.*"

an odd boy

"*Yeah—it would—you'd get me along to that*" Meryl agreed. "*You can read your poetry to us though – but I guess it's not quite the same as having something set up.*"

"*Thanks for the offer—maybe if you three had material you'd like to read —but I know what you mean. A venue where a number of poets gave recitals would be a different thing from reading at home. What I used to like about it was the responses you'd get – and of course at Farnham Art School it was tied in with Related Studies – so we'd get people like Adrian Henri and Roger McGough down. Constructive criticism from them was always interesting and they had a lot of enthusiasm for our work.*"

"*It sounds as if you might be happier in some ways at the College of Music and Drama – although we don't get visiting poets*" Meryl commented.

"*I suppose what I'd really like would be an Arts School ... a place where people could explore all the Arts.*"

"*That would be interesting ...*" Meryl replied "*I suppose there's no concept of anyone writing a play in the Drama Department. There is set design – but that's separate from acting. It seems that a lot of things are separate ... when they could weave in and out of each other.*"

"*That's why I loved the Foundation year – and why—in some ways—I'd have liked to have continued there – y'know just have it turn into a degree course. What would be so interesting about that would be that you'd always be exposed to people working in their different areas.*"

"*Yes*" Meryl replied "*But ... maybe that couldn't exist as you're thinking of it ...*" Pause "*... because the thing that creates what you're describing only exists because all those people are destined for different courses. If you had people who wanted to be on a four year Foundation course – they might not offer the breadth of interest you'd want.*"

"*Mmmm ... I'd not thought of that – but you're right.*" Pause "*It looks as if what I want would be to take serial Foundation courses.*" Pause "*That would only be possible if you were rich and could afford to pay for everything yourself.*"

"*And of course the Art School would have to agree to it too ...*" Penelope remarked.

"*Right ... well ... that idea's doomed then.*"

We live in an age in which only results seem to count, not processes – but life is liquid, not solid; a process, not a result; the present, not the future.
Keith Jarrett

Both Penelope and Meryl apologised for pouring cold water on my scheme – but I shook my head "*No—not at all—I may be crazy but I don't like to be unrealistic. It's useful to be able to bounce ideas around with you. When I find myself a lecturing position on a Foundation course somewhere – these ideas will be useful in terms of how I approach all that.*" Pause "*I realise ... that I may not find students like the students I used to know and I suppose I will have to roll with the changes.*"

"*Y'know—some time back—'dette told me that no one at the Art School discusses anything beyond the stereotypical student interests*" Meryl said. "*Y'know – going to the pub or playing whatever wretched sport on weekends ...*"

"*Right ...*" Rebecca replied. "*They go to Greece for holidays and ride around on hired motor-assisted bicycles. Then the worst part is that they write their theses on it – on the excuse that they can throw in a photograph or two of the Coliseum or something ...*"

"*Yeah – I've seen them ...*" Meryl yawned "*... types who listen to head-banging Pop and find philosophy as interesting as asbestos insulation.*"

"*Apart from you three ... and 'dette ...*" I replied. "*I feel like some sort of pterodactyl perched on the outer perimeter of somewhere or other.*"

an odd boy

"*Yes ... that's what it—feels—like sometimes ...*" Rebecca agreed.

"*I used to—speak—to people and—people—used to—speak—to me.*"

Rebecca was silent for a few moments before she answered "*I think that there—was—a time when that happened – and I think it still happens here and there. The problem ... is that things are changing.*"

"*They've been changing for a while. It used to be normal to talk about Art, Music, and Poetry – but the intellect's fallen out of the whole freak scene and now most of what's left is mindless head-banging Pop culture.*"

I knew it was true – but I was a little shocked to hear someone else make the statement "*Really? That's ... how you see it?*"

"*Yeah ... but, I mean ...you were never a—freak—anyway ...*" Rebecca commented "*...you said so yourself.*"

"*Yes ... but at least there—were—other people like me around.*"

"*People who were literate and passionate about the Arts?*" Rebecca queried.

"*Certainly. There were interesting intelligent freaks too – I mean not the kind of people who said 'it's all words man' when you attempted to discuss something slightly difficult.*"

"*Yes ...*" Rebecca sighed "*... probably they're still around somewhere – there are just fewer of them.*"

"*Maybe for some it was just a fashion – and they changed with the fashion.*" Meryl suggested "*Maybe that's why no one plays Blues anymore – as you pointed out.*"

"*And that's why there's no purpose in my being a vocalist any more.*"

"*Right ...*" Rebecca recalled. "*There are a few Bristol bands ...you had sessions with a few of them didn't you?*"

"Yes ... but only due to various people hearing I used to be a vocalist with a band. I'd go along and chat – just to be friendly but they were all into the new Californian Soft Rock. I should have said no straight away – because ... well, I can't see the point any more."

Penelope raised an eyebrow indicating that I'd need to explain further. "*Dance music and so forth ... is ... fine in its own way – but I can't find any heart in it.*"

Meryl grimaced "*Yes ... I know what you mean. That's why I turned to Baroque and Early music. There's no musicianship anymore. There was a time when there were virtuosos – but now it's either volume or fluff.*"

"*See your point*" I said. "*I enjoy Early Music and Bach far more than anything recent I've heard.*"

"*So what happened with the bands?*" Rebecca asked.

"*They all seemed to like my voice well enough – but they'd no interest in playing Blues; especially slow Blues. They enjoyed my tempo rubato—especially on the Van Morrison numbers—but, they weren't up for musical composition and had no interest at all in doing anything with my psychedelic lyrics.*" I'd shown Penelope my old lyrics and she'd enjoyed them. "*Unfortunately, the Art School band—Gravy Train—got to hear about me too.*"

"*Yeah ... that was probably, 'dette. She mentioned you having been in a Blues band a lot in the first year when she came over to the College of Music and Drama. She must have done the same in the Textiles Department*" Meryl replied. "*When you were first together she seemed to —really—like the fact that you'd been on stage as a Bluesman.*"

"*Past tense?*" I queried.

"*Oh ...*" Meryl dissembled "*... didn't mean anything by that – it's just ... the way the words came out. I meant to say that it was new at the time ... and ... now she's probably grown used to the idea.*"

an odd boy

"*Right … it's all old history anyway*" I replied with some sense of unease in my mind in respect of Meryl's failure to dissemble sufficiently to eradicate the question she'd placed in my mind. "*Still … I tried out with them one lunchtime—at their request—but it didn't work out for me or for them. They couldn't use a harp player. They had a saxophonist and seemed to see harp as unsophisticated or some such thing. Said they wanted a 'tight sound' … and, that's what they've got. They're all competent players though.*"

"*Run-of-the-mill bulk-standard wedding and bar mitzvah band?*" Meryl asked.

"*No … but nothing exciting either. They didn't say so – but it was obvious that they considered me a relic of a by-gone age. I may as well have asked them if they played 'Chattanooga Choo Choo' as ask about 'Spoonful'. They're just too West Coast for me and I'm too Mississippi / Chicago for them.*"

You're obsolete my baby – my poor old-fashioned baby, / I said baby, baby, baby you're out of time.
Jagger/Richards—Rolling Stones—Out of Time—Aftermath—1966

Penelope thought it was a pity that there was no place for music, purely as music. "*Even a dance band ought to be able to have a few slow numbers in its repertoire.*"

"*You'd have thought so … but …y'know … I'm actually relieved it didn't work out with the College band. I only went along with it because of some idea I have that Steve and Ron would've wanted me to go on … to be a performing musician on stage. It's somehow hard for me not to act as if Steve and Ron weren't out there somewhere observing me. I still occasionally feel as if I'm letting them down. I know I'm not – and so the whole thing is ridiculous.*"

Penelope didn't entirely agree with my conclusion. *"Yes ... but it's* —not—*ridiculous. I think it's very touching that you remember your friends. The only thing that's ridiculous is feeling guilty. It's not your fault that Pop music's made such a big comeback – and that it's swamped everything else."*

It was good to hear that and I thanked her for what she'd said. *"I'm glad I was able to tell you about it. The idea of investing in another microphone and* PA *system is too much outlay if I'm not going to play Blues. I'd much rather play sitar. It doesn't require an audience or contact with the outside world."*

Without *the three ladies* Bristol would have been a musical desert. There'd been groups of three ladies in my life at various points – and I started wondering whether there was something about me that cultivated such situations. There'd been Alice Trevelyan and her friends Bethany and Gillian. There'd been the three friends of Lindie Dale who'd said *"We wish she was with you – you were so good together."* There were Susan Wilcox, Sarah Bradley, and Daphne Morgan. We went to London in December 1970 to look around Art galleries – and had a thoroughly fine day. I'd offered to buy them all dinner – but they insisted on paying for mine instead. There'd been Emily, Rose, and Valerie back in the Autumn of 1971. There'd been Anne, Ruth, and Mary – three ladies I'd met in Betws-y-Coed in North Wales in November 1969. It was a Geography field trip that lasted a week. Pupils from schools across the country were in attendance and Anne, Ruth, and Mary had become friends as a result of the predatory pursuit of two fellows from Leeds. The lads had their eyes on Anne and Ruth and were trying to elbow Mary out of the situation. This annoyed Anne and Ruth.

an odd boy

I agreed that it wasn't gentlemanly behaviour – and in so saying, I became their sole male companion – mainly in the rôle of entertainer. The fellows from Leeds confronted me about horning in on 'their territory' and asked in an offensive yet evidently nervous manner *"What's so special about you then – eh?"* I grinned and pulled out my harp *"Bluesman."* And gave them a long bent note and a trill of fast notes that plummeted into another low bend. That was a few months before Ron died. It was a time I could still say that 'I'm a Bluesman' with some conviction.

Penelope, Rebecca, and Meryl were like the three sisters I never had and I was continually delighted with their company. There were often concerts at the College of Music and Drama and we attended with glee. We always dressed for the occasion and made a night of it. It was glorious and the perfection of life was sumptuous. Penelope had a way of being able to like almost anything with a genuine enthusiasm that was infectious. She played 'cello extremely well. She could swing that thing up sideways and play it like a guitar. That was a revelation to me. Rebecca played bassoon and had eyebrows that seemed to remain permanently arched – in the style that woodwind and flute players have when they play. Meryl played oboe. She was the least skilled of the three – but she was proficient and graceful in her playing. She'd learnt at school – but had decided on drama rather than music as her forte. They loved Baroque pieces and sometimes I would just sit and listen to them in a state of languid rapture.

Claudette would sit and listen – or sit and read. She was a great reader. Meryl sometimes had to sit out because she was perpetually learning lines from plays.

I never enquired further of Meryl as to her comment with regard to Claudette—nor did I take it up with Claudette—but the idea that Claudette had changed in some way was not something I could deny or shrug off. I had no desire to be placed on any kind of pedestal – but neither was I keen on being demoted from whatever position of high grace I once occupied for her. Somehow I was no longer Mister Renaissance man. That was no particular problem because I didn't see myself like that. The Renaissance approach was an aspiration, certainly – but I didn't see aspiration as equivalent to accomplishment. Whatever respect or admiration I was accorded—or had been accorded— had morphed into … the very faintest derision? Maybe it was the way that so many couples came to take each other for granted?

But what could be done about it? It was as if she'd gone to bed with Leonardo Da Vinci and woken up with Nigel Higgins the averagely talented nowhere man from the Illustration Department. There was nothing I could do about that. I couldn't demand to be seen as anything other than I appeared to be. I could point out that some kind of change had occurred – but that would have seemed petty and somehow narcissistic. Something about what I was sensing reminded me of the way that Helen had changed over the duration of the Foundation year – and I had to admit to myself that it might go the same way. Still there was Jazz to imbibe and Jazz to play – so I could put such morbid conjecture on the back burner.

I obtained the three album solo piano '*Bremen and Lausanne*' set in 1974 and was fascinated by Keith Jarrett's seemingly limitless ability to improvise. It struck me that Keith Jarrett's fabulously extended piano improvisations could be a bridge between their Baroque interests and my Blues orientation.

Jazz is there and gone. It happens. You have to be present for it. That simple. Keith Jarrett

The Indian Classical tradition was also opening up for me and I talked about it with Penelope. "*I've been fascinated with those sounds since I first heard the Indian-themed George Harrison tracks.*"

Penelope smiled "*That started with 'Norwegian Wood' didn't it?*"

I'd forgotten that. "Yes ..." I replied. "*And then 'Love to You' on Revolver and 'Within and Without You' on Sgt. Pepper's. I wish there'd been more.*"

"There were – Traffic used sitar on their 'Mr Fantasy' album."[3]

"I didn't know that ... I'd like to make a collection of all those tracks so that I'd be able to get a sense of where I could go. It would be interesting to compare them."

"The Pretty Things used sitar too – so I imagine there must be more out there."[4]

"I'm sorry George Harrison never took those ideas further."

"I can see that *Avant Garde Jazz* is a better medium than Rock music in terms of sitar" Penelope commented. "Rock's a little rhythmically limited."

I could see that. We talked for several hours and played around with themes of 'cello and sitar. It wasn't long before I found an importer of Indian musical instruments in London and acquired a set of tabla drums and a tambura. The tambura produced a fabulous buzzing drone sound and *sat well* behind oboe, bassoon, and 'cello.

---

3 'Utterly Simple', 'Paper Sun', and 'Hole in My Shoe'.
4 'Bracelets of Fingers' and 'Private Sorrow'.

bower ashton – almost a giraffe-hide greatcoat

Our quartet manifested an ebullient ambiance. Our music was always there – and went nowhere other than where it was. That was perfect—and when I realised it was perfect—I finally felt that Steve and Ron could be satisfied with me. I had not let them down. I was still a musician.

Orpheus with his lute made trees,/ And the mountain tops that freeze, / Bow themselves, when he did sing: / To his music plants and flowers / Ever sprung; as sun and showers / There had made a lasting spring. / Every thing that heard him play, / Even the billows of the sea, / Hung their heads, and then lay by. / In sweet music is such art, / Killing care and grief of heart / Fall asleep, or hearing, die.
William Shakespeare—Henry VIII—Act III—Scene i—1613

10

the second year: april 1974 – may 1974

bower ashton – heroines of art

Take me down little Susie, take me down, / I know you think you're the queen of the underground, / And you can send me dead flowers every morning – send me dead flowers by the mail. / Send me dead flowers to my wedding – and I won't forget to put roses on your grave.
Jagger/Richards—Rolling Stones—Dead Flowers—Sticky Fingers—1970

There were three theatres in Bristol – the Old Vic, the New Vic, and Colston Hall. Claudette and I saw a shoal of plays together in these venues.[1] It was a fabulous education and I felt privileged to be in the audience. I wondered why no one else from the College ever seemed interested – because we attended as often as I could afford. Claudette could always afford – and sometimes she afforded me rather than attend alone.

"*Theatre's magical*" I observed. "*I'm just ... spellbound by the sheer skill of the actors.*"

"*Impressive aren't they—especially these players—notice how the lead actor speaks with his body when he's peripheral to the main action.*"

I observed him and it was exactly as Claudette had indicated.

"*That—really is—quite something. There's almost too much to take in – you have to be incredibly keen in your observation – kind of darting from wide-angle to telephoto moment-to-moment*" I whispered.

---

1 Plays by Shakespeare, Chekhov, Jean Genet, Samuel Becket, Harold Pinter, George Bernard Shaw, Oscar Wilde, Jean Cocteau, TS Eliot, Dylan Thomas, Tom Stoppard, Oliver Goldsmith, Peter Shaffer, and Henrik Ibsen.

"I've never really understood acting as an Art – I mean, I've never understood how people manage to become other people quite so convincingly. It seems such a fantastic skill. A person just turns into a canvas and paints themselves – right there in the moment in front of your eyes."

"Well, they—do—learn their lines and rehearse you know ..." Claudette replied, intimating by her tone that I was stating the obvious.

"Yes certainly ..." I replied mildly, as if I'd not noticed her tone, and settled in to watch the remainder of the play. There was no dampening my amazement, however. After the show I continued "I was thinking about what you said ... about actors rehearsing – and it occurred to me that even though they'll have their lines memorised – they have to come out and—live—for an hour or so as whomever."

"Yes – but that's also their training. I don't quite see what you're trying to say beyond the 'willing suspension of disbelief' that's required of everyone who wishes to enjoy a play."

"Right ... but there's never any 'willing suspension of disbelief' involved on my part – I seem to believe without effort as if ... I wasn't even—in—a theatre."

"And so, what does—that—mean?" Claudette asked suspiciously – as though she feared I was about to become abstract in my musings.

"Well ..." I answered warily "... I don't become 'other-conscious'—as opposed to 'self-conscious'—I just fail to find myself outside the experience of the play as reality – and I find that amazing."

Claudette glazed over at that point. She'd never really joined me —in my escapades into what she considered *ætheric regions*—but since the commencement of the second year, I'd noticed that she'd started to look irked when-*ever* I started to talk about anything perceptual or experiential.

I tried to make my *artistic-excitement-about-life* interesting for her – but there were only so many angles of approach she'd want to take on any subject. I tried another tack. "*The use of coloured lights and props is fantastic – it seems to have so much in common with Surrealism.*"

"*Surrealism?*"

"*Yes ... the way that reality and illusion are each an allusion to each other. I met an American lady called Juliet at the Reading Festival a few years back who was studying set design. She told me quite a lot about this kind of thing ...*" I internally berated myself for having mentioned a lady from the past. I continued as if there was no problem "*... she had a pronounced sense of the Surrealism of set design. It's amazing to see it in operation though.*"

"*You've ... not mentioned a—Juliet—before.*"

"*Really?*" I replied with the closest I could come to nonchalance.

I wished I'd not mentioned Juliet. It was hard not mentioning people I'd known and appreciated – but whenever they happened to be female Claudette would want to probe for information and attempt to coerce me into revealing something that would make her seem superior in every respect to the lady I'd mentioned. It was gruesome and my refusal to make negative comments infuriated her.

"*I must say, you—are—a treasure trove of liaisons.*"

I wondered how to reply. My romantic liaisons certainly were a treasure trove. I thought kindly of all my previous lady-friends – but how could I say that when it was obvious Claudette was going to be touchy on the subject?

"Well ..." I replied as ingenuously as I could *"... my life has been ... what it's been – and I've enjoyed it ... despite some sadness and grief. I suppose most people have a—*history—*of some sort. 'Life's rich tapestry', I believe, tends to be the apposite cliché ..."* I ran out of ideas.

*"Yes it—*is—*a cliché ..."* she replied. *"So why use it?"*

"Good question ... maybe it seemed appropriate ... because I picked up the sense that you were seeing me as clichéd ... y'know, with your remark about a 'treasure trove of liaisons'."

"Touché." Pause *"So ... exactly how many lady-friends—*have—*you had?"*

"I've not exactly been keeping count."

"No need to be evasive."

"I'm not. It would be bizarre if I could answer immediately with an exact number."

"Accepted ... so I'll give you some thinking time."

*"Mmmm ... that might well help – but I don't understand—*why—*you want to know."*

"I'm interested ..." Pause *"... and I think that you want to be mysterious about it for some reason."*

"Mysterious!?" I laughed. *"Not—*at—*all—there's just a strange sense of being on trial – y'know: 'No one expects the Bath Inquisition!' It's like a re-write of Eugene O'Neill by Monty Python ...Y'know 'Long Day's Journey into Relationships Past.' "*[2]

"Sorry. I didn't mean to sound like that" she conceded – and I indicated with a nod that I accepted her defence.

---

2   Reference to 'Long Day's Journey into Night' by Eugene O'Neill.

"*So … if it's alright, will you tell me*—how—*many?*" she asked in a friendlier yet still insistent tone.

I really didn't want to acquiesce to Claudette's insistence – but we were in relationship and that required me to be as open as I could be, in terms of my life. The problem was that it put me into internal conflict. I loathed the whole business of discussing previous relationships – but I also disliked being secretive with Claudette. If I'd been certain that she'd just accept a description of people's good qualities I'd have been happy enough – but I knew she'd want to hear about faults. Why did she always push me for details on past lady-friends that I considered intimate? I felt I wanted to say '*Leave it out, 'dette – I've had it with your prurient curiosity*' but that would have seemed aggressive and self-protective. One day I was going to have to find an answer to this. "*Well alright …*" Pause "*… if you're*—that—*curious …*" I replied with supremely understated exasperation. "*I*—could—*think about it … but*—*you'll*—*have to keep count. I can't really do that … due to my poor grasp of arithmetic.*"

"*Go on then.*"

"*Let's start with Juliet – as I happened to mention her.*"

"*And what can you say about her?*"

"*Well I only knew Juliet for a weekend and we got separated in the crowd on the last day of the Reading Festival … and never saw each other again.*" I gave Claudette a brief account of the festival and our conversations and even how we met, skinny-dipping in the river. Claudette was revolted by the idea of skinny-dipping but was polite enough to make no comment. Public nudity was anathema to her – as were rivers likely to be infested by rats and other undesirable pollutants.

"*And so ... although it—was—extremely brief I count Juliet as a real relationship ... inasmuch as it could have developed and moved into the future. I might have moved to Charleston ... or anything.*"

Claudette looked surprised. "*You'd have moved to America?*"

"*Well ... why not? Anything's possible.*" Pause "*I might even have taken up guitar again and played the Chitlin' Circuit*³ *like Jo Ann Kelly. I'm not utterly tied to Britain and a person has to be free to fly in any direction ... if the time's right and if they have no ties.*"

"*That ... sounds a chaotic way to live ...*" Pause "*... it's as if you – well ...you—never—sound happy being where you are.*"

"*No ...*" Pause "*... I don't recognise that.*" I shook my head "*That doesn't sound like me. I'm happy where I am. I—almost—always am ... and ... I've got no—great—desire to be roaming the world or trying new places for the sake of it. I'm just saying what was in my mind at—that—time. I had no idea of going to theatres – and then I met you ... and now ... here I am Vic of the New Vic.*"

"*Very droll—I'm sure—so what about the others?*"

"*My other—lady—friends?*" I asked – whilst knowing exactly what she meant. She made a face that expressed agreement and irritation at my feigned uncertainty as to the nature of her question. "*Well you already know about Alice, Anelie, Lindie, and Helen. That's about it really. The other ladies were brief situations ... where ... two people just found each other insufficiently synchronised or whatever. There were a number of girls from Farnham Grammar School.*"

---

3   The Chitlin' Circuit – the string of Blues venues throughout the southern and eastern States of America. Chitterlings are the boiled small intestines of pigs – a popular food stuff in the Southern States. Jimi Hendrix played the Chitlin' Circuit before he came to Britain.

She asked me for an approximation *"I dunno ... nine maybe ... D'you require names, or will numbers suffice?"*

"No need to be prickly" she said softly – aware that she was pressing me for information that I wasn't easy with giving.

"Sorry – but it stills feels a little uncomfortable."

"Yes – I would like their names, if you please."

"Right ..." Pause *"Mary Chambers ... Rachæl Rotherwell, Janet Macintosh, and ...Veronica Drew..."* Pause *"Mary Claremont ... Joan Cuthbertson ... Deborah Fielding ... Margaret Cholmondeley – and Linda Peerce."* Pause *"Then ... mmmm ... did I mention Stephanie Mathews?"* She told me I hadn't. *"Alight then ... Bridgette Morgan, Sarah Andrews ... and Linda Brandon."* Pause *"Ruth Vickers – oh, and Miriam Remington."*

"That's more than nine" Claudette responded. *"I make it fifteen."*

"Alright then—fifteen—as I said, I never was good at arithmetic ... but y'know ... this—is—starting to feel a little creepy ... why d'you want to know all these names. Some of the ladies I've mentioned only went out with me for a week or so."

*"It's more the fact that you—*remember*—them all that I find surprising."*

"It would be sad if I'd forgotten them ..." Pause *"Why should I forget them? If they were interesting enough to ask out – they're interesting enough to remember. The problem was that either they found me too weird ... or they were very bright and had well-to-do middle class parents who hated me on sight."* Pause *"Oh, and by the way, there was also Andrea Rawlinson but that was only three days because she was kind of violently repulsed by my Captain Beefheart and Frank Zappa albums."* Pause *"Anyhow ... I tend to see these ladies as ... heroines of Art... as magical emblems of life."*

an odd boy

"*So that's what I am too?*"

"*Certainly – why d'you need to ask?*"

"*Well it feels a little as if I'm just another 'emblem' in the long list of 'emblems'.*"

"*No ... 'dette. It does not mean—that—at all. And since when has a heroine been a mere emblem anyway.*"

"*Sorry ... I forgot the heroine part – but it's still a long list.*"

"*There's only a—*long list*—'dette ... because—you—asked me to provide it. I really do not see the ladies I've known in terms of a list.*" Pause "*I don't chant the names every night before I go to bed like some kind of prayer. Besides – what about you? I'm sure—you—must have your history?*"

"*Not really.*" Pause "*But ... then you've never asked have you?*"

"*No ... it's not really what I do.*" Pause "*I mean, why would—I—be asking you, if—you—weren't telling me?*" Pause "*Why would I want to know? To what use would I put such information? I think if you'd ever mentioned anything connected with a fellow – I might have asked something. And—of course—I also don't really like to pry. Talking about past relationships can be a little ... tacky sometimes. I don't think it's an easy topic of conversation – but as you've brought it up, tell me about your previous beaux.*"

"*Nice old fashioned word ... however – there was only one.*"

"*Was ... that by choice?*"

"*No ... not really, if you—have—to know ... no one else ... asked me out.*"

"*Well—that's—surprising!*" I exclaimed both in genuine surprise and in an effort to lighten the exchange. "*What's wrong with the men in this part of the country?*" I laughed "*They all—brain-damaged or something?!*"

That made Claudette laugh – and I felt rather relieved.

"So … anything you want to tell me about him."

"No."

"I think you owe me a—name—at least … after all you know about Alice, Anelie, Lindie and Helen."

"*Alright*" she replied with an expression that betrayed utter disgust. "*John Willoughby.*"

"Yes … and?"

"I met him when I was 16. We were both on the Foundation year at Bristol – and then he left me for someone else —just before Christmas. I have—nothing—to say about him other than that he was a vile—contemptible—despicable pig."

"That sounds extremely sad … I'm sorry." Pause "I suppose it's just as well I never asked before – but … maybe it would help to talk about it? You seem to hate him quite …" Pause "… well … I don't think I've ever hated anyone."

"Not even Brigadier Dale!?"

"Mmmm … well … I think I—was—angry with him for a while – but … in the end … I recognised that he was only trying to protect his daughter from a criminally depraved drug-fiend."

"But you're not."

"No … but I dress like one—in his mind—the blue tinted national health spectacles and all that … and … that's all he has to go on."

"Isn't his mind—his—responsibility?"

"Yes … ultimately … but he's a product of his society – and I can't hate him for that. I hate the ignorance and closed-mindedness he represents … but not—him—personally."

"I think that's your—philosophy—speaking rather than how you actually feel."

"You're probably right – but I'm hoping to become that 'philosophy' ... as you put it, at some point." Pause "So d'you want to tell me something about John Willoughby and what happened? I'll listen you know ... extremely seriously ... these things are important ..."

"Not to me. I'm content to hate him. I hope he dies of cancer or gets burnt to death in a car accident."

I sat staring at Claudette feeling slightly numb. I couldn't exactly chastise her for her vituperation. I couldn't morally condemn her extreme wishes – but I couldn't exactly go along with them either. I really had no idea of what to say next – but she broke the horrible spell after a moment.

"No ..." she exclaimed through gritted teeth "... *but I hope he's treated—by someone—as cruelly as he treated me. He just flipped from me to this other girl on Foundation—overnight—and then proceeded to be love's young dream with her right in front of me for the rest of the year.*"

"Yes ..." I let out a long sigh. "*That—is—horrible* ..." Pause "... *that's worse than anything that's ever happened to me in relationship ... that must have been ghastly.*"

"Yes. It was—*at the time*—but ... I was naïve and ridiculously innocent. I've developed a healthy cynicism since then."

"I don't think innocence is—necessarily—*a state to regret*" I replied. "I'd rather retain a degree of naïveté. I don't think I'd want to become cynical whatever happened."

"*You'd rather be hurt?*"

"Yes." Pause "I think I would ... I'd rather be hurt repeatedly than become cynical."

"I think ..." she said with a regal air *"... of cynicism ... a little more as it was discussed by Antisthenes and Diogenes."* She'd suddenly lost all trace of the mixed mien in which cold anger cudgelled sadness into submission. She was now the stoical empress of emotional stateliness.

"Well you've lost me there, 'dette. I've never read—that—much Greek philosophy. Didn't Diogenes live in a barrel or something?"

"Or something" Claudette shook her head at my ignorance. *"What I—mean—is that I don't believe in romantic idealism any more. I don't believe in giving everything up purely on the basis of erratically violent emotional stirrings."*

"I don't think ..." I pondered, wondering where that left me *"... that I'd like to put limits on myself like that."* Pause *"However ... I've—never—left—anyone—for—anyone—else."*

"Never?" she asked incredulously.

"Never." Pause *"And I never will. If I'm going to leave a relationship I don't wait for another to come along first. If I leave – I leave. I'd never cheat a partner in that way. I don't respect that kind of behaviour. It's vile —contemptible—and—despicable ... just as you say. My partings have— all—been more-or-less amicable – and pretty much mutual decisions."* Pause *"I have been—left—a few times, I suppose .. "* I laughed *"... once after a couple of hours."* I told her about the incident around Greg Ford's Beach Buggy to give her some distance from John Willoughby.

She was highly amused by my account *"Especially being jilted in the middle of 'Hello-Goodbye'*[4] *– what a hoot ..."* Pause *"... well as you describe it."* Pause *"So that was the Grammar School girls. What next?"*

---

4   Lennon/McCartney—Beatles—Hello, Goodbye—Magical Mystery Tour—1967

an odd boy

I could see that Claudette was in for the kill. I was not going to escape this line of questioning 'til I'd enumerated everyone. The alternative was to refuse to go any further on the grounds that it felt tacky – but somehow I hated taking the 'high moral ground'. There were some things that I wasn't prepared to mention— such as the night with Rose and Valerie—but I decided to conclude the enumeration as rapidly as I could without seeming withheld. "*Fiona Featheringstonehaugh, at Farnham Art School – after Helen left ... and when I got back from India.*"

"*Ah yes ...*" Claudette interrupted with a jocular sneer "*... the Highland Swearing Champion.*"

"*I—wish—I hadn't told you that*" I responded with a weary shake of my head. Claudette asked why that was, as if I was some sort of hyper-sensitive. "*Well ... it turns her into a caricature ... and that doesn't sit well with me – and it's unbecoming in you too. You don't know her – so labelling her in—that—way is as gross as swearing as far as I'm concerned. Although for the most part I—don't—swear, I—don't— quite share your revulsion for it – and I—don't—enjoy Helen being derided in that way.*"

"*Sorry I didn't mean to insult her ... sorry to have interrupted ... I was just being flippant – I didn't mean anything by it*" Claudette conceded. I nodded with a smile to indicate that I'd not taken any great offence. "*So ... would you complete the picture?*"

I was going to have to get this over with once and for all – and never return to the subject again. "*Alright ... there was a French lady called Ortense. Never caught her last name – it was too French, too fast, and too late at night.*" I explained the weird way we lost contact and Claudette opined that it was probably just as well. "*... and Cindy Sutherland a sculpture student. There was Cynthia Cheswick – we met at a wedding reception where I played a set. It was held in a huge field where two bands played. I was on in between.*"

I sat musing for a moment wondering how to account for Rose and Valerie. "Then ... before I went to India there was Rose Johnson – I met her in Carlisle where I played a gig. Then there was Valerie Camberwell – from Exeter Art School. I played a gig there too." Pause "Then in India I spent some time with a lady called Annabelle Hastings from New Zealand. I liked her a lot – but ... New Zealand's a long way away and it just didn't look possible." I told Claudette about various rambles we'd made up into the area of Chamba in Himachal Pradesh as Annabelle had been a great hiker. "Then there was the lady in the Chapter and Verse book shop – but she was married."

"*You had an affair with a married woman!*"

"*No*" I laughed. "*I wouldn't act in that way. I just asked her out in the shop when I was buying a copy of 'Trout Fishing in America' ...y'know —Richard Brautigan—and she told me she was married ... I would have married her if she'd been single ...*" Claudette asked me why I would have married a person I'd met in a shop for five minutes. "*She seemed interesting, intelligent, lively, and ... she sparkled. She reminded me of Alice.*"

"*You'd marry someone just because she reminded you of your first girlfriend?*"

"*Not exactly ... or maybe quite possibly ... we would have had to have burst into flames—as well. She was from California ...*" Pause "*So ... that's my story ... sad but true – about some girls that I once knew ...*⁵*And now ... here—we—are.*"

"*Here—we—are, indeed*" Claudette replied somewhat resentfully "*And you're not—itching—to be on the move again?*"

---

5   DiMucci/Maresca—Dion—Runaround Sue—1961 'Here's my story, sad but true, It's about a girl that I once knew.'

an odd boy

"No ... I'm—itching—*to change the subject of this conversation – and* —itching—*to see you in a more pleasant mood ... but other than that ... I ain't itching.*" Pause "*The reason I've had a few relationships ...*" Claudette spluttered derisively at my use of the word 'few' "*... has ...*" I continued at slightly increased volume "*... got nothing— whatsoever—to do with 'itchy feet' or any other form of dermatological complaint. I think my life's just been ... kind of turbulent. I'd be married to Lindie Dale now if it wasn't for her—insane—parents.*"

"You really—are—*a curious mixture. With you it's either some kind of Grand Prix circuit of liaisons or marriage. That's ... quite a contrast.*"

"Yes ... if you—insist—*on polarising it in that way – but, old fashioned though it may sound, marriage is what I've always wanted. I've never really had any 'counter culture' views on marriage. It's always seemed an ideal state – for the right people of course.*"

"*Really ... what an extraordinary creature you are ... to be sure.*" Pause "*I can see why you've never talked about your career as a serial monogamist before – it's ... quite ... well ... quite a marathon.*"

"*Quite ... and*—that—*would be the reason I've never talked about past lady-friends.*" Claudette raised the eyebrow of incomprehension.

"*You make it sound as though these were all 'sexual conquests' and that is* —not—*the case. I'm not keen on ladies I've known being trivialised, sensationalised, caricaturised, bowdlerised, dehumanised, homogenised, cauterised or whatever.*

"*The ladies I've known have all shared ... a vision of wonder with me. They all saw the world as Art – and that's what we had in common. We had a shared excitement in being alive and enjoying what we saw and heard. They were my friends ...*"

"*Sorry...*" Claudette accepted culpability as much as was her wont – with a slight shrug "*... but you must admit it's a little out of the ordinary.*"

"*Perhaps – but I've never made a particular study of human conventions – and I have little interest in what's ordinary.*" Claudette shrugged as if to say 'fair enough' and I continued with some deliberation "*And 'marathon' is not a word I would use about romance – so I do*—not—*intend to accept it.*" I was confused and a little annoyed. "*I haven't talked about my life in terms of relationships before … but*—not—*for any mysterious reason. I just don't go in for talking about previous relationships. So, whatever*—you—*might be seeing, is something that has more to do with*—you—*than me.*"

"*Alright … point taken*—*point taken*—*but there must be a reason of*—some—*sort for your reticence beyond the idea that I'm going to be censorious.*"

"*Yes. There is. It's the privacy of the ladies in question. It wouldn't feel honourable.*" Pause "*You might consider how*—you—*might feel if it occurred to you that John Willoughby was describing*—you—*to someone else.*" Claudette froze. She sat in silence seemingly torn between grief and anger. "*I'm sorry, 'dette … I didn't intend to say anything hurtful – but I needed you to understand something. I'm big on the 'do as you would be done by' thing.*"

"*Alright … I suppose I can see that*" she replied after a moment's tense consideration. "*So you won't even tell me what they were like?*"

"*Yes. If it's*—good—*things you want to know – but I wouldn't want you being comparative about it, or getting haughty or whatever.*" Claudette agreed and I gave some descriptions—mainly of mutual interest in poetry and music—but also of humour and the hilarious times that were prevalent in the late '60s and early '70s.

"*Margaret Cholmondeley had guinea pigs. She loved those little creatures and I found it quite astonishing the way they just sit on you for hours. We used to talk about animals a lot and it was always delightful how she opened that world up for me.*

"*The world was teeming with animals – and they lived lives that had almost nothing in connection with human stupidity. She reminded me of Steve in some ways because he was interested in animals when he was younger. Did you ever have pets?*"

"No. They smell."

"*Fair enough – just as well I'm relatively hygienic then.*"

"*It's one of your fundamental virtues – so beyond potential zoologists ... what about art?*"

"*The guinea pigs were Art.*"

"*Were what!?*" Claudette sputtered "*This is very loony.*"

"*No. Art is what you see. Art is how you see. The whole visual field is Art – along with all the other senses.*"

"*That's a little too broad to make any sense to me but go on.*"

"*Rachæl Rotherwell liked to watch the rain falling – and we'd talk about how amazing wet slate looked. She was always showing me things that she liked – like pebbles in the drive that had strange colours. I thought it was a pity that she didn't go to Art School – but her parents, like most, had other ideas.*" Pause "*Most didn't like me – which accounts for why I had no long term relationships around that time. It wasn't because we fell out or anything.*"

Claudette sat there expressionlessly. "*And then?*"

"*Joan Cuthbertson ... was an amazing pianist. She'd had lessons practically since she was in the cradle and I could sit and listen to her for hours. She had to practise a lot and I was more than content to sit and listen. Deborah Fielding played flute and it was the same with her – I'd sit and listen. Their parents—of course—would ask me if I had music lessons and I'd have to tell them that my parents couldn't afford it.*"

"That was usually the death knell ... but anyway – we enjoyed the times we had together and talked about all kinds of subjects. I used to read Deborah my poetry – and she'd read to me from the poets she enjoyed."

Claudette looked as if she was about to yawn. "*Let's hear about Juliet then ... the 'Southern belle'.*"

"*Juliet was indeed a Southern Belle. She had an educated Georgia drawl that sounded straight out of 'Gone With the Wind'. She must have been something over six feet tall and had extremely long curly hair. She was interested in poetry – especially Walt Whitman and she loved Chicago Blues ...*"

Claudette interrupted me at that point "*She was involved with theatre wasn't she?*"

"*Yes ... theatre school in London—I never discovered which one—and she was interested in lighting effects. We had some wonderful conversations about light and the nature of form.*"

"*Could—she—follow your flights of fancy without glazing over?*"

What a question. "*I can't recall her 'glazing over' ... but maybe our conversation never went so far into the abstract. It was only a weekend ... and although we talked a great deal – it's a few years back and I've not really thought about our conversations that often since that time.*" That was untrue – but I really didn't feel like giving a more detailed account of subject matter that had nothing to do with Claudette.

I was still feeling uncomfortable with her line of interrogation and was looking for some non-punitive means of bringing the subject to a close. Claudette seemed to regret her 'flights of fancy' comment and changed tack "*So you discussed theatre?*"

"*Yes – but set design was her speciality and so we talked a lot about how different effects were created. She told me about the crossover between theatre and film – because set design is part of both fields.*"

an odd boy

"*Theatre—isn't—just the art form that came before motion films existed, as—some—people seem to think*" Claudette volunteered apropos of nothing I'd intimated.

"*I've never seen it that way*" I concurred. "*But I never thought the question was at issue either. I'd never have imagined there was a competition … they're entirely different art forms.*"

"*The supremacy of film over theatre is widely discussed—in some vulgar circles—but theatre will never be replaced by film*" Claudette pontificated. "*The fact that human beings are performing their rôles at so close a distance is electrifying. That can't be replaced. Theatre also provides the possibility of a unique experience each time the play is performed. A film is—always—the same film. A play is—never—the same play.*"

"*Good point, 'dette*" I responded with enthusiasm, glad to have moved away from the subject of previous relationships.
"*The unique quality of each performance is something that hadn't occurred to me before – but it should have been obvious from poetry recitals and being on stage with Savage Cabbage.*"

"*Theatre being replaced by film …*" Claudette continued – without reference to my previous remarks "*… is as ridiculous as talking about photography having the ascendancy over oil painting, or lithography being superior to letterpress printing.*"

"*Indeed – couldn't agree more.*"

Claudette—cheered by my support for her cherished art form—asked "*Which playwright do you enjoy most?*"

"*Of the plays I've seen … Shakespeare.*"

"*Why's that?*" she replied somewhat surprised.

"I'm intrigued by the way he pillaged British history for material and presented it in such a profoundly lucid manner. He combines strife and comedy and always introduces some profound perspective on life – and of course there's the language."

"Don't you find the language difficult?"

"Yes ... it's difficult ... but it's—always—worth the effort. And ... it means I can see the same play repeatedly and find something new each time."

"You never tire of archaic language?"

"No – it simply provides further scope for subtlety and ... multi-layered 'perceptual-costumes of interaction'. It's like you were saying about each performance being unique – but more so. Shakespeare is endless."

"My father used to take me to the theatre – but since we've been together he's taken a back seat ... as it were. He loathes Shakespeare – by the way, so it would be inadvisable to quote." Pause *"I know you like to do that – but it annoys him."*

"I shall desist in that case – whenever it is that I finally meet him."

"He's agreed to see you next weekend."

"He's agreed has he ..." I grinned *"... but have I—also—agreed?"*

"Don't be awkward now. There's no need to take offence – it's just his way."

"I haven't taken offence – I'm just commenting in order to maintain some sense of reality."

"Oh ..." Claudette replied – flummoxed that she'd misinterpreted me *"... so you're still coming?"*

"Certainly. I said I would and I don't go back on promises."

an odd boy

I was not looking forward to meeting Mr Gascoigne. I'd thought that his misanthropy would spare me the customary parental inspection – but, lack-a-day, it was not to be. "*How can you loathe Shakespeare?*" I enquired of Claudette. I'd agreed to attend the regal presence so I thought I deserved an explanation of his literary quirks. "*I can't see how that's feasible. I thought your father was an all-round epicurean?*"

"*He is – but he finds Shakespeare to be the proclivity of too many would-be intellectuals – and … that has rather soured the bard for him.*"

"*Really … I don't think I'd like to be governed in that way – but it's his loss not mine.*"

Claudette shrugged. "*So back to Juliet?*" she exclaimed. "*After two torrid days in a tent she managed to lose you.*"

"Yes …" I replied with a rather overstated sigh "*… and now … I'm going to—*lose—*this subject. I said nothing of 'torrid'. I said nothing of anything apart from our conversations – and I will not be drawn any further. What I—*will—*do, is ask—*you—*some questions. I've answered —*far more—*than enough. I'd now like a—*full—*account of what John Willoughby was like and how you first got together.*"

"*As I said he was a vile—*contemptible—*despicable pig and I have—* nothing—*to say about him*" she glared at me coldly.

"Then, 'dette … I have—nothing—*more to say either.*" Pause "*I'm glad you don't want to talk about him. I don't really want to make you talk about anything you'd rather not tell me. And …*" I stressed "*… I expect the—*same—*courtesy from you.*"

Claudette suddenly realised that it was time for her to leave. She always left at 10 pm. She looked a little shocked after my last statement as she'd never heard me be stern before. She'd never heard me be quite that determined and obviously didn't know what to make of my uncharacteristically emphatic demeanour.

"*There*" I smiled. "*Now we'll*—both—*be able to move on to more pleasant topics. I'm looking forward to meeting your father* – *he sounds an interesting man.*"

Claudette nodded and accepted the change of subject "*Yes. I'm sure you will find him interesting – although ... I'm not sure what he'll make of you.*" Pause "*I'm not sure what*—I—*make of you sometimes*" she almost whispered.

"*That makes two of us ... and three if you add the herring.*" I laughed without any great mirth and wished her goodnight. We managed to be relatively warm – but I returned to my room slightly baffled by the increasingly perplexing changes that seemed to be occurring in our relationship. It was as if the initial excitement of having me as a romantic partner had dwindled in a way that was unaccountable. I'd done nothing. I'd acted as cordially and thoughtfully as before – but I found myself progressively at fault for being what I was when she first met me.

The evening had taken some bizarre detours. I'd started out enjoying a theatrical production but had been waylaid by an impromptu inquisition – which ended with my having to be somewhat autocratic in terms of establishing boundaries.
I started getting the vague feeling that I was in some goddamn Eugene O'Neill play. I wondered how the plot would evolve and whether I was going to have to absent myself during the intermission.

I'd finally been invited to meet Claudette's father—the somewhat rarefied and societally reticent Mr Gascoigne. I wondered what meeting him would be like. What would he make of me? Why was I going to see him anyway? I felt 'too old' to be introduced to a parent; especially as she never took visitors home. We were hardly about to enter any kind of long term engagement.

an odd boy

Claudette was decidedly against marriage or even sharing accommodation and so the meeting made little sense to me. I wondered *why* I'd agreed to see him. Why? Well there was an easy answer to that: because I liked to agree to most things. Maybe that was a problem. I drifted off to sleep with a sense of unease.

11

the second year: a single day,
in your merry-merry month of May 1974[1]

bower ashton – the earl of groan

This tower, patched unevenly with black ivy, arose like a mutilated finger from among the fists of knuckled masonry and pointed blasphemously at heaven. At night the owls made of it an echoing throat; by day it stood voiceless and cast its long shadow. Mervyn Peake—Titus Groan

I felt out-of-sorts with myself the day Claudette was to take me to Bath to meet her father. I'd not seen her since the week before – when she'd played the part of Owen Glendower *'calling spirits from the vasty deep.'*[2] She'd instigated the séance, summoned *the ghosts of relationships past*, and suffered the haunting – but I'd suffered the visitation vicariously. I wasn't happy with the fact that I'd had to scold Claudette about her attitudes to previous relationships. Taking the high moral ground never felt wonderful. It reminded me of the time I'd had to excuse myself from having fun with Morticia on the basis that she was a smoker. How was it possible to have personal standards without them having to exist as traps and snares for others? I knew she'd been offensive with her line of enquiry – but somehow I felt that I should have been more light-hearted about it all.

---

1   Leonard Cohen—Who by Fire—New Skin For The Old Ceremony—1974 '*Who in your merry merry month of May.*'
2   William Shakespeare—Henry IV—Part I—Act III—Scene i—1597

I should have fabricated a liaison with an Eskimo and regaled her with tales of eating raw whale blubber in an igloo; a sojourn with a Zulu spear-maiden hunting lions in the endless savannah; or living in a yurt with the 111th princess in the succession to Genghis Khan – sipping fermented mare's milk and learning *khoomei overtone singing*.[3] No – that would have been problematic.

I decided to purchase flowers for Claudette and bought what seemed beautiful to me. They were Arum lilies.[4] I presented them to Claudette with a smile.

"*Funeral flowers?*" she asked in a horrified voice.

"*Pardon?*" I replied – entirely perplexed "*They're … beautiful … and … I thought you might … like them.*"

"*Yes—well—thank you*" she mumbled. "*Arum lilies are—funeral—flowers. You—obviously—have—no—idea.*" She shook her head as if I were a died-in-the-wool ignoramus.

"*No … I don't …*" I replied "*… but then … nor do they.*" Claudette looked confused. "*The flowers—I mean—they have no concept of themselves as 'funeral flowers' …*" I chuckled, feeling the situation was slightly deranged.

"*Very droll—however my father gets hay fever—so we'll have to leave them here anyway … what—ever—they think they are.*"

"*I'll put them in a vase in the kitchen.*" Pause "*Maybe the girls won't mind the morbid connotations – and therefore fail see me as a frolicking festival of faux pas.*"

---

3   Khoomei – Tuvan throat singing. It is produced from deep within the throat which rises to multiple harmonic tones.
4   Arum or Calla lilies (Zantedeschia of the Araceae family) – originally found in Africa, from South Africa to Malawi in the north.

"*Sorry ... I suppose it—was—nice of you to buy me flowers – so I— should—be grateful.*"

"*Yes ...*" I laughed. "*I would have thought so – but don't let it be a burden.*"

Claudette thanked me for the kind gesture as we drove off and apologised for her reaction to the funeral flowers. "*I shall tell you all about flowers and their associations*" she offered.

"*I'm always happy to enhance my education, into the floridly fabulous forest of flora.*" Pause "*Drive on Caruthers!*"[5]

Claudette—having informed me that I was 'very droll'—proceeded to tell me about flowers. We chatted amicably in the Rolls as we purred off in the direction of Bath. We finally arrived outside a large and impressive house. Bath stone[6] is a pale yet warm-coloured stone for which the town of Bath is famous – and the Gascoigne residence was a fine example. It was possessed of rather wonderful iron railings and an imposing front gate. The front door was also a thing of wonder with a huge bronze knocker—*and*—a bell pull. There was also a servant's entrance—which we took—as it led more directly to the kitchen where I was required to remove my shoes prior to entering further into the inner chambers. I was immediately aware that I'd set foot in some sort of ancestral home. It was bright and clean—spotlessly clean—but gave no great sense that anyone lived there. Claudette ushered me into the sitting room and provided me with a crystal glass of sparkling water.

---

5   'Lead on Caruthers' or 'Lead on Macduff' – reference to a genre of 'ripping yarns' in which British military types engaged in high adventure. 'Lead on Macduff is a misquotation of 'Lay on Macduff'.

6   Bath Stone – oolitic limestone originally quarried at Combe Down and Bathampton Down, Somerset. It is 'freestone' inasmuch as it can be cut or 'squared-up' in any direction.

She then departed saying that her father was on his way. I got no chance to ask where she was going or whether she would be joining us. Suddenly I was alone in the room – feeling as if I would soon be in the dentist's chair.

Mr Gascoigne—when he eventually appeared in the sitting room —was languidly lugubrious yet lithely surreptitious in his approach. I didn't hear him coming – and then suddenly, there he was. He evidently found me a repugnant specimen as soon as his eyes settled on me. He affected not to betray his opinion – but he was not as difficult to read as he imagined. I stood up *"Good afternoon Mr Gascoigne – good to meet you at last"* I greeted him extending my hand. He didn't take it. Rather, he nodded and indicated I should return to the chair from which I'd arisen to address him. I offered a peremptory *"Thank you."* I pondered my own words briefly 'good to meet you at last' ... I'd said the selfsame thing to Brigadier and Mrs Dale but at least they'd taken my proffered hand. He'd been discourteous – but I decided against commenting.

I sat waiting. It was his move. He dressed in a suit at home – on all occasions I learned later. A nasty pale grey narrow-lapelled silk suit. The blood-drip tie he wore with it was the same colour as the suit; and so—almost—was his shirt. His hair—severely brushed back—was also grey. The only contrast was his extremely pale pink skin – which gave him the appearance of a peeled prawn. He gazed at me expressionlessly with pale heavy-lidded grey eyes. The words 'emaciated albino lizard' crossed my mind. I admired his capacity to avoid blinking. I found him obliquely aloof—not *hostile* exactly—but as distant and uncommunicative as a crustacean from the crab nebula.

"*Victor Simmerson*" he began. "*I am a solitary man and I do not entertain visitors. I hope—however—that you will not feel affronted by my disposition?*"

"*Certainly not sir*" I replied, with as pleasant an air as I could muster. "*Everyone may choose their disposition. Please let me know when you wish for privacy.*" I'd changed from the 16 year old who'd tried to win over Brigadier Dale. I'd be polite – but I'd not attempt to impress him and I'd not be coy. If he loathed me – that was his choice. Claudette had obviously departed, to leave us alone together. That was unexpected – but I didn't mind too much.

Mr Gascoigne—evidently surprised by my candour—replied with great deliberation "*You are remarkably well spoken for a young man of your generation – but you are also precipitate.*"

"*Yes?*" I replied. "*I think that's true – but it's not necessarily a quality I greatly admire in myself. I think I was slightly surprised that you did not take my hand when I offered it.*"

"*A personal foible. You will excuse me.*"

"*Certainly sir – I have many of my own, so I understand entirely.*"

He nodded partially acknowledging my comment "*Yes.*" Pause "*You would do well if the cut of your clothes—not to mention the cut of your hair—matched the cut of your speech – but … there it is … that is today's fashion is it not?*"

"*It was the fashion in* 1966" I replied. "*I'm a little dated – according to current tastes.*"

He had nothing immediate to say in response to that – so I reached for my glass and took a sip of sparkling water from the rather fine crystal glass. "*Lovely house, Mr Gascoigne*" I continued after my sip of water. "*Bath is quite a remarkable town. It feels strangely familiar – I must have seen parts of Bath in films.*"

"*Yes*" he replied. "*Film-makers … they are almost a nuisance here.*" Pause "*You admire Georgian architecture?*"

"*Very much so—although I've not studied it sufficiently to comment—but, the proportions are—highly—pleasing. It must be a pleasure to live in a house like this.*"

"*Yes – it is …*" Pause "*… which is why I enjoy the solitude it offers.*" Then he stood up quite quickly "*Well—Victor Simmerson—we have met then. I … trust you will succeed in your studies at the Art School.*" Pause "*I now have other concerns that require my attention. I wish you goodbye. Claudette will—no doubt—take you home directly.*"

"Goodbye … Mr Gascoigne" I replied with the very slightest grin. I almost added '*Thank you for your time.*' But I saw no reason to compound my crimes or match his incivility. This man was stranger than fact or fiction—but I never saw him again—and never found out how the Gothic novel ended.

Claudette appeared after some minutes. "*I'll take you back to Hotwells now*" she announced hurriedly on entering the room.

"*I hope he didn't find me rude?*" I enquired.

"*No … in fact he thought you were not as 'wishy-washy' as he'd expected you to be. He'd expected you to be tongue-tied.*"

"*Wishy-washy?*"

"*Well … his words not mine – but … it's just that …you're a little too 'far out' for him – not that he'd know a term like that. He likes what he calls 'æsthetic proprieties' to be observed. He has highly particular views on the subject of taste and he tends to be offended by most aspects of the modern world apart from quality engineering. He's also … shy of strangers …*"

"*He didn't—seem—shy.*"

"*That's a cloak he wears ... although ... he's not actually shy – he's simply highly reserved – æsthetically.*"

"*I could almost say the same.*" Pause "*But ...*" I considered saying 'I like people' but chose another tack "*... what did you—think—would happen when he met me? You must have hoped we'd get on.*"

"*No ... not really ... he just wanted to see you ... and now he's seen you. He'll probably say more when I get home again – or not. He doesn't go in for discussing other people that much.*"

"*Right ... well ... that's kind of—weird—but who am—I—to complain about 'weird?*" Pause "*But ... if he wanted to—see—me ... why didn't he ask me anything? Last time parents wanted to see me they interrogated me – not that I enjoyed it that much of course.*"

"*Then everything is perfect. Let's leave now—so that I can get back—and ... well – if he's got anything further to say he can say it to me.*"

"*I have to admit ...*" I smiled "*... I find the mystery of it all ... intriguing. This is anything but average or humdrum.*"

"*Quite so*" she replied almost peremptorily.

"*Possibly—bordering on the Byzantine – in a ... monochromatic kind of way?*" I added reflecting her tone for my own amusement.

"*Now-now—let's have no sarcasm*" she grinned. "*I didn't think you—went in—for that.*"

"*I don't ... but I thought you might appreciate it – if delivered with ...*"

"*Finesse?*" she interrupted.

I nodded in casual—if partial—agreement, and concluded the exchange with an inconclusive "*Yes ...*"

an odd boy

We boarded the Rolls in silence and glided through Bath toward Bristol – with Claudette regaling me with the joys of Dorothy Parker in terms of being able to say '*What fresh hell is this?*' whenever she picked up the telephone. I said that I could see the humour of it—and laugh—but that I was glad that I didn't feel the need to employ sarcasm more than once a decade.

Claudette went straight home after dropping me off. She telephoned later that evening. "*Vic?*"

"*Yes*" I replied. "*What fresh hell is this?*"

"*Oh—very droll—so you're a Dorothy Parker emulator now?*"

"*I applied for the licence shortly after you left – they're sending my acerbium tomorrow?*"

"*Acerbium?*" she enquired

"*Yes—just made that up—it's a dictionary of acerbic comments, tailor-made for every occasion. Speaking of which ... what did your father have to—say—about that dreadful hippie you took home?*"

"*He took no great objection—other than I'd expect. D'you—really—want to know?*"

"*Certainly – in-f'r-a-penny, in-f'r-a pound.*"

"*Tasteless clothing—unsightly facial hair—foppish coiffure.*"

"*Tasteless clothing eh?*" I enquired with amusement. "*Fine by me—he doesn't have to wear them—but, wouldn't that apply to you too? I mean you're hardly a conservative dresser are you?*"

"*No ... but I'm female so I'm exempt. He says that women are not bound by the same sartorial rules as men – and that it's natural for them to move through different phases of experimentation with dress.*"

"*Glad to see he has—some—unconventional opinions, 'dette.*"

"*Oh yes. I wouldn't say he was conventional by any means.*"

"You could've fooled me ... but ... I'm no authority on subtleties of that nature. I suppose it's unconventional to be a recluse – unless you're a religious ascetic."

"Yes – or unless your level of sophistication doesn't endure crass popular culture."

"Right ... well ... in some ways ... we're quite similar then. I'm not a great fan of popular culture either."

"He'd not see it that way of course ..." she sighed "... he—can—be a little aloof in his opinions ... sometimes."

"Doesn't his ... mien ... make your life a little bleak?"

"No. There's a certain refinement to it that I find reliable." Pause "You see ... he prefers his home to be a place of privacy." Pause "He's ... a man in long term mourning. My mother—as you know—died of leukaemia and he'll never re-marry. I'm his 'only child' and he's cut off from any relatives we had. They were the kind of people who take advantage – you know the sort ..."

Well no, I didn't – but it occurred to me that I was probably in the same category.

"My father's a deeply solitary man – apart from work colleagues, he has no friends – just me."

"Well ... I suppose that must ... suit him ..." I replied, rather than risk a question that might seem intrusive.

"He's a little like Heathcliff"[7] she commented with subdued seraphic intonation. "It's hard to understand for most people but he's ... painfully romantic. He'll never get over the death of my mother. It was hard for me – but it's—totally—impossible for him. He just doesn't want to see people—and never will—but ... I do respect the elegance of that."

---

7 Heathcliff – a character in 'Wuthering Heights' by Emily Brontë, 1848.

an odd boy

"*Elegance ... I'm not sure whether I understand that – but I can see why you're drawn to the theatre ... it's almost as if you live inside a play.*"
I wondered if I'd gone too far – because Claudette went silent.

It occurred to me that my idea of 'living theatre' might be a little too close to her everyday reality at home and decided I'd better not dwell at length on that subject with her. "*I'm sorry ... that must be very difficult.*"

"*No—not at all—it's just different*" Claudette responded with frozen serenity. "*He's not grieving in any*—ordinary—*sense. He can often be quite amusing – it's simply that he doesn't want to deal with—other—people. He can't see any purpose in it. They all want to do things like try to 'lift him out of it' and nonsense like that. He has no interest in dinner parties where he'd have to endure endless twaddle. He has his cars, his books and the radio – and he watches the occasional television drama, so he's quite content. He finds most people banal and oafish.*"

"Banal and oafish ..."

Claudette sounded embarrassed "*He didn't find—you—oafish ...*"

"*Just banal*" I laughed.

"*Well ... he finds any kind of 'fashion clothing' banal.*"

"*Me? Fashionable? I'm as fashionable as Derek Crowe. We both dress in period clothing and so does your father. He's directly from the 1940s. I'm severely out-of-fashion now anyway – and getting further out by the month. Anyhow ... fashion's a state of mind. What I like has occasionally been in fashion but I've only ever dressed according to what I like. Although I'm partially 'tail-end Carnaby Street' I never went in for the whole deal. A critique of how I dress really can't use—fashion—as a criterion.*"

"*Even to your hair?*"

"*Even that. That goes back to the* 1950s *and seeing films about Roundheads and Cavaliers – and liking the Cavaliers because they had long hair and wore better clothes.*"

"*Now that's a concept that would intrigue him*" Claudette offered "*but he still wouldn't want visitors I'm afraid.*" Pause "*See you tomorrow – sorry if it was all a bit unusual.*"

I replaced the telephone receiver feeling as if I'd spent the day as a figment of someone else's imagination. I sat for a moment and wondered where meetings with Mr Gascoigne left anyone in any way connected with Claudette. A strange textural message started to form itself in my mind. It didn't have any meaning that I could discover. I didn't try that hard to unravel it – but I began to feel as if I was part of some tale by Emily or Charlotte Brontë. I wasn't keen on those books – and had a strong disinclination to have my life moulded in any way that resembled those tales. I decided that I'd not make mention of Mr Gascoigne again – with Claudette at least. He made no problem about our association – but I never saw the house again, even from the outside.

I strolled into the Hotwells living room. Meryl looked up as she'd caught fragments of my telephone conversation with Claudette. "*How did it go? I was meaning to ask.*"

"*It went*" I laughed. "*And it ain't never coming back.*" I meant the 'it' to apply to me.

an odd boy

She shook her head in dismay "*Right—yeah—know what you mean: the ghoulish Gascoigne ... I call him Sepulchrave – y'know the Earl of Groan ...*"[8]

"Mervyn Peake?" I enquired and Meryl nodded in the affirmative. "*I see what you mean*" I replied. "*I can see him welcoming the prospect of being eaten by owls in the attic of his mansion. He'd probably leave a note saying 'My perfect flesh shall not be sullied by worms'.*"

"*You should have taken Drama y'know – you'd've had fun as an actor.*"

"*Sepulchrave Gascoigne too – he stepped right out of a theatre production.*"

"*Y'know ...'dette thinks he's some kind of romantic figure of mystery...*" Meryl sighed "*... but I think he's a complete and utter creep. He's the closest thing to an animated waxwork I've ever seen. He has his nails manicured y'know – I can tell. And he keeps this little scented handkerchief in his pocket and holds it in front of his nose whenever people get too close to him.*"

"*A nosegay, eh ...*"[9] I chuckled "*... how very mediæval – still, I admire the ... style of it.*"

"*He really is quite a cranky man*" Rebecca offered. "*Saw him when he came to the Art College with 'dette. We'd all gone to see her show at the end of the Foundation year one evening and—he—turned up. He only came because he felt obliged to attend her show – but he never spoke to anyone. He looked expressionlessly at each piece of 'dette's work.*

---

8   Lord Sepulchrave, the Earl of Groan – a melancholic character in the 'Gormenghast Trilogy' by Mervyn Peake. He is burdened by his endless duties as Earl and his only relief lies in reading. When his library is destroyed by fire he loses his already insecure sanity and goes to live with the death-owls in the Tower of Flints. They eat him alive.

9   Nosegay – a posey—small bunch of flowers—typically given as a gift. Also a scented handkerchief. In mediæval culture, a nosegay was carried or worn to mask unpleasant smells – literally, to keep the nose gay (happy).

"Then he nodded to her and left. That was it. He didn't even speak to the tutors — hardly even spoke to 'dette. He just floated in as if he was on castors—discharged his minimal parental duty—and walked out."

Even the ubiquitously kind-hearted Penelope was of the same opinion. "Yes ... he—is—sort of sinister ... 'dette has to answer every phone call because he won't answer at all. If she's not there he just lets it ring. He lives in part of the house where he can't—hear—it ring.

"Of course 'dette thinks he has every right not to have to deal with the world. He goes out to work — and she says that's enough for him. The rest of the time he just reads or tinkers with vintage cars."

"I suppose it's good that he works on cars" I suggested. "That sounds a little more real than the rest of it. I suppose he has to get a bit dirty and greasy when he does that."

"Not on your life!" Meryl laughed. "He wears surgeon's gloves or something — and an apron and felt galoshes to keep his shoes clean. When I said he tinkers, I mean he—tinkers. He sees himself as some sort of scientist. He makes fine adjustments — 'dette told me all about it. He has a whole load of dials and gauges and he writes things down in notebooks. If serious mechanical work is needed, then someone else has to do that. He regards—that—as menial work." Meryl was especially annoyed by this because she loathed snobbery.

It was one of the most outlandish accounts I'd ever heard. "It's like something out of Dickens."

They all nodded. "And ..." concluded Penelope "... it accounts for a few of 'dette's peculiar preferences."

"Like me?" I laughed.

That had them in hysterics "No—you're—the most—normal—thing in her life!"

an odd boy

"Me normal? That's—entirely—surprising!" I laughed. "But then ... I never set out to be ab-normal. I suppose I should be pleased. 'Mister Normal' eh ... there should be a superhero costume for that rôle ... with a mask like a hammerhead shark or something – and pair of pretty pink strawberry-pattern bloomers."

Penelope choked on her wine at that image. "*You—could—sometimes wait and check to see if anyone had a mouth full of something before saying things like that ...*" she laughed

"*... but yes ... 'dette's really had quite a strange time of it with her father being as he is.*" Pause "*And then there was that really awful time she had with—total bastard—John Willoughby on Foundation. She really fell for him quite badly when she was 16. They both arrived on the Foundation Year together and were—very much—the inseparable couple. Sepulchrave seemed to have a little more time for John Willoughby ... he had relatively short hair and wore a suit when he visited – 'dette apparently put him wise to that – and being from the same sort of private school background he had that kind of get-up.*"

"I have it too ..." I replied "*... but 'dette never mentioned that I should dress any particular way.*"

"*You have a suit?*" I replied in the affirmative and Penelope continued "*The white one and the green leather one you mean?*"

"No – a regular dark grey suit. It's Edwardian double breasted with a waistcoat – I could have worn that."

"*Does 'dette know about it?*"

"Certainly – I wore it to the theatre the first time we went out together."

After silently cogitating for several moments Meryl said "Maybe ..." Pause "*... she's got rebellious in her old age ...*"

"Maybe" I replied. "So ... anyway – what happened with this Willoughby fellow?"

"Well ... as I said, he was an utter shit." Pause "He dropped her like a stone, just before Christmas for ... what was her name now ..." she pondered "... oh yeah—Sophia Grey. Snooty blonde girl who flashed her bosoms around." I raised my eyebrows at that description. Meryl noticed the movement of my eyebrows. "Nothing to cause any—great—furore you understand ... but she made sure everyone was aware that she had breasts."

"In Jane Austen's day the term was 'Cupid's kettledrums' ..."

"Yes that's right—amusing term and quite appropriate in her case—she was an expert in making a lot out of a little." Pause "Anyhow she was one of those 'Nouveau Riche—Alfa Romeo—skiing holiday in St Moritz types'; y'know—moon boots—perfect teeth—diamond bracelets."

"Yes ...'dette mentioned he'd gone off with someone—but she gave me no details—and didn't want to tell me anything more than that. I understood because it's obviously an extremely painful memory. It was kind of ... peculiar though because she'd spent most of the evening getting a detailed list of my love-life."

"Well yeah ... she's kind of cautious like that now, I suppose."

"Right ..." I replied out of a haze of aimless conjecture. "Is there anything I ought to know – just to be ... aware ... or whatever ..."

"Well ... it hit her like a bombshell. She clammed up. Shut herself up all over Christmas. We'd invited her to parties but she never came and didn't answer the phone. We didn't see her at all and then she wouldn't speak to anyone. She started looking as if she was turning into her father or something. We practically had to force her to go back to Art School after Christmas – and at least old Sepulchrave agreed; although he was glad to get us out of his house." Pause "When she went back to Art School she would hardly speak to anyone and used to come and see us every lunch break.

an odd boy

"*Then we—Penelope, Rebecca, and I—had to talk her into applying for the degree course in Fashion and Textiles. She was about to give up on everything and stay at home like some sort of Miss Havisham.*"[10]

I wasn't entirely at ease hearing all this – but somehow it seemed that I ought to know, so I didn't curtail the flow of information.

The eerie thing about what I was hearing, was that it all added up to something. The sensation was in no way comforting or reassuring. It occurred to me that knowing the reason why Claudette was as she was – should have made a positive difference. I should have thought '... *ah, I see – now I will know how to proceed. All I have to do is reassure her – or avoid this and that when I talk with her ...*' but no ... To me, it sounded like a book or a play – where the author has planned a tragic end. There seemed little room for manœuvre. Claudette certainly didn't seem as if she was going to tell me anything more than I'd just learnt – and in fact not even that. It was her private life and she wanted no one invading it.

She'd discovered a great deal about me – whilst remaining an emotionally closed book herself. That couldn't be healthy ... and couldn't lead anywhere good – not unless she changed.

"*I'm happy she has you three as friends. I sort of wish she'd spend more time with you.*"

Meryl shook her head and said "*Well ... 'dette's never been violently social – and we did see her whenever you took off to see friends.*"

---

10 Miss Havisham – a character in Charles Dickens' 'Great Expectations', 1860. She is a wealthy unmarried woman who lives in a dilapidated mansion. Having been jilted on her wedding day she spends the rest of her life wearing her wedding dress.

"That's good to hear – she never told me she'd called while I was away … I suppose there was no great need. I think she likes to be private and keep life in separate compartments." Pause "The thing that … concerns me … a little …" I continued "… is that she takes after her father in some ways, y'know – insulating herself from the world." Pause "I know everyone should be free to cut the cake however they like – but I'm not sure it's good for people to hide away."

"Well she's got this money coming you see – and … well … she doesn't really—need—to work or get a career or anything – so … she seems to think that being self-contained suits her – especially after being jilted by Mister Willoughby."

At that moment Penelope appeared from her room and overheard Meryl saying "I'm not really sure she'll—ever—get over that … she's become kind of hard edged and frosty or something."

"What was she like before?" I asked.

"Well … she was a lot … softer – kind of … much more open and light hearted."

Penelope entered the conversation "We were all—really—glad when she took up with you."

"Right!" Meryl nodded vigorously.

"Because … well, you're … so—nice" Penelope added sheepishly. "And anyway …" she continued in a bolder voice "… we've all been hoping that 'dette would relax again and be more like she used to be …she's warmed up—don't get me wrong—but she still seems a little … fragile in some ways – you know, kind of brittle."

"She can get angry about really silly little things" Meryl added. "Like you can just say the wrong thing and she'll stiffen up like a broom handle … and … to be honest … it—can—be a little bit of a drag sometimes."

an odd boy

I knew exactly what she meant – but left my response as a slight nod of the head.

"*I think it's all her father's fault—I don't think we should blame her—he was almost—pleased—that 'dette had been emotionally hurt so that he'd have her at home more*" Penelope suggested.

"*Right?*" Meryl interrupted. "*Because it meant she could join his bloody 'walking-dead club' or whatever it is.*"

"*Yes …*" Penelope ventured. "*You're really—very—normal in comparison to the rest of her life.*"

I pondered—briefly—what 'normal' might mean.

"*It occurs to me that 'normal' and 'abnormal' depend almost entirely on where you're coming from. I suppose it's not normal—for me—to be travelling in a Rolls Royce to see a play. If I didn't know 'dette I'd probably never see the inside of a Rolls.*"

"*Going to Bath for tea and scones at the Pump Rooms …*" Meryl grinned. "*… is—fairly—abnormal for an Art student.*"

I'd not considered that. "*That's not—so—strange for me I suppose, because there's a string quartet – and it's a free concert if you take it as such. It reminds me of a place in Nepal – the adjectival 'Johnny Gurkha Restaurant'. There was a bandstand there – a little pavilion where a music teacher and his students played every evening … as the fruit bats flapped silently over head. The teacher and his students played the most excellent Indian classical music. It's not easy to hear Indian Classical music in India. It's on a par with going to Glyndebourne.*"

"*It requires formal dress?*" Penelope asked.

"*The Classical concerts – yes*" I answered.

"*Not for the bats I hope*" Rebecca laughed – falling backwards into the settee.

"Certainly – they wore evening tails." Pause "Anyhow ... I never got to go. It was far too expensive. The music at the 'Johnny Gurkha Restaurant' was entrancing though and probably somewhere in that league – but it was free."

"What did they play?"

"Sitar—or sometimes surbahar—veena, tambura, tablas ... and the teacher on five string violin. But again, people just talked over it as if they had something monstrously important to say that couldn't wait till some other time. Y'know ..."

I held forth with hardcore hippie mumble "...Yeah man, like Kulu shawl verbiage—yeah really man—Manali ashram verbiage—like I mean man, Green Manalishi verbiage—Maharishi Guru verbiage—Maharooni macarooni monsoon verbiage—I mean really Rishikesh verbiage man—like we could score some totally ganja guru verbiage—like really guru verbiage ganja karma—and trekking too—far out man—like really—and so Kulu cool yeah, like Yeti verbiage—y'know, she was only the abominable snowman's daughter – yet'e loved 'er."

"Hysterical!" Meryl shrieked with laugher. "You'll have to give a rendition at the Drama College."

"Happy to oblige—or maybe not—but really ... it was like that everywhere I went in the East" I groaned. "Sometimes it got a little much. A young lad followed me along the street one day offering to sell me ganja. Every time I said no he lowered the price – until finally he said 'You cannot buy cheaper than this!' and I replied 'I believe you – but I want you to believe that I really don't want to buy any.' He just stared at me in disbelief."

"Out of step – again Vic ... it must get you down ..." Penelope offered in her kindly way.

"Well ... I don't mind it too much. I don't go out of my way to be the odd man out – but it seems to happen of itself. I mean ... I was sitting in the park one day reading the notes on the Ravi Shankar album I'd bought when a hyper-hippie fellow walked by with that languid lope ...you know the one I mean?"

"Yes – people have started doing that haven't they ..." Meryl interjected. "And – talking in some sort of soft West Coast American accent – it's really peculiar."

"Peculiar indeed" I replied. "People I used to know have either become bastions of society or they've turned into caricature freaks."

"So what happened then – with the loper?" Meryl asked.

"Well he asked 'Whadya score man?' – and I answered 'Ravi Shankar album.' Then he said 'Who?' and I replied 'Ravi Shankar – a master of Hindustani classical sitar.'"

"That would have clarified his question" Rebecca laughed.

"I would have thought so" I chuckled. "Then he said 'Yeah man ... like cool' and sped away as if I had the plague or something—right appearance but wrong voice—he must have thought I was an undercover narcotics agent." Pause "But that's only half the story. On another day I walked into a gentleman's outfitters on Park Street—where I bought my sitar—and got a very frosty reception. The man asks 'Can we be of assistance?' in a tone that meant 'You're in the wrong shop – go away.'."

"I can just imagine ..." Penelope commented "They usually only get Land Rover owners in places like that – y'know people like Todd."

I recognised the accuracy of that idea. "Yes ... So, anyway, I replied 'Thank you, yes. I would like to purchase a pair of grey woollen socks.'"

Penelope fell about laughing. "I can just hear you. So what effect did —that—have?"

"His attitude changed immediately. 'Certainly Sir – what would your shoe size be?' I was suddenly a recognisable human being—wrong appearance but right voice—the world's an adjectival lunatic asylum."

"Perhaps we should all go to the Pump Rooms" Penelope suggested.

"I'd like that – but ...you might not enjoy it that much ... because it's the same as at the Johnny Gurkha Restaurant'. The other people quaffing tea and scones don't usually seem that interested in listening to the music ...'dette and I have to sit as close to the string quartet as we can in order that we can hear them clearly over the background hum. Y'know ..."

I held forth with a Sloane Ranger twang "...Yes—verbiage—and as hitherto and notwithstanding—verbiage and semi-visible verisimilitude—indubitably my dear fellow—verbiage and variegated valences—quite so vicar—verbiage, verbiage, verbiage. Verbiage? Really? Verbiage and Verbiage? And they were there too with Viscount Verbiage— Verbiage you surprise me ... vertigo verbiage vestibule. Really ...you don't say ... Yes indeed, Balderdash and Basilisk Barangrill[11] with their children Boris, Doris, Horace, and Maurice—not to forget verbiage and Horatio Hunchback-Haddock. Cry haddock and let loose the cods of war!"

"It's really quite fun listening to you rant!" Rebecca laughed.

"Yes ... there aren't that many causes for ranting."

"Maybe ..." Penelope suggested "... it's just because it's rare. You're usually so ... considered and easy going about everything – even on subjects like Todd and the Earl of Groan."

---

11 Barangrill – a place in a song of the same name by Joni Mitchell from 'For the Roses'.

12

the second year: may 1974 – july 1974

bower ashton – speaking with ravens

Twilight ravens may be calling – seeking speaking through to me, / Circling through the fog lights – of the frost enshrouded trees, / There's cloud that's sitting silent – dreaming uncertainty, / And the morning waves are rolling – out across the boiling sea. / There's a tempest that's a-blowing – and a wilful howling gale / But ravens will be with me – when the night sky sets its sail. Frank Schubert—Ravens—1974

Attending the theatre and the occasional sojourns at the Bath Pump Rooms—with its fine four-piece chamber orchestra—had become all the time I allowed myself away from illustration and painting. Claudette enjoyed these outings and we spoke about them with delight. She seemed to have lost interest in the fact that I'd had an intriguing past. That was a relief in some ways – although it also felt slightly uneasy in terms of her not being interested in an area of my life that had intrigued her before.
It wasn't that I wanted to talk about the past—or dwell on past glories vis-à-vis Savage Cabbage—but it seemed as if the subject had somehow become blocked. That was no big deal however – as I was quite happy to move on. For my part I attempted not to plunge into speculative philosophical or Artistic theoretics with Claudette. I found it solved the problem as far as she was concerned.

It wasn't frustrating – as I had Meryl, Rebecca, and Penelope with whom I could discuss anything—at any length—and in as much detail as required.

an odd boy

I had too many ideas to contain or explore. I kept a notebook of future plans and worked through them as the ideas slotted into the broad evolution of my work. Sometimes I'd write the poetry or prose first and illustrate it in the conventional illustrative sequence – and sometimes I would create the image first.

The sphere of *word and image* as a *combined Art-form* seemed to be my niche and I revelled in its possibilities. There was no reason —for example—why a word and image combination should not be framed like a painting. It was illustration—that was for sure— but it did *not* have to be small scale. A stained-glass window in a church was an illustration – so a person didn't have to be limited by books and magazines. Posters were certainly a part of the illustrator's province. There was no rule I could see that prevented me from working large. John Martin, the Victorian artist, produced huge mezzotint images and so I felt I could take illustration into realms that transcended the tidy truncated minimalist images that Dick Taylor believed illustration to be.

I continued work on the series of Raven paintings that I eventually called 'Speaking with Ravens'. The paintings became gradually more involved and the different systems of removing partial layers of paint became more complex and time-consuming.

As Claudette retired as my life-model—with respect to my raven paintings—I painted my main image of the Art School model with whatever background there was in the studio. I'd allow the paintings to dry and then overpaint them with the colours that seemed to be hidden in the room – the non-obvious colours. The Fine Artists would peer at me when I painted over the top of my paintings and sometimes they seemed almost interested – especially when I seemed to be moving toward something that looked abstract.

But then I'd sand it back and they'd see that I was up to 'some tawdry illustrator's trick' and lose interest. This was the technique I'd started exploring when I was at Farnham Art School. I was keen to see to what extent I could develop it. It was a remarkable way of working but it was not long before I started branching out into other ways of creating texture.

Sometimes I'd allow the overpainting to dry to the point where it could be rubbed back with a cloth soaked in turpentine – or I'd scrub the canvas with a stiff bristled scrubbing brush. The scrubbing brush would striate the paint and then I'd paint over it again so that the new layer of paint would settle into the striations. I'd let that dry and then sand back again. I'd carry on this way adding layer after layer and sanding back. The textures I achieved by this means became exceedingly intricate and convoluted – and often gave me ideas for the next painting, even though there was no way I could reproduce the effects with any great exactitude.

Rebecca was looking at my latest 'Speaking with Ravens' painting and asked me *"I'm interested in the intricate textures you create. They're obviously crucial to the composition because …you spend so much time evolving them. Can you tell me how they come about?"*

I was always happy to talk about painting *"What's most important to me—with these textures—is the quality of light. The painting has to glow. I'm seeking radiance – an atmosphere of colour which expresses the environment in which the model—and ravens—are flying."*

Rebecca stared at the painting for some minutes *"I'd like to be flying like that."* Pause *"D'you think …'dette would mind … me, posing for a painting?"*

"Think you'd better ask 'dette …" I replied *"… but I'd be happy to paint you next – 'dette doesn't sit for me anymore – because it's hard work sitting still."*

"Hard work?"

"Yeah – hard work. I spent six months as a life model in Farnham Art School so I know all about that. It's—not—easy to sit still for a long period – even with rests."

Rebecca continued to peruse the textures in the painting.
"How do you choose the colours? They're not really the colours of any environment ... I mean, they're not the colours of your room ... and I can't imagine that they're the colours of the Art studio at Bower Ashton."

"They're exaggerations of flashes of colour that reveal themselves ... through the act of staring. They have to communicate something that resonates with the posture of the model. The colours ... are based on the colours I see in the studio – but ... I take them further ... in the direction of light. I turn everything into the play of light – because ... that's what everything is."

"That's exciting." Rebecca was fascinated with these ideas of light and colour *"I think it would be amazing to be personally transported into that field of light ... through painting I mean."* Pause *"When did you first have ideas like this about painting light?"*

"Dates back to the first life model painting at Hatch Mill."

"Seems as if you could explore this endlessly ..." Rebecca opined *"... because you'd never know what's going to happen or how the texture's going to reveal itself next."*

"Right ..." I grinned *"... there's a certain richness and subtlety that always starts to emerge – which is when I add the ravens."*

"You don't copy them from books?"

"No. I used to – but that was far too limiting. That's why I started going to Bristol Zoo. There're ravens there – and I occasionally need to replenish my references. In Farnham I used books for the ravens I painted – but that didn't provide enough detail – or ... the 'life' that's necessary."

Rebecca sat staring at the painting. *"These ravens are all from drawings you made at Bristol Zoo then?"*

"Yes ... mainly – but they're from photographs as well." I could see Rebecca looking confused *"But that's entirely different from relying on the photographs in books. Firstly I take the photographs myself ... and secondly I distort the ravens by tilting the bed of the enlarger. That creates stretched ravens, flattened ravens, and long-beaked ravens."*

"D'you have any here?" Rebecca asked and so I opened up my folder. *"There's bloody hundreds of them!"* she shrieked with delight. *"I love—this—one ... can I be painted with this one?"*

Rebecca—after a day or two—plucked up the courage to enquire of Claudette whether she minded her sitting as a model for my next painting. Claudette said *"I'd be more than pleased. It was fun at first being immortalised on canvas – but I think I've served my time on the painter's podium."*

It was agreed. Wednesday evenings became painting evenings in the Hotwells house. During the remainder of my time at Bower Ashton I produced numerous drawings and three 6 foot square paintings.

Rebecca appeared at the appointed time in her dressing gown—obviously highly anxious—but she hadn't disrobed for long before she felt as if she'd been life modelling for years. *"I don't feel ... 'looked at' as I imagined I might have felt 'looked at' – it's really ... quite ... curious."*

That was as it should be. *"Yes – I can relate to that having been a life model – and of course, the painter is in some other state of mind ... when painting."*

That phrase made her ponder. *"I suppose that's the same as playing music – when you know the piece so well that you forget you're playing."*

"I got into that frame of mind with Savage Cabbage when I'd learnt a bass riff well enough to simply roll with it."

That interested Rebecca. *"So it's probably the same for Meryl when she's acting."*

We put the idea to Meryl. *"Yes ... it's the same."*

There's a crystal dew a-coiling – in a fuselage of snakes, / Spinning down and writhing – where the platform terminates, / There is no clear distinction – of all the sights you've seen, / Beyond the silver turnstile in the departure lounge of dreams. / The mercury's falling fast now – in the mirror of my tale / But ravens will be with me – when the night sky sets its sail. Frank Schubert—Ravens—1974

Conversations in the painting and life modelling situation were interesting because silence was the norm. This meant that ideas arose slowly in relation to whatever the last comment was and the end result was usually some form of profoundly circuitous theoretical exposition. It wasn't long before Penelope and Meryl were eager to take their turns as a life model for paintings.

Rebecca sat staring at herself in her en-ravened image. It was a long time before she spoke. *"There's something sumptuously forceful about this. I think I'd like to live in that world for a while. How d'you get into that world?"*

"You can get into that world playing your bassoon."

"Well yes ... but when I play bassoon I'm always playing music composed by someone else ..." Rebecca replied *"... and I feel ... I'd have to be playing raven music to find myself in this painting."*

"Raven music ... now that sounds interesting" I mused. *"Maybe we could compose something. I can see bassoon, oboe, and 'cello being the perfect instruments for ravens. I don't know about sitar or tambura though ..."*

"*Perhaps we could borrow the double bass ...*" Rebecca pondered "*...you—did—say you played bass with Savage Cabbage?*"

"*Well ...yes ... I did ...*" I replied "*... but I was on rhythm bass – and the bass I played had frets. The idea of a fretless instrument kind of ... unnerves me ...*"

Rebecca found my trepidation surprising "*I thought you liked experimenting – and I'm sure that Penelope would help you.*"

"*Yes I'm sure she would – but it's my ineptitude that concerns me. I'd love to try a double bass—of course—if you three wouldn't mind me hitting bum notes.*"

"*We'll bear with you*" Rebecca chortled.

Penelope gazed at her painting silently musing for some time. "*It makes me feel ...*" she said eventually "*... as if I went to some other dimension of reality and was visually ... captured there – in some other state of mind ... with some sort of mind-camera that ...*" Pause "*... showed what I was feeling in colours rather than words.*"

I was delighted by her comments. "*You'll be writing poetry soon – with ideas like that.*"

Penelope grinned "*I'll give it a try – even though ... I've never attempted poetry before. I'm a musician – and it's never occurred to me to try my hand at lyrics let alone poetry.*"

"*That's one of the problems with the educational system*" I told her. "*It divides subjects. Anyone can be anything – especially in the Arts. That doesn't mean that you can't specialise or that you have to look into every branch of Art – but I believe that Artists should always be open to exploring within the Arts.*"

Meryl burst into tears when she saw her finished painting. "*I've never thought of myself like that before – I look like someone in a film or a fairy tale.*

an odd boy

"It's weirdly ... more like me ... than any photograph of myself. I just can't quite believe that's—me—in there with those enormous ravens lying around me. It looks so reckless—so perilous—yet so ... serene. I find myself wondering what kind of play it would be and what I might be saying."

"You should script something for it" I replied.

"Right ... I'll keep that in mind ... maybe there'll be a project where I can use this painting as the theme. We will have writing projects next term and I think my tutor would be open to me working with this image as the basis of a soliloquy."

I told her I'd look forward to seeing that if it was one of the performances that were open to the public. Meryl said I could simply sit in – there'd be no problem with that. "*I just wonder whether I'd risk a nude performance – or whether they'd permit it, of course. Now there's an idea ... I'll look into it and see how I feel closer to the time.*"

"*I'll be interested to know what you decide*" I said. "*Maybe this'll induce me to write songs again – I've not put my hand to lyrics since I left Farnham Art School.*"

The idea did indeed induce me to write songs again and I produced a raven song for Meryl's performance.

There's a counter-clockwise chemistry – of ravens on the wing, / Swooping down on alchemy – as the sirens softly sing, / No one's ever situated – outside of time's recall, / So listen to me one more time before you make your call. / The river's flowing through the sky – in the misty evening vale / But ravens will be with me – when the night sky sets its sail.
Frank Schubert—Ravens—1974

I gave Penelope, Rebecca, and Meryl their respective paintings even though they wanted to pay for them.

Claudette was vaguely disquieted by Penelope's, Rebecca's, and Meryl's enthusiasm for my painting. It was as if she was on the outside of an internal adventure, even though there were far more paintings for which she'd been the model.

"*I like the ravens—they're marvellously strange—and, most of the time, I like myself in the paintings—but Penelope, Rebecca, and Meryl seem to be seeing something else in them. There seems to be something I can't quite see. Could you talk about them in more detail – so I'll get a better idea of them?*"

"*Certainly ...*" Pause "*I see the paintings as a ... plummeting trajectory ... into the core nature of ravens.*"

"*I can always rely on you to insinuate a pun in an unlikely situation*" Claudette laughed. "*That sounds intriguing ... but what does it mean?*"

"*I'm not totally clear what it means ... but it wasn't an intentional pun*" I replied. "*I'll try to say a little more – I'm not used to putting words to how I arrive at these images.*" Pause "*Since I started painting ravens—as superimpositions on life models at Hatch Mill—I've come to see them as ... self-existent messages.*"

"*What do the messages say?*" Claudette asked with a hint of suspicion in her voice.

"*By self-existent ... I mean ... that the meaning is simply there ... in ... an unstructured way. I don't think the messages can be understood in language ... or maybe I don't think I'll ever understand the messages – but somehow ... it's not crucial that I do.*"

"*So why call them messages then?*"

"*Why indeed ...*" Pause "*Message was just the word that came into my mind when you asked the question – so I'm not sure what it means myself just yet.*"

"*Well yes ... but that's not an understandable reply is it?*"

an odd boy

"*No ... I guess you're right – but ...you see ... as I said ... I don't really have words for any of this other than the words that suggest themselves when I'm asked to explain.*"

"*And you don't know what those words mean?*"

"*No ... not absolutely – not in the sense of conventional definitions ... no.*"

"*That's quite unworkable though – how can you speak using words when you don't understand them?*"

"*I can't answer that ...You are asking me to explain and I'm trying to put words to something for which there are no words – and this is what happens. I think it's about ... an openness. Maybe it's an openness to understanding—something—that's just—there—being as it is and manifesting its nature*" I posited – observing Claudette's internal consternation at not being able to follow my language. "*Maybe ... the message is an openness to discerning the impossibility of literally understanding an experiential texture.*"

"*Are you saying these things deliberately so that I won't be able to understand?*" Claudette asked in a rather crisp tone.

"*No ... as I said ... I'm not used to talking about the process. You see ... 'the experiential texture' seems to exist as a state of mind—complete in itself—without any need of an intellectual infrastructure.*" Claudette still looked bewildered so I continued to speak "*It's a creative ambience that's self-informed ... and—it informs me—if I'm open to it ... and 'that' continues as long as I'm painting. That seems to be what I'm calling the self-existent message.*"

"*That makes it no clearer*" Claudette sighed resignedly. "*That sounds more-or-less like your poetry – which means—nothing—to me at all.*"

"*Well yes ... but that's only because you're used to reading for meaning rather than word-sounds. I mean – you like* Under Milk Wood *... and Dylan Thomas certainly uses that mode.*"

"*Yes but yours never uses anything else.*"

"*True.*" Pause "*But then ... it's what I enjoy. I'm just sorry you can't enjoy it too.*"

"*Anyhow let's get back to the painting – maybe there's something in that – that I can understand. After all if Penelope, Rebecca, and Meryl can understand it – you ought to be able to explain it to me.*"

"*I'll do my best ... but whatever I say is likely to sound like poetry.*" Pause "*You see ... there are things it's impossible to say in linear terms.*"

"*So how d'you judge something when there are no criteria – what divides it from meaninglessness?*"

"*Your guess is as good as mine ...*" I replied with slight frustration. I could explain myself to the girls – but I always ended up irritating Claudette. "*It's intuitive I suppose ... I simply work according to what I feel about what I see. The questions of meaning and meaninglessness don't really arise – or if they do, they simply move in and out of each other.*"

That made no sense to Claudette either "*What about the model— what part does she play—or is she as inexplicable as the raven?*"

I thought about this for a moment. "*I think she's a creative accident of time and place who started at Hatch Mill. It was the first oil painting project and we had to paint the model. It just went on from there and there's something I have come to appreciate about exploring the juxtaposition.*"

"*Without—any—communicable sense of what you're doing?*" Claudette asked incredulously.

"*No ... or rather, yes ...*" Pause "*... thing is, 'dette ... I don't—need— anything to 'make sense' in terms of painting, lyrics, or poetry. This is why I've only ever illustrated my own writing – or why I only write pieces to fit with my own images.*"

"*Isn't that entirely self-referencing?*" she asked. "*I mean—how—do you know what you're doing or where you're going?*"

"*I don't*" I replied. "*I have no idea where anything's going. The whole question of 'I' doesn't really have to be involved. I don't think I'm referencing a 'self' – well … not excessively anyway.*"

"*Right …*" Claudette yawned "*… the wretched Buddhist thing about 'not existing' or whatever. I really don't get that non-ego business – particularly because you're about the—last person on earth—I know who looks as if they weren't concerned with self-image.*"

Claudette having once expressed some interest in Buddhism had hit the wall running in terms of trying to understand it. I'd suggested books by Chögyam Trungpa Rinpoche – but she soon became completely bored by the subject and thought it was all highly elaborate semantic sophistry. She didn't like the answers Chögyam Trungpa Rinpoche gave to people's questions and said that he appeared to be deliberately opaque. I then regretted ever suggesting his books – as I'd obviously done him a disservice by placing them in the hands of someone who wasn't open to letting the written word become an experience.

"*Firstly, 'dette – it's not courteous to refer to Buddhism as 'wretched'.*"

"*I'm sorry – that was going a bit far.*"

"*Yes it was – but it's fine. I'll now forget you ever said it.*" Pause "*Secondly … I'm no great example. Never pretended to be. Thirdly, I have to make some slight reference to Buddhism – because it's how I think. If I'm to explain my painting – I have to use the structures that are meaningful to me. Fourthly, the Freudian 'ego' word has nothing to do with it. It's just a question of 'what we are' being unstructured. It's not that there's nothing there – it's just that what's there is momentary. It just means we're in flux – and I try to have that sense of being in flux when I paint.*"

"*And ...*" Claudette began "*... what would be the difference between— that—and not knowing what you were doing.*"

"*... 'none' is the simplest answer – but ... I suppose I could say that I recognise the subject—the model—and I recognise the ravens—as—ravens ... so it's not as if these are works of abstract expressionism or anything.*"

"*Abstract expressionists go in for spontaneous subconscious expression ...*" I could tell Claudette was going to hold forth. She was good at this kind of thing. "*... and Fine Artists all seem to be able to talk coherently about the subject – I mean ...*" she emphasised raising her voice "*... books—are—written about it aren't they?*"

"*Yes ... true – but just because other people want to rationalise what they do ... doesn't mean that's a rule that everyone has to follow.*"

"*Ah yes ...*" Claudette clucked. "*Now—would—be the time to bring in the anarchist angle.*"

"*It's not an—angle—'dette ... it's just how I am – and ...y'know, I don't really need to prove anything by—any—of this. I just paint and— you're—just asking me about it.*" Pause "*You're not enjoying what I'm saying – but I'm not entirely responsible for that. I mean ... I didn't exactly set out to tell you all this stuff and I'm—not—pushing it ...*"

"*Well it just doesn't make any sense to me*" she snapped petulantly.

"*Fair enough ... but I'm talking about—enjoyment—rather than sense-making. Maybe ... if you enjoyed the word-pictures I make about my paintings rather than trying to understand literally ...*"

"*And that's what Penelope, Meryl, and Rebecca do – you're saying?*"

"*I don't know what they're doing – it never came to a point where we discussed it in that way.*" Pause "*Anyhow ...you'd have to ask them. All I know is that ... we talked about the paintings ... and it all kind of flowed.*"

"It—flowed—did it ... maybe that's because you're their pet artist and they humour you."

"Right, 'dette ..." I sighed *"... now I'm going to tell you a few things that are quite linear. What you've just said is insulting. It's insulting both to—your friends—and, to me. Now—before—you get indignant ..."* I could see her fuming *"... I don't go in for feeling insulted – but I can get to a point when I have had enough with a conversation that feels like assault and battery. I think you need to look at your relationship—with your friends—and with me ... and figure out what we are to you. I'm not trying to put anything over on you. You're the one who's—demanding—to understand in a certain way ... and I'm just not coming across satisfactorily. I'm sorry about that – but it's not—my—fault if Penelope, Meryl, and Rebecca get—whatever it is they get—and you don't. This is a silly conversation – and I'd rather I wasn't having it. Have I ever attacked you in this kind of way? And—before you answer—I'm not interested in the fact that 'I could if I wanted to' or that 'your work is all intelligible'. All I am asking is whether I have ever attacked you in this way?"*

Claudette looked a little shocked. This was the second time I'd had to 'get serious' in this way – and this time I'd sounded a little more serious than before.

"I'm sorry" she offered quietly.

"Thank you. I appreciate that."

"... it wasn't really what I meant to say ... Penelope, Meryl, and Rebecca—are—good friends and it's unfair to say things like that about them or you – it's just that your world is so strange to me."

"Yes ... well ... I suppose we do live in slightly different worlds in some ways – but I'll always—try—to give you a picture of what I'm doing if you ask me." Pause *"Maybe that's the problem though ...you want to know about my pictures and maybe all I do is give you another picture."*

"That's always what it seems like — and I can't seem to find a way through it without feeling angry — and I don't want to feel angry, especially with you."

"Thank you, 'dette" I smiled. "I appreciate that a great deal." Pause "So ... what can I say ... that would be useful?" I pondered "Y'know ... I think the only factor that's crucial with what I do ... is hard work and ... the refusal to compromise on the quality of what I create."

"Now that is something I—can—understand. I suppose that will have to do for now."

"There's all the time in the world, 'dette ... 'til the sun implodes that is."

The question of hard work and refusal to compromise seemed to satisfy Claudette's need of quality judgements — but she still found my pictorial and linguistic amorphousness perplexing.

Claudette spoke to Rebecca about my intellectual opacity — but realised that Rebecca could be as intellectually opaque as I appeared to be.

"I think 'dette sees you as an intriguing yet ... gauche mixture of ad hoc erudition and plebeian naiveté" Rebecca opined.

"That sounds ... absolutely accurate. I have no real education — it's mostly autodidactic ... apart from one wonderful English teacher, Steve, Ron, and my lady-friends ..."

"Very funny — the plebeian ignoramus who professes an—autodidactic—education" Rebecca chuckled. "But then ... she finds me as hard to understand as you ... when it comes to speaking about the Arts and how I feel about music." Pause "Seems to me ... that 'dette's really quite concrete in the way she thinks. She's a literalist ... she likes things to be linear and kind of obvious ..."

The light from the window was brightening and fading intermittently as if some gigantic Norse god was playing with the dimmer switch. The dark clouds were only allowing odd streams of bright light to illuminate the room. It was vaguely like being on stage in an impromptu play – where two people were discussing 'dette.

"*I feel ...*" Rebecca mused and lapsed into silence for almost a minute "*... that 'dette's been indoctrinated by—Sepulchrave—her father ... into thinking that everything has to be intellectually validated on sound conventional academic principles – so that even if something is avant guard ... it has to meet established criteria ...*"

"*Yes ... I can buy that ... having met the man ...*" I said, pausing to observe the strange fluctuating light. "*I imagine from what I know that he has extremely tight ideas about how everything—should—be.*"

"*Yes – Sepulchrave's got his own rule book and there are twenty-three volumes of it gold-blocked and bound in leather. I've heard a lot from 'dette about that. He has a critique about anything and everything and very little meets with his standards of perfection.*" Pause "*I think ... that the real problem with—you—is that you are quite like Sepulchrave in—some— ways.*"

"*Me!?*" I almost squeaked.

"*Yes ...you have some strong views and you're certainly a perfectionist – but you're not an imperious, censorious, elitist autocrat.*"

"*And ...you think 'dette wishes I was?*"

"*To some degree ...yes ... I think that you are almost perfect—in her eyes —but that you fall short of Sepulchrave's standards of culturally sanctioned orthodoxy.*" Pause "*Y'know ... she told me you were unusually widely read – but you'd not read—any—of the books she'd imagined you'd have read – to have become the kind of person you appear to be.*"

"*That's ... well ... I'm not sure what to say about that*" I laughed. "*And she's the one who thinks—I'm—a convoluted thinker.*"

"*Yeah ... really ... I think she finds it a little alarming—from an intellectual point of view—that you admit to disliking books with miserable conclusions.*"

"*Oh—yeah—right ... like Thomas Hardy and George Eliot. I tried them just to show willingness – but ... blimey ... I enjoy their written language – but they're terminally despondent. I suppose that makes me a moron in terms of cultural æstheticism.*"

"*Me too ... wouldn't catch me reading that either ... I'd rather read the telephone directory.*"

"*Yeah ... but I'll spare 'dette that point of view when she next raises the topic.*"

Claudette did raise the topic when we next met – being interested to see what I'd made of the Thomas Hardy and George Eliot books she'd loaned me. "*They're marvellously well written ... but they don't offer a great deal of hope, do they?*"

"*True – but they're writing about the reality of the time.*"

"*Wouldn't argue with that. There's some very interesting information in those novels ... valuable perspectives on the times – certainly.*"

"*So what's your problem?*"

"*Well ... if I want to read about history via novels ... I'd prefer it without having to empathise with characters who're heading for the long drop.*"

Claudette mused on that point for a while before speaking again "*It does one good to be stirred.*"

"*Mmmm ... maybe I'd prefer to be shaken rather than stirred.*"[1]

"*I thought you Buddhists were big fans of reality?*"

"*We—the Buddhists—object to that generalisation*" I laughed. "*Reality is one thing, 'dette ... but I don't need to—read—about the bleak aspects of it. Reports on Vietnam supply me with'em. I'm surrounded by reality every day. I want to read about how reality could be – rather than how it sometimes had to be in the past. Reality isn't all misery in any case.*"

That was a novel concept for Claudette who queried "*Are you not at risk of advocating Mills and Boon.*"[2]

"*Certainly*" I chuckled. "*I'd rather read Mills and Boon than several hundred pages of misery – but maybe ... the Mills and Boon I'd choose ... would be Georgian.*"

"*Do you know—many—Georgian Mills and Boon authors?*"

"*... only one ...*" I replied with a grin.

Claudette raised her eyebrows in question "*... and whom might—that—be?*"

"*Jane Austen. She wrote excellent novels with happy conclusions.*"

"*Outrageous!*" Claudette remonstrated – but at least with a degree of mirth.

"*Yes – but I felt you had it coming. There's some sadness in Jane Austen too – but she writes a more balanced account of human life. I could re-read her books – but not Thomas Hardy and George Elliot – or at least what I've read of them. Maybe I shouldn't presume they're all the same.*"

---

1 'Shaken, not stirred' – the famous phrase of James Bond (Ian Fleming's British Secret Service agent 007) with regard to the way he wanted his vodka martini prepared. It first appeared in 'Diamonds Are Forever' in 1956.
2 Mills and Boon – a British publishing company which specialises in romantic novelettes.

Claudette could not assure me that they were not – but we both agreed on Jane Austen as a fine author. Claudette was still conceptually bewildered by me when it came to Art.

Our conversation returned to the ravens. Claudette loved ravens, as Helen McGillvray had done.

"Although what you said about them is utterly bizarre I still find it worth exploring – if only to find out what it might be that Penelope, Rebecca, and Meryl find in them."

"As I said before … I think you'd be better off asking them …"

"I did – but they weren't that communicative … they said they'd understood what you said – but that it wasn't easy to repeat it. – so can you just tell me what you told them?"

It occurred to me that Claudette might not have wanted to admit she was discomfited by the fact that Penelope, Rebecca, and Meryl were far more excited about the painting than she was – so I pondered my reply with that in mind. *"I told them mainly about the way I'd created the textures – and they didn't ask the kind of questions you asked me last time we talked. Their sense of my paintings seemed to come … simply from looking at them. Maybe it's because they're musicians?"*

"Maybe …"

"There's one photograph in which the raven's eye contains a pool of light" I said, opening my folder and finding the photograph. *"It speaks volumes concerning the—*mind*—behind the eye. It's like a doorway into the raven … and … I try to reproduce that in my paintings."*

Claudette thought that was intriguing. *"Yes it's beautiful—as you know—I love ravens … but why do you need anyone to sit for you as a model, when the ravens obviously appear to be taking over?"*

an odd boy

"*Yes ... the ravens—are—getting more predominant aren't they ...*"
I agreed "*... but the ravens wouldn't make sense without the model glowing behind them. The painting isn't really just about a life model and any number of ravens – it's the interplay. The raven's feathers—and outer-space blackness—are a dimension ... and the human lustre ... is another dimension – and yet ... there's a communication between the two that conveys something ...*" Pause "*... when I can capture it.*"

"*The fiery-haired theme remains ... is that important to you?*"

"*Yes ...*"

I had no desire to be painfully honest at Claudette's expense and went into a momentary silent reverie. It was Lindie's hair and ... it always had been. I'd realised that in the first term of the second year. I'd woken up too early one morning and had sat staring at the oil painting in my room. The sun was rising and the ginger hair was the first colour to emerge from the darkness of the painting. Then the painted image of Rebecca began to appear – and for a moment it looked a little like Lindie Dale. Then it hit me that I had always been painting Lindie – as far as the hair was concerned. Suddenly I emerged from the reverie and Claudette was staring at me in consternation.

"*You don't suffer from petit mal seizures do you?*"

"*Sorry—I drifted off—into ... some sort of ... idea about the painting, and ... trying to find an answer for your question ...y'know ...*"

"*No ... I don't know. What ideas – you'll have to spell them out or I won't know at all.*"

"*Hair like fire ...*" I replied, dissembling here so as to avoid her jealousy "*... and ... the inchoate birds of Odin.*"

"*Huginn and Muninn?*" Claudette queried. "*Why d'you call them inchoate?*"

"Well Huginn is 'thought' and Muninn is 'memory' – and ... that's the recipe for chaos."

"According to whom?"

"According to me ... I suppose." I noticed Claudette bridle at what she usually classified as my cavalier attitude toward academic exactitude *"... that idea ... I think ... comes from the fact that—every morning—Odin's two ravens, Huginn and Muninn, fly out over Midgaard. Right?"* I looked to Claudette for confirmation and she nodded. *"Well, Odin always fears that Huginn—thought—may not find it's way home – but his fear about Muninn—memory—is greater."*

"And that's chaos?"

"Yes ...y'see ... because Odin's a vast presence with only one eye and he sees either thought or memory with that one eye – but never the two together." Pause *"There's apparently something like this in particle physics – where you can determine either the position of a subatomic particle, or its speed – but not the two together."*

"Apart from the—fiery—hair" she grinned. *"I'm not much taken with this theory – especially bringing science into it."* Claudette was pretty much an expert on such matters.

"Well ... it's more of an Artistic intuition and ... an aspect of my own relationship with these images" I attempted to explain. *"I get images related to Thor too – and the Midgaard serpent."*

"And where do Thor and the Midgaard Serpent fit into this?"

"They're reflexes of a ... female Odin." I knew I was in trouble as soon as the words were out of my mouth. *"I know it's outside the remit of standard mythology ... but it all makes sense to me in terms of painting."*

"But why do you—have—to theorise in the abstract about things that are already understood?"

"Well, 'dette ...you're the one who asks me questions about—what I do —and my theorising is just my way of answering."

"But the subject of Norse mythology is already well researched by eminent scholars – and no one has said anything to suggest that Odin might be female."

"True ... I'm not saying that this idea has anything to do with Norse history. I'm exploring this in terms of painting rather than academic mythology." Pause "Look, 'dette ... I know this is—your—subject ... so maybe you shouldn't ask me about my paintings – I'm not trying to convert you to my ideas of anything ... and ... I'm not trying to say I have some secret insight into Norse mythology either. I see the Norse gods as 'atmospheres' ..." Pause *"It's just that I don't see these 'atmospheres' as limited by history or mythology. I see them as 'dynamic gestalts' who emerge for me as ... an artist ..."* I observed Claudette glazing over – but decided to stumble on to the end of my sentence *"... they emerge in different ways than they emerged for Norse warriors."*

"Yes ..." she replied in a vaguely sneering manner "... *Loki's wager, I would say.*"[3]

"You're going to have to explain that to me, 'dette. Loki's wager?"

"Loki's Wager is a logical canard—a fallacy that is."

"Yes ... I know what canard means" I chuckled. *"I usually try to duck them when they're thrown at me."*

"Oh very droll—you're quick, I'll give you that—however, the canard in question is the irrational insistence that a concept cannot be defined, and therefore isn't open to logical discussion."

---

3   Loki – a trickster god in Norse mythology.

"*Always*—did—*have a soft spot for Loki*—he kind of reminds me of Papa Legba—but ... what's the connection with Loki and logical canards?"

"You should know this kind of thing if you aspire to make free with the mythology ... but anyway Loki had made a wager with some dwarves in which it was agreed that the price—should Loki lose the wager—was his head. Loki lost the wager – but when the dwarves came to collect his head, Loki said that although he was willing to pay with his head, that the dwarves had no claim on any part of his neck. The dwarves had a protracted debate with Loki and although they adjudicated that parts were clearly head, and other parts were evidently neck – no agreement could be reached as to exactly where one ended and the other began. As a result, Loki kept his head."

"When all round are losing theirs and blaming it on me?[4] Most instructive ... I seem to remember that story now."

"And now Rudyard Kipling rears his ugly head ... very droll ... So—anyway—how is—Odin—an atmosphere or a dynamic gestalt? What does that actually mean?"

"Well ... take the 6 string HAGSTROM bass Steve Bruce used to play – I always saw that—imaginatively—as some sort of lightning conductor that functioned as a conduit for Thor. Steve Bruce playing slide on that thing was like a sonic key to the Bifröst Bridge to Asgaard."

Claudette burst out laughing "That sounds like one of those awful American super hero comics! Did you ever read that awful one about Thor? It—sounds—as if you did ..."

---

4 Reference to Rudyard Kipling's poem 'If', 1895. '*If you can keep your head when all about you are losing theirs and blaming it on you.*'

an odd boy

"*Alright, 'dette …you've got me there. Yes … I did read Thor comics when I was 10.*"[5]

"*I—thought—as much.*"

"*However … owning up to it does make my explanation more difficult – being as I have to assure you in some way that this is not at all connected. It's not that I see Thor …*"

The opportunity for a pun was too much for Claudette who proceeded to lampoon me on that basis "*Thitting on a thee-thaw …*"

"*Quite so. Ath I woth thaying before I—thee-thawed …*" I lisped – hoping to be amusing but failing "*… it's not that I see Thor … or anything of that nature—I'm not some sort of naïve neo-pagan—but … the Norse gods have always been an eidetic form for me. The imagery of the Norse gods haunts my poetry and paintings as … emblems of tensile vibrancy. The question of their existence or non-existence is irrelevant to the world of colour, sound, and language I inhabit.*"

Claudette understood what I was saying to a certain extent "*But why are you never content to enjoy mythology without wanting to climb inside it and stretch it outward into the air you breathe?*"

"*Thought you weren't a poet, 'dette?*" I smiled. "*That was—very—nicely phrased.*"

"*Naturally.*"

---

5   Thor—as a fictional superhero—appears in Marvel Comics. The character first appeared in 'Journey into Mystery' in 1962, and was created by Stan Lee, Larry Lieber, and Jack Kirby. The character is loosely based on the Thor of Norse mythology.

"But as to an answer ... I'm here at Art School doing what I always imagined would be possible at a place like this – but, it turns out that I'm more or less on my own with it. I just do what I do and I'm moved by the things that move me. I've not got some huge logical thing about it. This is just—me—*being me ..."* Pause *"I'm just sorry that it irritates you. I'm not an intellectual – so I can only explain what I do in terms of poetry – and even that doesn't accord with anything linear."*

Claudette looked sad at that point – and seemed to regret the fact that she'd called my creative vision into question.

"I wish I could be more like you in these ways ..." she said *"... but I feel I'm happier being in the audience rather than standing on the stage or writing the play."*

Claudette suddenly backing down was touching and I appreciated it a great deal – maybe because of the contrast between that and her previous acerbic questioning. *"That's alright by me – but you might change your mind one day. It is*—always—*possible. It's just a matter of finding yourself on the threshold of enthusiasm for some stunning possibility that comes screaming out of nowhere. That can happen at any time. I can't believe you can see all these plays and not have plays waiting to jump out of you."*

"To hear you talk you'd think it was still 1967" Claudette smiled wanly. *"Not that that's a bad thing – but there aren't many people with that point of view any more. Maybe I*—will—*write a play one day – but no one will publish it."*

"Well, 'dette ... you're a pragmatist – and I have to admit that reality takes your side of the argument rather more often than mine."

Later that week Claudette read my poetry concerning how Odin, Thor, and the Midgaard Serpent manifested in the world as aspects of phenomenology. *"You don't mention them by name though"* Claudette questioned.

"No ... I'd consider that too gauche and cloying – maybe too much like childhood enthusiasm – or the Thor comics. I merely hint – and extend the hints thinly and sporadically. They're partial sightings in a wilderness of weather."

"Weather?"

"Yes ... they're the quality of rainfall in eddying gusts of wind ... the colour of the sky modulated by the rumbling of thunder ... the fleeting image of lightning as an after-image against a tangle of gnarled oaks."

"Oh ... I like that image."

"Coils of mist and fog that stain the air with damp persistence."

"That too – it's lovely."

"They're the weather conditions – and, the personal emotional contexts which dance with weather conditions."

"I can enjoy these images – but I can never understand anything you're telling me when you use poetry to explain" Claudette commented with a slight edge of irritation in her voice. "I suppose I shouldn't really ask you ... I always seem to have the same reaction don't I?"

There was no answer to that which wouldn't sound as if there was some kind of barrier or insoluble issue. "I'll attempt to be less opaque – but it's difficult ... my poetry's highly emblematic – but ... the emblems are ... amorphous. They've been sanded like my paintings – to reveal the over-painted layers that lie beneath."

"I can see that with ... painting – but ... with your words ... it's too difficult" Claudette yawned.

"Yes ... maybe this is something that only I can understand" I replied – carefully avoiding any mention of the girls.

"Don't you think that's ... a bit of a cop-out?" she yawned. "If you can't talk about it ... how ever do you think ...you'll be able ... to teach ... on a Foundation Course?"

"*Well, that could be a question ... but I'd be working with students in terms of*—their—*ideas rather than mine. I'd also be giving guidance with respect to technique as well. I guess if they wanted to ask me about my work ... they'd get the same answers you're getting – and some people ...*"
I paused to think of a way of avoiding citing the girls
"*... Derek Crowe—for example—seem to follow the drift in terms of what I explain.*"

I was cornered by my inability to tell Claudette that I had fascinating conversations with Rebecca, Meryl, and Penelope – and that they never seemed to find me incomprehensible. She seemed half asleep however, and so her standard cut and thrust had faded into a game of blind man's buff in a maze of beige flannel.

"*Derek Crowe understands you does he ...?*"

"*Yes – he isn't particularly thrown by metaphors ...*"

"*Metaphors ...?*" Claudette asked in a sleepy yet vaguely interrogative tone. I had no answer so she continued "*You have to be able to say ...*" she yawned "*... something...*" she yawned again "*... about your metaphors ...*"

"*Yes ... but I can only explain that with another metaphor.*"

"*Go on then.*"

"*They appear as opalescent ghosts from the canvas of chaos.*"

"*Mmmm ...*"

"*They appear outside the field of linear meaning—even though they inhabit the syntax of meaning—and ... I accept them as they are.*"

"*Mmmm ... opalescent ghosts ...*" she said very softly.

"*Yeah ... it's as if I see them through a nimbus of life images ... taken from the life that coils around me ... in my ... peripheral meanderings through time passing.*"

"*... meanderings ...*" she yawned "*... through ... time passing.*" Claudette repeated faintly with consummate flatness of affect.

"*Yes ... the interplay of the sense fields and the elements – they express themselves as weather conditions – as a language of dramatic flux.*"

"*Dramatic ... flux . .* " Claudette repeated extremely quietly.

"*Yes ... weather conditions as the language of the elements which can be modulated and modified as the grammar of the senses and the fields of the senses in ways that are unpredictable.*"

Claudette was asleep.

"I ... have ... become—exceedingly—*boring*" I enunciated entirely to myself. I felt colossally tedious. Even the subject of painting and poetry felt tedious. There was no joy in discussing painting and poetry when it was the cause of such turgid dialectics. I wondered why it was so easy and stimulating to converse with Rebecca, Meryl, and Penelope – and sometimes so difficult and enervating to be interrogated by Claudette. I kept hoping for a breakthrough – some point at which I'd hit the light switch and Claudette would understand Art nonconceptually. I tried hard with every explanation but my language always conspired to make me more opaque than before I started explaining.

I decided to wake Claudette when it was her regular time to go home – and began to sketch her as she reclined against the cushions. The shapes of the cushions made a curious interplay with the strangely coiled shape that Claudette created. There was something beautifully serpentine about it. I wondered what she found of interest in me, when I made no sense to her. I could find her fascinating when she talked on subjects that interested her. She could be delightfully witty – but ... 'I' ... often felt like a huge disappointment.

I'd have to discuss it with her at *some* point – but in the meantime—having finished my rough sketch—I'd sat gazing out of my attic window at the rampant colours of night. These colours never asked questions of me – or if they did, they never seemed dissatisfied with my silent answers.

There's hypnotism hiding in a tapestry of hail, / And consequential tokens of remembrances in braille / There is no contradiction in the plumage inky sheen, / Of ravens glowing in the dark of visions we have seen. / The conundrum's are rotating – within the same portrayal / But ravens will be with me – when the night sky sets its sail. Frank Schubert—Ravens—1974

13

the third year: september 1974 – december 1974

bower ashton – silk blancmange rottweiler

Well you've been living in the big city, broke and had to get along, /
But you can hurry back to Mississippi, cause Bilbo is dead and gone.
Andrew Tibbs—Bilbo is Dead—1947

I was sitting in my spacious attic room—early evening—looking out at the lazy tidal river. I often sat alone for short periods of time, when I wasn't working. I'd gaze out of the floor-level window next to my bed and marvel wordlessly at the rampant exquisiteness of existence. I sometimes felt overwhelmed by my good fortune. I was an Art student. I lived in a marvellous house with three good friends – three fellow Artists and each a fine conversationalist. What greater felicity could there be?

Distant sounds of Penelope, Rebecca, and Meryl occasionally spiralled upward – weaving through the polished beechwood banisters. Sound of an ironing board clapping closed. Sound of one hand clapping. Clinking wine glasses being set on the dining table. We'd be having dinner later. I wasn't cooking that evening – so I was biding my time. After dinner we'd play music together – then *I'd* be cookin'. I loved our musical evenings. Claudette had gone home for dinner in the late afternoon. She always spent Sunday evenings at home. We'd settled into an unusual pattern in which our times together were scheduled according to Claudette's sense of existential perfection. She'd always have Sunday dinner with her father and she liked early nights before Art School days. I fitted in with the scheme quite easily as I had a parallel life with Penelope, Rebecca, and Meryl.

an odd boy

Thoughts of my first year at Bower Ashton flickered – as if I were surveying my sojourn from a remote mountain peak. It was a disjointed picture show and I was haphazardly—though serenely—intrigued by the puissant pirouettes of the pastiche. Episodes flowed past each other—in and out of each other— and I realised it wasn't easy to understand the exact sequence of events. Each image was entire unto itself. Whilst absorbed in any one vignette, the others discreetly withdrew – as if they were conscious of their lack of relationship with previous images.
I had a picture in my mind of Claudette – not long after we'd got together. She'd been a diaphanous mystery. I remembered pondering the fact that I always ended up with Grammar School girls – or girls from private schools. Why was that? Maybe they liked the fact that I was literary – but in an obscure way that didn't match with the usual ideas of what that should mean.

Resting in the ambience of memory, a vignette of Claudette sailed up the river of disparate meanderings. It had been late one rainy Friday afternoon in February 1973. She'd entered stage left in a flurry of dusky green satin skirts and dark blue cloak—and asked *"Have you read 'Lord of the Rings'?"*

"No, 'dette – I haven't."

"The Hobbit?"

"No … haven't read that either. The breadth of my reading still leaves much to be desired."

The truth was that I had a prejudice against these books on the basis that every tarot dealing cardsharp on the astral plane had those books on their shelves.

I knew about *Gandalf's Garden* in London – but I'd not been there either, nor met Muz Murray.[1]

I'd kept these ideas behind my eyebrows and replied "*I'd certainly like to read 'The Hobbit' if it's a book you've enjoyed.*" I was not about to be closed-minded. I never enjoyed closed-mindedness in others so I was not going to hang onto churlish notions concerning JRR Tolkien's books. Claudette gave me the books and left for an appointment to look at the new leather upholstery her father was to install in her Silver Cloud.

So—there they were—the two books. I browsed 'Lord of the Rings' for a while – but decided I should probably start at the beginning. I was half way through the first chapter when Penelope came down from packing her rucksack. I was sitting in the living room with my pint of Mocha-Java coffee—acquired from the excellent coffee roasting shop in Park Street—and Penelope noticed the book I was reading. "*'dette's obviously assigned you your task for the weekend.*"

That caused me to emit a mild chuckle. "*For the month I should imagine.*"

Penelope didn't respond as light-heartedly as I'd expected. "*Well 'dette's not shy of educating you where she feels it necessary, is she?*"

That *was* true – but I was never peevish about it. "*I'm always interested to look into unknown areas*" I replied.

Penelope skewed her nose sideways, in token of something that was on her mind.

---

1 Gandalf's Garden – the name of a mystical community in London in the late 1960s. They ran a shop and magazine by the same name. Muz Murray – a prominent figure and editor of the magazine. The author met Muz Murray briefly in 1989 at Element Books in Shaftesbury Dorset and supplied a calligraphy for his book.

She said "*Well yes—that's what makes you such an interesting person—but 'dette could try to be more open to influence from you. I don't see her making quite as many changes or investigating as many new directions.*"

That was also true. "*Maybe it'll go that way in time*" I ventured. "*She's not really experienced much in the way of relationships before she met me – and maybe she'll grow into it.*"

Penelope looked a little grave and pensive. She agreed – but in a manner that left me with the impression she'd prevented herself taking the subject any further. "*Yes ... she's not used to compromising.*" Pause "*Anyhow, I'll see you on Sunday afternoon when I get back from Cirencester.*"

When I started the book – I wondered why I was reading a children's story. I found it odd – but persisted. After a while I discovered it was actually somewhat charming – especially against the sound of rain and wind whipping furiously outside. Rebecca and Meryl were going home for the weekend as well. All three were to attend a class reunion party in Cirencester. They bade me goodbye. "*I shall have leeks au gratin awaiting your pleasure on Sunday evening.*" They both smiled broadly and said they'd furnish the wine.

"*So?*" asked Claudette when she appeared several hours later "*How're you liking it? Where have you got to?*"

"Well ... the wizard and his goblin pals turned up. They've eaten the pixie out of house and home – and ... he's just imagined himself struck by lightning due to some tale about a dragon."

Claudette burst out laughing with that shake of the head usually reserved for incorrigible children. She decided that she had to sit me down and read it to me.

Right ... so Bilbo wasn't a pixie, he was a hobbit ... and they were dwarves, not goblins.

"The goblins will come later – and most amusing they will be, when we get there."

The Bilbo with whom I'd previously been more familiar was a senator from Mississippi who was not exactly popular in the black community in Chicago. Knowing the song 'Bilbo is Dead' I kept humming it in my mind whilst reading 'The Hobbit'. This didn't help me take the story too seriously. Claudette had an excellent reading voice however, and read the entire book to me over the course of the weekend. I soon forgot about the senator from Mississippi – and, as she read, I found I was enjoying the story more than I'd expected. I forgot it was a children's story and it stopped being 'a children's story'. It was simply a story. It was well constructed and developed as it proceeded. Claudette then went on to the 'Lord of the Rings' – and hearing her read became a fixture of our relationship.

I was suddenly roused from my reverie by the sound of my name and I rose quickly and clattered down the stairs. Penelope had called several times but I'd been so lost in musings that I'd not heard her immediately.

"*Where were—you?*" Penelope laughed as I plummeted into the ground floor hall as if I'd flown.

"*I was elsewhere ... sorry you had to keep calling ... I was recalling events – y'know ...*"

"*Yeah ... I like to do that sometimes. The past is quite mysterious – especially Badminton—I look back at it and wonder who I was—or where I was—or where it's all going.*"

"*Yeah ... where is it all going? Sometimes I wonder.*" Pause "*I think I've had so many directions ... and they all seem to take me to another crossroads ... it's curious.*"

Pause *"Don't get me wrong – it's a hell of a ride ... but apart from my work and living here ... it—is—sometimes hard to know exactly what's going on."*

Penelope smiled at me in a strange way. There were thoughts in her mind but she didn't express them. Instead she said *"We'll be five minutes yet—apparently—there's sauce to make."* She passed me a glass of wine. *"You may as well go watch the river—like you do—in the living room. We'll call you when we're ready."* We enjoyed preparing meals for each other – and so I went and sat in the vast armchair that overlooked the river. I sat pondering Sauron – the fellow from Lord of the Rings who made Hitler look like a rank beginner. What was in it for him – I wondered. He had power—sure—but he lived in a poisoned wasteland surrounded by terrified minions who made Todd Whelcomb look like the archangel Gabriel on a goody-two-shoes day. After dinner I mentioned Sauron and my thoughts on the subject of evil.

Rebecca said *"Sauron's the primeval evil—that's for sure—but the final section of the book when the hobbits return to the Shire is the most spine chilling episode for me. Saruman had turned the Shire into a miniature Mordor"* she continued. *"We're seeing that now with our own eyes. The very people who ought to be maintaining hard-won freedoms of personal eccentricity seem to be clamouring to re-form the establishment."*

"Yes—you're right—that's happening everywhere" I replied. *"Art Schools in Britain seem to be changing into academies of the establishment. If it weren't for Derek Crowe – I don't think I'd be enjoying the situation. Todd would be the standard-issue-mindset and we'd all be revamping margarine containers."*

"The School of Music and Drama's fine – but the sense of open-ended experimentation's no longer as fiery as it was when I visited in 1970" Meryl sighed.

"The thing that I find sad is that those who should be committed to freedom have turned out to be self-interested self-seeking fashion chamæleons who merge with whatever happens next."

"Is it as bad as that?" I asked. *"Can an entire philosophy of life—be it ever-so-obscurely defined—merely be another fashion."*

It took a long time for someone to answer. Rebecca twiddled her hair in the way she had when she was pondering. Eventually she said *"Yes ... I'm afraid it can."*

Penelope nodded *"The sense of possibility I felt in the '60s seems doomed somehow."*

We sat in silence for some time with that ominous thought.
"The world's not going to change in the way we thought—that's a shame—but individual human beings can still change" I eventually volunteered. *"Appreciation enables us to sidestep fashion."*

"Right?" Meryl asserted. *"We're still here. We haven't bought into the establishment – and we're all still free to explore."*

Suddenly—almost unanimously—we all felt it was time to retire for the night. We'd each had days of strenuous work and wanted a fresh start in the morning. I could have talked longer into the night – but then I was always inclined to go that extra mile when it came to conversation. I was actually grateful to get an early night as I fell asleep almost as soon as my head touched the pillow. I had strange dreams. I was back at Virginia Water School talking with Lindie Dale. I knew what had happened or was about to happen – but I didn't know whether the date was before of after the fateful interview with Brigadier and Mrs Dale. I was hoping it was before that point as then everything would be alright. Steve and Ron would be there too and I hoped the dream would continue long enough to meet them again.

Then I awoke feeling extremely strange. I'd had some sort of partial lucid dream. I partly knew I was dreaming – but not sufficiently to change the course of events. What was I doing having dreams of the distant past? It occurred to me that it wasn't optimal to be plunging back into a time—albeit in dreams —that was presenting itself as a golden age. I was happy where I was – even though I was aware that my relationship with Claudette was not comparable in most respects to my relationship with Lindie. I was not pleased with myself having such thoughts in my mind and wondered what I would do with them. Best forgotten. Life was what it was and my situation was just what was happening. After leisurely ablutions I decided that I was merely dawdling in the hangover of a dream and that it was meaningless to ponder further. Breakfast would cure that. I made my usual sprint down the stairs.

"You're going to break your neck one day" Penelope laughed as I sped past her bedroom. I got to the kitchen in time to help rustle up a batch of boiled eggs. I was good at boiling eggs as I used my mother's system. I had a German 'egg piercer' which made a tiny hole at each end of the egg. This—in conjunction with starting the eggs off in cold water—prevented the egg bursting when boiled. I volunteered to wash up after breakfast and left Rebecca and Penelope at the breakfast table continuing to converse. When I returned Rebecca was alone at the table and she returned to the subject of the previous evening.

"Penelope and I were talking about the way appreciation's become cramped or something … and the atmosphere of Music College becoming less experimental" Rebecca commented.

"Yeah … I see that happening too." Pause *"I've wondered about it and whether it's just Bristol."*

"I don't think so ... Sandra—an old friend of mine up at Leeds—says the same."

"Well ... it's different from Farnham – that's for sure."

"It almost seems like some kind of rejection of the '60s – as if you have to be embarrassed about that time just to show you're serious. Y'know experimentation seems to have run its course – like: 'We've done that, and now we have to do something stolid rather than continue to experiment.' It's as if there was a generation who were allowed to experiment – and we're not. Y'know they were the ones who—did that—and there's no need any more."

"Yeah ... there's a lot of 'normality' going on. It's strange because it's not coming from people like Derek Crowe. He actually tries to encourage us to experiment. At the Art School the conservatism's coming from the students – in the Illustration Department at least."

"Openness ..." Rebecca pondered "... is required in order to explore, otherwise stuckness occurs – and stuckness is what I see in too many people."

"Right ... that is the thing about Art School at least in terms of working with Derek Crowe. He's always open to exploration. Real appreciation isn't inclined to disappear just because the flock of normality-worshippers have ceased to appreciate whatever-it-is or whatever-it-happened-to-be. There'll always be people at Art Schools who remain open to experimenting – it's the nature of the place."

"I think that's maybe a little too optimistic" Rebecca commenced tentatively. "I'm not convinced that 'dette's as open to exploring as you are. She's not exactly open to change – especially in terms of getting into your life and interests. I guess that must be ... alright with you ..."

"Yeah ..." I commenced, feeling a little caught off guard.

"I once wished she'd avail herself of a little more of my spheres of interest – but ... I'm kind of resigned to the fact that 'dette's got her life worked out pretty exactly in terms of what interests her." Pause *"She feels she's only got space for what really suits her temperament – and I guess time's limited isn't it."* Pause *"Can't blame her for that."*

"Well ... I suppose not ..." Rebecca interjected *"... but what about —your—time Vic."*

"How d'you mean?" I asked – knowing exactly what she meant – but feeling a little awkward about the line of questioning.

"Well ... isn't that—also—limited?"

"Yeah ... my time's limited too – but 'dette doesn't prevent me enjoying what I enjoy or following the interests that are important to me."

"Y'know ... 'dette's my friend ... we've been friends since early on at Badminton ..." Rebecca responded noticing that I was slightly ill at ease *"... so ... I'm not—intending—to be critical ... it's just that you're—also—my friend ... and ... actually ... I'm kind of closer to you now ... than I am to 'dette – even though I have more history with 'dette."* Pause *"I don't really know what I'm trying to say exactly – but I just wonder sometimes whether the relationship with 'dette—actually—suits you. It doesn't seem like the kind of relationship you really want – not with what you've said about it ... and what you told us about ... what was her name?"*

"Lindie Dale" I replied – wishing the name hadn't sprung so quickly to my lips and wondering whether she intuited my recent dream. *"But—y'know—I only told you girls that because you asked me about my history of romance ... and ...you only asked me because 'dette told you I was touchy on the subject ... and I was sort of concerned to let you know that I wasn't touchy at all. As you know – I'll talk about anything. It's just that 'dette has some weird angle on it all."*

"Yeah well ... it's more-or-less obvious that she's jealous or twisted up about the fact that you've had so many more relationships than her." Pause

"In fact ... she's only had the one ... and I think that's a bit of an issue with her – especially as it ended so badly."

"It would seem so ..." Pause "... maybe she'll get over that ..."

"Well yeah you'd think she'd have got over it by now – because you have been very nice to her as far as I can see ..." Pause "... but—nonetheless —you two seemed to share so much at first ... and now ..."

"And now ..." I mused "...yeah ... right ... I can't deny that I'd prefer to have—more—in common with 'dette ... I suppose we don't spend enough time together ..."

"Yeah – but she does seem to organise it like that doesn't she."

"Yes she does ...yes she does ..." Pause "... but then ... I suppose ... that does seem to suit me—most of the time at least—as I put in a lot of hours working ..." Pause "... and ... I suppose that living here with you, Penelope and Meryl ..." I left the sentence unfinished as I heard sounds outside the front door.

Rebecca sat poised with an expression of curious expectancy and vague dread – but the door clicked open and Meryl strode in. She noticed the contemplative atmosphere.

"*Have you come to any conclusions since this morning?*" I asked in order to shift the subject away from Claudette.

"No ... not really ... is that what you and Rebecca have been talking about?"

Fortunately Penelope chose that moment to descend from her room on the 1st floor "Yeah ... well ... I've given the thing some thought since breakfast and it occurs to me that some people are re-investing in the whole bourgeois scene.

an odd boy

"*They'll do anything to make themselves seem relevant to whatever it is they think is important ... but—if—you really do experience your senses, you're not going to climb onto any bandwagon merely to make it in that corrupt corporate world.*"

"*Well right ...*" I replied. "*I've no intention of climbing on any bandwagon.*"

We all retired to the living room. Meryl sat down and stretched her legs out. "*Right ... the bandwagon's—owned—by the establishment*" Rebecca observed. "*All you can do is hire it ...*"

"*Yeah ...*" I replied "*... and pay for the hire with your integrity and the loss of genuine creativity.*"

We sat gazing through the living room window for a moment – and Rebecca said "*I hope we're not going to end up back in the '50s again – but I don't know what to do to fight against it.*"

"*It took me a long time to realise that you don't have to fight*" I interjected.

"*I don't think you have to fight anything*" Meryl agreed. "*You can't win anyway—not that way. Cultural revolutions never seem to work out for lasting freedom in the end.*"

That made perfect sense to me. "*The only way you can defeat the trend toward conformism is by staring it out in your own mind. It's a staring competition. We just have to stare it out.*" Meryl agreed emphatically and I concluded "*It's up to us to be as we are – and to continue being as we've been since we first discovered the freedom of our senses.*"

No use blaming Devil ... No use polarising personal phenomena, as if 'nice' and 'nasty' were menu options at 'Restaurant Reality' ... It's that Silk Blancmange Rottweiler! You gotta stare that thing in the eye!
The author—Silk Blancmange Rottweiler—1974

14

the third year: january 1975

bower ashton – waterloo sunset

I was sitting in my room looking out at the river. The melody line from the Kinks' song—Waterloo Sunset—stole across my mind *'dirty old river must you keep rolling – rolling on through the night'*.[1] It was one of Lindie Dale's favourite songs. The lyrics conjured something approaching deep contentment – even though the melody line could sometimes bring tears to my eyes. Not on this occasion however. Waterloo Sunset imbued the River Avon with an ambience passing strange. Something about the silence of the moon. The quiet of the room. Vague flames of distant stars. Slow drifting quirks – the tidal river shimmying through infinitesimal shades of indigo-grey. Occasional memory-figments surfaced – independent of any obvious connectivity. Memories were anomalous flatfish. They'd been scouring the river bed for nourishment and—suddenly surfeited—they hit the surface of the present as … flying fish.

I decided I'd apply to the Royal College of Art. Obtaining a 1st or an Upper 2nd degree[2] result would get me there. Derek Crowe thought I'd get an upper 2nd without doubt. "*It's not something I can personally guarantee …*" he said "*… but, I'd be very surprised if you didn't get a 1st.*"

He thought it was a good idea to apply to the RCA.

---

1   Ray Davies—The Kinks—Waterloo Sunset—Something Else—1967
2   BA and BSc university degrees in Britain are awarded as following: 1st, Upper 2nd, Lower 2nd, and Pass.

"You enjoy the Art School environment and I think you should make full use of what is available. The grants ³ are there and all you have to do is continue in the direction you have taken."

"Marvellous – and yes, I really do enjoy the Art School environment. I can't think of anywhere I'd rather be. The first day at Farnham Art School was a revelation. I would liked to have lived there – or at least close enough to have walked there everyday."

"It's not as easy as it used to be to slot into a lecturing rôle …" Derek replied and I could see that it gave him no pleasure to add this cautionary note *"… but I'm sure you have the tenacity to find yourself a position. The only thing is … that it might not be Bristol. How would that be?"*

"Well … that'll have to be as it is." I could tell what was on his mind – but I said nothing. I knew Claudette was married to the idea of staying in Bath and working in theatre there and in Bristol – so I knew there'd be some choices somewhere down the line.

"I think I'd like Falmouth, of all places. I've always loved Cornwall and I can see myself settling down there."

"I've got contacts in Falmouth Art School, when the time comes" Derek responded. *"They might well like the idea of someone with an MA from the RCA – especially on the Foundation Year."* That was excellent news – although what it meant for my relationship with Claudette was entirely uncertain. Long distance relationships were not ideal – and something in the back of my mind was not convinced that Claudette was entirely in tune with me. Her life was a thing of her own creation – and it didn't seem amenable to alteration.

---

3   Grants – financial education support.

"*What I'd like most ...*" I said to Derek "*... would be to be sitting where you are—somewhere—and offering the help and encouragement you've always shown me.*"

Derek looked moved by that comment and said "*I'm only too happy to have made your time at Bower Ashton a good experience.*"

"*It's been more than a good experience ...*" I replied "*... it's been ideal. The only aspect missing has been a peer group – but I seemed to find that anyway. And ... I think that's really taught me something.*" Derek tilted his head and adjusted an eyebrow in token of a question, so I continued "*I've learnt that you can always find situations that suit – if you're open to what is happening.*"

"*You've obviously made good friends with ...*"

"*... Penelope, Rebecca, and Meryl.*"

"*Yes indeed—charming names, they would have come back to me eventually —their music and drama studies have certainly enriched your experience of illustration – and I have no doubt that you have provided an interesting sounding board for them too.*"

I admired Derek Crowe as a human being – and could think of nothing better than becoming some other version of what he was. I admired his kindness and openness – his belief in education for its own sake. It would be marvellous to facilitate opportunities for others as he'd facilitated them for me – and, of course, I'd continue to write poetry, paint, and play music. The idea of Falmouth betokened that I'd need to talk to Claudette ...

The last glimmers of evening light eddied into my mind – and the flying fish of memory followed as the glimmering fish scales of dreams. Claudette liked the idea of my becoming an Art School Foundation lecturer and thought it would suit me well.

"*It will be a matter of a vacancy coming up at Bower Ashton won't it?*" she asked.

an odd boy

"Well yes ... it would be good if it did – but ... what if that doesn't work out?" She was silent for a little too long – so I continued "*I think ... it's going to be a matter of finding a vacancy—somewhere—maybe, anywhere. If a vacancy comes up at Bower Ashton, I'll certainly apply – but I don't think I could sit waiting for that to happen; not if it took too long.*"

"*How long is too long?*"

"*Too long ...*" Pause "*... too long—might—be a matter of months 'dette ...*"

"*What!?*" she gasped.

"*Well ... it could be a year – or even years, couldn't it?*" Pause "*I'd have to take a place wherever a vacancy came up.*"

"*So you'll apply for other places straight away?*"

"*I have to be realistic about it – these places don't come up that often.*"

Claudette looked strained at that point. "*You—do—find odd moments to be rational. I thought you were going to live in Bath with me.*"

I was speechless for a moment or two. 'Live in Bath with me.' That was a peculiar description of what she really had in mind.

"*Well certainly—if—that's possible ... but what we'd like and what's possible, might not coincide. We can try to coincide – but you're as determined to live in Bath as I am to be a Foundation lecturer.*" Pause "*I mean – you'll sit it out in Bath waiting for a theatre opening – because you want to live in your family home. I can't do that. Bath is too expensive and I don't have the deposit to get a mortgage, even—if—I landed a job at the Art School. I wouldn't be able to go home and hang out there 'til something opened up here ... especially if it took too long. I couldn't let time tick by like that.*"

"*So ... what d'you mean by too long?*"

"*That's hard to say ... Besides, I'll be in London at the RCA and I have no idea what might arise out of that situation. But at the end of my time at the RCA – what if there's a connection and an opportunity I can't refuse?*"

Claudette snorted "*It's purposeless to speculate about the future in this way.*"

"*I agree entirely – but ... what about your future speculation about us both living in Bath?*"

"*That's different. That's not speculation – that's talking about an ideal.*" She'd explained the idea to me on several occasions. She was entirely committed to living with her father and there was no possibility of me sharing that domestic arrangement.

"*Buying a house on the opposite side of your street ... is ... wonderfully picturesque.*"

"*And why not? Visiting each other on a daily basis—back and forth—as the mood takes us. We'd be able to wave to each other from our front windows – wouldn't that be jolly?*" She had the whole thing worked out. I was slightly baffled by the idea.

"*Y'know ... a situation like that would be—exceptionally—difficult to arrange. The chance of the house opposite—or any house in your street— coming up for sale at the right time, is even more remote than my getting a Foundation lecturing post at the time I'll need it.*" Pause "*Y'know, 'dette, this 'two houses idea' is more than a little impractical – and ... it's not exactly ... my idea of a long-term living situation.*"

"*I think you're – suffering from some remnant of conventionalism. You—of all people—should be able to broaden your horizon of what's possible.*"

"*Maybe I'm more conventional than you think ...*" Pause "*... maybe I'm more conventional than—I—think ... but ... I'm just speaking about how I feel. I don't have a fixed point of view about it.*"

"It could be perfect—and you might be surprised—you can't say that without trying it" Claudette insisted.

"Trying it ...yeah ... well ..." I replied. *"I suppose ... if I won the pools*[4] *I could—try—it ... not that I play the pools anyway ..."* Pause *"... but ... the financial viability of it lives in the world of day dreams ..."* Pause *"If we were both rich, it'd be simple. I don't know exactly how rich you'll be at some point – but I get the impression that you'll be fine whatever happens."* Pause *"You'll inherit your family home."*

"Well maybe next door might not work out – but it could be a house in Bath—somewhere."

"Yes ... it could. Although Bath is more expensive than Bristol – and even Bristol is expensive. There ... are cheaper areas in Bristol of course ...Totterdown—is—on the Bath side of Bristol ... I suppose ..." Claudette looked hopeful at that point – but I'd left my sentence unfinished. The image in my mind was not workable. Being some kind of poor cousin was not an intelligent solution in the long term. Nor was it emotionally feasible. I could imagine the conversations:

'So ... how long have you lived in this lovely House in Bath, 'dette?'

'Oh all my life – and I do so love it here. I have—all—sorts of plans for it.'

A patronising eye turns to me 'And you Vic ... 'dette tells me you have your own place – an artist's studio I believe?'

'Yes ... it's a two-up, two-down hovel in Totterdown. It has a charming outside lavatory and a stunning view of a railway line. I'm hoping to be able to repair the roof in a few years if I can sell a few paintings.' This would be greeted with a condescending smile 'Excellent arrangement ...'

---

4   The pools – the football lottery in Britain.

No—*that*—it was not ... but the scenario amused me.

Bath and Bristol were expensive towns and Falmouth was not. A pleasant home in Falmouth was a workable proposition for someone who could get a deposit together with a few years of work. Bristol—let alone Bath—however, was not a sensible proposition whichever way you looked at it. Then there was Claudette and whether our relationship was actually viable.

As time proceeded I felt increasingly uneasy about the viability of our long-term future. We had our good times – but there were issues that refused to make either emotional or practical sense to me. Claudette's plan would work out fine for her as she'd inherit her home. I didn't have that luxury or anything remotely close.

"Can you explain—one more time—why the idea of sharing the proposed apartment in your father's house is out of the question?" This question always upset Claudette.

"Because it will only be a—real—apartment when the external stairs are built that'll cut it off from the rest of the house – and then there'll be a kitchen to be installed ... and that can't happen—that—soon. Until then my father's adamant that he—never—wishes to meet any person other than—me—in his own home. You know what he's like now – so you must see that it isn't possible."

"Yes ... I know what he's like ... and to be honest I don't think I'd feel—that—comfortable around him either. I'd have no problem living in rented accommodation for a while – that's not really ... what I'm thinking about."

She asked me what I was thinking about.

"Well ... I am wondering what the problem will be ... once there—is—an independent apartment. I'd imagine ... it would be pretty large ... being on the top two floors – or three if you count the attic."

an odd boy

"*We have different tastes ...you know as well as I do!*" she exclaimed in what seemed to be high anxiety. "*You know that I love my environment! And you'd want to change that! And that wouldn't work for either of us! And why would you want to compromise your tastes and interests!?*"

"*Right ...*" I felt like saying that I'd already compromised my interests. Penelope, Rebecca, and Meryl had commented on it – but to mention that would have opened an enormous can of worms.

I decided to stare into space instead. Having stared into space for some minutes, I said "*Y'know ... the question of not compromising my tastes ... well ... it works for clothes. It works for the things I can afford – but houses—or even apartments—don't fall into that category.*" Pause "*I think you—know—that.*"

"*Yes—but ...*" she launched in "*... it's such a—*blinkered*—view—especially—for you! It's as if you're preaching predestination and you're not supposed to believe in that!*"

"*True ...you've remembered well.*" Then I burst into song "*I don't believe in destiny. I don't believe in fate. I don't believe in providence, – I don't believe in 'me' ...*"

"*Yoko and me ... very droll I'm sure.*" Pause "*... but song lyrics apart – you agree that you can't know how the future might work out and what might become possible.*"

"*Quite right, 'dette ... I don't know—what—might be possible in the future. I'm talking about what happens after the RCA – when I'm applying for lecturing posts. Everything's fine at the moment because I share a lovely house in Hotwells.*"

"*Well, I arranged—that—for you didn't I?*" Claudette almost snapped.

"Yes you did ... and I remain—extremely—grateful ... but when the tenure's up – I'll be back in bedsit-land again – and to be frank I'd rather go back home and get a job on a building site before moving to London. You know how it is with work down here – I can never find anything. I've stayed down last Summer and only managed to pick up crumbs of work here and there. That's meant my having to subsist on quite a miserable grant ... I could have added to that a lot more if I'd gone back to Farnham last Summer. You know my father's situation. He's classed in an earning bracket that means he has to subsidise me – but he cannot do that because of the alimony he has to pay ... and for incomprehensible reasons the grant authorities refuse to take that into account."

I was supposed to tailor myself according to what was best for Claudette – but how was I to point that out, without being unnecessarily hurtful to her. The approach that spared her sensibilities however, was the same thing that neglected mine.

The very thing that, makes you rich – makes me poor. Sidney Bailey—The Very Thing That Makes You Rich—performed by Ry Cooder—1979

Claudette was nebulous in the realms of practical life – and I was epistemologically nebulous in the realms of Art.

"I can't understand why you can be so infinitely abstract when it comes to painting and poetry – but you can't be imaginative about life. You always want to see the difficulties and the reasons why things won't be as we want them to be."

"Well ... as you want them to be." Pause *"I'm not trying to muscle in on your future apartment or anything – but I have the feeling that you want me—at your disposal—but also at a convenient distance."*

"You know perfectly well, that—that's—not got anything to do with it. I just don't believe in all this nicey-nicey nest-of-tables, ducks-on-the-wall, happy-families, home-sharing business – it's both puerile and Palæolithic."

an odd boy

"*I don't quite see myself as the archetypal caveman*" I laughed –the irony of her statement being too bizarre not to comment.

"*As you well know, we each live our own lives at home—and, as you also know, I have no choice. I get no grant.*"

"*That's true, 'dette—that's true.*" Pause "*I—do—get a grant – but … I also have to work in holidays or I'd never make it through the year – especially with theatre tickets to consider. And …*" I empathised before she could complain "*… I'm entirely happy to earn money for theatre tickets. I—love—the theatre.*" Pause "*That's the thing really … I—do —have choices.*" Pause "*I've had personal choices since I took weekend work at the age of 14.*"

Claudette looked as if she were about to speak again – but I shook my head "*I've not finished yet, 'dette.*" Pause "*You see, you have your vision of the future – and you want me to fit in with that. That's not a great problem—if—it's possible … even though it's not my ideal – but I don't think it's viable to let your idea of 'our future' prevent me from choices I might—have—to make. If I'm offered a post in Falmouth, Carlisle, or Edinburgh – I can't turn them down in case a post at Bristol comes up, especially if I have to live in a bedsit—on the adjectival dole* [5]*— waiting for it.*"

"I see that … the thing I don't understand is that you're unprepared to dream with me about a future that—could—be."

"I'd be more prepared if it looked as if you wanted to help make it possible – but you have your fixed notions of what's impossible – for you."

Claudette went silent and glum – so I sat and waited to see what she'd say next. "*It's … that you seem to want to brutalise my dreams*" she finally asserted.

---

5 Dole – Social Security unemployment benefit in Britain.

"No … I'm sorry it feels that way to you …" Pause "… but—I—don't want to be brutalised to support your dreams. My experience of life—so far —has been … that—very—few dreams come true. Even the dreams that —have—come true haven't lasted long. I'm not complaining and I'm— not—being pessimistic. I'm just talking about my experience. Unless you find yourself in a dream—quite accidentally—they tend to be rare."

"What about working for your dreams?" Claudette asked in a slightly stentorian manner. "You said you can—always—make your dream real if you work hard enough."

There was an implication in what she'd said that I couldn't leave unchallenged. "I've worked hard—all—my—adjectival—life, 'dette."

"But not at school by all accounts!" she rebuked. "You told me you only did what you wanted to do!"

"I didn't—want—to work every weekend at Farnham hospital or the Army kitchens. And, I never—said—Netherfield School was 'my dream'. Art School's my dream now – and so I work hard at that, as you know. If I get to be a Foundation Year lecturer I'll count it as a dream come true – but 'til then it's only a dream. I don't mean to turn this into some kind of proletarian rant … but have you—ever—had to earn money? I bought my own clothes from the age of 14 – so … if you please, I'd rather not be hauled over the coals for not working for a dream."

Claudette backed off. She could tell I'd become somewhat adamant. "That's fair … you work much harder than I do" she admitted. "And you've worked harder than I've ever done … to earn money – but you should take confidence in that in terms of the future."

"I could do …" I sighed "… but I've learnt that hard work and effort aren't always enough. Being a Bluesman was a dream. I invested a great deal of work in that – but the dream died. I'm not complaining about that either …" Pause

"You have to play the cards as they're dealt. I've had my share of hearts—as you've pointed out—but diamonds have—never—come my way unless I've—bled—for them with my time."

Claudette found my pragmatism a little hard-edged and started looking tearful – so I concluded *"Alright ... I don't know—everything—and ... maybe I've gotten a little closed down ..."* Pause *"Let's go for the impossible dream then. You'll get your dream theatre job and I'll get my dream lecturing job ... at Bower Ashton. I'll find a house right across the street from you, with a mortgage I can afford from selling my raven paintings ... because I'll have become a famous artist or something."*

"So ..." Claudette almost croaked *"...you see! It isn't impossible!"*

"No ... it's not impossible in a world where everything's possible. Nothing's impossible apart from avoiding death." Death was another subject that Claudette didn't like to discuss – so the subject was neatly placed back in its box.

When the girls heard about Claudette's housing idea – Meryl looked a little shocked. *"I hope you don't mind my saying this ... but – I can't help wondering why you think the idea is workable. I think 'dette's lost her marbles."*

Rebecca and Penelope had 'concerned looks' on their faces which I found touching. *"I appreciate your being frank with me – although I'd rather you were Penelope, Rebecca, and Meryl."*

They laughed but not as mirthfully as usual. *"Sorry – I didn't intend to be flippant. It's just that I don't really know what to say. I probably agree with you – but that puts me in a strange situation. Maybe the idea sounds workable to me from the position of living in this house with the three of you—because you're my friends—and ..."*

Rebecca raised her eyebrows *"Don't get us wrong. We don't want to make problems where there aren't any – but …you—do—tend to go along with things as far as 'dette's concerned."* They all nodded.

"Right … well … I do like to be amenable … where it's possible" I said – wondering slightly at the fact that I'd been observed in relation to Claudette.

"That's one of the reasons you're so easy to live with" said Penelope.

Meryl nodded *"Right—absolutely—when 'dette first suggested renting this house with you, we didn't think it was such a great idea – but it's turned out to be brilliant—we love you being here. You're such a great friend, it's hard to imagine living without you."* Meryl blushed slightly and got up to open another bottle of wine.

"I'm really touched by this—don't get me wrong either—I understand what you're saying and … if pushed … I'd have to agree …" Pause *"… entirely … I suppose … I'm simply floating—at the moment—in this … field of implausibility. I'm … wondering which way it'll all go."* Pause *"I think that decisions—are—going to have to be made at some point … and —when it comes to decisions—I know I—can—make them. I can— always—be decisive – even if it's painful."* Pause *"I don't allow myself to be tortured by irreconcilable alternatives."*

"It's a relief to hear that" Penelope stated, looking me square in the eyes.

"I just … want to give Claudette the chance to see—for herself—how her plans'll fare at the hands of reality. I don't want her to get the idea that I'm steering the situation away from her notion of what's possible. She'll see for herself what happens. I mean … if Derek can help me with contacts at Falmouth – there's no way I'm—not—going to apply for a post there … and …" Pause *"… then … that'll have to be … goodbye."*

an odd boy

Helen McGillvray—was—right about long distance relationships. Even though I didn't like it at the time, I could see she'd been right.

We talked on for a while. I had no absolute notion of what would happen in the future. "*If you go to the RCA, you'll be in London for two years*" Meryl commented. "*Does 'dette plan to visit you at weekends? 'cause I know her father's not going to have you or anyone else staying over at his house. He doesn't even have relatives stay at his house. He doesn't even—see—relatives. He doesn't—see—anyone.*"

"*That's certainly true ... her father runs a tight ship*" I said. "*That's probably where Claudette inherits her singular notion of residential singularity.*"

Meryl spluttered with irritation. "*Tight ship's nothing in it – it's the bloody Marie Celeste. The man's a loony.*"

Rebecca nodded sagely "*We did point this out to 'dette ... that she was like her father – but she refuses to see—*any—*similarity.*"

Penelope looked to me for some comment and all I could find to say was "*Yes ... well ... I think I can feel three years of random images suddenly coming together ... the jigsaw puzzle's coming into focus – and the picture's not something I'd buy if I saw it hanging in a gallery.*"

They laughed but not excessively – as they knew I was trying to slip away from the facts.

"*I think it's great that you can be humorous about the situation ...*" Penelope remarked charitably "*... but the fact that 'dette's in denial about certain things that have a direct effect on your life and future together worries us – being that we're your—*friends—*and we care about you.*"

They were my closest friends. I told them as much. They were actually closer friends than Claudette. Saying that however, would have been loaded with ideas that were too poignant to discuss.

Penelope returned to the subject *"You know ...'dette's never been keen on travel and she's horribly tied to her own bed and home comforts. She's not even as wild about staying over here as she was when you first moved in. She always likes to get home at night. ... now ... that wouldn't have suited me."*

I'd already put all these facts together – but having them brought to my attention made me uneasy. *"No ... I know that I'm floating – but I'm not exactly rudderless. I've not agreed to this separate houses idea – I've just said I'd no overriding objection to living in parallel – but you're not to worry that I can be talked into anything emotionally impossible. That's not on the cards. I may seem to be—too amenable—but I'm only ever as amenable as it seems kind to be ... and ...'kind' eventually has to include me."*

"Well ... if that's how it is with you ... and you—are—the master of your own destiny" Penelope said. *"I'm a lot less worried about you."*

"I'm glad you're going to apply to the RCA too" said Meryl. *"I'm sure you'll be accepted after what Derek Crowe said about your work."*

"Yes ... I think being in London will probably change things. That's why I'm in no hurry to ... well y'know 'dette tends to get upset if I get on one of my 'realism jags' as she calls them."[6]

Meryl shook her head *"Well yeah ...'dette never likes realism when it's not the reality she wants. She's watched her father create his own bubble so she sees no reason she can't have the bubble she wants."*

"So anyway ..." I said to change the subject. *"I'm on course ... and things'll fall out as they will ... because of that."*

The rain had increased and become a noisy downpour.

---

6   Jag – an intense period of indulgence in a particular activity or emotion. 19th Century US colloquialism.

an odd boy

"*I love the sound of the rain …*" Pause "*Anyhow … I just don't want to pre-empt what happens … when it's not necessary – especially with the degree shows coming up – 'dette's quite tense about it …*"

"*Yeah …*" Rebecca sighed "*… last time I saw 'dette – she was a little more anxious than I've ever seen her before. I don't think she's happy with what her show is going to look like. I think she realises she should have worked a little harder.*" Pause "*I think that's why she's sometimes a bit touchy about how hard you work – even though it doesn't impinge on her.*"

"*Yeah …*" I replied. "*I'd worked that out – more-or-less …*"

"*So …*" Penelope interjected – changing the subject "*You'll be going back to Farnham at the end of term?*"

"*Yes … I'll be going back to Farnham … well … as soon as the lease is up here – and then … well … it'll be what it is.*"

"*… be what it is …?*" Penelope asked with a curious expression.

"*Well yes … I'm—not—going to get a bedsit in Bristol. That would be absurd. The only rational option is to go home and find a job for the Summer. It wouldn't make—any—sense at all to stay here. I've already made my life difficult staying in Bristol last Summer when I could have got labouring jobs round the Farnham area. I have a lot of building site contacts there – and I had a decent reputation as a brick hodder.*"[7]

"*Oh dear …*" Meryl winced. "*Isn't that rather … backbreaking work …?*"

"*Some people say a man's made out of mud – but a man is made outta muscle and blood—muscle and blood, skin and bone—a mind that's weak and a back that's strong – Ah 16 tons and whaddya get …*"

---

7 Brick hodding – carrying bricks up ladders on building sites in a device called a 'hod', a 'v' shaped container on a pole.

"*You must have a song for everything!*" Meryl laughed. "*But seriously, that—is—very hard work.*"

"*Yeah ... can't deny it – but it's a friendly atmosphere.*"

"*Wouldn't it be easier to take factory work?*"

"*No ... the work on building sites is far more humane. It isn't as full-on high-pressure as it is in factories. The foremen are friendly too – not like factories where they crawl to the boss and lord it over the workers. I'd far rather have intermittent hard work in a friendly atmosphere than work at Stalag Arbeit ...y'know what was written in wrought iron over the gates of Auschwitz? ...'Arbeit Macht Frei' ...*"[8]

"*Ouch ...*" Penelope winced. "*I think I prefer 'le travail rend libre'*"

"*Y'know I've picked up a whole slew of French from you three—and 'dette —it always intimidated me a little when I was at Frensham Art School because they threw it around there sans la pitié*[9]*... as it were.*"

"*So much for the mind that's weak then ...*" Meryl grinned.

"*Maybe ... but I'm still not the academic or intellectual that ...*" I cut myself short. I was going to say 'that 'dette would prefer' but decided the discretion was the better part of verbal incontinence. Rebecca knew the end of the sentence immediately and carried on where I left off.

"*That ...'dette wishes you were ...?*"

---

8   Arbeit Macht Frei – work makes you free. It was placed over entrances to several Holocaust concentration camps. The slogan derives from the title of a novel by German philologist Lorenz Diefenbach ('Arbeit macht frei' – Erzählung von Lorenz Diefenbach—1873) in which gamblers and swindlers find salvation through labour. In 1928 it was adopted by the Weimar Government as a slogan extolling the virtue of their public works programmes to end unemployment. It continued when the Nazi Party came to power in 1933. The Auschwitz sign was made by prisoners in 1940.
9   Sans la pitié – without pity, mercilessly.

"Yes ... that is what I was going to say ... Going back to Farnham will mean that I'll also be able to help my mother out – y'know, looking after my father." Penelope, Rebecca, and Meryl sat looking at me as if I was a rare creature in a zoo – so I said "*Y'know ... life mainly works by itself. The times when you have to intervene don't happen too often in my experience. I tend to trust life to be what it is. That doesn't mean that I live by default – but that ... I don't find the need to paddle when I'm in a canoe that's moving with the current – and when the current's taking me where I've decided to go.*"

"*That sounds like a good idea – but don't forget to look at the scenery*" said Meryl. "*You wouldn't want to miss anything ... would you ...*"

Mysterious. "*No ... I'll keep my eyes wide ... the chance might not come again.*"

I went to bed early. I felt in need of private thoughts. I lay looking out at the points of light that dotted the river. The melody line from Waterloo Sunset stole across my mind once again: '*dirty old river you keep on rolling – rolling on through the night.*' Wordless sadness – wordless apart from the memory of Lindie. A melody line like that could bring tears to the eyes.

On this occasion it did.

15

the third year: february 1975 – march 1975

bower ashton – you 'girls' are quite the sensation

"*I would be most interested*" Derek smiled "*if you would tell me about these Bacchanalian amphibians.*" Derek Crowe was always enthusiastic about my projects and keen to help in any way he could. One 'illustration' I devised was a series of photographs of a bronze sculpture I created. Derek arranged my time in the sculpture Department and I was there for two weeks. The result was entitled 'Frogs in Amplexus'. It depicted two frogs in blissful union standing on a hemisphere. I planted the finished sculpture in a shallow pond infested with vivid green weed and photographed it from a variety of angles – some seen through willow branches. The photographs illustrated a piece of extended prose-poetry which explored the idea of amphibian perception; not in a zoological sense – but in the sense of living in two worlds.

"*Well ... the idea arose out of a kind of pivotal notion. It's something I've felt most of my life—or at least since I first started performing in public—the notion of celebrity and anonymity. I've come to feel as if I live in both worlds simultaneously – it's just that celebrity is now simply unmanifested and ... most likely it's going to remain so.*"

"*And this relates to the frogs in some way ...*" Derek interjected.

"*Yes ... the frogs are content with their situation as amphibians – and I'm also content being amphibian.*"

"*Ah ... I see—dipping in and out of the waters of celebrity ...*"

an odd boy

"*Yes – but at the moment I'm* ..." Pause "... *well* ... *I no longer feel trapped on either side of the illusion. Fashions come and go. If you're in the right place at the right time – and if your passion for the Arts dovetails with something that's gaining momentum, you fly – and if not* ... *then you simply get on with your life.*"

"*That sounds healthy to me* ..." Derek nodded "... *but* ... *what about choice?*"

"*Choice?*" Pause "*That's an interesting question* ... *choice—for me, in terms of life—mainly seems something of a luxury.*"

"*Really?*" Derek looked incredulous.

"*Yes—well—that's what it feels like* ..." Pause "... *it's not that I've not —made—choices. I've made some important choices. I chose to apply here and I'm choosing to apply to the RCA – but beyond that* ... *I make choices and then roll with the changes. It seems that the results of choice leave you with situations – and then you roll with the results.*" Pause "*It seems that once choices are made* ...*you're then only free to the extent that you can adapt to the outcome.*" Pause "*Which is a limited kind of freedom.*"

"*The die is cast?*"

"*More-or-less* ...*yes.*" Pause "*I seem* ... *to make a choice and—then—a whole story commences – and, the only way to change it, is to take an entirely different direction.*"

"*Somehow* ...*Vic* ... *I don't think you're talking about your work* ..." Pause "...*your work seems entirely self-directed* ... *I think you're talking about other parts of your life.*"

"*Sorry—yes—the choices in my work are all open ended* ..." Pause "... *my work here seems entirely free and I feel open to explore without any sense of getting locked into anything.*" Pause

"You're right ... it—is—my life that seems a little locked in. It's not a—deal—though ... although I do sometimes wonder about life in general and where it could go." I was actually thinking of my situation with Claudette – but it didn't feel right talking with Derek as if he were a marriage guidance counsellor. "You see ... having been on the brink of celebrity once ... I always find myself wondering what life would have been like if Ron and Steve hadn't died."

"That's natural" Derek smiled. "I expect that idea will always be with you. I don't think it's possible to forget such friends or such circumstances. Is that what you meant by 'flying' in what you said before about choice?"

"Yes ... flying is something that—has—to involve choice – or the flight's as much of a prison as anything else. But as you know ... the prime movers have the airways mapped. They've put me in holding patterns in the past – so that's just as likely to happen in the future."

"How does that feel to you though?"

"It feels like a space-between-illusions – but I'm no longer interested in the oscillating illusion of failure and success. I've followed that too long."

"You'll treat those two impostors just the same?"[1] Derek replied.

"Yes ... that's a basic Buddhist principle ... and one I try to remember. Failure and success—as a pair—are a way you can make yourself crazy ... there are others like shame and fame; gain and loss; meeting and parting; pleasure and pain ..."

"It might be hard perhaps to live cheerfully regarding them all as imposters ..."

---

1 Allusion to Rudyard Kipling's poem 'If' '*If you can meet with triumph and disaster, And treat those two impostors just the same.*'

"Well ... it's not that success and pleasure are to be avoided – it's more the struggle that needs to be avoided. That is to say doing anything to avoid pain or gaining pleasure. It's the tension between the two and making them your master. For example, Derek ... being a conscientious objector during WWII can't have been easy ... so you didn't make a choice that involved avoiding pain."

"Ah ... I see, that now makes complete sense."

"For me ... there's no choice about that if you want to remain sane" I laughed. "Not that I ever wanted to be rich – I just want to function – within whichever Art will let me through the door."

"It's not Art that stands as the door keeper ..." Derek mused "... it's fashion and the franchises people fabricate. I think you—will—open the right door in the end. You're far too persistent to fail at leading a creative life – and the RCA will be a rewarding experience – I have no doubt about that. Maybe you need to be in London ...yes ... I can see you living there and meeting the kind of people with whom you could exchange creative ideas."

"That's what I'd want to be doing – and ... maybe ... Penelope, Meryl, and Rebecca will pass through – I have some idea that we could get together on some kind of multimedia project in the years to come."

"And Claudette ...?" Derek enquired tentatively.

"Claudette's not so ..." I was going to have to choose my words carefully "... hugely interested in multi-media projects." Pause "She mainly wants a career in theatre wardrobe ... I know that's creative – but she doesn't really want to instigate anything personal." Derek sat observing me in a kindly way – as if he knew I had more to say and was waiting for me to be more open. "We've talked about it ... and ... although I've had all sorts of ideas about incorporating costume into my work ... she really only wants to deal with costume in the context of plays."

"*Ever thought of writing a play?*" he asked – diplomatically refraining from asking anything further about Claudette.

"*Yes ...*" I chuckled somewhat grimly "*... but Meryl's more interested in that than Claudette ...*" Pause "*... far more interested. I'll be keeping in contact with Penelope, Rebecca, and Meryl when I leave and we plan to work together whenever we get the chance. I think play writing would be a bit of a leap for me. I've never written dialogue and I've never written—anything—with a narrative.*" Pause "*So ... I'd have to spend a fair few years developing that before I'd feel confident about involving Meryl.*"

"*Yes ... writing plays is certainly a different area of skill – but you have a natural flair with language. Once the degree show is over you could try your hand at it and see what happens.*"

"*That—is quite an idea. I think I've taken poetry as far as I can take it at the moment – lyrics too. Trying my hand at a play could be—just— what I need to develop a new direction. I think I really—need—a new direction ... something challenging and ... open ended.*"

Derek Crowe was not tainted by fashion. He was an individual. Over the three years at Bower Ashton, Claudette and I were periodically invited to dinner by the Crowes. They were splendid evenings because Derek and Susan were more of *the lost time* than the students they taught. They could discuss the Arts and philosophy. They were keenly interested in ideas and seemed entirely open to examining any new point of view on any topic. They liked us and regarded us as friends. I considered that a privilege because I had a great deal of respect for them. The Crowes were not famous – but they *had* what the famous *had*. They had much more in certain respects. They were creative high flyers who were not world renowned – but happy where they were. They didn't need to be anywhere else.

They'd 'arrived' as Artists. They *lived* as Artists in an ambience of knowledge and fascination with life. They were living life as it should be lived and I admired that intensely.

The only difference between the Crowes and the internationally famous within the Arts was the illusion perpetrated by Moloch. The Crowes however had side-stepped Moloch entirely – and here they were, *being who they were* with charm, dignity, and grace. They were the Count and Countess of Creativity who held court without needing to hold court. They came to dinner in Hotwells too and met with Penelope, Rebecca, and Meryl who enjoyed their company immensely.

Their home was a ceiling to floor bookcase – crammed with fascinating objects. There was an old phonograph and flower presses sitting around the place. They lived in what seemed to be an antique shop and enjoyed life in a way that I could understand. Whenever we had dinner with them I felt as though I was seeing a future that I hoped to inhabit. I'd like to grow old like the Crowes and invite likely students to dinner. I'd be an Art School lecturer and try to keep the ethos of Art School alive for whomever had that certain synapse for the heart of creativity.

My social association with the Crowes didn't go unnoticed. Todd Whelcomb expressed his perplexity to Janet Ferris one day while arranging plans for a party. "*Why should he want to spend evenings with the Crowes rather than associating with people his own age? They're an elderly couple and Derek Crowe's a little quaint to say the least.*" Derek Crowe was of his parents' generation and so the fact that a latter-day weirdo found more in common with the Crowes than those of his own generation was incomprehensible to him.

"*Maybe they have a lot in common ...?*" suggested Janet. That was not the reply Todd wanted – so he turned to me imagining I'd not heard his whispered remarks to Janet.

"*Been anywhere interesting?*" he asked in an offhand way which indicated that he was not frightfully interested in any answer he was likely to receive.

"*Yes – had dinner with Derek and Susan Crowe—splendid people—it was a real pleasure to invite them to Hotwells.*"

Todd grinned like a gargoyle. "*Really—niiiiice*" he responded in an ostentatiously derisory tone – shuffling back to his art desk like an agitated crab. I continued drawing and overheard Todd mumbling to Veranda "*Maybe once or twice – but every other week is abnormal. I'll be happy to see the last of that freak-of-nature.*"

"*You don't need to account for yourself to anyone*" Janet said in a quiet voice.

"*Thank you Janet. It doesn't really trouble me that Todd and Veranda view me as a freak-of-nature. I just find it a pity that they're plagued with such irritation on my account ... I wish a little more acceptance of difference were possible – but ...*"

Todd and Veranda went back to their party plans. After a while Todd asked in a snide tone "*I don't suppose—you'd—want to come to something as normal as a—*party*—would you?*"

I wondered what to say for a moment. It was obviously a rhetorical question—asked to be awkward—and it occurred to me that maybe I should call it out as such. I had no need to challenge Todd however, so I tried to be humorous. "*Sure – what kind of party will it be 'Come as a Goblin' or 'Bambi meets Godzilla'?*"

"*Neither – it's for sophisticated adults*" Todd pronounced as if that were likely to put me in my place.

"*Well – that counts me out then. I hope you have a splendid evening. Whenever it is.*"

I think it annoyed Todd that he was unable to annoy me.

an odd boy

The party was to have been the following Saturday night. Todd seemed to regret the effect his sarcasm might have had on the others in the room – and said "*You—are—of course, welcome to come …*"

"*Thank you Todd. I'd accept gladly—but I'm afraid Claudette and I have a previous appointment—made last month.*"

"*What's that then? If you don't mind my asking?*"

"*Not at all – we've got tickets for Stravinsky's 'Rite of Spring'.*"

On hearing that Janet Ferris burst out laughing.

"*What was so funny?*" Todd asked Janet.

"*Well*" she replied. "*I think you need to be a sophisticated adult to enjoy that …*"

I pretended I hadn't heard the comment "*Sorry I won't be able to join you.*"

I later thanked Janet for observing the irony of the situation and said her comment made me feel less isolated.

"*I thought you wanted to be isolated?*"

What an idea. "*No … I don't—want—to be isolated. I just don't—mind—being isolated. I find Todd a little too stereotypically male for my style of conversation. He likes to lock horns and always has some sort of stance in terms of how people should be.*"

Janet pulled a wry face and said "*And you don't of course …?*"

I smiled at that. "*Well yes—I have all sorts of ideas—but I don't expect people to adjust themselves according to my vision of the world.*" Pause "*I think the problem is that my—mien—is an innate criticism. My philosophical position is evident in what I do. I don't have to—say—anything to be offensive.*"

"*It's like being a vegetarian in a room full of carnivores. Even if the vegetarian says nothing – the criticism is self evident.*"

"*Hadn't thought of it that way – but I can see the situation ...*" Janet commented "*... so ...you don't make comments on Todd's likes and dislikes – but he sees you as different ... and that just irritates him?*"

"*That seems to be how it is*" I replied. "*When he's nominally cordial I respond in a friendly way – and when he's hostile ...*"

Janet laughed "*When he's hostile you say weird things that make his blood pressure rise.*"

"*Well yes ... I have to admit ... I do that. However ... that's mainly 'me being me' and saying the first thing that comes into my head. I should really attempt to be less weird – but sometimes ... I have no idea of what's going to annoy him. I'd have thought that Pythonesque humour was part of common experience – and that most people would relate to that, especially in an Art School.*"

Janet mused for a moment "*I wouldn't have thought about your humour as Pythonesque – but that's a useful way of describing it. I think Todd probably makes a distinction between Pythonesque humour in Monty Python's Flying Circus and other people adopting it in everyday situations. It's not usual for people to use language like that – but I find it amusing. It's quite clever too – because you don't repeat yourself.*"

"*I'm glad I don't irritate you as well.*"

"*Not at all – but ... it—is—kind of eerie how easy it is to talk to you. I thought you'd make fun of me or something.*"

"*Why should I want to make fun of you?*"

"*Well ...Todd thinks you try to be superior and look down on the rest of us in the studio. He thinks you think you're some kind of Sultan with what he calls your 'Harem' in Hotwells.*"

"*My what?!*" I laughed.

an odd boy

"Your harem ... he means your ... girlfriends."

"Girlfriends?" I almost spluttered. *"They're friends ... and they're ladies – but they're not my 'girlfriends.' I just share a house with them ... They just*—happen—*to be female. I think Todd's got a vivid imagination or something. So ... what's he said about that?"*

"He says you gloat about it."

"That is strictly bizarre. How can I gloat when I never mention them? What's there to gloat about apart from having three good friends anyway? I suppose Todd has friends too in the Hall of Residence where he's chosen to live. I mean—that's—rather more peculiar than sharing a house with three ladies ... if you ask me."

"Yeah ... I'd have thought that the Hall of Residence was for only for 1st *years"* Janet replied. *"I didn't want to live there even as a* 1st *year – it seemed a little too much like being babied."*

"Quite – that's why I didn't take that offer. It seemed like everything that Art School wasn't."

"I suppose it goes with the Polytechnic scarf and the whole late-adolescent image .." Janet shrugged *"... but this gloating business ... he must be jealous or something."*

"Maybe ... I don't know ... I thought he was supposed to be overjoyed with Veranda ..." Pause *"... anyhow, I never*—mention—*the subject of my living situation, let alone gloat about it. If I was going to gloat, I'd talk about the view from my bedroom window. Y'know ... Todd turned up some time back to borrow my palette knives."*

"Yeah! We heard all about—that!*"* Janet interrupted.

"What's to hear? I just offered him the loan of some of my pallette knives and—attempting to be friendly—*invited him to stay for tea ..."* I replied a little bewildered.

"Yeah ... that was friendly of you after how he's been – but he said it was like a cross between an encounter group and Satyricon or something."[2]

"Satyricon eh ... that's funny ... that's also ... sad. He's a sad fellow. All I know, is that he hightailed out when Penelope, Rebecca, and Meryl started discussing literature with him. He did end up—looking—as if he'd walked into a cannibal soirée in the Marquis de Sade's Satanic Apiary – but ... Satyricon was entirely in his head."

Janet shook her head giggling. *"That's a—very—different account to the one Todd gives. He said you'd sat there smirking and offered him tea as if he was an underling or something – while your harem tried to spook him out."*

I felt saddened by that – because the nature of Todd's projections were fairly transparent. *"Well I can't account for Todd's mind ... apart from asking you how you find me. D'you find me supercilious?"*

"No ... that's the really weird thing about it – you're completely unlike Todd's picture of you" Janet replied. *"I'll just ignore Todd's remarks in future. I'll let the others know too ...y'know ... he's got some loony problem that doesn't have anything to do with you. I mean you're actually kindly and pleasant – and quite easy to talk to."*

"Thank you Janet – that's really kind of you – but I'd rather you didn't cause yourself problems on my behalf. I wouldn't want Todd and Veranda being unpleasant to you as well. I'll just be happy to chat with you on a day-to-day basis ... and maybe the others'll notice that humiliation's not involved."

"Yes ... that would make a better atmosphere when you're around. Can I ask you something else though?"

---

2   Satyricon – a Roman work of prose-poetry produced by Federico Fellini in 1969, which details the erotic mishaps of Encolpius and his lover Giton.

an odd boy

"Certainly."

"Todd said—apart from you making him feel unwelcome—that your 'girl friends' started babbling mindlessly and gawping at him. He said he thought they were all on drugs. Said he had to leave because it was such an abnormal creepy situation."

"Right ... that could be almost funny ...y'know ... I don't really care much about what Todd has to say about me – but talking about my friends in this way is really too much." I told Janet what actually happened in the debate about Tolkien and CS Lewis.

Janet was fairly wide-eyed by the end. *"So he just made all that up ... just because he was intellectually upstaged by a girl ..."*

"*Well—two actually—but yes*. I must admit that Meryl did make him look a little silly ... but then he more-or-less brought it on himself. He just decided to vaunt CS Lewis as a master of English Literature with a theatre student. Dumb move if you ask me – but ... fools rush in, as it were ..."[3]

"He really has quite a big problem doesn't he ..." Janet shook her head. *"Well ... I'm glad it's all come out ... it makes sense of some things. Y'know I've wondered if Todd's lied about other things too. Some of the things he says sometimes are just a little – unbelievable."*

The situation lightened after that – with all but Todd and Veranda. They continued to eye me with unveiled contempt. I made a special effort not to employ Pythonisms or personal linguistic eccentricities when I responded to them – but that tended to make me a little stiff and humourless.

---

3   Johnny Mercer/Rube Bloom—Fools Rush In (Where Angels Fear to Tread)—1940. The origin of 'fools rush in where angels fear to tread' is Alexander Pope's Essay on Criticism.

'Good morning' Todd would say – and I'd reply *'Good morning Todd'*—rather than *'Good morning Todd – grrrrrrand day for roasting a hammerhead shark in a magnesium contra-bassoon.'*

I asked him how his project was coming on and he replied "*You probably wouldn't be that interested – it's an illustration for a packaging design.*"

All I could say was "*I hope it goes well.*"

Janet noticed my attempts to be normal "*I'm surprised you can just drop your usual style so easily.*"

"*It's not entirely easy – but I took what you said on board. I thought I'd work on trying to ease the atmosphere.*"

"*I wouldn't bother if I were you*" Janet laughed. "*He's just morose – and some of us miss your loony comments.*"

"*I'll boil a few up with the pickled walrus spleen I've secreted in my subcutaneous chemical vat.*"

"*D'you have a catalogue of these insane phrases or d'you just make them up on the spot?*"

"*I have some favourite animals and objects that recur ... but they largely just spout out of me. I've been saying these things for years and so I guess it comes quite naturally. The more you invent this kind of stuff, the easier it gets and the quicker it flies.*"

I continued to be 'Mister Normal' with Todd – but threw occasional 'loony stuff' around when he wasn't in the direct vicinity. The ladies in the Illustration studio warmed up considerably after my discussion with Janet and we all decided to give our Degree shows in the same room. A photograph was taken of us sitting under the trees in Ashton Court and we agreed to place it at the entrance of the room.

The image was composed of a large central photograph surrounded by smaller photographs which were all slight variations of the main photograph. All sixteen photographs showed us laughing – our heads turning this way and that as if we'd just heard the funniest joke in the history of the galaxy.

"*Don't you think that photograph montage might be found ridiculous?*" Todd commented without want of an answer.

"*Thank you for your view Todd …*" Enough was enough. "*… good to know what you think.*" Todd had no sense of irony and was always speechless when I thanked him for his rudeness. I wished I had other responses to offer that wouldn't floor him quite as decisively – but there seemed no way out of it.

I mentioned this to Janet, who said "*Well … I've seen you try with him – but he doesn't appreciate it when you do. Anyway – he always sets himself up to be humiliated. I know you don't do it on purpose. He gives you little choice. I told him once that you weren't how he thought you were – but he had some idea that you were devious and acted in different ways with different people. I tried suggesting he might be a bit paranoid – but he wouldn't hear a word of it. Now he doesn't seem to like me either – and wherever he leads … Veranda follows.*"

I told Janet I was sorry to hear that. "*Todd's right in one way though … I—am—different with different people.*" Janet looked quizzical. "*Not that I set out to falsify anything – but different people bring different things out of me – and I enjoy that. I don't like to have some sort of personality that dominates every situation and forces the outcome to be a certain way. There's no freedom in that.*"

"*So what effect do I have on you?*" Janet laughed. Her question took me back a little.

"*Well I don't plan what happens or how I'll be so I can't say I could define it – I mean, I've not got you codified or anything ... but now I'm thinking about it ...you are quite a serious person and you consider everything in depth. That's unusual – and so ... what tends to happen is that I become a little more contemplative and earnest.*"

Janet found that interesting "*I'll have to pay attention to how I am with people ... I think I'd like to be thought of as a little more light-hearted.*"

"*I hope I haven't given you the impression that I think you are dour, Janet. It's more that I see you as a thinker – that's a good thing. You don't fire off with the first thing you think and that's an admirable quality. I have no concept of you not being light-hearted – in fact ... I'd go so far as to say you'd tickle the fuzz off any peach within reach.*"

Janet grinned "*I'm glad you can also feel free to be loony with me.*"

The Degree show was looming and I'd been gathering together the best of my three years illustration work. I was looking for my Dürer-esque photographic grass image – but it was nowhere to be found. It had been in my cupboard with my other first and second year work – but no matter how many times I sorted though the work I failed to find it. "*I know it was there last week – y'know the green tinted photograph and hand-scripted poetry*" I said to Janet.

"*I know the one – I love that.*"

"*Well ... it doesn't seem to be here.*"

"*Can I help you sort through again? I'm sure it'll be there somewhere.*"

We went through each piece more methodically than I had done on my own – but in the end it was definitely not there. "*I don't understand that Vic ... I saw it last week – y'know, when Derek said ... it was one of your best pieces.*"

an odd boy

"Mmmm ... someone else must have thought so too ..."

Janet looked nervous. "*D'you think the print and negatives have been stolen?*"

"*It's difficult to know what else to think ... as I haven't taken them home. I put it all back in the cupboard after Derek's appraisal.*"

"*Oh Vic ... I am so sorry ... and I suppose there's no time to reproduce it is there?*"

"*No ... doesn't matter too much though. I've got more than enough without it and Derek told me I'd have to cut back on my show. They only want to see a selection of work.*"

Janet asked the obvious question. "*Are you going to tell anyone about it?*"

"*Well ... I don't think I'll tell Derek about it ... I don't really want to create a problem for him. I won't get it back anyway – so there seems no purpose.*"

"*I see your point ... but it might not be a good idea—not—to say anything. I think that Derek would want to know. I mean ... he's the head of Department and he'd want to know that your work had been stolen.*"

"*Yes ... there's no good way round this is there ... I suppose ... if Derek asked me why I'd not exhibited that piece I'd have to tell him anyway.*"

"*So you'll tell him?*"

"*I think I'll have to. Sometimes I tend to let things drift their own way and it's not always a good idea. I can tell Derek that I don't want any fuss made on my behalf – and that might be a way to answer the problem, both ways.*" Moloch was creeping up in the most unlikely places.
I couldn't fathom why anyone would do such a thing as stealing another person's work at an Art School.

"*Good – I think that's the right choice*" Janet responded in an encouraging way.

"*Thanks for your help with this … just talking it through with you has been helpful*" I replied.

I told Claudette about my conversations with Janet and she was intrigued by the fact that changes were occurring. "*Thought they all despised you for being a Fine Artist in the Illustration studio?*" Claudette could be extreme sometimes.

"*No, I don't think anyone but Todd and Veranda ever—actually— despised me … and I don't think 'despise' is quite the word I'd use.*"

Claudette tittered "*Loath, vituperate, deride, disdain?*"

"*I'll opt for 'disdain' as the closest word – and now that's just Todd and Veranda.*"

Claudette then proceeded to lampoon Todd and Veranda for their sartorial destitution.

"*You're most amusing 'dette – when you take a dislike to anyone's dress sense.*"

Claudette seemed pleased that I'd agreed with her – but I never felt much inclined to encourage her too far in that direction. I never enjoyed disliking people and although humour could be found – it seemed slightly problematic to indulge it beyond a certain point.

"*I think I just make them nervous. They're keen on setting up a graphic design illustration agency. They're full of marriage plans and a whole range of notions we've never discussed. They have no idea why we're not living together or planning to live together or whatever and why I'm living in a house with three ladies when you're living somewhere else.*"

an odd boy

I'd not actually planned on saying what I'd said about living arrangements – but Janet had told me that this was one of Todd and Veranda's jibes about me.

Claudette was thoughtful for a moment "*As you have said before ... they're absurdly conservative—in the bourgeois sense—and easily scared by ideas they don't understand.*" I agreed. "*But ...*" she continued "*... are you saying that you're still keen on this conformist idea of living in the same house just because you're involved with someone?*"

We were back to the difficult subject again. "*No ... not exactly – it just came up because we were talking of Todd and Veranda.*" Pause "*I'm hardly a conformist. I'm just not entirely convinced—as yet—that your idea is one hundred percent workable.*"

Claudette pursed her lips "*I can't say I'm entirely convinced about your* —lack—*of conformist tendencies.*"

I grinned attempting to bring some humour into the discussion. "*I think this 'conformist idea' is a bit of ... an ad hominem red herring ... in a blind alley ...*"

"*Tu quoque—Brute.*"[4]

"*You're going to have to translate that, 'dette.*"

"*You will know it better from Shakespeare. 'Et tu, Brute?*"[5]

---

4   'Tu quoque, Brute, fili mihi' is one variation attributed to Julius Caesar as he lay dying from assassination. Tu quoque—you, also—is Latin for a type of logical fallacy. One party would use the logical stance of 'tu quoque' to assert an opposing position is false because its proponent fails to act consistently within that position. The argument attempts to prove that the opposing position applies equally to the person making it; it is therefore, a comment against the person rather than on the position (*ad hominem*).

5   Et tu, Brute – 'And you, Brutus?' or 'Even you, Brutus?' The last words of Julius Caesar from Shakespeare's 'Julius Cæsar'. Quoted in the context of betrayal. On the Ides of March 44 BC Cæsar was attacked by senators, including Marcus Brutus, his closest friend.

"*Ah ...*" I was not that keen on being classed as a betrayer of principles. "*I don't see myself that way. I'm neither conformist nor nonconformist. Conformism's not about 'what' – it's about 'why'. I'm too partial to—freedom—to want to be either.*

"*I need to be free to like what I like rather than bow to the dictates of either persuasion.*"

Claudette—never keen on this style of approach—replied "*Why do you—always—have to dive into intellectual abstractions rather than admit to anything?*"

"*I can admit to things, 'dette – let's start with the fact that I never learnt to tie shoelaces. I just tie a variant on a reef knot where the final twist is made with loops.*" Pause "*But in terms of intellectual abstractions ... you're—the one who quotes Latin?*" I sighed "*I hope you remember that I was the one who used to mispronounce Aristophanes as Aristo-faines.*"

"*Very droll ...*" Claudette glowered.

She never enjoyed it when she lost her intellectual footing with me – and I never made a point of arriving at the position unless she pushed me. I didn't like upsetting her – but sometimes her concept of a relationship was a little too vague for me.

"*Y'know ...*" I continued in a flat monotone "*... these are all just —ideas—at the moment ... so there's no purpose in speculating.*" Pause "*I don't know how I am going to feel about it after the RCA. I've lived with a lady-friend before in Farnham and it worked out well while it lasted – and she was actually as unconventional as you are – although in a different kind of way.*"

"*Yes—the Highland Swearing Champion—she must have been exceptionally original.*" Pause "*Well ... as you said 'while it lasted'. It just didn't last very long – did it?*"

an odd boy

"*Y'know, 'dette, I really*—don't—*appreciate it when you caricaturise in that way* – *and, it doesn't help your argument in the least. Helen and I were*—not—e*ntirely suited but we did have a lot of fun together.*

"*She was an extremely talented painter* – *which is why she wanted to be with someone equally dedicated to painting. That's all there is to say.*"

"*But the fact*—is—*that it didn't last. Did it?*"

"*No, 'dette …*" I replied with a long drawn out sigh "*… it did not.*" The next words could have been '*and I don't think this will last either*' – but I didn't want to broach the subject with the degree shows looming. That would have been unpardonable. "*Y'know, 'dette. I think you've won the argument*—*as you always want to*—*but I'm not going to promise anything. All I can do is keep an open mind to it. That's what I'm*—*trying*—*to do* – *so …your attempting to force the issue will not help. It'll just drive me away.*"

Claudette knew when I started a sentence with her name, there was no purpose in attempting to prevail. It had happened increasingly since the final term of the second year. We still mainly enjoyed each other's company – but as the end of the degree course came closer, thoughts of the future began to writhe. Penelope, Rebecca, and Meryl had asked Claudette if we were planning to live together at some point and she'd been unsettled by the question. She wasn't keen on them knowing about her 'private life'. "*Did you put them up to this?*"

"*No …*" I replied with studied nonchalance. "*I don't need their assistance* – *and I wouldn't put them in that position, in any case.*"

"*Then why did they ask me a question like that?*"

"*That's for you to answer, 'dette*—*they were your friends before they became mine*—*you went to Badminton with them for a decade didn't you?*"

"*Yes* – *and?*"

"Well ... let me guess ... Mmmm ... why—did—they—ask—you—a—question—like—that ...?" I asked as if I was really pondering a difficult question "Could it have been ... that ... maybe—being that they've known you for so long and you're their oldest friend—they're ... interested in your life?"

Claudette—uncharacteristically—missed the irony in what I'd said and snapped "I don't like having my privacy invaded." Claudette somehow gave me the impression that it was my fault whether I'd said anything to the girls or not. I didn't answer immediately. It was another situation in which I felt as if I wanted to say that our relationship was not as pleasant as it once was. It was not as happy—delightful—inspiring—or any of the good words that could once have been used.

"Well, 'dette ... that has nothing to do with me ... does it? You will have to take the 'invasion of privacy' matter up with them — because I'm not going to say anything on your behalf. That is entirely between you and them."

"Well ...you certainly feel strongly about it don't you."

"Yes and no – any strength of feeling I have on this subject is a reflection of your anger about having your privacy invaded. I'm simply stressing the fact that I am not responsible. I had no idea that conversations had taken place 'til you told me in the evening."

"It's just that I hate this kind of thing."

"Fair enough, 'dette – but it's just a little alien to me. I mean – my life's an open book. Not that I'd wish to suggest you—should—welcome having your privacy invaded ... it's your choice." Pause "But ... couldn't guarding your private life with friends be construed as a socially conventional position?"

an odd boy

Claudette stood up and walked out, slamming the door behind her. She came back an hour later in a better frame of mind – but I'd grown wary of her, and weary of her manner.

"*Seems I can tread the conventional-unconventional tightrope as well as you can – but … I just don't like being caught out at it.*"

"*That's brave of you, 'dette – I respect you for saying that. Thank you.*"

"*Can we be friends now?*"

"*I was never anything else, 'dette*" I smiled rather slightly. "*I just need to be as free … as you want to be … and I'm heading for the RCA in September … I'll be in London for a few years – so … I really don't know what will happen after that – or where I might have to go to find a post in a Foundation Department.*"

"*Yes … I suppose I can see that.*"

"*I don't have—any—issue with you living at home.*" Pause "*Apart from the fact that it locks me back into bedsit land when the lease is up here.*"

"*Yes … I can see that too.*"

"*I've got used to living in a house – and the thought of returning to 'bedsit land' is—not—exactly alluring. I'll do it if and when I have to—and it'll probably be fine—but I'm not looking forward to it.*" Claudette nodded and I continued "*I know that it makes sense for you to live at home. I'm not out to make your life difficult …*" Pause "*I'm hardly lonely you know – us 'girls' have a fine time of it.*"

Claudette tittered "*You 'girls'—very droll—you 'girls' are certainly— quite—the sensation.*"

I wasn't quite sure what she meant by that statement so I simply sat observing the fading light in the room. Claudette was not used to long conversational silences from me. "*Don't you find it a bit peculiar that they call you 'one of the girls'?*"

"*No … why should I? It's just humorous.*"

"Humorous?"

"Yes ... merely a mirthful statement of inclusivity ... and ... I enjoy the way it transcends the stereotypical gender nonsense."

Claudette frowned at that "*You seem to delight in being unconventional as-and-when it suits you.*"

"Well yes—of course—but as you said when you came back – we both do that." Pause "The only thing I'd say in my defence ..." I grinned "... is that I don't do it to gain advantage or win an argument. My main wish is to be free—to be creative—and to be ... happy, whenever feasible. I'm an anarchist and always have been."

Claudette gave a slight snort "*The anarchist advocate of married life.*"

"Anarchism means freedom and responsibility. Anything that's freely chosen is fine. I'm not advocating it for anyone else ..." I replied, ignoring Claudette's jibe "... so although I may flit between bizarro counter-culture eccentricity and bourgeois conventionalism I have no—plan —with it. It's just—me—the way—I—happen to be ..." Pause "... and ... I hold myself accountable for that. I don't say that anyone else should live the way I live – or value what I value. I'd like everyone to be free to live whatever life suits them."

"I think ..." Claudette replied "... we should agree to disagree and enjoy the rest of the evening – Penelope, Rebecca, and Meryl have just walked in – and there suddenly seems to be no more to say on the subject."

"So guess what happened today?" I called out. "I discovered that my grass photographic piece was stolen from my art cupboard."

"You never mentioned—that—to me" Claudette stated with slight consternation.

"Well ... we got onto other subjects ..."

Claudette nodded in comprehension of my diplomacy.

an odd boy

I told the story and all four ladies were aghast. They'd all seen 'The Grass' as I called it and they all thought it was a sad loss.

"*Personally, I'd suspect Toad*" Claudette stated and I asked what brought her to that conclusion. "*Well ... was he there when Derek said it was one of your finest pieces?*" He was. "*Well then ...*" she continued "*... the degree shows are coming up and he wants to make sure you don't get a better grade than he gets.*"

Penelope thought that was improbable but Meryl and Rebecca—who'd had the CS Lewis argument with Todd—thought otherwise.

"*Have you looked through his cupboard?*" Meryl asked.

"No ... I guess I could. I get in early enough ... but—that—would feel creepy."

"*Not as creepy as Trophy-head stealing your work!*" Meryl replied – and I told her I'd think about it. It was a difficult question for me. Claudette thought it would be the best idea to look for it and then tell Derek as soon as he came in so that a search would be made and Todd would be discovered as the thief and tarred and feathered or whatever.

"That's right outside anything I'd consider, 'dette. If I found it in Todd's cupboard – I'd just take it back again. I have no desire to punish anyone. I could just move my stuff to the lower shelf of Janet's cupboards as she's got one of the lockable ones. She offered to let me do that – so it's not a problem."

"*What I'd do in—that—case ...*" offered Rebecca "*... is to leave a note for Trophy-head in your empty cupboard saying 'Good Luck Todd' – then he'd know you knew.*"

"Now—that—I could do. Maybe ... 'Good Luck Todd I won't grass on you' – that might serve."

Everyone fell about laughing at that – but I noticed Claudette look a little peeved that I'd gone with Rebecca's suggestion. So I made a point of supporting her whenever I could – with whatever came up next in the conversation. We all talked together for a while – then Claudette made her customary night time departure. The girls and I talked on into the early hours. I felt strangely guilty that I was having a far more enjoyable time alone with Penelope, Rebecca, and Meryl.

I never felt I became tedious to them – and they never made acerbic comments in relation to my ideology of creativity. It wasn't that they didn't challenge me—they did—but it was light-hearted and I never felt derided. We all had our areas of special interest and respected each other's expertise. We also had music in common. I sometimes wondered if Claudette felt left out. I'd asked her about it – but she said "*I like hearing you all play – and it gives me a chance to read books.*" I enquired whether it ever made her feel excluded. "*Not at all – how could I feel superfluous when I'm the regal audience of one. It's like having my own chamber orchestra.*"

Penelope, Rebecca, and Meryl seemed to brighten ever-so-slightly when Claudette left – even though they *were* all ostensibly good friends. It was not the kind of thing I could ask about – so I didn't enquire. Then I noticed that it was not only Penelope, Rebecca, and Meryl who brightened ... I seemed to brighten as well. It was as if I was able to relax and say whatever came into my head – but then I realised there was no 'as if' about it. It was definitely what happened. I could say whatever I wanted and it was always alright. Penelope, Rebecca, and Meryl were never offended by me. I was never offended by them either. We just flowed with each other and the conversation tumbled in every direction, peppered with laughter and unexpected insights.

I realised that Claudette was right in what she'd said about us – but not in the way she'd intended. We—were—*quite the sensation*, to each other. We were the best of friends. We shared a sensation of *ease* that made delight, fascination, and laughter possible; through trust and respect – openness and appreciation. Being with the girls was as good as being with Steve and Ron.

16

the third year: april 1975

bower ashton – a woeful ballad made to his mistress' eyebrow

All the world's a stage, and all the men and women merely players: / They have their exits and their entrances; and one man in his time plays many parts, / … At first the infant, mewling and puking in the nurse's arms. / And then the whining school-boy, with his satchel and shining morning face, creeping like snail unwillingly to school. / And then the lover, sighing like furnace, with a woeful ballad made to his mistress' eyebrow. / Then a soldier, full of strange oaths and bearded like the pard, jealous in honour, sudden and quick in quarrel, / Seeking the bubble reputation even in the cannon's mouth.
William Shakespeare—As You Like It—Act II—Scene vii—1599

Financial circumstances had finally swung in favour of giving Claudette a treat. She'd always wanted to go to Stratford to see Shakespeare. She'd never wanted to go there alone – and her father had decided to abjure Shakespeare as the stock-in-trade of nouveau intellectuels faussaires [1] – people who liked to pretend they were culturally high and mighty by virtue of a falsely assumed love of Shakespeare. I thought Mr Gascoigne was a card-carrying neurotic and dyed-in-the-wool misanthropist.

He was a man who lived to take vituperate positions that placed him above others – and he all but poisoned his daughter's mind with his narcissistic bigotry.

---

1 Intellectuels faussaire – intellectual falsifiers.

Be that as it may ... I'd sold one of the bronze castings of *Frogs in Amplexus*—for what seemed to be a princely sum—and so it was a done deal. We stayed overnight in a lovely old hotel. The room had cost an arm and a leg – but that came as no surprise. The sign in the car park requested 'Please Park Prettily' and I'd amused myself with the idea that a sign in the room couldn't have requested 'Please Behave Prettily'. Sadly she found the bed impossible with regard to sleep. I'd slept on the floor to give Claudette more room – but she failed to register that as any kind of sacrifice, as I'd once spoken of sleeping on blanketed boards in the Himalayas. I wasn't saddened or aggrieved by Claudette on this score – because I'd come to a point where I merely teetered between amusement and bemusement.

Writing a play. That was Derek's idea – and it remained fermenting in my mind. It glowed – sporadically dappling my vision with possibilities. I'd started observing plays with a new and sinuous curiosity. I was wondering what I could create in this arena. What words would I place in the mouths of as-yet-unborn characters? I was eager to see what this production of 'As You Like It' might spark.

'*All the world's a stage, and all the men and women merely players.*'

"*Hmmm* ..." I hummed like a mutant bumble bee – causing Claudette to squirm in the theatre seat next to mine "... *merely players eh?*" I whispered to myself. I was not quite as sub-audible as I thought and Claudette arched her eyebrows in disapproval.

'*Seeking the bubble reputation even in the cannon's mouth.*'

I emitted an almost noiseless "*Yesssss!*" that startled Claudette.

I explained later – as we were leaving "*Sorry 'bout the hiss, 'dette ... that was just me thinking aloud.*"

"You've taken to thinking like a pressure cooker then?" she snapped with slight yet evident irritation.

I decided to be humorous rather than take offence. "*Yes, 'dette* …*'Jack' is a word I reject absolutely. It's a word I put into my galvanised pressure cooker. Whreeeeep! Jack's dead.*"

"*What?*" Claudette replied with a partial splutter.

"*It's a line from 'The Ruling Class' – you know, that Peter O'Toole film I told you about … a long—long—time ago.*"

"*Oh yes …your essay with Rick Frampton.*" Pause "*So—anyway—what caused you to hiss like a galvanised pressure cooker?*"

"*It was that line 'Seeking the bubble reputation even in the cannon's mouth.' That could just as easily be 'seeking Art even in the cannon's mouth' or 'seeking Art through the explosive windows of the senses'. I love Shakespeare!*"

Claudette pronounced a sound which indicated irritation. "*Then—why—are you always rephrasing him?*"

That was simple. "*Well … it's an important part of my appreciation of him.*" Claudette had a quizzical expression – but said nothing, so I continued "*I may be 'bearded like the pard' – but I'm not a soldier, full of strange oaths' … I'm an Artist full of strange ideas.*"

"*That's a neat sidestep*" Claudette replied.

I exhaled an entirely silent sigh. Claudette had become increasingly adversarial.

"*What have I sidestepped? You'll have to explain, I thought I was simply having a conversation with you …*" I enquired – not really expecting an answer that applied to anything I'd asked.

"*Using Shakespeare out of context to support your argument*" she replied as if she was talking to a dimwit.

an odd boy

"*It's not an 'argument', 'dette ... it's merely a reflection*" I replied as mildly as I could. "*I'm just excited about the play. I'm just talking about ideas ... I'm not intending anything definitive.*"

"It didn't sound like that when you took issue with Shakespeare ..." Claudette stated "... *on the idea that all the men and women are merely players.*"

"*Mmmm ...*" I exhaled in a cross between a moan and a groan, which sounded not entirely unlike a mediæval woodwind instrument.

"Why the moan if you claim to love Shakespeare?"

"*Were I as tedious as a king, I could find it in my heart to bestow it all on your worship.*"

"*And the origin of*—that—*would be?*" Claudette answered stiffly.

"Dogberry to Leonato in 'Much Ado About Nothing' – *after Leonato tells him he's tedious.*"

"*So*—I'm—*tedious am I?*"

"Not in the context of the quotation. I was alluding there, to my being as tedious as Dogberry." Pause "But as you mention it ...*you*—do— become tedious when you get adversarial in this way and turn a conversation into a closed loop – *yes.*" I regretted it as soon as I'd said it "*I'm sorry ... that's not entirely accurate – you probably speak as you do because you find me tedious ...*" Pause "*So ... it's not you*—or—*me ... I think it's the situation that's tedious. I don't particularly want to make you the tedious part of the equation.*" Awkward silence "*Anyhow ... to answer the question*—truculent though it may appear in relation to Shakespeare—*it was merely the word 'merely' ... and then I was merely 'taking issue' with the word in relation to an idea I have. You see men and women*—are—*often 'merely' players – but they have the potential to be far more. My idea is merely this: men and women can*—write—*the play.*"

Claudette clucked her tongue "*You'd do—anything—to be back on stage again wouldn't you?*"

"*Fabulous non sequitur, 'dette – but, no ... not anything ... if I'd do—anything—I'd be singing soft Rock with the Gravy Train.*" Pause "*I've got this feeling that you're—*angry*—about something. Everything you know about my—being on stage—is stuff I told you two years ago – so ... I'm kind of perplexed as to why you're throwing this at me now.*" Claudette opted for silence in response – so I went back to her previous point "*What I—*meant*—was, that people can write plays with their lives—and perform in them—if they have a sense of creativity. We're all on stage in that way. It's not reserved for the famous. Everyone could be glorious in their own plays.*"

"*Everyone?*"

"*Yes—everyone—why would I leave anyone out?*"

"*Why are—you—so intent on raising—everyone—to heights they don't deserve?*"

"*Who's to say who deserves what? Wouldn't you wish the—*best*—for everyone?*"

Claudette was on me quick as a flash "*Maybe you just want—everyone else—to be on stage so that you can be there too.*"

This was becoming exasperating "*Quite so . .*"

It occurred to me that I was in a rather a ridiculous situation. I had just spent a great deal of money with the purpose of giving Claudette a pleasurable experience. It was an experience she desired to have. That is not to say that it was not highly pleasurable for me too – but I'd wanted to repay her for the clothes she'd made for me and to give her a token of unwithheld generosity. It was vaguely bewildering therefore – to be subject to such (I silently struggled for words) venomous ingratitude.

What was I to say? Should I call her out? Should I expose the situation for what it was? That would pretty much precipitate the end of our relationship – and I didn't want to throw Claudette into emotional chaos just before the degree shows were staged. I was also curious—to a certain degree—as to just how brutal Claudette would become if I simply continued to tolerate her vindictive edge. In a moment of derangement I commenced to quote *"Towers of death and silence. Angels of fire and ice. Saw Alexander … covered with honey and beeswax in his tomb. Felt the flowers growing over me. Oh, a man must have vision. How else could an English judge—and peer of the realm—take moonlit trips to Marrakesh and Ponders End? See six vestal virgins smoking cigars? Moses in bedroom slippers? Naked bosoms floating past Formosa? Just time for a quick one. Be of good cheer Master Ridley – and play the man! There's plenty of time to win this game and beat the Spaniards too. Form square, men! Smash the Mahdi and Binnie Barnes!"*

"*Another quote from The Ruling Class, I suppose?*"

"*Yes … as you were talking about my lust for glory on stage … I thought I'd recite.*"

"*And you learnt this drivel by heart?*"

"*Yes indeed*" I replied with a slightly deranged laugh. "*I learnt— this—by heart!*" Claudette asked why – but without any evident interest. "*It's something I enjoyed at school – learning poetry and prose by heart, that is. I can still quote most of Tennyson's Morte D'Arthur.*"

"*Can you now …? That would surprise me.*"

"'*So all day long the noise of battle rolled / Among the mountains by the winter sea; / Until King Arthur's table, man by man, / Had fallen in Lyonnesse about their Lord, / King Arthur: then, because his wound was deep, / 'The bold Sir Bedivere uplifted him,/*

Sir Bedivere, the last of all his knights, / And bore him to a chapel nigh the field, / A broken chancel with a broken cross, / That stood on a dark strait of barren land. / On one side lay the Ocean, and on one / Lay a great water, and the moon was full. / Then spake King Arthur to Sir Bedivere: / The sequel of today unsolders all / The goodliest fellowship of famous knights / Whereof this world holds record. Such a sleep / They sleep – the men I loved. I think that we / Shall never more, at any future time, / Delight our souls with talk of knightly deeds, / Walking about the gardens and the halls / Of Camelot, as in the days that were. / I perish by this people which I made, / Though Merlin sware that I should come again / To rule once more – but let what will be, be, / I am so deeply smitten through the helm / That without help I cannot last till morn' ... and ... there I falter. I can't remember it all ... I find it valuable to be able to quote – and of course ... I had to learn lyrics by heart with Savage Cabbage." I replied, in an effort to pull the conversation in a less belligerent direction.

"*So you're thinking of the theatre as a career now are you?*"

"*That hadn't occurred to me yet, 'dette – but I don't rule*—anything—*out.*"

"*I know ...*" she sighed wearily "*...you think you can do*—anything —*as if you were some kind of Leonardo Da Vinci or whatever.*" Pause "*Penelope, Rebecca, and Meryl seem to have that opinion of you.*"

"*Do they ... Well ... if they do they never said anything to me about it. They're my friends – that's all I know.*"

'Leonardo Da Vinci' ...Yes ...That seemed a long time ago ... Claudette had called me Leonardo once. It had been in fun – but it has also pertained to a respect she had for me at the time. That respect had dwindled over the three years and now ... where was it?

Where was any kind of respect or appreciation other than sexuality – and that seemed increasingly impersonal. Maybe that's the wrong word – maybe un-romantic is closer to what happened. Sexuality seemed to have become Claudette's fix-it when we couldn't relate in any other way and it had become one of the few aspects of our relationship where she found no fault.

I felt close to calling an end to our relationship again—in that moment—but was determined to hold out 'til the degree show was over. I didn't want to damage her chances – but I felt that I could no longer avoid calling her out. I had to say something to encourage her to examine her state of mind "*I really don't understand where you're coming from, 'dette. You seem to want to pillory me with this stage business ... for reasons that I just don't understand. I mean ... this discussion's not—just—about my Shakespearian theorising is it? It's as if you want to punish me for something – and ... I have—no—idea why. Let's get this clear – I've just taken you to Stratford to see a play – and I think I deserve a little friendliness if only as a matter of common courtesy.*"

"*I'm sorry—if—I sounded unfriendly ... I didn't mean to ...*"

"*Thank you.*" Pause "*Y'know ...you're often quite ... adversarial.*"

"*Well ... I'm just responding to you, as you seem to me. You—are—always suggesting high adventure, daring exploits, and the like, and you—are—obsessed with being on stage and I think that's a romantic delusion that will ruin your life.*"

"*Well ...you're certainly convinced about my obsession – but whether it'll be the ruination of me is unknowable, isn't it?*" I replied impassively.

"*However ... whatever my obsession is or isn't – you seem to be obsessed with my obsession. And—that's—equally as problematic.*"

"*Touché – and then?*"

"*And then, 'dette?*" I replied in as soft a voice as I could manage. "*Touché is for fencing ... and I don't really go in for that. I can't afford it. I'm working class and you need money for that kind of thing.*"

"*The class thing again.*"

"*No really, 'dette – it's just me taking you up on the fencing term. I've got no desire to score points ... not with Todd—not with you—not with anyone.*" Pause "*I'd rather have a friendly conversation. All I'm suggesting —purely as an idea—is that we're all on stage anyway, whether we like it or not. The world's a stage and we're players – and that has nothing to do with the fact that I was once on stage. It was wonderful being on stage with Savage Cabbage and I enjoyed it – but it's—not—obsessing me. It was just a part of my life that I enjoy thinking about from time to time.*"

"*My, my, you have an acrobatic imagination*" Claudette sniggered. "*The way you build your home-grown hippie philosophies out of Shakespeare ... is – hardly the height of accomplishment. You can't just offer these ideas up as if you were an acknowledged expert on the subject you know.*"

"*No, 'dette ... I don't*—know—*that ...*" I stated slowly with subdued yet emphatic enunciation "*... and you don't*—know—*that either.*" Pause "*It's just what you're telling me ... because*—you—*want me to hear it. It's fine for*—you—*to think as you do ... but I don't*— have—*to agree with you.*" Pause "*If you're not interested in this topic, I can*—as easily—*drop it. I have no desire to change your opinion – or to argue that your opinion isn't as valid as mine.*"

"*It's not just*—my opinion—*you're always trying to bring things down to 'personal opinion' as if there were no intelligible cultural consensus on anything.*"

I felt like replying '*Jawohl mein Führer!*' because the ridiculousness of the situation seemed to escalate no matter what I said.

an odd boy

"*Well there may well be an intelligible cultural consensus – but that would not—need—to be the only allowable view on any matter. You're free to harangue me as long as you like whilst we're in the car together – but eventually ...you will have to leave me in Hotwells.*"

"*So you're not prepared to listen to a word I say?*"

"*I can hardly avoid it can I? But, no I'm not prepared to listen to a word you say – not when what you say is delivered with such ... animosity. I'll discuss anything with anyone as long as it's a friendly conversation – but this is not friendly is it?*"

"*I don't see how it's possible to be friendly with you when you're so fixated on being right – and refusing to accept acknowledged authorities.*"

"*I am interested in what acknowledged authorities say, 'dette – but what happens when I find myself taking a different view? I signed no contract when I enrolled for Art School to the effect that I'd believe the word of every acknowledged authority ... and I'm not about to change it, just because—you—disagree with me. I don't—need—you to agree with me. I don't want you to change your mind either. I don't want to win the argument – but I don't intend to be bludgeoned into acquiescence either.*" Ghastly hiatus. "*Y'know ...'dette ...you're right from your side, and I'm right from mine. We're both just 'one too many mornings and a thousand miles behind.*"[2]

"*And so you'll quote Dylan at me when you run out of Shakespeare?*" Her sneer was evident.

"*Ain't no law 'gainst it yet, 'dette*" I sighed. I'd been tempted to say '*Goodbye is too good a word gal – so I'll just say fare thee well*'.[3]

---

2   Bob Dylan—One Too Many Mornings—The Times they Are a-Changing—1964
3   Bob Dylan—Don't think Twice, It's Alright—The Freewheeling Bob Dylan—1963

The decision not to say anything final was proving increasingly hard to maintain.

"*The law—if you have to put it that way—concerns the serious study of literature and history. Had you studied Shakespeare you could theoretically make comparisons – but you haven't studied Shakespeare. So your comparisons don't actually mean anything beyond idle conjecture.*"

"*Maybe they are, 'dette – maybe they are – but that's*—me—*isn't it? You are who you are ... and I am who I am.*" Pause "*... or maybe it's idle conjecture – and I'm an idolater as my old Religious Instruction teacher used to say ...*" I replied hoping that would be the end of the matter.

"*Then why do you*—insist—*on doing it!?*"

"*I know ...*" I sighed "*... that it offends you that I make no distinction between Bob Dylan and Shakespeare – but I've never gone in for obeying societally sanctioned cultural rules – as a blanket procedure. I come to my own conclusions about*—everything—*and remain open to learning. As far as I'm concerned*—*Dylan's a philosopher who couches his philosophical considerations in song form. Shakespeare did the same in plays. All I do ... is respond to them according to what seems interesting to me. If I didn't respond to his plays in this way – I wouldn't be interested in seeing his plays, or anyone's plays.*"

"*Well ...*" replied Claudette after a lengthy pause "*... I suppose I'm glad you enjoy plays – I just can't contend with your eternal philosophising about them.*" Pause "*Meryl does that too. But*—she's—*studying theatre. At least she knows what she's talking about.*"

That was designed to close the subject and put me in my place at the same time. "*Fair enough, 'dette. I'll keep my ruminations to myself – that's not too demanding.*"

an odd boy

I decided that I'd better simply sit in my 'dette-ors prison and occupy myself in some more productive way – such as admiring the scenery. My thoughts turned to Penelope, Meryl, and Rebecca. My three friends back in Hotwells always welcomed discussion. They often instigated it. I'd been recalling these enjoyable discussions for some minutes in peaceful silence when Claudette asked *"Why can't you just enjoy a play – and let me enjoy it as well!"*

"As I said ..." I replied. *"I'm keeping my ruminations to myself."*

"Saving them for Penelope, Rebecca, and—Meryl—*I suppose."*

"Well yes ... 'If the words sound queer or funny to your ear; a little bit jumbled up and jivey – sing: Mares eat oats, and does eat oats, and little lambs eat ivy.'"[4] I quoted simply to reflect the nonsensical nature of her question.

"Well we may as well see plays each without the other then ..." she snapped *"... if you're going to live in a private world of vaudeville references."*

My immediate inclination was to agree – but I decided on a less dramatic approach. *"I'm sorry I spoil the plays for you ... I—can—just enjoy seeing a play – but seeing a play I enjoy, sparks me with ideas and it's not easy to separate the ideas from the enjoyment."* I felt that it was important somehow to remain in communication with Claudette.

It would have been easy to have said that I'd been on the brink of leaving her for a while and that this discussion had just precipitated the end – but that seemed aggressive somehow. I didn't want to become another John Willoughby in her mind.

---

4   Al Hoffman/Jerry Livingston/Milton Drake—Mairzy Doats—1943. Quoted by Jack, the 14th Earl of Gurney, in 'The Ruling Class'.

She *seemed* to want out as much as I did. We were simply unsuited – and I wanted her to come to that same conclusion. Maybe she'd be relieved if I took what I thought was her cue … but maybe I was incorrect in my reading of her.

Claudette remained silent. After a moment I asked *"Is there … some aspect of the play, you*—would—*discuss other than the philosophical side?"* Claudette shrugged—she was determinedly vexed with me —but I was committed to maintaining a degree of civility. I never was one to sulk, or to allow moods to predominate over the possibility of cordiality. *"What about the costume?"* I proffered *"Theatre's your area of expertise – so, I'd be interested in how you thought they handled that."*

Claudette was highly tense. I could feel her searching for a caustic response. Just as I was about to comment on the beauty of the countryside as a means of changing the subject, she blurted out *"I'm not*—always—*at Art School like you are! You*— never—*take time out! Ever*—ever—*ever! Even when you're taking time out it's a constant Art seminar! Everything in your world centres around the damnable creative process … and I … just find it exhausting! It drains the pleasure from everything! I enjoy costume design – but having constant conversations about it just ruins everything."* Lengthy pause. *"I've just got nothing much to say. I thought it was good – but there's no more I have to say about it."*

"Right …" I replied. *"I think … I'm about through too."* Pause *"I think I'll just enjoy the scenery."*

Claudette drove on in silence – and I was just beginning to enjoy the landscape and forget about Claudette's harangue when the silence became too much for her and she launched in again.

"Philosophy's—your—*peculiar penchant … there's nothing particularly wrong with it, I*—suppose—*but it's just not*—my—*interest! I'm just*— not—*that kind of person and I never will be!"*

There was an unspoken final message that came across as loudly as if she shouted it '... *and if you don't like it you know what to do!*'

'... *and if you don't like it you know what to do.*' Yes ... I knew what to do. I was just uncertain as to the how and when of it. I was no longer exactly '... *the lover, sighing like furnace, with a woeful ballad made to his mistress' eyebrow.*' I was already out on some lonesome highway.

Well I'm walking down that long lonesome road babe – where I'm bound I can't tell. Bob Dylan—Don't Think Twice, It's Alright—The Freewheeling Bob Dylan—1963

I considered Claudette's remark and decided that it would be an aggressive stance to ignore her. "*I suppose it can be useful to know what kind of person you are.*" Pause "*I've been all kinds of people – and ... I have no idea of what kind of person I might become.*"

Claudette looked as if she was on the brink of screaming when I said that – but decided to say nothing instead. We drove on in silence and I returned to gazing at the green rolling hills and drystone walls. There were occasional lovely stands of trees on the crowns of hills and the wonderful jigsaw puzzle of small fields – grazed by sheep and horses. If Penelope, Rebecca, and Meryl had been with me we could have talked endlessly about ... the countryside and its effects on English literature. The girls were always open to discussion – and ... unending conversation.

I valued my friendship with them immensely – and it dawned on me that without them, my relationship with Claudette would not have endured as long as it had. There were a few points in our conversation when I'd almost said '*Would you mind stopping the car —I'd like to hitch back to Bristol*' but that would have made me late for dinner back in Hotwells with Penelope, Rebecca, and Meryl.

That would have been monstrously discourteous – so I was stuck in the passenger seat wondering what the next exchange might be. Fortunately silence reigned for a considerable time.

Claudette finally remarked—as if nothing had happened—that she'd bought a double album of songs sung by Fred Astaire. I asked her about it – as if nothing had happened. Claudette was good at these transitions and I'd become adept at going along with them.

"*There are songs from 'Dancing Lady', 'Flying Down to Rio', 'Top Hat', 'Shall We Dance', and 'Damsel in Distress'. It's quite a collection – and there are some nice photographs too.*"

I asked her what songs were on the album and she regaled me with a list. I asked if she could sing one – but she said she'd do them an injustice and I'd have to wait to hear them properly.

"*I look forward to hearing it. I really enjoyed the other Fred Astaire album you played for me … quite a surprise really because I wouldn't have imagined I'd have enjoyed that kind of music. It's a*—whole—*other world isn't it.*" I stopped short of speculating on the lyrics and how lyrics have evolved. That would have taken me into discussions of *my* lyrics and Claudette was likely to bridle all over again.

I'd initially been bemused by the way that Claudette— intellectually bright as she was—had so little interest in exploratory discussion. It wasn't that she *wouldn't* discuss anything – but there was always a cut-off point. These 'discursive terminations' occurred at incrementally shorter periods as the first year moved into the second year – and now she'd made it clear that she wasn't open to *any kind* of conceptual exploration.

an odd boy

The play we'd seen was 'As You Like It' but very little surrounding the play had been anything close to *as I might have liked it*. The trip to Stratford brought me closer than I'd ever been to bidding Claudette farewell – but I kept remembering that the eve of the degree show was—*not*—the right time to say '*I need to spread my wings and fly.*'

Ah, that's what Shakespeare said: There would be days like this, / Say you'll be in Paris, playing the Blues. And I never believed it. / Now I believe everything Shakespeare says. Champion Jack Dupree—Million People Live the Same Way—The Tricks—1976

17

the third year: may 1975 – june 1975

bower ashton – don't think twice ... it's alright

It didn't seem long before the third term was drawing to a close. I was setting up my Degree Show. The photograph of myself—with Janet Coleridge, Stephanie Lyndhurst, Angela Grey, and Linda Essex—had been framed in simple hardboard, glass, and clips – but the glass was a type of bathroom glass that was slightly green and distorted. The sepia, blue-toned, and green-toned photographs below it had been faintly and delicately hand-coloured by each of us. The central image was black and white and depicted us all staring directly into the lens. It gave a strange feel to the image as we were smiling, yet vaguely demonic.

You gotta to have what it takes—Lord—you gotta to have what it takes, / You can't get what can be had if you ain't got what it takes.
Jack Jones—Betty Hall Jones—You Gotta to Have What it Takes—1943

Todd Whelcombe—skulking at the doorway to our exhibition room—passed further gratuitous comments as soon as I hove into view "*Pity ...*" he observed with a studied sigh "*... that the girls let you draw them into your obsession with weirdness.*"

"*Thank you for your critical observation Todd.*"

"*You're welcome*" he replied.

"*No*" I grinned. "I'm—*Simmerson*—you're—*Whelcombe.*"

Janet, Stephanie, Angela, and Linda burst out in riotous laughter. Todd turned on his heel and stormed down the corridor.

an odd boy

"*You've done it now*" Linda observed. "*But he deserved it! I just don't know—why—he acts like that.*"

"*I'm afraid your laughter probably upset him more than my making a pun with his name. You know ... I've tried hard to understand Todd and Veranda – but the best I could come up with was that they're aspiring-middle class who wish to be seen as upper-middle class and ... feel I should know my place.*"

"*I don't know about the class thing ...*" Janet observed "*... but what I do know is that Todd and Veranda are both like Dylan's Mr Jones. Something's happening and they don't know what it is.*"

"*Yes ...*" I grinned "*... too true ... maybe I'm happening ... and they don't know what I am. Either way, I'm a reflection of something they don't want. I don't know what happened to them during the '60s – but it must have frightened them. I'm by no means as weird as some of the people I used to know at Farnham – but my existence is some sort of on-going insult to them – or to the kind of life they want.*"

It was strange to present a display that represented three years of work. Once I had my selection arranged Derek came to survey the scene. He made some good suggestions and I took his advice about the balance of material on display. He told me I didn't need to crowd my exhibition. Derek told us he liked our room and thought we'd all do well. Just before the external assessors arrived Dick Taylor made his rounds with the Graphic Design tutors in tow. He paused in front of my exhibited work —a slight smile playing beneath his nose—and said "*Well—Victor—Simmer—son ...you never quite—came to the—boil—as an Illustrator ... did you.*"

How long had he planned this I wondered? Since my Dick Taylorship remark in the first term? "*No Dick ... I suppose I didn't ...*" I replied "*... but then ... I suppose ... I never became a codpiece couturier ... either.*"

Muffled sounds of amusement arose from the tutors who'd followed my word play – but this time Dick Taylor was unmoved. The slight smile remained. It was a little eerie.

"*You know ...*" he commented calmly "*... he who laughs last, laughs longest.*"[1] Pause "*It's a wise saw ... and you would do well to remember it.*"

"*I shall ... I like wise saws.*" Pause "*After all ... an abscess makes the heart grow fonder.*"

This produced further chuckles and Dick Taylor—still with his slight smile—moved on to the next display as if nothing had happened. That was no problem to me as I had no desire to triumph in any battle of wit. I only took him on because he was there and ... because authority figures still had the power to make me take them on. I drifted down to the refectory to use my mouth more valuably on a plate of fish and chips. The fish and chips were still as good as ever – but Dick Taylor's slight smile remained in my mind as an uncomfortable memory.

The assessors came and talked to us all. Then it was the turn of the public to view the exhibitions. My application to the RCA had been sent and I had a slip to attach to the folio I was to take there – *if*, I got a 1st or upper 2nd.

The final exhibition came and went. The Illustration studio became an arena of expectation and anxiety waiting for the results. Todd eyed me from time to time but said nothing.

"*Todd finds it irritating that you don't appear to be concerned about the degree results*" said Janet.

---

1   15th Century proverb. Also expressed as '*He who laughs last, laughs best.*'

"*That's a pity ...*" I replied "*... but I don't think I'd oblige him as far as feigning anxiety. I think he enjoys having reactions to me – as if it was my rôle in his life.*" Janet asked me what I meant. "*Well it's almost as if he defines himself in terms of his dislike of me. I think if he ever entertained the idea that I was likeable he'd have to review his notions of reality.*"

Janet nodded "*Yes he does seem to have an investment in seeing you as he does.*"

"*I just wonder how he'll live without me after the term ends ...*"

Eventually the day arrived. Our degree results were released and posted on the wall outside Derek's office. As soon as the news reached us – the Illustration studio suddenly emptied.

I remained. I was in the middle of a collage based on cut-outs from my own drawings. Todd and Veranda were incredulous as to why I wasn't anxious to know my result but didn't stop to brow beat me about it. What would I have said? '*I think I know what I got.*' No. I wouldn't have said that – even though I believed I *did* know. They came back after a while. Some highly pleased – others not. Todd was practically shuddering with emotion.

I continued to cut out sections of my drawings.

Janet came in last and said with a big smile "*Congratulations – you got a* 1st!"

I looked up with a smile "*Thank you for letting me know – what did you Stephanie, Angela, and Linda get?*"

"*We all got* 1sts! *We—all—did! I can't believe it!*"

"*Fantastic! I'm really pleased! You really deserved it – all of you!*" I said. "*Your show was superb—especially the etchings—I love that one of the bulrushes. I've always wanted to produce an etching as good as that.*"

Todd—unable to restrain himself any further—turned to me and said "*I bet—you're—surprised.*"

It was not a question. I should have replied '*I wasn't surprised*' but as it was the last time I was going to see Todd and Veranda – I decided I'd have to be weird, just for old time's sake "*Yeah Todd – surprised as a stag beetle in a possum's posing pouch.*"

Todd looked icy – but this time he was not about to turn on his heel. "*And*—you're—*telling*—me—*you're not surprised?*" he almost barked.

Sigh. "No ...Todd ... *I'm not telling*—you. *You're telling*—me. Are you ... surprised at my result?"

"*Yes*—I—bloody—well—am—*surprised!*" Pause "*Surprised*—and —disgusted! I wouldn't have credited that frivolous self-indulgent weirdness deserved a 1st."

"Well maybe it doesn't Todd ... but ... that's what I got. What d'you expect me to say?"

Todd stood there glaring – his eyes darting slightly in token of rapid thinking. He said nothing so I continued "*Y'know* ... however weird my work is Todd, I worked—extremely—hard ... and I have quite a lot of work." Pause "*Y'know* ... I think you're actually far more of a professional graphics person than I am ... but ... I just put in a lot of hours ... so maybe ... I got a 1st *on sheer quantity.*"

Todd looked a little thrown by my compliment and didn't know what to say for once. I didn't ask Todd about his result because I somehow guessed he didn't get a 1st.

"*It was kind of you not to ask him what he got ...*" Janet said "... and ... kind of you to tell him what you told him about being more professional – but ... did you—mean—*it?*"

"Certainly I meant it. He's got a far better sense of product-marketing, corporate identity, and the whole sphere of commercial image making. He's got a natural talent for presentation that I don't.

"The thing is ... he just never worked that hard. If he'd worked harder I imagine he could have got a 1st. *What did he get by the way?"*

Janet shrugged *"Lower* 2nd *like Veranda."*

"Ouch" I grimaced.

"They're pretty livid about it. They're going to complain or something."

I suddenly felt sorrier for Todd and Veranda than I'd ever been. *"Well ..."* I said *"... we all get what we deserve ... whether we deserve it or not."*

Janet grinned *"I don't think I know what that means."*

I laughed *"Nor do I ... but I think ... it's vaguely sympathetic. I don't like to see people unhappy."* Pause *"I don't like to see people fail to get the things they want. It's happened—too—many times to me. I know I got a* 1st *... and I wanted it – but there've been a fair few times ... when I lost what I wanted ... on a regular basis."*

"Claudette got an upper 2nd *– did you know?"*

"Yes—she's really happy too—she wasn't expecting a 1st *y'know, and she doesn't need it for the line she's taking. I'd better go off and celebrate with her – it's the mid-morning break and she'll be expecting me down there"*

For once, Claudette wasn't there. She'd stayed up in her department – and ... I decided not to venture up there. I'd see her later back in Hotwells.

That was the last time I saw Todd or Veranda. They vanished that day even though the term wasn't finished. I never found out whether they made an appeal against their results but—whether or not—it made no difference to me.

The other ladies remained a little longer and we exchanged addresses – but I was on my own on the last day of term. I was still completing an oil painting.

I'd collect it when the paint dried. It took me back to the final day at Virginia Water when I'd left my completed painting to the school – signed Frank Schubert. That seemed a lifetime ago – but it was impossible to think of that last day without remembering that it was the day on which I knew I'd never see Lindie Dale again.

Somehow she always rose in my memory at these transitional phases. That was five years ago and the painting of a young version of myself with Mr Love was hard to recall. Lindie was not hard to recall. It was as if I'd seen her yesterday. Bristol had been good – but life as I'd known it was drawing to a close. I'd decided on becoming a Foundation lecturer – anywhere there was still an Art School. I had little choice about where I ended up – but I had hopes about Falmouth. Falmouth hadn't been absorbed into a polytechnic. Bower Ashton—along with the various technical colleges—were being absorbed into Bristol Polytechnic. Its character was going to change irredeemably. It was the beginning of the end and it was evident that the Illustration Department wouldn't survive Derek Crowe's retirement.

I'd applied to the RCA in London for an Interdisciplinary MA degree that could go on to a PhD. I seemed to have made the right choices. I was going to London for three or four years. As I prepared to set off for London with my folio I knew the time had come to talk with Claudette. I was going to have to be as gentle as I could be. There was nothing to complain about – because I had tolerated her behaviour when maybe I should not have done. I'd just let the situation roll when I should have been more realistic. I'd allowed her to undervalue me – and that was my fault. I'd given her a false impression of what I was.

I'd allowed her to think that she could treat me as she did without consequences – and now ... the consequences were just going to have to hit the fan. We were simply too different. We would—or could—always be friends. There just wasn't enough to hold us together as a couple. I knew she'd not come to stay with me in London when I was at the RCA. She'd have to acknowledge as much. It was a given fact that her father wouldn't have guests in the house – so she'd have to see that it was as much her decision as mine.

"*Y'know Rebecca ...*" I mused "*... it occurs to me that there's more to 'dette's separate house idea than she lets on.*"

"*Her father, you mean?*" Rebecca replied. I nodded. "*Well ... we could have told you—that—but ... we thought you knew ...*"

I was somewhat taken aback "*Well ... I know now ...*" Pause "*... or at least I've just worked it out.*"

"*Yeah ... her father warned her on Foundation about the possibility of losing half her inheritance if she shared it with a partner who wasn't in a financially equal position ... we got to hear about it when 'dette was having that scene with John Willoughby. She told us about it then because they— were—to have got married! Can you imagine that!? 'dette being up for marriage! She was totally and utterly besotted with that creep – and for once I'd say her father was right – he was in for the main chance, the bastard. Anyhow ... she probably forgot she'd mentioned it to us—she was totally out of it at the time—otherwise she'd probably have had to have owned up about it. I can't imagine things have changed at home.*"

"*Right ... so ... I'm a 'menial on the make' – and the whole idea of sharing a house with me must have been described as a blunder of the worst kind. This is like something out of The Forsyte Saga.*"[2]

Rebecca nodded sagely "*That world's still there ... I should know and so should Meryl and Penelope. We're all—Badminton gells—you know.*"

"*Yes ... I know that – but you seem to wear it differently from 'dette ...*"

"*Well ...yes ... maybe that's because us three are not—*proud*—of it. Don't get me wrong—it's a good school, albeit a little fusty—but we don't see that having gone there gives us any kind of status. None of us have any desire to trade on it or even mention it – but 'dette's different ... she and her father definitely see themselves as aristocrats of some sort – even though ...and this is going to sound completely stupid ... but Meryl and Penelope's parents are a lot higher up the social ladder than old man Gascoigne.*"

"*And you?*"

"*Well ...yeah ... my parents too, I suppose.*"

"*I wouldn't have known ...*" Pause "*... what—is—it about me that always ends me up having relationships and making friends with the upper echelons ...?*"

Rebecca shook her head "*I hope you've not seen us like that—as being different or whatever—because we're not like that at all.*"

"*Have no fears on that score – that's never occurred to me and doesn't occur to me now. It never affected me with Lindie – but then ... however little difference she saw—in who we each were—her parents had a pretty clear idea. It's never my friends – it's always their—parents—who decide I'm a gutter snipe ... and y'know ...*

---

2 The Forsyte Saga – a series of novels by John Galsworthy—published between 1906 and 1921—describing the lives of an upper-middle class family.

"*I'm getting a little—*tired—*of it. This situation with 'dette and her family home is a re-run of Brigadier Dale – but it's clandestine.*"

"*Yes ... 'dette's vampire-father trickle-fed her with pathological indoctrination to a point where she has little emotional understanding of her life.*"

"*Right ... at least Brigadier Dale confronted me personally.*"

"*It's not just Sepulchrave ...*" Rebecca sighed "*... it's Claudette's need for comfort and security. If it comes to having a partner or security ... the house would win—every—time. You see ... she's in this position ...*" Pause "*If she plays her cards right financially – she'll never have to work. She's not going to be rich – but she's going to be able to support herself very comfortably 'til she pops her clogs and she's—*terrified—*of losing that situation.*"

"*Y'know ... this may sound stupid or whatever ... but ... it'd never occur to me to deprive someone of half a house on the basis that I'd lived with them or married them. As far as I'm concerned you only have the right to take out what you brought in.*"

"*Yeah ... but that's not—*the law—*is it?*" Pause "*And 'dette's strictly against marriage for just that reason. I don't think that Sepulchrave had to do much persuading. She's talked to us about her beautiful future ... and how she'll be able to pick and choose with theatre work – but she won't be dependent on employment for her income.*"

"*Right ... the picture makes sense ... and—y'know—I'm glad it makes sense ...*" Pause "*... it makes everything simpler in my mind. It makes it easier that I'm ... well, vaguely redundant to her situation. I'm a private convenience rather than a public convenience.*"

"*It's almost eerie ...*" Rebecca smiled wanly "*... the way you can find humour in any situation.*"

"*Yeah ... well ... it's a Blues perspective ... but I wouldn't say—any— situation.*" Pause "*Y'know ... I feel sorry for 'dette.*"

"*So you—are—going to leave her.*" Rebecca wasn't asking a question.

"Yes ... without a doubt." Pause "Y'know ... I remember oblique comments, that you've all made from time to time about the future – and ... it's all pretty clear."

"Yeah ... well ..." Rebecca replied cautiously. "We went about as far as we could in trying to tell you – but ...you never really looked as if you'd welcome us saying any more than we said."

"Yeah ... I'm sorry ... that was dim really. I'm aware of that ... but 'til recently, I just haven't been willing to have anything spelt out. It's been increasingly evident ... and ... now I see it – it's made my decision ... obvious. I can't possibly stay in this relationship. It makes no sense to me at all. It hasn't made sense for a fair while. I don't think I'll say anything to her about her father or the financial thing."

"*Why?*"

"There's no need. It would only complicate things." Pause "I'm leaving ... simply ... because I don't want to stay."

Rebecca nodded sadly. "What if she changed her mind about living together though?"

"It would make our separation more difficult ... being that I would feel she'd made a huge concession – but ... it'd make no difference to my decision. It's too late for that. It was ... actually too late for that a fair while back."

Rebecca said she was relieved—wished me good luck—and I went up to my room to wait for Claudette to arrive.

Well I'm going to Paris in the morning soon, / If I don't leave in the morning, I'm gonna leave in the afternoon.
Champion Jack Dupree—Going to Paris—The Tricks—1968

an odd boy

After a quarter of an hour—she was always punctual—Claudette rang the bell, entered, and ascended the staircase to my attic room.

"*I'm going up to the RCA tomorrow, 'dette, I've got to take my folio for the pre-interview selection process.*"

"*Yes. I already know that.*" She'd already formulated her position. "*I'm not up for travelling there with you if that's what you have in mind.*"

Claudette had set the scene for me – and I was relieved that she was not in one of her sprightly convivial moods. "*No, 'dette … it's not … in fact … that's the last thing on my mind.*"

She looked relieved – but a little disconcerted that I'd made no attempt to persuade her. "*I've never liked London—you know that— it's filthy and I have to wash my hair and clothes when I get back.*"

"*Yeah … train full of smokers – totally vile …*" I tried to chuckle. "*I knew you wouldn't want to take a trip to London.*" Pause "*And – I know it'll be like that, 'dette … when I'm living there… that's why I'm bringing it up now.*"

Claudette had heard me use her name thrice – and sensed something amiss. "*You're sounding portentous*" she said as an attempted quip.

"*There's no—right—way to say this, 'dette … but, I need to go to London … alone.*" Pause "*I need to go there alone and … stay alone for a while. In fact … for a—long—while. I need to begin a new life – on my own*" Pause "*I suppose you know for yourself … that things haven't exactly been easy between us. It's been like that for … a while now hasn't it.*"

"*But … we …*" she gulped – but it went nowhere.

"I think we—can—be friends – and we should—be—friends … I think we could be better friends than we've been …" I suddenly didn't know what word to use for what we were to each other.

"Your father wouldn't allow me to stay if I were to come to visit in any case – and … paying for a bed and breakfast to be in Bath would be absurd – quite apart from the fact that I wouldn't be able to afford it on whatever grant I get."

"But this is all about practicalities … what has—this—got to do with us?"

"It has everything to do with—us—'dette … everything." Pause "You see … practicalities mean a—great deal—to you. That's why you want your own home. That's why you don't want to share a home with anyone else. That's important to you – and there's no reason you should change anything that's so important to you." Pause "The practicalities that seem irrelevant to you, 'dette … concern how—I—have to live life from day to day. Certain things aren't a big deal if you can afford them – but I just can't afford the life you want – and there's no place in your scheme of things for me once I leave the house in Hotwells."

Claudette was silent. Sitting staring at me. There were a few more things I had to say – so I thought I may as well plough on "So … I think you're going to—have—to accept that there are things that are more important to—you—than a partner – or at least … a partner like me. I think you need to find someone who's more important than whatever it is—you—want."

"What do you mean!? I don't understand what you're saying!"

an odd boy

"D'you really—want—to know?" She did. "Well ...you want life to be as—you—want it to be – and ... when I want something different ... I have to do it on my own. You'll never travel with me. You can't abide strange beds, shared bathrooms ... it's a long list you know ... quite apart from the fact that you have absolutely no interest in Buddhism even in terms of talking about ideas ..." Pause "You see ... I've always lived—your —life with you ... but you've never lived—my—life with me." Pause "You see ... the tearooms and ... the antique shops ..."

"You always said you liked that!"

"Yes ... I did – and I do ... but that was—your—life. I was happy to join you there ... but you never wanted to join—me—anywhere." Pause "You could have come to Samyé Ling with me—just once—but that always totally was out of the question." Pause "I'm not saying it wasn't fun, 'dette – but you can't deny it was—always—your way."

"This is all out of proportion!"

"Yes it is, 'dette ... our relationship's been out of proportion for almost two years. It's out of proportion that you'd never visit me in London. It's out of proportion that there wouldn't be a place to stay in your house if I were to visit. It's out of proportion that you'd expect me to go along with that. It's all out of proportion that you seem unable to understand that none of this is workable." Pause "Then ..."

"There's more?"

"I'm afraid so, 'dette ... and this is probably the thing that makes it final. There's the constant irritation I cause with what you describe as my 'philosophising'. It's no fault of yours 'dette ...you just—are as you are —and I'm ... just as—I am. I'm not saying my way's any better than yours ... we're just—too—different – and there's no reason why we should make each other suffer because of it." Pause

"There's no good reason why you should have to learn to enjoy 'my philosophising'—or talk with me about Buddhism—and there's no good reason why I should have to inhibit 'my philosophising' and never mention Buddhism ... Neither approach is emotionally feasible."

Claudette sat staring at me in what could have been perplexity.

"Yes ..." she eventually replied "... I suppose you're probably right. I've actually been waiting for you to say something like this for the last year — especially ... on that ... awful journey back from Stratford. I don't really understand why I was—so—horrible to you ..."

That was a little unexpected. Should I ask why, I wondered? I decided it was not useful to either of us to dissect our situation. "... I ... wondered if you were going to shout at me ... and ...you never did." Pause "You never have." Pause "That's not a complaint ... but ... it's unearthly — especially when I've shouted at you." Pause "Maybe that's why I've never liked the idea of Buddhism — it's so ... I don't know what to say or how to describe it — but it's somehow inhuman and robotic ... People get angry when people are horrible to them — because it's natural to get angry — and ...you—never—do!"

"No ... that's true ... I never did and never will."

"But it's just that, that always made me feel lonely and stupid!"

"Y'know 'dette ... 'stupid' is the very last thing you've ever seemed — and the very last thing you've ever seemed to show." Pause "This is the first I've ever heard of you feeling stupid ..."

"That's because you're emotionally two dimensional." Pause "I'm always the one who acts badly — and all you ever do is to look ... wearied. That's so unnatural!"

"I never told you I was mister natural, 'dette ..."

"Oh really!"

"I never intended to look wearied, 'dette — it wasn't deliberate ..."

an odd boy

"No—I could see that—and that made it even worse!"

"I mean I wasn't trying to cause an effect with how I looked."

"No—quite—that's just what I said, that's what made it even worse!"

"I'm sorry ..." Pause "... at those times ... I guess I was just frustrated with not being able to answer questions – or ... like with the ride back from Stratford – simply not accepting a definition of *myself* that didn't feel real."

"Sorry ... but your lack of anger is something I should have talked about a long time ago."

"I can't blame you for that, 'dette ... I could have spoken up earlier too ... I should have done – and if I'd started talking about the things that didn't suit me, you have felt free to do the same ... so I take the blame for that."

"Why should *you* take the blame! Why d'you have to be so damn good all the time! I don't think that Buddhism is any good for people – my father says that this Buddhist passivity and acceptance comes from a culture where it's needed – where most people live in poverty and die before they're forty."

"Your father may have a point there—culturally speaking—but passivity and acceptance aren't ideas that can be used as simplistically as you're using them ... As you said on the way back from Stratford ... there are subjects which are only open to discussion if you've studied them – if you're an acknowledged expert." Pause "I'm not expert – but I have studied ... and can only say that I have no reason to consider your father having more than a rudimentary understanding of the religion – especially as it's practised in the Nyingma Tradition."

"But this refusal to be angry *is* Buddhist, is it not." Claudette stated emphatically.

"Anger is regarded as a problem ... yes ... but my dislike of anger predates Buddhism by a fair few years. You see ... my father was an angry man – or rather he could become extremely angry – and I never enjoyed that aspect of him. I never respected it – and I hated the fact that my mother was subject to it." Pause *And I must say ... that I have to disagree entirely with the idea that anger is either natural or healthy. Anger is a learnt habit and ... frankly ... I find it far more repulsive than you find swearing – in fact ... I—fucking—abhor it ..."*

That was the second time I'd used the Saxon expletive since I'd first met Claudette. Initially it was shortly after we met – and it had been part of comical badinage.

It seemed somehow fitting now, that I should use it again, at the end. I noticed 'dette hearing that word. Something seemed to register with her – as if that word had said more than everything else I'd said. That word was the full stop at the end of the sentence.

"We're ... not ... alike ... at all, are we?"

That had to be admitted *"No, 'dette—not ... sufficiently—no ... not enough to have a relationship beyond ... being friends ..."*

Claudette turned her face to the window and—avoiding my gaze —said *"Penelope, Rebecca, and Meryl have—all—talked to me about how I 'dominate' you – 'so called'. They said you'd not mentioned anything about that to them – they'd just seen it."*

"What did they see?"

"It doesn't matter. Most of it made no sense – but there were a few things I suppose." Pause *"So ...you never spoke to them about being dominated?"*

"No, 'dette – I never said anything to Penelope, Rebecca, and Meryl about our relationship – that would not be dignified. I would never discuss my partner with anyone else. I never have done – and I never will do." Pause "In terms of 'domination' however – even if I had spoken, I would—not —have laid that at your door. I did actually—allow—whatever of that nature may have occurred … but …y'know, 'dette … I was always free to say 'no' any time I liked. I don't—allow—people to dominate me … I stopped allowing that when I was 16 – with my father …you may remember." She remembered.

"I think they're right in—some—ways …" Claudette sighed "… although … you always—looked—as if you were enjoying yourself."

"Yes, 'dette … I enjoyed myself with you in many ways … it's … just that I can't live—your—life anymore … and … I need to be able to have the kind of conversations I enjoy without driving a partner frantic."

"Yes-yes-yes!" she snapped – but then softened. "Oh well … it's just that … I used to think you were more like me than you turned out to be. I thought you enjoyed being with me and enjoyed the things I enjoyed."

"I think I—am—like you in those ways, 'dette – and … I—do—enjoy many of the things you enjoy. I appreciate you in many ways. It's just that there are aspects of 'me' that are far too different—aspects that you don't enjoy—aspects that are …" I didn't finish the sentence – but Mr Love's words '*a little too lively*' came to mind. Mr Love had said that Blues was '… *a little too lively, for the English.*' Bath and Bristol were emotionally central to Claudette's career map and life plan – but not to mine. Neither of us had an alternative. We acknowledged that – and neither wished the other to abandon their choice. We sat in silence for some minutes. I gazed out of the window at the slow gliding river.

bower ashton – don't think twice ... it's alright

The Kink's song came to mind again and I threw a silent parody on it: '*Lonely old river, must you keep rolling – flowing right out of sight, It makes me feel dizzy – when she's in a tizzy – the ripples are shining so bright, But there's no beginning or end, As long as I gaze through my small Hotwells window, I am in paradise ...*'.

It was Summer but there was an overcast sky. It had rained intermittently through the night and there was a clean fresh smell in the air. It was cool and slightly damp. I loved that weather – as it cleared away the Summer fug of heat and dust.

When it rained – everything that was airborne simply hit the deck – made a clean slate of the atmosphere. In a flash of a moment—absorbed by the beauty of the scene before me—I'd forgotten that Claudette was there.

"*Which—one—is it!?*" Claudette shouted and I flinched slightly as my autonomic nervous system reacted to the suddenness of the sound. I turned my head—slowly—and faced Claudette.

"*Which one is what, 'dette?*" I asked—as gently as I could—having no idea what she was talking about.

"*Penelope, Rebecca, or Meryl!?*" she virtually screamed.

"*What about them?*" I replied in an even, uncomprehending tone. "*I have—no—idea—what—you are talking about, 'dette.*"

"*Which one are you leaving me for!?*"

"*Are you out of your—mind—'dette? Where on—earth—did this notion come from?*"

"*Just answer my question!*" she shouted.

"I am not leaving you for anyone, 'dette. I am simply leaving—you." Pause *"I'm leaving—you—because I want to be on my own. I'm leaving—you—so that I can begin to make simple decisions that affect only—me. I'm simply leaving you 'dette ... and it makes me sad that it makes you sad ... but I simply cannot stay in this relationship with you. I simply can't be with someone who's ... lost respect for me."*

"And what do you think of me then?" Claudette asked in a fairly restrained manner.

"I've not lost respect for you, 'dette—or admiration for your knowledge and skills ... but I no longer love you, 'dette. You've been ... too censorious for—too—long and it's worn me out – or worn out my capacity for love and romance."

Claudette burst into tears, apologising—amongst giant gulps for air—for having shouted at me.

"It's alright, 'dette ... I can understand how an idea like that could make a person ... shout ..." Pause *"... but I'm not affected by it. It doesn't make me upset with you, only ... upset—for—you. I don't like to see you upset."*

It was a while before she calmed down enough to say anything.

"It wasn't—so—bad was it?" she asked – meaning the final year of our relationship.

"No, 'dette ... not—so—bad ..." I lied *"... but ... it really wasn't that great sometimes either ..."*

"We had fun though, didn't we?"

"Yeah ... we had fun. I'm not saying I have no regrets about leaving you, 'dette. I'd have left a while back if you weren't dear to me ... I do still remember the first year y'know – when you seemed to like how I was ... but then ...you just got angrier and angrier with me as time went on ... just for ... being who I've been all along." Pause "I mean ... I haven't changed have I?" Pause "Not in terms of my 'philosophising' I mean – I was always like that wasn't I."

"...yes ... I suppose you were ..."

"... and, at first that was alright ... then later ... well ... I don't know what to say ..." Pause "... later my ideas became a source of irritation to you ... and that just became more intense ...'til ... I didn't want to experience any more of your displeasure. It wasn't pleasant for you, it wasn't pleasant for me – and we've just ended up wasting each other's time."

"I can't argue with that ... I don't understand what happened ... I just don't understand why it all changed and why it ... why you ... why I ... why I just couldn't—go—there with you. It was all just too 'far out' and you ...you ... were always saying things that couldn't be understood by— **any**—one."

I decided not to say that Penelope, Rebecca, and Meryl never had problems understanding me "I'm sorry, 'dette – I didn't mean to be unkind ..."

Claudette smiled tearfully and said "You weren't unkind ...you were never unkind – even when you were obviously fed up with me ... on the way back from Stratford." Pause "Life doesn't always work out does it?"

No answer was needed – but I replied "No, 'dette – it doesn't ... I know that only—too—well ..." I was thinking of Lindie. I was also thinking of Steve and Ron. Suddenly I was in tears. We were both in tears and it was over – apart from a final embrace.

Then—*suddenly* and *mysteriously*—I was on my own.

an odd boy

It was almost as if I hadn't expected to be alone. Claudette left the house in Hotwells for what was probably the last time. We'd planned a theatre visit. I'd already bought the tickets. I said I'd still be delighted to accompany her – if that was alright with her. She said it was – but it wasn't.

She had something arranged on that evening. She was going out to dinner with her father – to some prestigious restaurant.
I'd thought of asking Penelope, Rebecca, and Meryl if any of them would like the spare ticket – but decided against it. I had an uneasy feeling that Claudette might get wind of it and assume I'd lied to her in respect of cultivating a liaison with one of her three friends. I went to the theatre alone. I saw Julius Cæsar. He said *"Et tu, Brute?"* just before the senators plunged their knives into him.

Claudette had quoted that for my benefit on one occasion – for reasons I could hardly remember. I came home feeling uncomfortable about having left her. I had to remind myself why I'd left her – and remind myself that I'd not been unfair.

I sat up in my room looking at the river as I often did when discombobulated about anything. I decided not to listen to 'Waterloo Sunset' – because it was all too poignant. I finally got tired and went to bed. Slept like an entire lumber yard.

"Are you sad about 'dette?" asked Penelope observing my slightly sombre mien over breakfast.

"Yes—in some ways—I did really feel ... a great deal for 'dette ... She was a completely magical being at first ..."

Penelope nodded slowly *"Yes ... we could see that. You looked really good together at first ... she was nice to you and we all ... well we thought that was lovely. It was lovely to see 'dette looking so happy ... but ..."*

"... but she killed that incrementally ..."

"Yes ... we all saw that too – and it was, perplexing ... the way ... the way you put up with it. You'd always make allowance for her ... and make excuses for her. Sometimes ... we felt quite annoyed with 'dette – I mean— really—annoyed." Pause "Meryl almost bit her head off once ..."

"Never knew that ..." Pause "... 'dette never said a word – 'til I said goodbye ... then she mentioned that you'd all said she dominated me."

"Did she own up to that then?"

"Not really ... she said that most of it had made no sense ... but added that there were a few things – she supposed ..."

"I think she understood us fairly well ... but ... maybe she had no choice about it with the three of us telling her how it had looked." Pause "... y'know ... 'dette never does accept anything that doesn't fit with her own private reality."

"Yes ... that's how it was ... and ... that's how it is." Pause "So ... to answer your question ... although I'm sad about 'dette ... I'm also hugely relieved." Pause "I'm happy that it wasn't an angry parting."

I thought it unwise to refer to Claudette's shouting '*Which one is it!?*' ... that would have opened a certified, pre-cooked, carbon-dated can of worms."*It just had to happen.*" I concluded "*And ... she saw that it had to happen. Actually ... it really should have happened a year or more back.*"

That was plainly obvious to Penelope "*I'm glad it wasn't a bad scene for either of you. I talked to 'dette and she seems fine. Said it'd been a three year companionship to accompany a three year degree course – and that seemed somehow fitting. Only 'dette could say a thing like that.*"

"Yeah ..." I chuckled "... *she always had a nice turn of phrase. I'm glad 'dette was alright about it.*"

"*Well she rationalised it with her usual ... linguistic aplomb.*"

"Can't blame her for that ... a person needs to maintain some sense of dignity when they've been left."

"Only you could see it like that."

"Well ... she's been a good companion and I've valued having spent time together with her. She—was—always there for me – and I have to appreciate that."

Penelope pondered for a moment. *"Yes ... she was there for you ... but in her—own—very peculiar—way ..."* Pause *"She wanted convenience and comfort more than she wanted a partner."*

"Yes ... That's certainly true."

"'There's a lady who's sure all that glitters is gold – and she's buying a stairway to heaven ...'" Penelope sang.

"...'When she gets there she knows if the stores are all closed with a word she can get what she came for ...'"[3] I sang the next line. *"That's the first time I've ever heard you quote a Rock song."*

"I've always liked the way you do that ... so ... I thought I'd give it a go."

"For a first attempt it was perfection itself." I grinned ever-so-slightly *"Yes ... 'dette's just like that ... just like the song."*

"I think I'll try that more often in future – it's quite interesting. There's a sense of doom in that song that reminds me of 'dette ... Y'know ... you and 'dette ... it really—was—doomed from the start."

"Mmmm ... yes and no." Pause *"It was only doomed in terms of habit ... her habit and my habit. Hers you understand quite well – but my habit also played a part."*

---

3 Jimmy Page/Robert Plant—Led Zeppelin—Stairway to Heaven—Led Zeppelin IV—1971. The song is composed of several sections, which increase in tempo and volume. The song begins as a slow acoustic-based folk song accompanied by recorders before electric instrumentation is introduced.

"What did you ever do?" Penelope almost squawked. *"That's outrageous — unless you were aggressive with her when we weren't looking — and 'dette never accused you of anything like that. She only said you were philosophically and intellectually opaque ... and well she said a lot of things like that — but she never had any complaints about your manner."*

"No ... I am as-you-find-me ... but ... what I'm referring to is my habit of ... being non-confrontational ... and ... non-critical." Pause *"I should have told her what I didn't enjoy a little more directly ... I should have made certain things clear. I should have told her that I couldn't go on unless things changed ... and then ... it got too late and I didn't want to upset her before the final degree show ... And then ... in the end ... it didn't seem to upset her as much as I feared."*

"I can follow the logic of that — but it makes no sense emotionally ... I mean ... I think you're taking responsibility for things that aren't your fault." I shrugged — and Penelope continued *"So ... can I ask ...? If it's the habits that doomed it — what was the other side? Where might it not have been doomed?"*

"Well — to have continued as we were when we first got together." Pause *"I think it's possible to do that ... and when habits seem to be spoiling what you have — you simply apologise and return to how you were before the habits kicked in."* Pause *"You can stay in love forever — if you maintain courtship behaviour — and ... that's always what I try to do."*[4]

---

4 See 'Entering the Heart of the Sun and Moon' by Ngakpa Chögyam and Khandro Déchen—Aro Books inc—2009.

an odd boy

Penelope looked as if she wanted to say something – but sat nebulously fixated on the wall. She seemed to have suddenly become upset – but there was nothing in what I'd said that could have had that effect. I wondered whether I should ask her why she suddenly seemed so sad – but for some unaccountable reason, decided against it. Some moments of silence passed in which I simply took in the amazing pleasantness of the room I would soon be seeing for the last time. The end of the lease loomed. Then, as if someone else were speaking, I spoke to the air in the room. I felt as if I were in a play and my lines were scripted "*Weird thing is ...*" I sighed. "*... now it's all over ... I seem to have known it all along.*"

18

june 1975 – july 1975

ain't no djinn called alegbara[1]

Within hours Bower Ashton began to recede into an Ingres paper sketch of memory. A time that appeared almost eternal three years before – suddenly felt like a matter of months. Strangely however, my time with the lads and Savage Cabbage seemed to expand as if it were filling the vacuum. The gigs and conversations wove themselves into a story that was luminous and dense. I even remembered Gazzer Mitchell fondly and wondered where he was. I wished a similar rapprochement had been possible with Todd – but it hadn't.

It was the morning of the day I took the train to London. An *almost-orange-glow* was suffusing the living room from a sky that betokened rain. I sat gazing through the bay windows at the river and Penelope joined me hardly making a sound in her approach. I suddenly caught her image in my peripheral vision. She looked somehow intriguing and it occurred to me strongly —in that moment—how much I valued her friendship – and my friendship with Rebecca and Meryl.

---

1   Djinn – a spirit from Arabian North African mythology, of a lower order than angels and able to appear in human / animal form in order to exercise supernatural influence. Alternative spellings: jinn / djinni / jinnee / genie. Alegbara – the name of the one who comes to the crossroads and to accept your 'soul' in repayment for unprecedented skills on the musical instrument of your choice. Legba is identified in societal Christian terms as 'the Devil' – but he actually emanates from West Africa. Both a trickster and an inspiration of music and language, he makes claims on the aspirant other than the Christian sense of the 'soul'. 'Legba' is a contraction of 'Alegbara'.

"Y'know ..." I said to Penelope "... *I've been thinking back to my last exchange with Dick Taylor* ..." Pause "... *he made some lame joke about my name—Simmer-son—and not having come to the boil as an illustrator.*"

"Yeah ... that—is—pretty lame. So what did you say?"

"I agreed – but said I hadn't become a codpiece couturier either."

It took a moment – but the penny dropped "*Dick*—tailor" Penelope laughed. "*Oh that's really—too—funny.*"

"Well maybe ... but I didn't—have—to say that." Pause "I—could— just have let it go. I don't know what it is that makes me bridle like that. It's as if I can't resist it – with authority figures, that is ..."

"Well he sounds as if he deserved it – but maybe ... if you want to get psychological about it – you could still be fighting your father."

"Yeah ... you're probably right about that ... although – I get on with my father pretty well now. Of course ... it—could—all go back a long way too. It's not in my—mind—at the moment though. I suppose there've been other people too."

"Yeah ... like that Brigadier fellow."

"He's the one who springs more readily to mind – I must admit." Pause "You see ... in the end I—won—with my father ... but I—lost—with Brigadier Dale. So ... maybe it's him rather than my father. Winning the hair battle with my father heralded two—amazing—years in which almost everything just—kept—going right ... apart from Brigadier Dale that is." Pause "I know it all went horribly wrong in the end – but that had nothing to do with my father."

"You're probably right ..." Penelope said with a tilt of her head.

"But getting back to Dick Taylor – there was something—weird—about the whole thing. He had this slight smile all the time ... and he said 'he who laughs last laughs longest.' And I wondered what he meant by that."

"*Oh c'mon – that's just a cheap retort. Makes him sound as if he's got something up his sleeve.*"

"*Yeah ... that's quite possible – but it was his strange serene smirk that was ... well, it was uncharacteristic.*"

Penelope thought that was just another kind of ploy that people used to cover their embarrassment. I took her point and decided not to ponder that matter any further. After all I was never going to see Dick Taylor again – and I was on the eve of my train ride to London.

"*You must feel quite excited about going to deliver your folio to the RCA.*"

"*Sort of ...*" I replied. "*I've never been one for looking forward to anything too much.*"

"*Really?*"

"*Yeah ... I feel more ... amorphous.*" Pause "*I'm sort ... of caught up in the machinery now and whatever happens is just going to flow outward.*"

"*So you're not looking forward to the RCA?*"

"*Don't know whether I'll be accepted yet. Delivering the folio's just the first stage. Then there's the interview.*" Pause "*And then ... I'll have to find somewhere to live in London. I'll have to ask my half-brother James whether he's got any contacts. I think I'll get excited when I'm up there and about to start – but now ... is ... I don't really know what I'm feeling – apart from that I'm going to miss you, Rebecca, and Meryl. I wish we were all going on to London together.*"

"Yeah ... right ... that would be great fun – but we're all three going our own ways now. I'm going to the Scottish Academy, Rebecca's going to the Royal Welsh, and Meryl's going to Manchester ... so – who knows where we'll all end up."[2] Pause *"You'll keep in touch?"* Penelope asked – as if she wanted some slight reassurance.

"Without a doubt" I replied with almost indecent haste. *"I really do hope we'll be able to work on some kind of project together in the next years. Shame you couldn't all have gone to the London College."*

"We can't all be high flyers like you" she laughed. *"It would have been great ... but ... we all had to go where we could specialise and where we had a chance of being accepted."* Pause *"And ... none of us are anywhere near as close to our heads of Department as you are to Derek Crowe. You've got a golden road ahead of you."*

"Well ... it could have been with you to keep me company – who knows what I'll find in London. Maybe the place will be thick with Todds and Verandas" I laughed. *"Still – I'm sure we could keep an eye open for chances of joint enterprises."*

"That would be brilliant!" Penelope said with an uncharacteristic blush. *"And ..."* she faltered *"... I'm sure there are all sorts of possibilities in the future. You just can't tell."*

I'd finished preparations for London and was as satisfied with my folio as I could be. Derek had helped me choose the pieces. It had been difficult to make the selection – but I trusted Derek's judgement. He'd suggested that I left out the whimsical material – even though he liked it.

---

2   The Royal Scottish Academy of Music, the Royal Welsh Academy of Music and Drama, and the Manchester University Department of Music.

"You have to be careful with humour sometimes ..." he pointed out *"... because people don't always react well to it. Dick Taylor's of—that—persuasion. He sees humour as ... indulgent – and you never know who is going to look at your work at the RCA."*

I thought that was a good point. *"Yes ... I'm glad I didn't have to spend three years with Dick Taylor."*

Derek looked surprised *"You did ...you know ... He—is—the Head of the Graphic Design Department."*

"Yes ... I suppose I must have chosen to ignore that ... as I never had to speak to him about my work. I always saw you as the Head of Department – of the Illustration Department I mean."

"I—wish—I was ... but Illustration is a subset of Graphic Design and Dick makes—all—the major decisions. I—do—have my influence and I'll probably manage to keep Illustration separate 'til I retire." Pause *"It sometimes involves fighting the good fight and all that ... speaking of which I heard about your—duel—with the aforementioned—most—amusing. I wish I'd been there to hear it. You were obviously on good form – and, fortunately ... he doesn't have to write you a reference."* Derek looked at me with a mixed expression of kindliness and grave concern *"If I were—you—though Vic ... I would tend to employ a little more ... circumspection at the RCA – if you run into—another—potential nemesis that is. Your wit could cost you more than you imagine – with the—wrong—person."*

I nodded. I understood exactly what he meant *"Yes ... I hope that I haven't caused any difficulty for you with Dick Taylor ..."*

"No-no-no. Not a bit of it—not a bit of it—nothing to concern yourself about. It's just that the world is not always a generous environment. I also feel that it—is—important to stand your ground – but I would advise you to choose the time and place with care.

an odd boy

"It's sometimes better to savour your wit in private than risk making an enemy of someone in the position to cause you real damage." Pause "Being a conscientious objector in the last war taught me a great deal. There's a time to fight and a time to retreat – a time when discretion is the better part of valour."

"Thank you Derek ... that is good advice – I won't forget it." Pause "I think ... I should say, that ..." Pause "... it's the kind of advice I could probably only take from you. I'm not the kind of person who takes that sort of advice easily – especially when it comes to authority figures. Maybe I'm going to have to stop fighting my father ..."

"It's kind of you ... thank you. I appreciate what you just said – but I would not like to think of you not standing up for yourself either. I don't see you as a person with authority issues – because you've never kicked over the traces with me – and I've not always been able to go along with everything you've wanted to do." We parted with a warm handshake and a promise to meet up again for dinner the following week.

Traintime. The appointed hour arrived and I took the bus journey that would take me to Temple Meads – Bristol railway station. I climbed aboard the express with my carefully chosen selection of work. I remembered the last time I'd boarded a train from Bristol with a folio. I'd just been accepted at Bristol. I'd gone to sleep on the train and woken up in London. Now London was my destination. I remembered Gloucester Mews and my brief torrid sojourn with Ortense – almost as if there'd been no interval. I had a sense of sadness about my farewell scene with Claudette – but it was an emollient permeated with wistful wonder and spaciousness. I felt splendidly free and slightly apprehensive.

I delivered my folio to the RCA and realised that I could spend a few hours in London before needing to return to the train station.

ain't no djinn called alegbara

What would I do? Visit Art galleries? No—there'd be time for that in the future—I'd go to Dobell's and peruse Blues albums. Penelope, Rebecca, and Meryl would be returning to their respective homes in two weeks – so our musical quartets would not continue much longer. I looked longingly at an old NATIONAL RESOPHONIC guitar that sat in a glass case in a nearby guitar shop. Its nickel plating was dull and mysterious – like looking into a murky pool that held secrets in its depths. Some Mississippi Delta Blues player had probably sat on a porch playing that thing, as the crickets rattled the sun-baked cotton stems of their legs; like miniature washboards in the evening fields.

The Mississippi river, is long and deep and wide, / That gal I'm loving – she's on the other side, / That where she gone, and I don't worry / because I'm sitting on top of the world.
Howling Wolf—Sitting on Top of the World—1956—originally by Walter Jacobs/Lonnie Carter of the Mississippi Sheiks—1930

I remembered the DEBIL. I'd not thought about it in 3 years. I missed the bizarre contraption—as Jasper Stanwell had called it —and the way it looked. I missed the way it felt – smooth and lustrous like a vintage Chrysler car body. I chuckled remembering Jasper's spontaneous nickname for me: Voluble Vic Alpenhorn. That was in response to my loud voice and his reaction to Anelie Mandelbaum my Swiss au pair girlfriend. Where was Anelie now – and where was Jasper? Why had I lost contact with them? Why had I done and not done so many things? More to the point however – was why I was feeling slightly maudlin? I was on the brink of a whole new world of Art.

I missed the DEBIL because I knew I'd never make another. I was no longer 15 – no longer gripped by the same intensity. My feeling about the DEBIL seemed similar to my situation with Claudette.

I couldn't re-build the DEBIL and I couldn't time-travel to the point I'd first met Claudette – the point at which she appeared to value me for what I was. I'd gone along with too much. I'd assumed she'd be as malleable as I could be – that she'd see that it was more fun that way. I'd been wrong. I'd also allowed her to assume that I hadn't become increasingly estranged by living her life at the expense of mine. It wasn't a great expense— and it was not as if there weren't wonderful times—it was simply that the future made no sense. It had worked as long as I lived as 'one of the girls' in the house in Hotwells – but without them it was doomed. The four ladies had merged into an extended relationship in which Penelope, Rebecca, and Meryl made up for what was absent with Claudette.

I'd opted to apply to the RCA for the Interdisciplinary MA rather than Illustration as I wanted to make sure that I had the right background to be a Foundation Year lecturer. Maybe there could be the chance to build another DEBIL. Son of DEBIL. Daughter of DEBIL. DEBIL Rides Again. Maybe with Art school facilities I could make something with more volume? Maybe I could attach a 12 string neck to a steel body of my own construction ... it could be welded perhaps ... It was pleasant to muse on these possibilities as I strolled 'round London.

Back in Bristol I attempted to play Blues on my sitar. It sounded intriguing but unconvincing. A person couldn't sit on the floor like that and play Blues. I was going to have to sell the sitar— delightful as it was—and buy a guitar. Maybe I'd see if they'd take a deposit on that old NATIONAL RESOPHONIC style 'O' and let me pay the balance over time? I started wondering what I was doing having these thoughts about guitars.

ain't no djinn called alegbara

I'd come to some understanding about Legba. I remembered that deal I'd tried to make with him, 12 years old and sitting naked and half frozen at a crossroads with my bicycle and plastic guitar. I laughed at the thought. Legba never showed. Mr Love had been right, Legba was simply *genius* – or the lack thereof. There ain't no djinn called Alegbara at any crossroads anywhere – but I'd signed the contract nonetheless, a deal with my own mind. Legba was my own *impossible dream* habit.

Legba and his deal had always been available to me – but I always refused the deal. I was never prepared to sell *everything* down river for the deal. I always held back in some way – and I was glad I had. The *impossible dream* rarely turned out to be as amazing as what was actually happening. My life had always been a movie – a stream of glorious scenes. The cast had been perfect, even though they left the story at various intervals – and left me sad for their loss. I was happy to have stood on the stage with them all – even those I didn't like added to my experience of existence. I wouldn't cut their scenes. Old Legba had no power over me now. I'd simply play Blues for the joy of it – as I did with everything: the poetry, painting, and whatever else might come next.

The rent had been paid to the end of July and so none of us were in any tearing hurry to leave. We enjoyed each other's company and our Jazz quartet bloomed like some sort of sonic last rose of summer.

"*I wasn't really expecting to see 'dette on a regular basis*" said Rebecca "*but I didn't expect her not to come 'round at all.*"

"*Well ...*" I replied "*... I'd imagine it might be difficult for her. Have you invited her 'round?*"

an odd boy

"*Well ... I told her we'd be here and that we'd like to see her before she left. She said she'd call – but she hasn't ... and ... I've not exactly felt like pushing it. Anyway ... it might not be a great experience for you.*"

"*It'd be fine with me – or I'd make it as fine as it could be. I'd like to establish a regular friendship ...y'know, I feel it might be a lot more pleasant to be friends with her than ... well ...*" I ran out of ideas.

"*I don't know ...'dette became quite distant with us over the last year. I think she sensed that we were more your friends than hers ... and ... when we suggested she could be a bit nicer to you – she blew up at us.*"

"*Mmmm ...'dette did mention that you'd brought the question up with her – but she didn't mention she'd got angry with you about it.*"

"*Well ...*" Rebecca commented – evidently somewhat shy of the subject "*... it was ... quite a scene really. It was like we'd opened Pandora's box. She accused us of deliberately influencing you. It was all quite mixed up ... but blamed us for your 'philosophising'—as she called it —as if you weren't always like that.*"

"*What!?*" I exclaimed with unabashed startlement. "*That is just the —weirdest—thing I've heard for a long time.*"

"*Said we'd encouraged you in your 'abstract speculation'. Said it didn't suit you 'cause you weren't academic – and you just got lost in ideas that you didn't really understand.*" Pause "*We said that you'd always been entirely understandable – and ... that you might not be—conventionally academic —but that you were incredibly widely read and knew a great deal about music and painting.*"

That was a bolt from the blue. I sat gawp-eyed at the outlandishness of it all "*She ... never mentioned any of this to me ...*"

"I just bet she didn't ... because we had quite a shouting match about it ... she claimed we'd turned you into a freak-show – and she didn't mean that in the hippie sense of the word. In the end she stormed off saying she'd never see us again." Pause *"Later ... she phoned ... and made as close to an apology as she'd allow herself to get ..."* Pause *"... of course ... we accepted her apology and said it was all forgotten – but that was mainly because we didn't want to land you in an acre of merde."*

I sat there nodding – and probably giving a good imitation of one of those ridiculous toy dogs in the back of a saloon car. I was pondering—in an unstructured manner—how exactly I was supposed to have changed. *"That's a sad story ... but ... thank you for thinking of me ... as you say ... it would have been an acre of merde at least ... so ... when did this happen?"*

"About ... six months ago ..."

"Mmmm ... well that would fit with a few difficult times ..." Pause *"Maybe ...you should have just landed me in it – but ... it's probably better you didn't. At least she can't blame you now."* Pause *"But ... thinking about Dr Jekyll becoming Mr Hyde ... I've definitely—always—been like this. You've known that from the time I moved in here."*

"Yes. That's obvious to us all – so we didn't know—what—to say." Pause *"I think ... well ..."* Rebecca ground to a halt looking slightly anxious. I said I'd be interested to know what she thought. *"Well ... I think she—thought—you were someone with whom she could be superior ... because—y'know—she went to Badminton and all that. Then ... of course ... she discovered that she couldn't keep up with you ... and ... that was—totally—contrary to her idea of herself. Y'know ...'dette's not quite as bright as she thinks she is ... not at all ..."*

an odd boy

"*But she can spool out yards of French ... She drops Latin into every other phrase and provides the Greek roots of words at the drop of a hat ...Y'know '... when she goes to embassy parties – she talks in Russian and Greek ...*"[3]

"*Yeah ... she can do that ...*" Pause "*... but then, so can most Badminton girls. She knows a lot of facts – but she doesn't really know what to do with them beyond impressing people who never learnt that stuff.*"

"*Well right – but I was impressed. I learnt a great deal from her – and I love etymology ...*"

"*Yeah ... and I think she enjoyed impressing you ... It's just that she didn't enjoy being impressed—by—you. That's the—last—thing she wanted – unless you could impress her in ways she could understand ... but you always came out of nowhere as far as she was concerned. You'd use language in ways that baffled her – because she just wasn't used to thinking about anything that didn't fit into her preordained boxes.*"

"*Couldn't that have been ... exciting ... in some way?*" I mused.

"*Well, it would if she'd wanted to broaden her horizons – but it's all 'elite and exclusive information' to her – so ... when you start juggling with her 'facts of Art and culture' and treating them as if they were fluid – she just —doesn't—know where she is.*"

"*I ... never intended to juggle with concepts so as to confuse her – it's just that she kept asking me what my paintings meant and was never satisfied with my answers.*"

---

3   Peter Sarstedt—Where Do You Go To My Lovely—1969. It reached number 1 in the British Pop charts for four weeks in 1969 and was awarded the 1969 Ivor Novello Award. It is speculated that the song concerns Sophia Loren, who was abandoned by her father to a life of poverty in Naples. It is also speculated that Peter Sarstedt wrote the song about a girl with whom he fell in love in Vienna in 1965.

ain't no djinn called alegbara

"*Well ... that would have been her only way to win, wouldn't it ...?*"
Pause "*... by telling you that what you were saying was not valid as an explanation.*" Pause

"*So ... she was always—way—out of her depth with you ...*" Pause "*... and—to be honest—with us too ... It was always a subject that was out of bounds with us and 'dette ... if we said anything she couldn't follow, she'd simply say something imperious as if she was 'above all that' ...*" Pause "*... although ... she never got hostile or anything. I think she reserved that for you because you were close enough for it to be an emotional war zone. She always liked it that you were interesting – but she never liked it that she felt intimidated by your ideas. She hates anything that makes her feel inferior in—any—way at all. She desperately needs to be the mighty bastion of cultural intellect she feels her father to be. And of course, he's brought her up to think that she's the crème de la crème – you know, almost like Miss Brodie: 'I am in the business of putting old heads on young shoulders, and all my pupils are the crème de la crème. Give me a girl at an impressionable age and she is mine for life.'*"

"*That's pretty grim ... it reminds me of Great Expectations ...y'know how Miss Haversham educates her adopted daughter Estella to be emotionally unavailable.*"[4]

"*Well ... that's what Sepulchrave has done to her – and she really believes in her innate superiority even though ...*" Pause "*... I hate to say this ... but ... she doesn't really have the intellect to back it up.*"

---

4   Estella – a character in 'Great Expectations' by Charles Dickens, first published in serial form, from the 1st of December 1860 to August 1861, in the publication 'All the Year Round'.

an odd boy

That was upsetting to hear – but it made sense "*Y'know ... I never treated 'dette in—any—way that was meant to make her feel inferior. I only ever talked about what was on my mind. I know she'd often try to fathom the meaning of what I painted and wrote – but she was always the one who made a big issue out of it all. I had no design to overwhelm her with weirdness.*"

"*I know that Vic ...you'd have done it with us too, if you were like that – but you're not. I've never known a person less interested in one-up-man-ship than you.*"

Meryl—having just descended from her room—called out from the stairs "*It's just that 'dette's not the princess on the steeple.*[5] *She'd like to think she is – but she isn't. Sepulchrave's full of—insane—grandiose ideas about status and superiority. He's brought her up to think she's some kind of aristocrat or something. We all—actually—wondered how you stuck with it.*"

"*Well ...*" I mused "*... she does have regal airs – but I never minded that. I saw it as an amusing personality trait – and I'm sure a lot of it's tongue-in-cheek.*"

"*Kind of you to see it like that ...*" Meryl replied "*... but I'm afraid it used to bug the three of us. We sometimes worried that you might end up being like that as well – but you never did.*" Pause "*In fact ... it used to bug 'dette that you—always—reminded her you were working class. She'd ask us why we thought you did that – and we told her it was because you—were—working class – and weren't ashamed of it either.*"

---

5   Bob Dylan—Like a Rolling Stone—Highway 61 Revisited—1965

ain't no djinn called alegbara

"*You're right—I'm not.*" Pause "*If anything ... I'm probably proud of it ... and ... in a way that's not exactly ... laudable.*" Pause "*But I thought the comments I made to 'dette were more concerned with the fact that I'm just not interested in status or—any—of the whole class issue. People are just people as far as I'm concerned and I have no need to be other than I am.*"

Meryl nodded "*That's how we see it too.*" Pause "*I'd like to talk about this ... maybe later – because I've got to meet Penelope – we have some food to buy.*"

Rebecca and I bade her farewell and after a momentary silence Rebecca returned to the subject of 'dette "*...y'know ...your being so obviously easy about being working class never really suited 'dette's sense of rank and elevated cultural station. It really used to enrage her when you'd quote Blues and Rock alongside of her cultural icons.*"

"*Whoa ... that's a—sad—account. I thought it was just men who went in for that kind of thing.*"

"*That's 'cause you idealise women ...*" Rebecca smiled "*... which is nice for us ... but we are—quite—as objectionable as men can be – maybe even more so.*"

That bemused me momentarily "*Well ... I suppose that's reasonable ... but, apart from a few extremely good male friends – I can't say it's not been my experience. It's not that every lady I've known has been perfection personified – but percentage-wise there'd be no question ...*"

"*Maybe that's why you get on with us though. You're always primed for something positive.*"

"*I try to be like that with everyone – as best I can ... I don't see any other way to be, that would be enjoyable.*"

Unfortunately I never got to ask her why my lack of one-up-man-ship worked out so rarely with men because we went on to talk about the whole class issue and 'dette's elitist proclivities and once we were through and we'd exhausted the subject I said *"I find myself wishing I'd had the conversation we've just had a year or so ago ..."* Pause *"... I know you gave me opportunities – but I always shied away out of some sense of being loyal to 'dette ..."*

"Yes ...you always looked uncomfortable ... that's why we always backed off." Pause *"None of us blame you for that though – in fact, we all thought you were amazingly honourable in that way ..."* Pause *"... and ... we ... we felt ... well ..."* Pause *"It's not that—we—didn't have feelings about being loyal to 'dette – but ... it seemed as if ... as if we'd rather be loyal to you – if you'd have just let us ..."* Pause *"So we always felt torn ... and if we hadn't had all the history we've had with 'dette at Badminton and all that – we'd have been far more pushy. We'd have advised you to leave her ... even back at the end of the* 1st *year."*

"This is all ... slightly perturbing ..." I mused. *"Don't get me wrong – I understand your position completely ... It's just that it sounds like some kind of ... movie narrative ... with delicately balanced reasons why something has to be the way it is."*

Rebecca nodded *"Yes ... that's more-or-less what it is. In theatrical terms it's the basis for tragedy – although I don't think it's your tragedy."* Pause *"I really do think though ... that it—is—'dette's tragedy."*

And on that note we retired to attend to various tasks we each had to complete before Meryl and Penelope returned with the constituent elements of the evening's dinner. After completing the letters I needed to write – I lay and gazed through my favourite little floor level window.

I thought about *Claudette's tragedy* – and although I couldn't really see it as a tragedy that she'd lost me – I could see it as tragic that we couldn't have had a better time over the last year. If only I'd called her out much earlier. I could have made an ultimatum. I could have said '*Quit berating me and trashing my ideas or I'm leaving. Treat me with the respect and acceptance I offer you – or I'm outta here. Start sharing my life a little more – or I'm hitting the road.*' I could have said that and more – but … I'd hoped she'd simply learn from my mien. I hoped she'd learn to treat me as I treated her – but … that never happened. I was going to have to learn something from this – *because being as I had been* … had been no help to Claudette at all. I'd just allowed her to think that her behaviour was acceptable – and as such I couldn't blame her for it. I'd insinuated Claudette's behaviour toward me was acceptable, merely through failing to make—what were to the girls—thoroughly reasonable complaints. I must have gnawed on that wretched bone for a few hours – because suddenly I heard Rebecca call up "*Meryl and Penelope are back from town and I'm finished with my work.*"

"*Thought we'd have fondue!*" grinned Penelope when I arrived in the kitchen. We all occupied ourselves and the task was soon completed.

"*Saw 'dette in Broadmead!*" said Meryl "*she was … a bit … lugubrious … to say the least.*"

"*I think we'd have to—*expect*—that!*" Penelope offered.

"*Yes – but it was as if she didn't even know us!*" Meryl replied.
"*I did say she—*should*—come 'round for fondue – but she made some remark about it being uncivilised and unhygienic to eat out of the same bowl as four other people.*" Meryl laughed "*Said it would be like pigs eating at a trough.*"

an odd boy

"*That's 'dette*" Rebecca commented with a wry smile. I remained silent – feeling a little uncomfortable and hoping that we weren't going to spend the evening discussing 'dette in a negative way. I still felt some kind of loyalty – and, somehow it wouldn't be honourable to be part of a conversation that disparaged a previous partner – especially if humour were involved.

"*If you're ever up in London …*" I opened – in order to change the subject "*… it'd be really good to see you all – either all together or …*"

Penelope smiled "*Yes – that'd be fun. It's not—so—far away. We absolutely—must—stay in touch. I hope there'll be possibilities for projects like your play! You—will—write and tell us what's going on won't you?*"

"*Absolutely. It's always been part of my—vision of life—to work with creative geniuses.*"

The three ladies laughed at that image. "*Good to be included in that category – but I wonder what we—will—be …*" Meryl pondered.

That was enough to swing the conversation and we talked about our possible futures and possible artistic interactions. We were four extremely good friends and a number of evenings were spent simply delighting in each other's company. I avoided any mention of 'dette and she avoided contacting any of us. I felt saddened by her sudden disappearance, not so much because I missed her – but because I felt she'd suffer from the loss of friends. Penelope, Rebecca, and Meryl were willing to be her friends – but she seemed intent on rejecting them. I'd not wanted that – but there was nothing I could do about it.
I accepted the inevitability of the situation and decided I'd have to leave well alone.

A few days passed in which we lived in a bubble of liveliness – playing music and talking about anything and everything.

ain't no djinn called alegbara

Claudette occasionally arose in our conversations and all I could find to say was "*Well ... we had some good times—there's nothing I regret—I'm going to the RCA so ... it's just as well.*"

Penelope, Rebecca, and Meryl would look a little wistful when I made comments like that – and I got some sense that they were thinking thoughts. I figured it was probably thoughts about 'the end of the Hotwells era' and felt that was entirely understandable. I'd miss Penelope, Rebecca, and Meryl – in fact, I'd miss them a great deal. I'd not had such close friends since Savage Cabbage.

Finally, in mid-July, the letter arrived from the Royal College of Art. I'd been rejected without interview. I went up to London again to pick up my folio. It was a little like being forced to carry your own coffin to the wall where the firing squad was waiting.

I'd not anticipated rejection – let alone rejection without interview. It came upon me as an almost incomprehensible horror. It was as if I'd gone to see the doctor with a sprained ankle – and been informed that I had a week to live. The idea of going to see the NATIONAL RESOPHONIC seemed futile. It was not that one thing depended on another – but the shock of refusal, together with the fact that the rest of my life suddenly looked like an amorphous ocean of empty perplexity, threw everything awry. So—rather than investigating the NATIONAL—I decided to find Gloucester Mews. It wasn't hard to find. I walked there from Paddington Station before collecting my rejected folio. I didn't really understand why I'd gone there and had no idea what I was going to do. I walked the length of Gloucester Mews looking at each house in turn – but nothing jogged my memory. I don't know what I would have done if I'd found the Mews house – and I had no interest in ringing bells on the off chance.

I had no inclination to make enquiries either. I just stood there like an idiot waiting for a fortuitous coincidence like '*Hey Frank —man—where yer been?*'

If someone had actually called down to me from a window in that manner, it might have changed my life. No one called out and no one passed me on the street who looked like anyone who'd ever play Blues. I wondered whether it had been a mistake not to have made this investigation three years earlier – but decided that would not have helped. I should have gone straight there from my unpleasant encounter with Mister Jakes – before he had the chance to tell everyone I was persona non grata. I'd have to enter that on the list of 'mistakes I have made'.

Then I wondered about mistakes. What's a mistake, anyway?
I walked back to Paddington and caught the underground.
I went to collect my folio from the RCA – having toyed with the idea of leaving it there.

I realised I'd put it off as long as possible – and wondered why. Then I understood. The moment I picked up my folder – the story was over and I'd have to go back to Bristol. Picking up my folder was like watching the articulated lorry slam the DEBIL into the tarmac.

19

july 1975 – september 1975

traintime's almost here

No use in grieving, well I'm leaving – Well I'm leaving town / Leave town, ain't coming home no more / Traintime—baby—traintime's almost here. Jack Bruce—Cream—Traintime—Wheels of Fire—1968

Meryl came to sit next to me on the couch in the living room. I'd been staring out of the window for almost an hour. *"D'you believe in mistakes Meryl?"* I asked. *"I mean … are mistakes—always —mistakes?"* Pause *"Or … are there just choices and the results of choices?"*

"You might have to spell this out a little more, Vic."

"Well …" I told her about my failure to return to Gloucester Mews back in 1972. *"That was a mistake – but … it might have turned out badly if I'd gone back there. It might have all been a waste of time …and maybe I'd have postponed applying to Bristol … but, it all turned out well didn't it."*

"Well for us, it did – me, Penelope, and Rebecca."

"I'm glad. I've had a wonderful time living in this house with you three …" Pause *"… and the three years with Derek Crowe. I wouldn't have missed any of it for the world."* Pause *"But … that's not quite what I mean. What I'm wondering about … is whether mistakes are called 'mistakes' just because we don't like the outcome. There are things that—are— mistakes like filling your petrol tank full of diesel fuel – but … there are other things that are just impossible to define.*

an odd boy

"*If 'not enjoying the result' is always the way you define a mistake ... then it's quite a limited approach to life. I mean ...you can't look back and wish you'd made different decisions just because something happens that doesn't fit with what you want. For example – you can't say 'I won't make—that —mistake again' – because you could just be closing the door on an opportunity.*" Pause "*And ... anyway ... who's to tell that it really would be the same mistake ... because circumstances are never quite the same.*"

"*Yeah ...*" Meryl sighed. "*I can see that – but ...*" Pause "*... can I say something personal?*"

"*Sure ...*" I replied with slight caution "*... I don't need to clean my teeth or anything?*"

"*No ...*" Meryl laughed. "*And ... that's thrown me off a bit – as I think you might have intended.*"

"*Sorry ... it may have been – but it was unconscious if it was. Tell me whatever it is – and I'll be serious.*"

"*Well ... I think it—was—a mistake staying with 'dette as long as you did.*"

"*Ah ...*" I replied nodding almost imperceptibly. "*Yeah ... I think you're right. The only thing is ... that I didn't want to leave her during her last year ... I was worried about it having a bad effect on her degree show.*"

"*That's ...*" Pause "*... not really what most people would do.*" Pause "*Not that it wasn't kind ... but ... I don't think it was appreciated.*"

"*Maybe not ... I don't really know what to say – apart from the fact that I don't regret it. I think I would have regretted it if she'd fallen apart or something.*"

"*Well yes ...*" Pause "*I don't mean this to sound as awful as it's going to sound – but ... I don't think you ever really matched up to John Willoughby in 'dette's eyes.*"

"*Didn't she call him a vile despicable pig?*"

traintime's almost here

"*Yes ... she did ... and she said worse than that too ...*" Pause "*... but ... he was an upper-middle class vile despicable pig – and he had all the qualifications ...y'know: French and Latin ... and all the names of all the people 'dette thinks you have to know about.* " Pause "*She never said anything ... but we all thought that she looked at you as second best or something – and we all thought that was horrible ... contemptible in fact.*"

"*Really ... well that's ...*" Pause "*... well ... that's just how it is I suppose.*" Pause "*... and ... I suppose I must have known it, in some way. Y'know ... I think I always tried to pretend that her elitism was just some kind of harmless affectation that she'd eventually drop.*"

"*Well yes ... we saw it that way too – but then ... we think it became more ... what she really was as the years went by. She'd also grown a shell and wasn't going to let you past her defences. She really did want everything her own way – and that whole deal around where you lived—was— completely insane.*"

"*Yes ...*" Pause "*... but whether it changed my life for the better or worse is hard to tell. My relationship with 'dette ended with my decision to attend the RCA ... and now ... apart from not having a relationship ... I ...*" I ran out of capacity to speak. "*That's ...*"

Meryl interrupted looking slightly startled – and changed direction "*I'm—so—sorry about the RCA. I hope this doesn't change anything ... does it? With you and 'dette, I mean.*"

"*No ...*" I sighed. "*It doesn't change—anything—at—all. My decision wasn't—*just*—based on my move to London or her loony accommodation arrangements with the Earl of Groan.*"

"*Good ...*" Pause "*... because ... there's ... really ... nothing for you in Bristol now ... is there?*"

"*No ... I'm*—not—*about to check the paper for a bedsit. Even though there'll be plenty up for grabs with everyone leaving for the summer.*"

405

an odd boy

"*Yeah ... I suppose accommodation will be easy for a while – but ... what I mean is, that you're a made-to-measure traveller ...You're cut out for adventures – and, staying here ... well ...'dette ... she*—always was—*a stay-at-home. I wouldn't like to think of you falling back into*—that—*relationship again.*"

"*You*—really—*don't need to be concerned about that. I think we'll always be friends – but that part of my life is over now. It's been over for a while – and I'm not the kind of person who falls back into a relationship for the want of something better to do. My goodbyes*—when they're made—*are permanent.*"

"*Good ...*" Pause "*... but ... speaking of 'friends' ...*" Pause "*... I think that she could*—also—*have been a far*—better—*friend to you when you were together.*"

"*Yeah in some ways ... I ain't saying she treated me unkind. She coulda done better – but ... I don't mind.*"[1]

Meryl chuckled "*She just kinda wasted your precious time?*"

"*No ... it wasn't*—quite—*like that ...*"

"*... don't think twice ...*" Meryl cautioned with a wry smile.

"*... it's alright.*" I chuckled mirthlessly "*No Meryl ... I'm really*—not—*going to reconsider. I'm sure that*—I—*could have done better too ... and ... I think ... I probably wasted*—her—*precious time.*

---

1 Bob Dylan—Don't Think Twice, It's Alright—The Freewheelin' Bob Dylan—1963

"If I hadn't lived here with you three – I think I'd have called it quits sometime in the second year. In fact ... I think I really should have done. I just found myself ... haunted by the idea of not wanting to be another John Willoughby in her life. I suppose at least I didn't leave her for Dolly Parton or whatever she was called." [2]

"*Sophia Grey*" Meryl replied seeming highly affected by what I'd said. "I wish you'd talked more about it ... but you were always so—loyal—when it came to discussing 'dette. We did—sometimes—give you opportunities to talk ..."

"Yeah ... I know ...you did, Meryl ..." Pause "... I'm sorry for being withheld." Pause "I suppose ... I—could—have talked about it." Pause "Maybe I—should—have talked about it." Pause "It was always the idea of talking behind 'dette's back that stopped me – and the fact that you were her friends so long before you were mine."

"Didn't ... mean it as a criticism, *Vic*" Meryl assured me.

"Didn't take it as such." Pause "*Ain't nobody's fault but mine ...*"[3] I sang. "That's what I meant by mistakes. It seems that you change history with choices and so I'm careful not to ... flail around emotionally. And ... of course ...'dette was always kind of concerned about me talking to you three about her – and so ... I never felt I could do that – especially after I told her that I didn't talk about her." Pause "Y'know ... I sort of ended up under contract not to do a lot of things." Pause "I'm just explaining this now – so you won't think I didn't trust you or whatever."

---

2 Dolly Parton [1946 –] – Grammy Award-winning singer-songwriter, actress, and author. The most successful female artist in the history of Country music. She is known for her distinctive mezzo-soprano, occasional risqué wit, flamboyant dress, and voluptuous physique.

3 'It's Nobody's Fault But Mine' is a traditional Negro spiritual and Blues song. The first known recording was by Blind Willie Johnson.

an odd boy

"No ... none of us ever thought anything like that. It's just that ... well —maybe—*it would've helped ... and we could have been more supportive or ... something might have worked out differently or ...*" Meryl ran out of words. She suddenly looked a little discombobulated. "*I think I need to start preparing dinner.*"

"*I'll help*" I replied ."*I think I need to be doing*—something—*useful.*"

We got a roast chicken going and sliced a great bunch of leeks – along with roast potatoes, peas, and cauliflower. It was a feast. Penelope and Rebecca were glad of it when they returned from town and we sat together by candlelight – delighting in the light as it sparkled through the wine glasses.

"*I told Vic what we'd been talking about ...*" Meryl ventured at one point. I noticed that Penelope looked a little uneasy.

"*I was glad—well maybe that's not quite the right word—but anyway ... it was valuable to know what you thought*" I offered. "*And ... it does make me feel better about my decision. It makes me feel that at least I managed to be kind.*"

"*At the very least!*" Penelope exclaimed. "*How could you think anything else?*"

"*Well ... it's always harder to be left. The person who leaves always feels stronger about it – even though it's harder to be the one who breaks the news.*"

"*Y'know ...*" Rebecca commenced. "*I really think that 'dette misunderstood you ... I think she didn't really understand that your tolerance wasn't weakness. I think a lot of people are like that.*" Pause "*And so she was really surprised when you decided to leave her. She really had no idea.*"

"*That's sad ...*"

traintime's almost here

"Right ... well – I was worried about saying that ..." Rebecca replied "... because I thought you might want to give her another chance or something – and I think that would be a big mistake."

I smiled slightly – considering the statement before replying. "*I'm strange with decisions you know. Once I make up my mind – it's made up. It's not just one simple thing with 'dette—even just a few—it was a whole state of mind. We're just not suited to be anything but friends.*" I decided not to say '*She may be a lover but she ain't no dancer.*'[4] Claudette was actually a fair dancer – but she couldn't dance with situations – and she had no idea at all how to dance with reality. "*There's really nothing that could happen now that would make any difference. I'm already a long way away – and I think ... maybe ... you can all stop worrying about me.*" Pause "*I bought a bottle of port this morning. If you fancy it – we could drink a toast to ... whatever it might be that'll be different.*"

I spent a week in Hotwells with Penelope, Rebecca, and Meryl before we had to vacate the house. It was a marvellous opportunity to talk – and talk we did, pretty much incessantly. We all knew that the countdown had started and that our trajectories were our separate destinies—though my trajectory was not at all clear with the RCA out of the running.

"*Even if you applied for Art School Foundation posts with the qualifications you have*" Penelope said "*colleges aren't taking on lecturers who haven't worked in 'the outside world'. It's the same at the Music Colleges.*"

That was the latest news. I'd heard the same from Derek Crowe.

---

4   Lennon/McCartney—Beatles—Helter Skelter—White Album—1968

an odd boy

"*Yes ...*" I replied "*... just a year or so earlier, it was a natural progression – but you can't even get a job as a technician straight from Art School now. Now you need professional experience or experience of being an artist and exhibiting, or whatever. You have to go out and establish a career in order to give it up and apply for a job at an Art School. How can I throw myself into a career that I plan to abandon from the outset? The idea's ridiculous—Catch 22.*[5] *The only people who can become Art School lecturers now are people who'd not had that ambition at Art School.*"

Penelope looked sad. "*There's no way—'round—this problem, is there?*"

"*No ...*" I sighed. "*It's just what it is ... and somehow that—has—to be workable. I've faced this kind of thing before ... so it's not the terrible blow it might appear.*" Pause "*Life goes on—if you'll excuse the cliché—but I just have no idea—where—to go at this point. If you three were staying in this house I'd probably stay here with you 'til something became clear – so maybe ... it's as well ... that's—not—an option.*"

Penelope gazed at me with a mixture of emotions crossing her face. I wondered what she was thinking – but she said nothing. Rebecca and Meryl had appeared at the front door – back from shopping for groceries and wine. "*I'd somehow assumed that if I worked like the Devil, that acceptance at the RCA was assured.*"

Penelope nodded "*Yes ... after all you got a* 1st *and the best recommendation a human being could have from Derek Crowe.*"

"*Yeah ... he backed me all the way.*" Pause "*It's kind of ... incomprehensible*" I sighed.

---

5   Catch-22 – a novel by Joseph Heller, published in 1961, which illustrates circular logic that contradicts itself. The logic of Catch-22 is descriptive of the way bureaucracy crushes individuality and liberty.

"I had—all—that ... and yet, I—still—hit the wall, running. What kind of sense does—that—make?" Pause "Baby—baby—baby, what's wrong with Uncle Sam? He's cut down on my sugar, now he's messing with my ham."⁶

Penelope shook her head laughing "*You've got a Blues line for everything—it's quite a thing—shame you can't make a living at it.*"

"*Yes ... it is.*" Pause "*But ...y'know ... it was at its best with Savage Cabbage and I know that'll never happen again. I'm at my best with friends and ... without friends ... the whole thing means a lot less. I'm not really a solitary performer. That's why it's been so much fun living here.*"

"It's been fun for us too." Pause "We've all had a wonderful time ... with you."

I told Derek Crowe about the RCA on the day we'd arranged to meet. "*Why d'you think I was rejected without interview?*"

"*I'm as perplexed as you are. All I can suggest is that they may have sensed you were too set in one style ... and that you might simply continue in that style rather than change.*"

Those words had a horrible ring of truth to them. "*Yes ... that's me. I also remained a Bluesman when the curtain opened and the coffin of the British Blues Boom disappeared down that long dark tunnel.*" Derek knew the story. "*Maybe the RCA pinpointed the fact that I just flog the life out of a thing. I've been refusing to change my dearly-held principles more-or-less since the day I was born.*"

Derek had been mulling the thing over as I'd been speaking "*You could apply again next year – with some new work to show that you have other facets.*

---

6   Jordan/Clark/Cosey—Louis Jordan—Ration Blues—1941

"*I'm sure you could easily do that*" he suggested. "*I'll help you in any way I can you know.*"

"*Thank you very much indeed Derek. I think I'll have a good long think about the situation and get back to you ... if you don't mind. It seems that there's*—something—*that I haven't got quite clear about it all – and I have a feeling ... that I'm not looking at my life ... as a whole.*"

Derek smiled in that way he had – the way that recognised a case of major ambivalence. I got the impression that he knew I was deeply disappointed and that I was likely do something oblique. "*You can call any time and come over to my house to chat about it.*"

"*I'd appreciate that ... I'll call later in the week when I've talked with Penelope, Rebecca, and Meryl.*"

"*Not with Claudette?*"

"*Well no ...*" I told Derek about how things had fallen out. He was not surprised.

"*Susan and I never felt that you two were*—that—*well matched. You have a fire in you and ... Claudette ... is content to find a niche somewhere. There's nothing wrong with that – but the two don't always work so marvellously together. Susan pointed it out to me first. She noticed that Claudette looked agitated whenever you whirled off on some intriguing conceptual pirouette.*"

"*Everybody saw it but me ... it seems ...*"

"*Well ... that's often the case. There's no need to berate yourself on that account.*"

I might have berated myself – but for the fact that I had to think about the question of whether to apply to the RCA again the following year. I thought about it 'til my neurones were blistered.

"*Somehow ...*" I said to Rebecca "*... I keep coming back to the idea that applying again next year seems like an act of desperation.*"

traintime's almost here

Rebecca looked quizzical *"Derek Crowe didn't think that though."*

"No – but applying to the RCA *again next year feels too much like the time I chased music after Steve and Ron died. That seems to have come back to haunt me in some way. Not a bad way but*—you see—*I still couldn't go to London without eyeing* NATIONAL RESOPHONIC *guitars."*

Rebecca smiled affectionately *"Maybe now you just want one, for its own sake."*

"That would be a healthy turn of events" I responded. *"Yes … maybe I do … but right now, I still have no idea*—where—*to go or*—what—*to do next."*

"You don't think … that Dick-head cretin had anything to do with your rejection do you?"

"Dick Taylor? No. That's impossible. He didn't have anything to do with my letter of recommendation."

"But … he is the Head of Department isn't he?"

"Yes – but Derek would have told me if there'd been any chance of that happening. I really can't see it. All I can see is that there are better illustrators out there. I mean—*I just worked hard*—*but what if there're people who're better*—and—*work harder. They'd be the ones accepted."* Pause *"I think the*—real—*reason is that I'm just*—too—*idiosyncratic. I'm a Surrealist – and I think there's something of a reaction against Surrealism going on at the moment – maybe because it reminds people of psychedelia. Maybe a few too many acid-heads have passed through the RCA."*

"Y'know … I think you—might—*have a point there. 'Backwards guitar' or backwards any other instrument is strictly out of favour at the College of Music and Drama."*

Rebecca wished me luck with my considerations and left me to my solitary vigil over the river.

She took her leave down the staircase and I started singing '*dirty old river, must you keep rolling – rolling on through the night*'. Rebecca's voice chimed in—taking up the song with me—although becoming increasingly faint as she descended to the kitchen.

After a day of internal writhing I suddenly decided that I was— *not*—going to pursue the impossible dream again, even though Derek Crowe had said it was entirely possible. Maybe the RCA was possible but the Art Schools were vanishing one by one. And who were the students now? Would I find anyone like *the odd boy* when I was the version of Derek Crowe I wanted to become? Art Schools were past history—just as I was past history—and as soon as that thought formed itself, my decision was made. I was going to leave. I was going to leave the dream behind. I was going to leave the whole thing behind. Everything. I suddenly felt alive.

Worked hard and failed now all I can say is "I threw it all away." / Oh, I was just a boy giving it all away / sail away, sail away / Ooh, I know better now, I know better now giving it all away.
Sayer/Courtney—Roger Daltrey—Giving it all away—Daltrey—1973

"*Right*—that's—*it!*" I whooped "*I'm gonna to live with the adjectival yetis!*"

"*What?*" Penelope laughed as I came bounding down the stairs. "*What*—are—*you talking about?*"

I plumped myself down in the armchair next to her. "*Well ... since my first journey to India and Nepal in the Autumn of '71 I intended —at some point—to return to the Himalayas to immerse myself ... in Vajrayana – y'know, Tibetan Buddhism.*"[7]

"*Is there no way to study here?*"

---

7   See Wisdom Eccentrics—Ngakpa Chögyam—Aro Books—2011

"Well ... not as I want to study. I visited Samyé Ling in Eskdalemuir, Scotland – but missed Chögyam Trungpa by months."

"That's a shame."

"Yes ... It is a shame, because—apart from Chögyam Trungpa—studies of the kind I want aren't really an option in Britain. I've read—all—the books there are to read—many times over—and have more questions than I've—ever—had before."

Penelope—taking it all in—asked "*Didn't you once tell me that you'd thought of going to the Himalayas when you were older—when you retired?*"

I nodded. That had been my idea.

"*So ... that's all changed now?*"

"Yes ... I think it has." Pause "*I think it had to change – because ... well ... life's performed quite a backward flip on me. You see ... when the career vanished – the retirement plan's vanished with it. The RCA has ... adventitiously provided me with instant early-retirement. The time seems right*—now—*and if I wait or try to take any other course – the chance might not come again. Each of my alternatives has run its course to*— exactly—*nowhere – so ...*"

Penelope finished my sentence in a horrified tone. "*There's no direction home – other than the Himalayas?*"

"There's no other—sense—*left to me. I've run out of*—all—*ideas apart from resurrecting the last idea and reapplying to the* RCA ... *and ... I'm* —not—*going to do that. All I need is building site work for three or four months and I'll save enough money to last a year or two. Then ... I'll be off.*" Pause "*I know where to go ... and ... who to see.*" Pause "*The more I sit with the idea*—*and talk with you about it*—*the more obvious it becomes ... and ... the more*—right—*it feels.*"

an odd boy

Pause "*I ... can't say it won't be a wrench leaving you three behind ... I had hoped we'd be ... in contact, y'know – with what we talked about with plays and music ... but ... I need to do something with my life ... and I'd rather not leave that to total chance. Going to the Himalayas has no career future—I know—but at least it will enable me to fulfil an ambition. Even if I eventually have to settle down somewhere-or-other ... and get some-sort-of job – at least I'll always know that I took the plunge.*" Pause "*Can you understand that? Or is it just too weird?*"

"*Yes ... I can understand that. It makes ... perfect sense ... for you ...*" Penelope said extremely quietly – and I was too dense to notice her state of shock. It took hindsight to understand that moment. "*It seems ...*" she whispered "*... like a good idea—and one that'd suit you—but ... it's sad ... that I won't see you again ... for so long.*" Penelope absented herself suddenly in order to utilise the facilities and I wondered if I caught some sense of her being tearful.

"*That's sad for me too ... I'll write to you—and keep in touch—and ... I'll be back ... eventually ...*" I replied when she returned moments later. "*But ... as I said ... it feels as if I've been chasing the impossible for—far—too—long. I thought the Foundation lecturer plan was ... well sufficiently ordinary not to be an 'impossible dream' – but, that's just what it's become.*" Pause "*So ... I'd rather throw the whole thing open wide than try to force something, that just isn't going to work.*"

"*Yeah ... I can see that ...*" Pause "*... and ... I think it—is—what you need to do – especially after all you've told me.*" Penelope looked down at her feet "*It would have been great fun for 'the girls' to stay together ... and—well—I've always liked you. You know—if it hadn't been for 'dette—well ...*"

That was surprising. "*I ... really appreciate you telling me that ...*"

Penelope looked tense and highly emotional "*You're the best friend I've ever had.*"

I wanted to say it felt reciprocal – but somehow I didn't feel I could say that without betraying my relationship with Rebecca and Meryl – so I said *"It's the same for me with you three too – I feel as close to you as I felt to Ron and Steve."*

Penelope continued *"Yes ... although ... I would have liked to have become ... closer to you – y'know, in particular ... but ... because of the three of us ... and ... there was no way to change that."*

I nodded *"Yeah ... I understand that ... all ... too ... well ...There's —no—way out of this, is there ...? It seems ... so ... very ... very ... sad."*

I didn't know what else to say – and my speech had become almost too attenuated to understand.

"I don't think any one of us would've stepped in, or could have stepped in ... it would have spoilt what we had together ..." Penelope sighed *"... and ... that was always so important."*

This was heartbreaking. *"Yes ... it was important to me too. I don't know what I would have done without you three."*

"We ... talked about it ...you know – and we all decided that we couldn't face ... a decision where ... two of us would be left out ... because there'd be bound to be bad feeling and seeing each other would be too painful." Pause *"Can you ... understand that ...?"*

I was suddenly back in the state of heart-and-mind that I'd experienced at Lindie's departure – but this exploded over me in minutes.

"Yes." I stared blankly, holding back the growing sensation that I was going to burst into a flood of full-blown sobbing. Penelope suddenly looked more beautiful than I ever known her to be even though her face was bewildered with pain.

an odd boy

Tears glided down her cheeks as she sat staring at me and it took me a while to recognise that tears had welled in my eyes despite my efforts to repress them. We each seemed to recognise the existential statement thus expressed and also that there was nothing either of us could say.

Penelope stood up suddenly saying she needed to attend to some letter – and went to her room. I sat there – vaguely reeling. Every way I tried to think about what had just been said was too poignant to encapsulate into *anything* that resembled a possible position from which to make a decision. My rejection by the RCA was a shock – especially combined with the knowledge that I'd never be an Art School lecturer. Now I'd been hit by the fact that there'd been romantic possibilities with Penelope. That had *never* occurred to me – but then … why should it? But—I wondered—had that—*really*—never occurred to me? Suddenly I was beset with figments of what might have been. I realised I'd probably been in love with Penelope for two years – without understanding it as such. There was no direction home from *this* crossroads.[8] So there I stood … staring into a nebulous realm in which there were no more sign posts and no more roads beyond the one I'd taken – and that road, led into an entirely uncertain future.

Rebecca found me sitting alone in the living room looking out of the window. She knitted her brows and said "*You know … out of 'us girls' … It's me that's supposed to be intense – but … seeing you …sitting there staring out the window like that … that's … difficult for me …*"

---

8   Bob Dylan—Like A Rolling Stone—Highway 61 Revisited—1965

It was true – Rebecca had never seen me troubled by anything *"…you … usually just ride everything that comes up – and …grin about it. You're usually the one who listens to—our—problems and puts things right for us."*

Did I do that? Well – sometimes, perhaps.

I told Rebecca about my Himalayan decision and—like Penelope —she could see the sense of it in terms of my interests. *"But you look so sad …"* she said *"… and … I don't like to see you unhappy."* Then she burst into tears. I passed her a handkerchief— thankfully a freshly laundered one—and sat there motionless. I'd have put my arm 'round her – but that would have changed the course of history. *"I'm not—that—sad … just a little tired … and … perplexed. I'm in an odd position … poised like this … on the edge of some kind of ledge."* Pause *"It's like … the way is up … along the road … the air is growing thin … too many friends who tried … blown off this mountain with the wind …"*[9]

"Fairport Convention … I'm surprised you like one of their songs."

"It's probably the only one I do like … but it's by Richard Thompson … and he really has a way with lyrics and melody. 'Meet on the Ledge' has this poignant wistful verse – and then it hits out powerfully with the chorus … and … that feels vaguely like I feel at the moment."

Rebecca looked at me wanly *"I wish I could help – but … anyway, the three of us have all wished we could …you know … from time to time … and, well … the last thing any of us wanted was to have been too obvious with how each of us felt about you. It would have ruined our time together in this house … and now … it's all a bit … late … isn't it."*

---

9   Richard Thompson—Fairport Convention—Meet on the Ledge—What We Did on Our Holidays—1968

an odd boy

Rebecca was being perfectly English in her obliqueness – but her message was quite plain. They'd each wanted to replace Claudette – and of course that's what had made it impossible.

"*I don't think I've*—ever—*been as grateful for friendship and affection and … somehow …*" Somehow I had no idea what to say next without telling Rebecca it wasn't too late and that … and there my tears welled up again.

How was it that I was suddenly head over heels in love with the three of them!? If either of us had said more—or made ourselves any plainer—I might have found myself with no choice but to have acted impulsively. Impulsively … but which impulse when there were three? It was like something in a play— some immense dramatic irony—and the theatrical inevitability of the situation started feeling like the most emotively poignant dream. I found myself in the middle of an emotional tragedy of harrowing proportions. I was at an emotional crossroads on which every sign post said 'no direction home' apart from the little narrow track off to the side that bore an ancient withered sign indicating the lost horizon.

Rebecca and I both understood the problem. I was her friend. Meryl and Penelope were also her friends. I was a friend of all three. We were all friends—and none of us could alter that situation without betraying the other three. I said nothing of Claudette's strident question "*Which one is it!?*" and nothing of my fervent denial. It was true when I said it – but now it had become a lie. I'd not left Claudette for any of her three friends – but now it had been made apparent to me – that I could have done so with alarming rapidity at any point in time over the last year.

traintime's almost here

If someone had written this as a play I would have had to have jumped up on stage and said '*Right enough of this! I demand a happy ending!*' just as I'd told Lindie Dale I wanted to do with Othello ... I'd have had to have said '*The playwright who wrote this is a sadistic emotional pervert!*' and I'd have been right. But it wasn't a play and there was no one to blame – just as there was no one to blame for the deaths of Ron and Steve.

The romantic availability of the three ladies wasn't like the situation with Rose and Valerie – but it still threw me. I've never found it possible to refuse romance when it was on the cards. Somehow the nature of human affection has always been so fantastically magnetic that there has never been any alternative to celebrating attraction by yelling '*Yes!*' at the top of my lungs. Here however, was a case where everything was simultaneously possible and utterly impossible. I'd not exactly joined the Foreign Legion – but I may as well have done. Once again, the die was cast and there was nothing to be done but roll with the changes.

Meryl came and found me later. The three ladies had arranged it so they'd all have their private talk with me. The same message came across the amorphous divide like sheet lightning. It was hard to comprehend how I'd lived in a house for almost three years with three ladies who would have liked me as a romantic partner – whilst I'd floated in a default situation for no reason other than I had no good reason to end my relationship with Claudette. I had reasons – but they were never pressing enough to cause me to upset Claudette. And now I'd parted from her – she wasn't as upset as I'd feared. On the other hand I was *far* more upset than I'd anticipated – but for entirely different reasons.

In some ways I could have lived with the three ladies in perpetuity – but Claudette had been the one who'd made it possible by making me romantically unavailable to the others. And now that Claudette was out of the picture – she hung over me like the guillotine. I'd told Claudette that I'd not left her for one of her three friends. I was double, triple, quadruple bound ... to no choice other than the loss of everything. Claudette was obviously more perceptive than I was, in certain ways. She must have intuited something I'd missed with Penelope, Rebecca, and Meryl. Or maybe it was Penelope, Rebecca, and Meryl's enthusiasm to pose for me?

I'd thought that was simply their enthusiasm for my paintings. Well ... maybe it was – but maybe that was just the beginning of their each thinking about me in a different light.

Maybe I'd meet up with Penelope, Rebecca, or Meryl in the future – but how would that work? They weren't going to remain single forever on the off chance that I'd return – and there was nothing I could say before I left to give any indication of anything other than mystery. And even if I did meet up with one of them again – I'd have her parents to encounter. From what I'd gathered their parents made the Gascoignes look like poor relations. I'd just be back with Brigadier Dale again – and I could do without that. The ladies would be almost a decade older however – and that might make a great difference – but what was I doing even cogitating on such arcane matters.

The situation was simply dissolving around me with great rapidity. "*You know*" I said to Meryl "*you three have been as good friends to me as Steve and Ron were ... I hope we'll always keep in touch. I'm actually sadder to leave here than I can say.*

"*I could've just stayed on here with you—and Penelope and Rebecca—forever ... but ... life doesn't seem to be like that, does it.*"

"*No ...*" Meryl sighed, her eyes brimming. "*I ...*" then it was all just too much for her and she plunged her face into her hands and cried. That was too much for me to bear and I just sat there leaking like a colander. The three ladies—one after another—drove a corkscrew into my chest that persisted in wriggling remorselessly.

"*So ...*" she began again "*...you'll write from Never Never Land?*"[10]

"*Yes Tinkerbelle – it'll be the first thing I do when I get to wherever I'm going ... I'll write before as well – y'know when I'm working wherever I find to work before I hit the road.*" Pause "*Speaking of Peter Pan ... d'you think I'm the boy who never grew up?*"

"*Sorry ... that's not what I meant ... but, why would you think of that?*"

"*Well ... it doesn't do not to reflect on how you are ... and it occurs to me sometimes that I'm hideously naïve. And ... what I see of 'adulthood' doesn't look violently attractive from where I stand.*"

"*I can see that in some ways ... maybe ... but in terms of maturity – I'd say you got there a long time ago. Your Swiss girlfriend probably had something to do with that – and handling the deaths of Ron and Steve.*" Pause "*I hope you'll always be like you are ... and ... I hope ... I'll ... remain Tinkerbelle too.*"

'The girls' had a final meal together – which was surprisingly light hearted. It felt slightly awkward at first – but that lasted no longer than a few minutes. They wanted me to sing a few Blues numbers for them and so I obliged. I had no guitar but that didn't matter to them. I sang St James Infirmary Blues, and a few Son House numbers. I was loud – and it made them grin.

---

10 Never Never Land – a place featured in the novels of J M Barrie—1904. It is the dwelling place of Peter Pan and Tinkerbelle.

I was the first to leave Hotwells. I needed to avoid the agent. He never suspected that Victoria Hillary Simmerson was male – and this was not the time to blow my cover. I'd be posted my part of the bond we'd all paid. I bade the ladies goodbye – and they went out into town so that I could bid farewell to Claudette on my own. She'd agreed to meet me at the house in Hotwells on the condition that I'd be alone there.

Claudette arrived and took a seat in the living room. She noticed that I was close to tears. She seemed—from the words she employed—to take my evident sorrow as pertaining to her. I left her with that impression. How could I have explained that I'd lost three romantic partners the day before – unobtainable by virtue of the fact that each one was a close personal friend to us both? How could I explain that she'd been right in assuming that romance was on the cards with one of her oldest friends – let alone all three?

It's a desperate game we play, throw our hearts and minds away /
On wounds that can't be mended on debts that can't be paid'
Richard Thompson— Keep Your Distance—Rumour and Sigh—1991

The pathos of my demeanour probably saved me from any recriminations that Claudette might have chosen to heap upon me as a parting volley – so all-in-all our parting was almost '... *such sweet sorrow* ...' After a short exchange of almost meaningless enquires after each other's lives, I climbed into the removal van – which contained all my worldly possessions.

I gave Claudette an extremely broad artificially-constructed grin – and wished her well with her career in the theatre. That was the last time I saw her. That was also the last time I heard from her. I did write a few letters but none were answered.

*Sound like I'm hearing moaning, death bell ringing all in my head /
I know that I was gonna leave on a chariot but I didn't know what kind of
chariot gonna take me away from here.*
Lightning Hopkins—Death Bells—1961

In four hours I was back in Farnham. My mother greeted me joyfully. My father sat in his old chair and smiled at me as I walked into the living room.

During the last two years of College—my father had a series of strokes. He'd become a gentle fellow – always pleased to see me. I was able to tell him about my life. He was conspicuously happy that I wanted to talk with him – and, somehow, I found that unusually moving. I loved my father in spite of everything – especially now that he was so vulnerable and frail.

My father's hair was white by the time he had his last and most serious stroke. When I'd seen him in the hospital I was shocked. They'd shaved off his Sergeant Major's moustache – that thin line of regimented hairs a quarter inch long that paraded in two lines halfway between his lip and his nose. He'd clagged that regiment of hairs with Morgan's Pomade in order to make it visible. I'd done the same at the age of 13 when I sneaked it out of his jar. Hospital staff had accidentally shaved away his moustache – because it was indistinguishable from his stubble. I felt deeply sorry for him at that moment. He was as proud of his military moustache as I'd been of my long hair. He'd been a proud man. I wanted him to be able to continue being the proud man he wanted to be – even though I'd not enjoyed that aspect of him when I was young.

My father had seen his share of sadness and tragedy – but he'd not been lucky enough to discover himself as an Artist. He was a working class lad—as were his parents—and he'd been flattened too many times by middle class rejection.

an odd boy

I'd been a working class lad – but I'd become indeterminate. My father also became indeterminate – but not in a way that led to contentment. He'd been a wartime-major. His rank gave him ostensible equality with brother officers – but not equal respect in their society. No one let him in. He'd been *made-up from the ranks* and that was a fact that could never be lived down – especially as he had no concept of how to be middle class.

Middle-class-ness was a mystery to him – and all he could do was emulate its obvious externals according to the manner in which it was manifested in a military setting. He was therefore snubbed on a regular basis. It was the bitterness of this experience—and 25 years of swingeing self-imposed alimony—that soured his life.[11]

My father was a self-made man – a working class hero in his own way. He worked extremely hard throughout his life but never attained the circumstances he desired. He started at the age of 13 as a dockworker – but joined the Army at 14, to better himself. He rose from the ranks through intense application with engineering studies and eventually became an officer. Promotion beyond Major however, failed to avail itself – even though he tried to educate himself in relation to literature. Fortunately his cultural aspirations set the scene for meeting my mother. She introduced him to music – particularly the German Classical composers. He came to love Handel and Wagner. He in turn read her Dickens – to help her English.

---

11 Major Simmerson allowed his adulterous wife to sue him for desertion rather than face the ignominy of publicly admitting that he had been the husband of an adulterous wife. Once divorced, his ex-wife never re-married or sought employment, and thus ensured unjust life-long financial support.

traintime's almost here

He'd wanted me to rise in the ranks too. Maybe I met the same fate – although in entirely different terms. We both skirmished with success and fell short of our aims. The main difference was that I never became bitter about missing the mark – because I'd come to understand that 'the mark' is an illusion. There's too much to enjoy—too much to appreciate—whatever the outcome shows itself to be. My father would sometimes wake up from a dream in which he'd been back in the Officer's Mess in Cairo or wherever – and he'd weep because the dream was over.

The dream is over, what can I say? / The dream is over, yesterday / I was the dreamweaver – but now I'm reborn / I was the walrus – but now I'm John / And so dear friends – you'll just have to carry on: the dream is over.
John Lennon—The Plastic Ono Band—God—1970

He travelled the world with the Army. He joined the Royal Engineers at 14 and proceeded to better himself. He took engineering examinations. In 1921 he was in India – in sole charge of a power station in the Khyber Pass. He was 19 then – and Wyatt Earp was still alive.[12] In 1927 he provided calculations for rebuilding the Great Wall of China – which had been damaged during the Boxer Rebellion. He'd been stationed in Turkey, Syria, Egypt, Lebanon, Singapore, and places I can't recall. He'd sailed on grand old ships—the Mauritania and the Lusitania—but he didn't have any strange tales.

He wasn't one for strange tales. I think I was his strangest tale – and I turned out to be more normal than he thought. I told my father of my 1st class honours degree. He was happy I'd made it. Said he was proud of me. I was glad—at last—to be the son he wanted. Glad for him. I said nothing about having come to a dead halt with my RCA application.

---

12 Wyatt Earp died in 1928.

There was no need for him to know that. There was no need for even for *me* to know—*that*—anymore.

My father saw that my life was working well. Nothing hideous had happened. I wasn't the heroin addict he feared I'd become. I wasn't in debt. I wasn't in prison. My mother told me that he admired the way I dealt with life – and the way I enjoyed myself in almost any circumstances. He thought I'd learnt some sort of secret about how to be happy. It was no secret. I would have told him that at any point – if he'd asked. I'd have said '*Just appreciate the world. If you appreciate the world you'll become an Artist. No one can ever take that away from you. You'll always have your senses and the sense fields will always be there – no matter what happens.*'

So I had the secret of happiness … Well yes … maybe I did. I *was* happy. Life occasionally evoked tears – but happiness was always there. Appreciation was always there. It's appreciation which creates the space for sadness – simply to *be what it is*. Appreciation ensures that sadness doesn't crimp anything for too long.

Hey Father Death, I'm flying home / Hey poor man, you're all alone / Hey old daddy, I know where I'm going.
Allen Ginsberg—Father Death Blues—Don't Grow Old, Part V—1976

I still had some months before the monsoon was over in India and Nepal.[13]

---

13 The author's life between Parts 5 and 6 of Volume IV of 'an odd boy' [1975—2005] is recounted in 'wisdom eccentrics' published in 2011 by Aro Books inc. Part 5 of an odd boy ends in February 2007 – whereas 'wisdom eccentrics' commenses in 1971 and concludes in 2010. The author's Art School years are only mentioned in passing in 'wisdom eccentrics'.

traintime's almost here

I didn't want to arrive in the intense heat and rain of the Burra Baresh.[14] That time passed like a prison sentence.

I worked every hour of overtime available at a large warehouse in Aldershot – and accrued more money than I'd ever had at one time from past holiday work. When I wasn't working – I was busy with preparations for the great journey. I had to get a cholera jab and purchase various travel medicines – such as Imodium. There was the Nepalese visa to obtain – which meant a trip to London. I had to research the largest available rucksack – as I'd be living out of it for a few years. There were letters to write to Penelope, Rebecca, and Meryl.

There were arrangements concerning my paintings – where they were to be stored whilst I was away.

Finally – the end of September hove into view. I picked up my final pay packet and went home to spend a week tying up loose ends. Before I left for the Himalayas, my father told me "*For all your strange ways of going about things ... you seem to have understood something about life—how to enjoy it, I mean—and how to succeed. That is something I missed. I never learnt the trick of it – you see.*"

I was almost lost for words. I thanked him for his generosity in telling me personally. "*We could have had more time like this*" I said – and he agreed. I suppose that's why Shakespeare wrote tragedies – as well as histories and comedies. It's a normal human situation to manufacture tragedy. This was his. I will not say that it was not also mine. I knew it would have been too great a leap for him to relate to *the odd boy* 'til the point when *the surrealism of existence* could no longer be denied. My mother and I sat there with him as it got dark – and ... finally, he was gone.

---

14 The Monsoon in the Indian subcontinent is comprised of the Burra Baresh (big rains) and the Chota Baresh (the little rains).

part six

november 2006 – february 2007

welcome home

*My parents never looked down on anyone because they had less
– or did not dress so well.*
Renate Schubert

*It's funny the way most people love you when you are dead.
Once you are dead, you are made for life.*
Jimi Hendrix

*They say playing Blues is like having to be black twice.
Stevie Ray Vaughan missed on both counts – but I never noticed.*
BB King

"*Of all the Blues guys I ever met [Howling] Wolf and Son House both
lived up to my ideal of what they would be like ... I learned from them
that ... you have to believe that what you're doing is the right thing and
that there's no other thing for you to do, and 'til the day you die you don't
ever stop playing. It's your religion.*"
Paul Rishell quoted by James Segrest and Mark Hoffman in Moanin' at
Midnight—The Life and Times of Howlin' Wolf—
Going Down Slow—page 289

*It was like a shooting star – it flourished and we were lucky to see it
– and then it was gone.*
Billy Connolly, on 'Clive's Incredible Folk Club' – from the chapter 'I never
took lessons from anybody' page 26 – in 'Some People Are Crazy' the
biography of John Martyn by John Neil Munro. Billy Connolly's comment
would apply equally to the lost time.

1

december 2005 – december 2006

renate schubert

Shall I compare thee to a summer's day? / Thou art more lovely and more temperate: / Rough winds do shake the darling buds of May, / And summer's lease hath all too short a date: / Sometime too hot the eye of heaven shines, / And often is his gold complexion dimm'd; / And every fair from fair sometime declines, / By chance or nature's changing course untrimm'd; / But thy eternal summer shall not fade / Nor lose possession of that fair thou owest; / Nor shall Death brag thou wander'st in his shade, / When in eternal lines to time thou growest: / So long as men can breathe or eyes can see, / So long lives this and this gives life to thee.
William Shakespeare—Sonnet 18–1689

Disassembled diaries: the 24th *of December* – 2005

My mother had a sense of irony. There was a great deal of laughter whenever she came to stay. She came whenever she could, to spend time with her grandchildren Robert and Ræchel – and to have amusing conversations with her irredeemably odd son and his wife Caroline.[1] She smiled across the dining room table – and I knew she had something amusing to say.

---

1   Caroline Togden is known as Khandro Déchen as a Buddhist teacher and author.

an odd boy

"*How his farzer vould have laughed, Déchen! To see Chögyam*[2] *vearing zeez beautiful*—shining—*Oxford shoes today – and, ziss*—lovely—*tweed riding coat he vorr viz us to town. He even has a vhite shirt. It iss hard to believe!*" she laughed.

"Yes … I'd have liked to have seen him laugh about that …" I grinned "… and I'd have liked to have bought him a pair of Grenson's – I think he'd have enjoyed them." Pause "But you know … if I—do—look a little like him now—in the way I dress—it's not …" I pretended to stand on my dignity "… that I've become conservative, learnt my lesson … or anything—quite—*as vulgar.*"

"*Oh no! I certainly vould*—never—*sink zat!*" she laughed. "*Vott— has—happened to you zen, uzer-vise?*" she asked mischievously.

"It's simply …" I said with mock gravity "… *that I've grown to appreciate a range of clothing that was in favour … somewhat prior to my birth.*"

"Which as we know …" Caroline whispered conspiratorially to my mother "… was in the late 1700s."

"*Zat vould be*—just—*like you!*" my mother whooped, thwacking me hard on the leg with her hand – as she often did when she laughed. "*You are like Vinston Churchill you know!*"

"Winston Churchill?" I said with surprised amusement.

"*Ja! You vill fight zem on the beaches; you vill never surrender*" she was beside herself with mirth.

---

2   The authors' legal name is 'Dr Chögyam Togden'. 'Chögyam Togden' was the name given to him by Kyabjé Düd'jom Rinpoche in 1971. The author uses the name 'Doc Togden' for his music and in everyday circumstances – and 'Ngakpa Chögyam' as a Buddhist author and teacher. 'Doc' is derived from the author's interest in Doc Holiday and from the fact that he received a doctorate from the Visvabharati University of West Bengal for his work in the field of Tantric Psychology.

"*Exactly!*" I exclaimed in my best pseudo-Churchillian. "*This is my finest hour!*" Pause "*Y'know ... seeing the way people dress today – makes my father's sartorial sense highly appealing ...*"

"*Charlie Watts of the Stones seems to have come to the same conclusion*" Caroline commented with a grin.

I tilted my head to intimate that I'd like to hear the rest of the story. "*Well ...*" she said "*... Jack Webb espied him in a Gentleman's outfitters in London ... looking—every inch—the English gentleman.*"

"*Really ... glad I'm not—alone—then!*"

"*So!*" my mother responded in high glee. "*No more Carnaby Street, zen?*"

"*No ... even if it still existed as it was back then ...*" I replied "*... but when did—you—last see me dressed like that?*"

"*I wozz just vondering ... I forget, you know ... it does not seem—so—long to me that you verr at Art School.*"

"*You may have a point there ... it sometimes doesn't seem that long to me either.*" Pause "*However ... everything colourful—and circa '66—went some years ago.*" Pause "*The only reason I stopped wearing those moss crêpe shirts is that they just wore out – and so ... I moved on – or backward in time ... I guess I—could—have them tailored – but where would I buy moss-crêpe now – especially in emerald green and indigo?*"

"*You'd still wear them?*" Caroline asked incredulously.

"*Sure – if I had something that suited them – but that old emerald-green leather outfit of mine bit the dust a long time back*" I replied with a slight sense of nostalgia for the flamboyance of the ancient appearance. "*And ... although it's appealing in some way to recreate the past ... I can't recreate my hairline – and it would take a full head of hair not to look ludicrous in that outfit.*"

"*I am happy to hear it!*" my mother chuckled.

an odd boy

"*Did I ever tell you about the giraffe-hide greatcoat I—almost—had made?*" Both Caroline and my mother admitted to being entirely ignorant of the aforementioned item – so I gave them a brief account paying particular attention to the giraffe-tail that was to have remained attached to the back.

"*Ja, ja, ja ... I can—just—imagine it. I am happy zat—now—you like to dress so vell. It suits you.*" My mother had and a twinkle in her eye. "*But ... it does make me—laugh—you know – after all ze—trouble—it caused you ... zat—now—you look so respectable.*"

"*Mmmm ...*" I pondered – thinking of the trouble it caused me. "*...y'know Mum, I'm not sure it caused me—that—much trouble. The hair was the main thing and I still have that – albeit tied up in a bun.*"³ Pause "*The other thing, of course, was probably the same problem my father had ...*" Pause "*I never expected to have thoughts like this – but our lives have been quite similar. He was a wartime major. Then—as you know—he was snubbed by middle class officers in the officer's mess.*"

"*Yes ...*" my mother replied "*... but how iz ziss like your life?*"

"*Well ... I kept finding middle class girlfriends whose parents hated me worse than a dose of dysentery. I know that the image I presented didn't help – but I would have thought that my speech and general manner would have pleaded my cause to some extent.*" My mother shook her head as if to say she didn't go along with my theory – so I continued "*Well ... of course ... the next thing is also my fault. My hair and the fact that I didn't go to Farnham Grammar School. That's nobody's fault but mine – but all the parents seemed to make something of our address. We just didn't live in the right place. They all lived in 'The Bourne' or somewhere equally as grand – and they didn't want their daughters high-stepping with someone from the outskirts of Aldershot.*"

---

3 Both the author and his wife maintain uncut hair according to the vows of their Nyingma Buddhist Tradition.

"*Ja ... vell ... ziss iss true.*" Pause "*Zeez people are silly. My parents had a cook and a maid – but ja ... zat vozz before ze Vorr. My parents never looked down on anyone because zey had less – or did not dress so vell.*"

"*Oma was a remarkable woman – I was fortunate to have known her.*"

"*Vell ... ja*—she—*always liked your clothes – even zo zey upset your farzer. She argued viz him about ziss you know.*"

"*Really?*" Pause "*I never knew ...*"

"*Maybe zair are many sings you do not know*" she grinned.

"*Right ... and there was I thinking I was so clever and classless and free ...*"[4] Pause "*It took me a while to learn you can't be free the way I was trying to be free – but ... I don't regret any of it.*" Pause "*It all—more-or-less—led to freedom in the end ...*" I laughed "*... just not the kind of freedom I expected.*"

"*You know, at*—zat—*time*" my mother laughed "*you had—many—very strong ideas about Harris Tweed.*"

"*Well ...*" replied Caroline on my behalf "*I think he realises that Harris Tweed—wasn't really the problem ... it was the mentality it used to signify.*" Pause "*Like the bestial Brigadier Dale.*"

"*Ah yes ... zat vozz*—so—s*ad viz Lindie. Vhy did you not—tell—me at ze time?*"

"*I don't really know ...*" Pause "*... well ...*" I chuckled "*... I'd have had to have admitted that my father was right about my appearance and hair – wouldn't I?*"

My mother shook her head. "*Voz zat ze—only—reason?*"

---

4 'And you think you're so clever and classless and free / But you're still fucking peasants as far as I can see.' John Lennon—Plastic Ono Band—Working Class Hero—1970

an odd boy

"No ... *probably not – but ... it's all rather long ago now.*"
I stared momentarily into the night beyond the dining room window – almost as if it were a DVD and I could hit replay. "*You know ... events are far easier to remember than having any idea of what my motivation might have been ...*" I knew exactly why however. My mother observed me curiously as if she knew there were other ideas in my mind – but said nothing. 'The 'other reason' was because I'd have had to have recounted Brigadier Dale's insolence concerning both my parents. My mother was 'a German' and my father was working class. These were subjects best left in the past. I had no desire to make my mother feel responsible for anything I may have suffered on their account. I changed the subject. "*Jack Bruce has this line: 'Well it's hang the girls and young men, on the ropes of tweedy minds.'*[5] *and ... that's*—really —*how it was when I was young.*"

"*Ja ...you always*—ver—*ze rebel. You vould not have cut your hair even for ze Brigadier!*" she laughed. "*And you are no different now. But I am happy you are happy – and*" she smiled "*zat you cook me ziss*—lovely —*pizza!*" Pause "*How much garlic iss zair in here?*"

"*Too much*" Caroline laughed "*as usual.*"

After dinner Caroline said "*You know, Mum ... I think clothing's a really peculiar issue in Britain. Any singularity of clothing marks you out as a Rock Star, Film Star, television celebrity, or eccentric aristocrat of some kind.*"

"*Her Majesty ze Queen never dresses eccentrically*" my mother pointed out looking up from her crochet work.

---

5   Jack Bruce—Ministry of Bag—Songs for a Tailor—1969

renate schubert

"*Yes*" Caroline agreed "*I suppose … that would lend weight to a story I heard. The Queen was once supposed to have taken refreshment, incognito in a Scottish tea room. She was apparently approached by a woman who said 'Excuse me—I hope you don't mind me saying this—but you look remarkably like the Queen.' To which the Queen replied: 'How very reassuring'.*"

"*Is ziss a*—true—*story?*" my mother enquired – being familiar with our propensity for humour.

"*I don't know … it may be apocryphal…*" Caroline replied "*… but I'd like to think of her as having given such an answer.*"

My mother nodded with a smile "*Yes – many people do not seem to know zat she has a great sense of humour.*" She admired the Queen and was always reminding people that she was descended from the House of Hannover. My mother was a Hannoverian – and born there, as I was.

"*Celebrities …*" Caroline opined, returning to the previous topic "*… are allowed to dress creatively – but not the run-of-the-mill citizenry.*"

"*Especially the middle-aged males of the species*" I laughed. "*They're supposed to dress according to the dictates of those who designate the regulation style.*"

"*Vott vould ziss look like?*" my mother asked with a cheery smile.

"*Well …you can find the rule-book in any high-street clothing chain-store.*"

My mother looked quizzical, so I continued "*Pseudo-sports clothing and fleece items with elasticated waists.*"

"*Really?*" my mother said in surprise and I nodded in the affirmative. "*Ah ja*" she sighed "*I do not see so much of ze vurld zees days – so I do not know about ze rule book.*" Pause "*Iz zair*—really—*a rule book?*" she chuckled.

an odd boy

"*Yes ... in a manner of speaking ... but it's not a book. It's the 'average-sartorial-ethic' – and it's enforced by citizen police. We know people just like that ...*" Caroline laughed "*... they like to point out that you're not in step. They give you that '... and who d'you think—you—are!' look.*"

"*It's mainly males though*" I added.

Caroline nodded to my mother "*Women are no better. You see ... what—you—think looks so smart – most people—now—see as eccentric.*"

"*Really!?*" my mother laughed with incredulity.

"*Yes. It makes the British nervous when the middle aged and elderly get sartorially inventive*" Caroline replied – and burst into song "*People tend to get enraged – just because I'm middle aged – talking 'bout my generation.*"[6]

"*So now*" my mother chuckled "*you are a different kind of rebel from ze von you verr.*"

"*I never—was—a rebel really ... I just wore clothes I liked – and still do, even though I'm run-of-the-mill.*"

"*You?*" my mother asked incredulously "*Run-of-the-mill?*"

"*Sure. I'm nobody special. I never set out to be special ... well ... I suppose there was my time on stage with Savage Cabbage ... but ... although that made me special for a while – I was far more in-love-with the sensation of being on stage with my friends ... and being ... or living the life of a Bluesman.*" Pause "*Beyond that ... I just set out to live as an Artist.*
I did once have ideas of making things happen ... but that never took off in any major way."

---

6   Author's parody—My Generation—The Who

"*Ja ... I remember ...you had highs hopes venn you verr young. It vozz so very sad venn Stephen and Ronald died. I still remember zem vell. Zey verr such—*nice—*boys. You must have deep regrets over vott never came to pass ... viz zem ... and viz your music.*"

"Well ...yes ... I—do—*still regret the loss of Steve and Ron – and even Jack ... but ... I still play Blues.*" Pause "*Being an invisible Artist isn't a matter for regret though. It's a limitation of sorts – but it's not a fate to bemoan. I'm content to be who I am. I'm also content not to be who I'm not.*"

"*I could still be a nurse ...*" Caroline pitched in "*... but the roulette of existence does what it does.*"

"*And don't speak too soon for the wheel's still in spin, And there's no telling who that it's naming*" I laughed.

"*But ...*" Caroline offered "*... whether famous or insignificant – appreciation is self-fulfilling.*"

"*Absolutely. My senses don't need acclaim. I don't need acclaim to pay the bills or buy guitar strings – and I certainly need none at all in terms of Buddhism and what we teach when we're with our students.*"

"*Once you learn to work within the remit of your situation ...*" Caroline nodded "*... and appreciate what it has to offer, fame*—can— *be an unnecessary inconvenience. I wouldn't like anyone recognising me in the street. You could waste your life dwelling on the inhibitions imposed by 'lack of fame', when you could be enjoying the beauty of what's there in the moment.*"

My mother nodded. "*Ziss is vize – and it is better to be happy*— alvaze—*but you have books published, is ziss not fame?*"

"*Of a kind, yes ... and all the fame we can*—sensibly—*use. As you say, we're 'famous' in certain small circles here and in America in terms of teaching Buddhism. We're happy being who we are.*" Pause "*With the caveat, of course, that*—I—*continue to improve.*"

an odd boy

"*I've certainly no desire to be in world headlines*" Caroline asserted. "*That would make our lives difficult and would attract attention that we would rather avoid.*"

"*No indeed ... that could be quite a burden.*" Pause "*I never became the Bluesman, poet laureate, acclaimed painter I once hoped to be – but it really doesn't matter. It would have got in the way of teaching – and that is really the heart of what we do.*"

"*You are not sorry?*" my mother asked.

"*No ... I'd have liked to have collaborated with John Martyn on a Blues album. I'd have liked to have had Bob Dylan use some of my lyrics – but it's not a tragedy that it didn't happen. I mean, if something like that's not on the cards – that's just what it is. These things either happen or they don't – but we have our work as Buddhist teachers, and beyond that there's nothing to be sorry about.*"

"*You used to write lovely songs—strange songs—but sometimes lovely vords.*"

"*Well – I still write poetry.*"

"*And we write Buddhist books – there's a list we're working through and we may never come to the end of it*" Caroline commented. "*Our work as teachers together involves a lot of creativity – so we're always busy and—always—working on new projects.*"

"*Yes*" I replied. "*I don't see absence of worldwide acclaim as meaning anything.*"

"*Yes*" My mother stated. "*Fame does not make an Artist.*"

"*Quite – an Artist's a person who appreciates – and therefore creates. It's a fact or force of nature – like the way rain falls downward.*"

"*I don't think it's possible to appreciate without becoming passionate about the sense fields*" Caroline added. "*As soon as you start loving colour, shape, texture, sound, fragrance, taste, and ideation you become an Artist.*"

renate schubert

"Yes" I exclaimed. *"The world starts making self-existent suggestions."*

"You are going into Buddhist ideas – you vill have to explain vott ziss means?" my mother asked.

"It's about how creative ideas occur ..." Pause *"...you see ... the world has no intention of making suggestions – it simply happens. It's a synapse that occurs between the world and how we sense or perceive. So ... I never stopped being an Artist merely because opportunities to make a living in the Arts evaporated. Essentially it has nothing to do with making a living – and making a living in Art doesn't necessarily make you an Artist. If all you do is make a living in obedience to Moloch – you're a Molochite."*
I explained Moloch to my mother and she suddenly recognised the name 'Moloch'.

"Zat iss ... from ze Bible ja?" I nodded agreement and she continued in German laughing *"Ah—ja—das ist Der Teufel!*⁷ *I did not know you read ze Bible?"*

*"Behold the lilies of the field—they toil not, neither do they spin—yet even Solomon in all his glory, was not arrayed as one of these."*⁸

*"Ah—*ja*—but I know this well—and you can quote from the Bible too – I vould not have sought ziss."*

"Yes ... It's from Mathew ... I may not have remembered it entirely correctly – but we studied the Gospel of Mathew at school. But you're right – I don't think I've looked at the Bible that often since then ... although it does contain some very fine poetry and – insights into our existence."
Pause *"I was quoting for a reason though ... I may be misinterpreting the Bible ... but to me, this says more-or-less what I said about '... the world making self-existent suggestions' ... that's what the lilies are. They're self-existent suggestions."*

---

7 '*... ja—das ist Der Teufel!*' – '...yes—that is the devil!'
8 King James Bible—Matthew—chapter 26—verse 28

an odd boy

"*Ja ziss I see.*" Pause "*And Moloch?*"

"*My reference for Moloch however, is second hand I'm afraid. It's from the poet Allen Ginsberg. He uses Moloch to describe the ugliness and greed in the world – y'know ... materialism in its grossest most selfish form.*" Pause "*Anyhow ... Molochites—followers of Moloch—know nothing of Art. In servitude to Moloch they become blind, deaf, and dumb to beauty. They eventually atrophy, calcify, and fossilise into trilobites that live merely to be carbon-dated.*"

"*Zat iss funny*" she laughed. "*But not—everyone—vonts to be an artist you know.*"

"*Yes ... true ... but I think that is a pity*" I replied. "*And Art doesn't have to be world-class genius for a person to think of themselves as an Artist.*"

My mother nodded "*Ja, naturally every-vonn can be creative.*"

"*That's just what I'm saying. Human beings don't have to allow themselves to be perceptually edited on the Procrustean bed of average expectations.*"[9]

"*Ja ...*" my mother chuckled at my Greek reference. She knew the legend of Procrustes but had never heard of his bed being employed as philosophical construct. "*So any-vonn can sink of zemselves as an Artist in everyday life.*"

"*Yes ...*" Caroline nodded "*... but, Moloch however, tends to own the franchises.*"

---

9   Procrustean – Procrustes—'the one who hammers out'—was a son of Poseidon. He had an iron bed into which he invited every passer-by to lie down. Those who were too tall would be truncated and those who were too short were stretched until they the appropriate length for the bed. No one was ever the right size for the bed because it could be covertly adjusted. Procrustes would alter its size on viewing his victims at a distance. Procrustes was eventually killed by Theseus, who 'fitted' Procrustes to his own bed by cutting off his head and feet.

"*Exactly ...*" I continued "*... in education, politics, medicine, science, philosophy, psychology, religion, and the Arts. Every area of human interest is the potential territory of Moloch if we're prepared to crush each other's fingers on the success ladder.*"

My mother rubbed her nose for a moment and expounded "*In spite of ziss dreadful*—Moloch—*however, people can still be as free as zey vont to be.*"

"*Yes ... there's a price however*" I replied. "*Always has been.*" Pause "*The price of freedom is public censorship – or lack of approval from those who worship Moloch. Sadly ... people of all religions worship Moloch.*"

"*Buddhist too?*" my mother asked with evident surprise.

"*Maybe Buddhists more than others, I'm sorry to say.*" Pause "*Most people like to follow fashion – where the fashion is literalism, fundamentalism, antidisestablishmentarianism, political correctness, spiritual correctness, aggressive puritanism, dogmatism, tight-minded orthodoxy, unquestioning traditionalism ... there's a long list ...*"

"*It sounds as if you are speaking of ze Nazis in ze vorr ...*"

"*Yes ... they've not gone away ... they exist everywhere in every country in every religion. They are almost always people who are afraid of freedom and afraid of individuality.*" Pause "*To be free ...you have to become an authentic individual.*"

"*And ...*" Caroline added. "*There aren't many who wish to take that step – if you discount misanthropes and attention-seekers.*"

"*And ziss is vott you try to teach people vhen you teach Buddhism to zem ...?*"

"*Ja – naturlich*" I answered.[10]

---

10 "*Ja – naturlich*" – literally '*Yes naturally*' but meaning '*Yes certainly or obviously*'.

an odd boy

My mother nodded sagely, quoting the Bible as was her custom "*Und er sah, daß es gut war.*"[11]

I served out more pizza and poured more wine. The candlelight glittered on the cutlery and glowed on the soft waxed surfaces of the woodwork.

A wind storm was blowing outside and the windows rattled a little in the frames – requiring me to adjust the wedges that kept them quiet.

My crown is in my heart, not on my head; Not decked with diamonds and Indian stones, Nor to be seen; my crown is called 'content'; A crown it is, that seldom kings enjoy.
William Shakespeare—Henry VI—Part III—Act III—Scene i—1591

Basically you have to suppress your own ambitions in order to be who you need to be. Bob Dylan

Disassembled diaries: the 5th *of December* – 2006

I'd climbed into the car. It was a bitter cold foggy morning – and it wasn't quite light, even though the sun had risen an hour before. I placed an overnight carpet bag and satchel on the back seat along with my laptop computer and Stetson hat. All was quiet apart from the milkman clattering down the street with milk bottles jingling in the crates. The fog seemed to dampen the sound and the post-woman surprised me as I closed the passenger door. She grinned and handed me a letter. I took a quick look at it and pushed it through the letter box.

---

11 "*Und er sah, daß es gut war*" – '*And he saw that it was good*' from Genesis 1, 3 – 23: '*So God created the great creatures of the sea and every living and moving thing with which the water teems, according to their kinds, and every winged bird according to its kind. And he saw that it was good.*'

renate schubert

Caroline would need to see it before I did as it came from our publishers. Time enough for that when I returned. I set out for Farnham to visit my mother. She'd been taken to Farnham hospital.

I knew exactly where to go, because I'd worked weekends there in my adolescence. I didn't need a map. My mother suffered a stroke from which she never recovered – and I didn't know that I was going to say goodbye. I shall not write about my sadness. It's not really for anyone else to read – as everyone loses their parents at some point. I will only say that my mother helped and encouraged me throughout my life.

Words are insufficient with regard to praise and gratitude. I've described her as supremely kind, cultured, humorous, and open minded. Beyond that, I can only say she was my mother – and that means only what it means to me.

Do not go gentle into that good night, / Old age should burn and rave at close of day; / Rage, rage against the dying of the light. / Though wise men at their end know dark is right, / Because their words had forked no lightning they / Do not go gentle into that good night. / Good men, the last wave by, crying how bright / Their frail deeds might have danced in a green bay, / Rage, rage against the dying of the light. / Wild men who caught and sang the sun in flight, / And learn, too late, they grieved it on its way, / Do not go gentle into that good night. / Grave men, near death, who see with blinding sight / Blind eyes could blaze like meteors and be gay, / Rage, rage against the dying of the light. / And you, my father, there on the sad height, / Curse, bless me now with your fierce tears, I pray. / Do not go gentle into that good night. / Rage, rage against the dying of the light. Dylan Thomas—Do Not Go Gentle into That Good Night—1951

Strange that I resonate with the emotional force of that verse – yet have no sympathy with its literal meaning. I shall be content to *go gentle* into *that good night*.

an odd boy

Whilst I can rage against the dying of the light for *someone else* or *something else* – for me ... it's not *that* important. I'll just say *'Goodnight.'* Or possibly, being the last Savage Cabbage member to leave the stage, I might try my own version of Rosebud: '... *and me on larynx, pharynx, œsophagus, harp, and rhythm-bass. Goodnight Planet Earth, wherever you are.*'[12]

On my way to my mother's ward, another hospital visitor stopped me.

"Excuse me – I hope you don't mind me asking – but ... are you a rock star?"

I replied with a smile and slight shake of the head "*No ... just visiting my mother.*" Odd answer ... but the question had thrown me. It took me back to the conversation that Caroline and I had with my mother the previous year. I suppose I could have said '*No – I'm an Artist*' but the word 'star' had funnelled me down a theoretical avenue from which I couldn't easily make a conceptual turnabout. I've played different rôles at different times – and had mixed responses. I'd almost been a 'star' once. Some people saw me in that light when I was the vocalist for Savage Cabbage – but Ron and Steve were the real stars. I could have been a 'star' alongside them – but not on my own. What a word ... a 'star' ... what was *that* – who were *they*?

Oh bright star, what would your greatness be if you had not those for whom you shine?
Friedrich Nietzsche—Also Sprach Zarathustra – Ein Buch für Alle und Keinen (Thus Spake Zarathustra – A Book for Everyone and No one)—1885

---

12 Citizen Kane—released in 1941—was the first film directed and co-authored by Orson Wells. The narrative is a fiction based on the life of Randolph Hearst, which evolves through flashbacks, as the research of a reporter attempts to unravel the newspaper magnate's final word 'Rosebud'.

renate schubert

I'd been a star for some and remained a star-of-sorts for others. It was irrelevant to me – and even more so now when I left the hospital. I was at a loose end in Farnham. I'd planned it that way. I wandered into the gardens of the Bush Hotel – I'd booked a room at the Hotel in advance and was going to spend two nights there. I found the place where I'd sat listening to Jo Ann Kelly singing 'Come on in my Kitchen' – but she wasn't there, even as a ghost. I didn't actually expect her to be there – but I had a sense of the past that seemed palpable. I would have liked to have thanked her for what she played and sang – but she died in the 1990s.

It's gonna rain, and it's gonna be cold, / can't survive the winter – out in that driving snow, / You'd better come on—in my kitchen—because it's bound to be raining out do.
Robert Johnson—Jo Ann Kelly—Come on in My Kitchen—1969

I spread my arms out—as if I were on stage—and said "*Thank you.*" I tend to solitary melodramatic flourishes at times. On the whole I don't really approve of it – but as long as no one is inconvenienced by it – it seems harmless enough. A passing waiter wondered whom I might be addressing. I grinned at him "*Just exercising my voice*" I called out so as not to alarm him with the prospect of a lunatic wandering in the grounds.

"*You're an actor then sir?*" he smiled.

"*In a manner of speaking*" I replied. "*Blues singer*" I added so as not to be obscure and sat down on a convenient bench.

"*They used to have Blues festivals here … a long time ago.*"

"*I performed at two of those festivals.*"

"*Really – the manager will be interested to hear that.*" The waiter turned just before re-entering the hotel and asked "*What was your name sir? Just so that I can mention it to the manager?*"

an odd boy

"*Dr Togden—room 33—but I'd have been Frank Schubert on the poster and programme.*"

"*Frank Schubert sir?*"

"*Yes ... that was my stage name at the time.*"

The waiter did not enquire about 'Schubert' – but gave me a broad grin and disappeared. I might not be a star – but I was history. That was amusing. I sat pondering the matter and eventually went to check the files in the office – to which the waiter had directed me. Sure enough, there was the poster and programme of the 1st Farnham Folk and Blues Festival.

I looked at the listings and there were Mike Cooper and Jo Ann Kelly. Even Harry Blandon's name was there as the organiser – but no Frank Schubert. Somehow there was no poster or programme for the 2nd Farnham Folk and Blues Festival. That fact—mysteriously—made me smile. I was interested in the fact that I didn't feel personally disappointed – even though such an item might have been useful in terms of writing an *odd boy*.

I gazed at the poster looking at the name Jo Ann Kelly – and memory flooded. I could hear her voice and guitar. Jo Ann Kelly had brought Robert Johnson alive for me in that garden. Her entirely Delta voice—juxtaposed against blond hair, blue eyes, and ample Gibson-perched bosom—made a lasting impression. Jo Ann Kelly and Jack Bruce taught me how to sing—not personally—but through the sound of their voices. I still hear them today without recourse to recordings.

If I hadn't heard the Robert Johnson record when I did, there probably would have been hundreds of lines of mine that would have been shut down – that I wouldn't have felt free enough or upraised enough to write.
Bob Dylan—Chronicles One—2005

renate schubert

I could say the same of Son House, Muddy Waters, Willie Dixon, John Martyn, Mike Cooper – and many others. Gratitude feels like a banquet that could nourish me the rest of my life. Thoughts like these were moving in distended coils through my mind as I stood in the garden of the Bush Hotel. Farnham is quaint – and where better to have lived in a time when its quaintness made a recherché rebel of me. Farnham's not exactly Dylan Thomas' 'Under Milk Wood – A Play for Voices' – but I can imagine writing about the similar 1940s quality that Farnham had throughout the '60s and '70s.

It is spring, moonless night in the small town, starless and bible-black, the cobblestreets silent and the hunched, courters'-and-rabbits' wood limping invisible down to the slœblack, slow, black, crowblack, fishingboat-bobbing sea. The houses are blind as moles (though moles see fine tonight in the snouting, velvet dingles) or blind as Captain Cat there in the muffled middle by the pump and the town clock, the shops in mourning, the Welfare Hall in widows' weeds. And all the people of the lulled and dumbfound town are sleeping now.
Dylan Thomas—Under Milk Wood: A Play for Voices—1954

Remnants of an earlier era lingered in Farnham and its surrounds. Field Marshal Montgomery [13] lived in Alton—not far from Farnham—and could occasionally be seen in the town – in uniform even in retirement. My mother saw him once and was surprised that he was so short. Montgomery—much to the approval of my father—had advocated against legislation for the legalisation of homosexuality in Britain.

---

13 Field Marshal Montgomery – Field Marshal the 1st Viscount Montgomery of Alamein [1887 – 1976], affectionately referred to as 'Monty', commanded Allied Forces in the Battle of El Alamein, a turning point in the Western Desert Campaign during World War II. Later he held prominent command in Italy and North-West Europe, where he oversaw all Allied Ground Forces during Operation Overlord and the Battle of Normandy.

He stated that the proposed Government Act of 1967 was '... *a charter for buggery ... this sort of thing may be tolerated by the French – but we're British, thank God.*' It's probably apocryphal – but it's said that he once addressed the House of Lords saying "*As God said – and I do think very rightly ...*" For those who are surprised by some accounts I've given of lost time conservative attitudes – it's as well to remember that Montgomery was not alone in his attitude. Field Marshal Montgomery once waved his walking stick at me, telling me that I was impeding his progress on the pavement.

I stepped into the street to allow the whole width of the pavement for his perambulation. The story made my mother laugh. It makes me laugh today – but I'm glad I met the man and remember him fondly as part of a world that made it possible to be as I was.

2

december 2006

the rooms above nowhere

Disassembled diaries: the 6th *of December* 2006

The next day—before visiting my mother for the last time—
I went to see if I could find 'Nowhere'. The 'Nowhere Café' in
East Street was where I'd sat in 1972 with a borrowed copy of
Johnny Winter's *Progressive Blues Experiment*. The cover showed
the reflection of Johnny Winter's face in the back of his
NATIONAL TRICONE resophonic guitar.

I walked the length of East Street searching in vain for
'Nowhere' – but there was no café to be found. The closest
location seemed to be a launderette. 'Nowhere' was no longer
there. I stood staring at the place that used to be 'Nowhere'.
It had somehow failed to become *somewhere*, or *anywhere*.
There'd been a party in the apartment above 'Nowhere' in 1971.
A strange young man in a purple cloak—psychedelically
mesmerised by the links of the lavatory chain—had
commandeered the lavatory for a little too long. I'd requested
him to vacate the place in order that I could avail myself of its
facilities.

He gazed at me not really seeing too clearly *"How man? The stairs
y'know ... the stairs of the chain ... they're—there—they're just—there
—man. It's ...y'know ... eternal ... gliding—there's nothing—I ... see it
...like nothing man... like everything ... everywhere. Don't know—how
—I know. I just know ... I really don't know man – no one knows.
That's how it is – no one knows."*

an odd boy

I smiled. I could almost hear the backwards guitar. "*Quite so—Tomorrow Never Knows—there've been times when I'd have said the same. So ... if you don't mind I—really—need to use the loo.*"

"*Like yeah man – it's yours.*" He then drifted past me – and fell headlong down the stairs. I rushed down the clattering flight to help him. It was an alarming fall – but he was fine. Nothing broken. Just bewilderment talking to the fairies.

"*Good luck*" I said and turned toward the lavatory.

"*Chains man – like just check ... the chain*" he called up after me as I ascended the stairs. The lavatory was engaged. Life's like that sometimes.

There is—*no*—reason why I should remember such a thing. There's also no reason I should remember Andrew Sculley—Scottish ex-RAF dog handler turned art student—who'd found a tin of emerald green paint and painted three interwoven lines from the door step of 'Nowhere' across the road, up an alley and into the entrance to the graveyard. He later said "*I wanted to show*—man—*that 'Nowhere' læds tæ fouking nowhere.*" He was quite a literal man. One had to admire him for that. His other major project was a huge wooden carving that he made from the bole of a tree. The carving became increasingly smaller 'til the eventual knob of wood was thrown into the river and floated away on the current. He took photographs of the carving at frequent intervals with an empty camera – and the final product was nothing. I never did enjoy conceptual work of that nature. He certainly worked hard and worked long hours – but I really failed to see the value of the exercise. I was glad however that the tutors gave him good credit for the work. No matter how much I find such things pointless it pleases me that the Art School world allowed it.

It pleased me because it all added to the ambience of Hatch Mill. Anything was possible – and Andrew Sculley had been a symbol of that.

There's no reason why I should remember the flurry of topless dancing at Nowhere Café either– but I remember being entirely charmed. I was impressed by the determination and fortitude of the young ladies in question. There was little or no heating and the room was chill to say the least. Johnny Winter sang 'Rolling and Tumbling' on an inadequate record player – but his music carried the day. I got talking to a lady called Cindy Macintosh. She was a sculptor. She told me she liked welding and I took some infrared photographs of her at work with an oxyacetylene torch the following day.

She took me to her parlour, she called me with her fan – she said I was the prettiest thing to dream a mortal man, / I wished I was an apple, a-hangin' on a tree – ev'rytime that Cindy would pass me by, she take a bite of me. Sonny Terry/Brownie McGhee—Cindy Cindy—1943

Cindy was bound for Liverpool Art School, so—although there was significant interest—neither of us fanned the embers too severely. Nonetheless – our goodbye was not without some sadness. There were many gatherings above 'Nowhere' – some more florid than others. There were usually a few people who employed these gatherings to be on another planet – or to pretend they were on other planets. I used the evenings to talk with people – and find out what inspired them.

I stood on the pavement, and—having conclusively failed to find 'Nowhere'—I decided to go someplace else. I walked back into town – eventually finding myself standing outside 'The Bishop's Table' – a restaurant and tearoom. It was the place where I'd once been moved on by a policeman for loitering with unknown intent. *"Move on"* he said. I moved on.

an odd boy

Now look-a yonder, baby, what I see? / A police and a sergeant, they is coming after me. Robert Wilkins—Police Sergeant Blues—1928

Discussion was unwise. I'd simply been observing the sunset as it streamed down the small cul-de-sac that led to the new Art School buildings – but *try telling that to the judge*. The policemen in Farnham in 1970 seemed to labour under the impression that anyone who looked like an Art student was necessarily depraved and degenerate – bristling with felonious intentions and Thelonious Monk.

Well, you know I was sentenced for murder, murder in the first degree. Judge's wife called up, said: "Let that man, Brownie go free. / 'cause he's a jelly roll baker, yes, bakes the best jelly roll in town. / He's the only man that can bake jelly roll, hmmm, with his damper down."
Sonny Terry/Brownie McGhee—That Good Old Jelly—1947

I stood there again in 2006, wondering what might happen. Loitering without intent. There was no sunset at which I could gaze – it being ten past three in the afternoon. I was amused by the memory of my illustrated tale 'The Long Ten Past Three of Reginald Jones' and wondered where it was and whether Mr Vanderpost yet lived. The tale returned to my mind as a scattering of words:

Reginald Jones is put to the rack – and whilst being stretched on a monstrous contraption bristling with cogwheels and ratchets, Monsignor Writhe—a black hooded torturer—asks him: 'Are you going to be long?'

Maybe Mr Vanderpost bequeathed it to someone – or maybe it grew shabby and was discarded. The latter was probably more likely. As I waited to see what might transpire – I thought back to Reginald Clarke and his patriotic machine. Reginald Clarke dubbed me '666 The Great Beast'. There is no answer as to why that was. I phoned him about it – but he can't remember.

the rooms above nowhere

It remains a mystery – as does the fact that I had no objection to the sobriquet. Reginald Clarke was a curious mixture of interests. His father was much like mine – having a military background – but he was of a far more genteel and benign disposition. It seems likely that this is the origin of Reginald's penchant for military uniform – and of course 'The Patriotic Machine'.

'The Patriotic Machine' was an old television – one of those walnut veneered televisions from the early '50s which had a door that could be closed to hide the offending screen. We had one in our home and you had to whack it from time to time to stop the pictures rotating. My father was an expert at that trick. Reg had removed the defunct television from the cabinet. The vertical sides of the inside of the cabinet were then lined with pale pastel floral wallpaper. A 'floor' had been inserted and carpeted with maroon velvet – in the midst of which stood a faux marble plinth. A small framed picture of Queen Victoria hung on the back wall gazing out at a Union Jack which waved languorously from the plinth. When you opened the walnut doors of 'the Patriotic Machine' a light came on inside the box, a tape loop of the chorus of 'Rule Britannia' started to play, and the Union Jack began to wave.

Reginald Clarke went on to operate as a publicist for Richard Booth, self-styled 'King of Hay' in Hay-on-Wye – 'The Town of Books'. Reginald accompanied Richard Booth in a faux general's uniform with rococo-nouveau brass epaulettes from some fuss and feathers Italian regiment. He was the Commander in Chief of Armed Forces for the independent Kingdom of Hay.

April Ashley, Britain's first sex-change[1] candidate was named First Lady of Hay and a National anthem was devised – I have the 45 disc of it somewhere.

Lord Host of Host, asleep on high, awake and cast a kindly eye on independent Hay-on-Wye. / Let long the liberal urn here flow, with fruits that from our labour grow: conserve them long, Lord, here below. / Let flourish here the lame and odd, the hazel twig, the unknown God, and this independent sod. / Let your goodwill establish by this river under neutral sky a truly rural Hay-on-Wye. / Let us at every parish crisis invoke Apollo, Dionysus, the I-Ching and even Isis. / Let us and our direct descendants, with you, O Lord, in close attendance, depend upon our independence. George Barker—National Anthem of Hay-on-Wye

As the melody of the anthem trailed away in my mind I noticed that the police had not moved me on. Nothing had transpired or became apparent – just the daily flow of civic life in West Street, with all its varied colours and shapes. If there *were* art students – I did not notice them amongst the general citizenry. I'd returned from trying to find 'Nowhere' in order to stand observing nothing in particular. I was some kind of ghost – or character in an unpublished book: The *Ghost of Hallucinations Past*. Something like Marley's Ghost but trailing swirling colours and Blues riffs in his wake – rather than dragging chains and money boxes. I had a black 1850s flared-crown hat on my head. I wore the ankle length Hassidic cashmere coat I'd bought from Hardstein's on New Utrecht in Borough Park.

A pair of high buttonhook boots with Cuban heels and square toes. The wind whipped the coat out wide and I stood there enjoying the sensation of the fluttering fabric.

---

1   Sex change – 'gender reassignment' surgery in the USA.

the rooms above nowhere

Eventually a young policeman passed on the other side of the street. He could have been the son of the policeman who moved me on in 1970. He evidently didn't suspect me of anything – but it's more likely that he failed to record my existence. That would make sense – as I'd just walked there from a 'Nowhere' that was no longer there. I turned with slightly amused bemusement and entered 'The Bishops Table'.

I'd never been inside the restaurant before. An Art student entering 'The Bishop's Table' might have warranted capital punishment in 1970. I looked around at the splendid wooden panelling. It was a fine place – it had been well maintained. I ordered tea and scones. They were good – but I didn't touch the cream and strawberry jam. The policeman may not have noticed my attire – but the elderly occupants of 'The Bishops Table' certainly did. They noticed my hat.

One elderly lady was kind enough to say "*Oh … I—do—like your hat!*"

I smiled, replying accidentally "*Why thank you kindly ma'am.*" I was not clear why I'd become Clint Eastwood's *Pale Rider*. I'd not planned to speak in such a way. It simply spilled out of my mouth. I offered them my cream and strawberry jam. They appeared to have run short – and giggled in sheer delight at the extra treat. Life could be like that *all* the time. You just have to side-step Moloch. I've had many charming encounters with elderly ladies and often wonder if they're the real weirdoes of the human race – whatever the decade or century.

I remember asking two elderly ladies directions on one occasion – and they'd replied "*Don't ask us – we're just two idiots out for the day.*" I found that entirely refreshing and hoped I'd be able to say the same myself when I reached that age. '*Don't ask me, I'm just two idiots out for the day.*' You have to allow for inflation …

an odd boy

During the writing of *an odd boy*, the manuscript was read by numerous friends. Many said they were surprised by how sad my life had been. Several said it made them cry. I was also surprised when I came to add it all up. Although my memories hadn't exactly been hidden away – I had no recollection of 'sadness' – only 'sad moments' within a flow that was otherwise delightful. If you'd have asked me about my life as an offhand question, I'd have replied that it had been mainly joyous. Even having written this book—when I look back at my life as a whole—I cannot say it was sad. When I read the sequence of events however, it surprises me how many losses there were. Loss is a strange and rare creature that inhabits the edges of thought. I glimpse it from time to time and it looks at me fleetingly before blending with other mirage images of time-passing.

I can't remember if I cried when I read about his widowed bride, / But something touched me deep inside, the day the music died.
Don McLean—American Pie—1971

That song wasn't written for John Lennon – but I can't sing it—or hear it—without thinking of him. I also think of George Harrison, Jimi Hendrix, and Jo Ann Kelly. I also think of the lads – Steve, Ron, and Jack. We were all pretty much married to Savage Cabbage from '68 to '70. There were too many Blues heroes and heroines to name, who went before their time – and remembering them is part of my life.

Expressing what their absence means is not possible – although I hope I've described their presence well enough to give indications of the parts they played.

The day the music died was not a solitary day. It was any number of days – and they didn't fall in any intelligible sequence. It wasn't always *death* that marked those days.

the rooms above nowhere

It was the day Cream disbanded. The day the Beatles split. The day the Edgar Broughton Blues Band became the Edgar Broughton Band. It was all the individual days on which other fine bands vanished from public sight. It was the day the public started saying they couldn't dance to slow Blues – when before they simply sat and listened.

I can still see the look of confusion on Ron's face. "*Whaddya mean?!*" he asked the promoter.

I had to lead Ron away before he hit the man. I explained "*... people seem to want a faster beat for dancing now. You told me—yourself —Ron – 120 beats per minute or faster—is—what the majority of the musically illiterate want.*"

Ron gritted his teeth "*Yeah ... bastards danced last week though ...*"

Sad moment. "*Yes ... they did ... but maybe they weren't the ones the promoter meant.*"

"*Yeah ... suppose you're right. There are people who still enjoy decent Blues – whether they bloody jump around or not.*"

"*Maybe they'll jump around again next Sunday*" I volunteered.

They did. Although most sat and listened – the '60s weren't entirely dead. It didn't change overnight. I was happy Ron didn't die hard on the heels of speaking to that promoter. He went on the crest of the wave – seeing the band at its best. Jack had made an unexpected leap after bidding Cynthia adieu. He'd plunged into practice as if there'd been a hell hound on his trail. We were all impressed – suddenly he was in a different league. Steve's improvisation had reached a level of fluidity and inventiveness that caused Ron to grin demonically.

Even I'd improved on bass to the point where I provided a solid rhythm section. We were all set to make history.

Dreams, indeed, are ambition; for the very substance of the ambitious is merely the shadow of a dream. And I hold ambition of so airy and light a quality, that it is but a shadow's shadow.
William Shakespeare—Hamlet—Act II—Scene ii—1599

I had an ambition to be on stage – but I had to relegate that ambition to the realms of the imponderable when I realised that the British Blues Boom had died. I could have sung with a few bands in Bristol – but they weren't Blues bands. They were soft Rock bands, so there was no question. It was either relinquish ambition – or play music for which I had no heart. My heart won over ambition. Always has done. There have been people who achieved great celebrity and fell from public favour for no reason I can comprehend. There are those who only achieved modest celebrity – who I perceive as having a high level of creative skill and virtuosity. There are those whose celebrity is deserved and those whose celebrity is more-or-less undeserved. Some have 'greatness' thrust upon them – by Moloch.

... *be not afraid of greatness: some are born great, some achieve greatness, and some have greatness thrust upon 'em.* William Shakespeare—Twelfth Night—Act II—Scene v—1601—Malvolio, reading a piece of prose

I would not have objected to having had greatness thrust upon me – but with regard to 'the media': *Moloch giveth and Moloch taketh away.* The world of fame is often the abattoir of Art.

Appreciation dies when you've been bought and sold by popular demand. Malvolio's full text on fame reads:

If this fall into thy hand, revolve. In my stars I am above thee; but be not afraid of greatness: some are born great, some achieve greatness, and some have greatness thrust upon 'em. Thy Fates open their hands; let thy blood and spirit embrace them; and, to inure thyself to what thou art like to be, cast thy humble slough and appear fresh.

Be opposite with a kinsman, surly with servants; let thy tongue tang arguments of state; put thyself into the trick of singularity: she thus advises thee that sighs for thee. Remember who commended thy yellow stockings, and wished to see thee evercross-gartered: I say, remember. Go to, thou art made, if thou desirest to be so; if not, let me see thee a steward still, the fellow of servants, and not worthy to touch Fortune's fingers. Farewell. She that would alter services with thee, the fortunate-unhappy.
William Shakespeare—Twelfth Night—Act II—Scene v—1601

Malvolio's being tricked into believing that he's in with the main chance – but he's too dim to see it. I'd been *that very same Malvolio* too often. The only good I can say of myself is that I merely wanted to manifest what was possible – without expense to those who wished the same. In striving for the possible—or the impossible—there's always joy, always loss. They're interdependent. Flowers to weddings—flowers to the grave. Sometimes the grave's dug earlier than we'd like—or earlier than friends would like—but it awaits everyone, the famous and the obscure alike.

Take me down little Susie, take me down, I know you think you're the queen of the underground, / And you can send me dead flowers to my wedding, / And I won't forget to put roses on your grave.
Jagger/Richards—Rolling Stones—Dead Flowers—Sticky Fingers—1971

If I didn't remember a life brimming with astonishing people, spectacular situations, and magnificent possibilities – the sense of loss wouldn't be apparent. But it requires authentic appreciation to experience authentic loss. The loss of the lads only heightens my joy in remembering them. Hey, I've got nothing to do today but smile.[2]

---

2   Simon/Garfunkel—Only Living Boy in New York—Bridge Over Troubled Water —1970 *'I can gather all the news I need on the weather report. / Hey, I've got nothing to do today but smile.'*

an odd boy

Disassembled diaries: the 7th *of December* – 2006

I'd booked into the Bush Hotel three days earlier – to wander round the town a little. It was a matter of research – I'd wanted to check my memories. I overheard some Tibetans—young men and women—chatting in the laundry room. The Pestalotsi Children's Village isn't so far away from Farnham and there've always been Tibetan children in the care of that establishment. They obviously grow up and get jobs. Maybe they were students working in holiday time – I never found out. I wished them *tashee del-ay*[3] as I whisked past. It's a greeting which means 'hello and good luck'. I caught a brief moment of surprise in their expressions as they realised they'd been culturally identified. I couldn't stop. I was meeting with an old Art School friend – and I was on my way to the dining room. I was happy to remain a mystery.

I turned out to be the most conservatively dressed person in that dining room – in spite of my bun. Black silk Hassidic jacket. Impeccable wool-serge waistcoat. Brilliant white shirt. Dark blue polka dot cravat. Stiff new dark blue Serge De Nîmes trousers. Highly polished brown Grenson Oxfords.

I saw Pete Bridgewater—my friend from Farnham Art School—and went across to the table I'd booked. Pete now runs a company: the Bridgewater Book Company.

"*Clever initialisation* …" I commented, and he laughed. He'd come to meet me from Brighton. He'd gone to Brighton Art School the year before I'd gone to Bristol. He'd been highly successful.

I'd invited Pete to take a meal with me.

---

3   Tashee del-ay – Tibetan greeting. Transliteration – Tashi delegs (*bKra shis gDe legs*)

We'd not met up for many years – and our conversation was interesting, yet nebulous. Interesting because it *was* genuinely interesting. Nebulous – because it had been so many years since we'd last seen each other, that neither of us quite knew whom the other was addressing. For a short while, it was as if each of us were addressing the other through marionettes – operated from a distance. The marionettes were *who we used to be*. The puppeteers were the *present day versions of who we'd been*. Time travel affects the senses in that way. It was a good meeting – but I'd been aware that I'd become an unknown quantity. We had no lack of subjects to discuss. There were too many. I mentioned the story concerning Greg Ford's beach buggy and we both roared with laughter. Pete told me that Greg had about a dozen sizeable tool stores in Australia. I was delighted – but not surprised. Greg had also become Crocodile Dundee to a certain degree and the notion roused me to exuberant cheer. Pete talked of meeting again in the future when Greg came to visit Britain. That sounded just fine.

"*A toast!*" Pete exclaimed.

"*Wha's like us? Damn few—and they're a' deid!* "[4]

Pete looked a little thoughtful.

"*Never thought you'd end up as a holy man.*"

Pete was referring to the fact that I spent a decade or so in the Himalayas and was now a teacher of Vajrayana Buddhism.[5]

"*There's nothing particular holy about me Pete.*"

"*Yeah – but you know what I mean.*"

---

4   A Scottish toast – '*Who's like us? Damn few and they're all dead!*'
5   Vajrayana – (Tibetan: dorje thegpa – *rDo rJe theg pa*) the thunderbolt vehicle of Tibetan Buddhism, also referred to as Tantra or Tantrayana.

an odd boy

"Yes ... but I've been interested in Vajrayana since I was in Junior School — you must remember that I'd mention it from time to time."

"Well yes — but everyone was a nominal Buddhist or something back in the day weren't they."

"Yes they were. I guess I was never nominal though — just ... quiet about it."

"Yeah." Pete laughed "And you're not exactly noisy now either."

"I am when I sing Blues."

"Like the guitar playing vicar — you used not to be too impressed with that kind of thing."

"I remember him." I chuckled "Yeah ... maybe it wasn't wise of me to have derided the fellow — but y'know we all had pretty strong opinions back then." Pause "I still have I guess — but ... these days ... I try to remember that they're all entirely subjective."

"So now you're the Blues singing Lama?" Pete exclaimed with ever-so-slightly derisory glee.

"Yes Pete, I am — but I don't cross the tracks. I don't sing Blues numbers with Buddhist themes — so I suppose I'm not that much like the guitar playing vicar. I just enjoy Blues as much as I ever did — and there ain't no rule about it.

"I still write poetry and I still paint — but Buddhist thematics are never really viciously evident in that."

"So is that a bit of a double-life or double-act or ...?"

"Yes and no ... Yes inasmuch as I'm a multiple act ... y'know: Bluesman, poet, painter, gunslinger, horserider, Confederate re-enactor, sit-down comic, and balding buffoon." Pause "... and no, inasmuch as none of the acts are discreet — they're no big secret."

"An indiscreet double-life then."

"*You got it in one.*" Pause "*That why I ain't no holy man ... unless you equate Art with holiness—y'see ... I never ever really divided things like that.*" Pause "*As you may remember ... that ladies were always Art to me.*"

Pete grinned and raised his eyebrows.

"*No ... I'm not talking about 'erotica' Pete. I'm talking about romance – and the inspiration of that in my life.*" Pause "*Ladies have always ... been ...*" Pause "*Mysterious isn't the right word – it's more mystery in the sense that Max Ernst or Magritte's paintings are mysterious. When I look at that Max Ernst painting 'The Robing of the Bride', it is both understandable and completely beyond comprehension.*"

"*Yeah ... women can be surreal.*"

"*The whole of life is surreal, Pete – but if you get me onto that I'll start talking like a holy man y'know – and I'd like to hear some more about your life.*"

Pete went into some details about his time at Thames and Hudson after he left Brighton Art School – and how he went on to be a freelance graphic designer. He talked of loves won and lost and how he finally established the Bridgewater Book Company.

We talked about how different our lives had been – and yet how easy it remained for us to converse: the creative business executive and the ... whatever I was. But what was I in this context? I'd never become a born-again-Tibetan or a post-modern newage psychotherapeutic politically-correct buddhaphile. It was almost impossible to explain what I was.

an odd boy

In some ways I was very much an orthodox Nyingma[6] – but my sense of that means tends to be expressed through language that sounds more like psychology or science expounded through the medium of poetry. Still crazy after all these years. It was no one's fault that I didn't fit any statutory box – and it wasn't even that I'd done it on purpose just to bug people. How could I drop my love of Art because I'd become taken a route that led to being a Nyingma Lama?

Pete saw the problem *"You were always like that I suppose – y'know with painting and poetry and music. You were always multi-media – and now you've added religion to your witches brew."*

"That's a good way to look at it Pete ..." Pause *"... but I think that the religion is the broth in which the other ingredients ferment."*

"Fire burn, and cauldron bubble ... eh ..."[7]

"Thrice the brinded cat hath mew'd. Thrice and once the hedge-pig whined ..."

"You always liked your quotes."

"Fillet of a fenny snake, in the cauldron boil and bake; Eye of newt and toe of frog, Wool of bat and tongue of dog, Adder's fork and blind-worm's sting, Lizard's leg and howlet's wing ..." Pause *"Yes indeed – I'll quote at the drop of a hat."*

Pause *"Scale of dragon, tooth of wolf, witches' mummy, maw and gulf. Of the ravin'd salt-sea shark, root of hemlock digg'd i' the dark, slivers of blasphemer's shoe, gall of goat, and slips of yew, sliver'd in the moon's eclipse, Nose of Turk and Tartar's lips, finger of birth-strangled babe – ditch-deliver'd by a drab. Make the gruel thick and slab. Add thereto a tiger's chaudron – for the ingredients of our cauldron ..."*

---

6 Nyingma – (*rNying ma*) the 'old translation tradition' of Tibetan Buddhism.
7 William Shakespeare—Macbeth—Act IV—Scene i—1606

Pete interrupted me at this point as the somewhat sombre waiter approached us "*By the pricking of my thumbs — something wicked this way comes.*"

"Now that was impressive Pete — *for someone who doesn't usually quote.*"

"I think it's the only line I remember apart from 'hubble bubble toil and trouble' ..."

The waiter came—delivered our brandies—and gradually became vague as he melted into the far region of the dining room. Some fragment of something had obviously swished its tail in the sea of remembrance and Pete asked "*Whatever happened to ... what's-her-name ... the ginger haired girl you were so keen on?*"

"Lindie Dale?" I knew her name immediately.

Pete looked surprised by my instant recall. "*Not still carrying a torch for her are you?*"

"Good gracious no." I laughed "*Well ...yes and no ...*"

"*You're big on these yes and no answers, I notice.*"

"Well yes and no Pete" I laughed. "*But now you mention it ... I probably am ... because nothing seems that clear cut to me ... I tend to think in multiplistic interconnections ...y'know, where everything seems to relate to a whole range of ideas.*"

"*Hearing colours and seeing sounds — I remember you were always hot on that stuff even though you were never an acid-head.*"

"Certainly. I haven't changed that much."

"*So ... Lindie Dale — I'm not letting you skip round that one.*"

"*Am I still carrying a torch for her?*" Pause "*I did for a fair few years. She had a habit of reappearing in my mind every time something went wrong in a relationship.*" Pause

"It was eerie ...y'know ... I'd repeatedly imagine I'd finally settled to never seeing her again – and then there she'd be in my mind again. And there I'd be, head over heels in love with her again. That happened a fair few times."

"That's ... quite a thing to hang on to all that time" Pete chuckled.

"Well ... I have a memory for ladies ... and I—have—been writing about that time."

Pete nodded. "Right ... but I thought the book was about the Arts rather than Lindie Dale?"

"It is – but ... ladies are ... inextricably bound up with Art as I said."

"Right ...you did say..." Pause "Well? So what happened to her then? Did you ever meet up with her again or anything?"

"No ... never did. She married mister soldierman—his name escapes me —so there seemed no point in writing to her on the off chance that anything had changed."

"Well you never can tell ..." Pete suggested.

"You're right – maybe I should have written ... well ... somewhere between '72 and '75 ... Interestingly enough, I discovered that Lindie divorced the soldierman in the Summer of '72" Pause "Ah ... now I remember, Sidney was his name – 'Sidney the Soldierman' ... so it seems that I could, or should, have written. That was precisely the time we could have reconnected."

Pete looked curious "D'you wish you had?"

"Interesting question. There—were—imes when I—would—have wished that..." Pause "... but not now – not for ... let's see ... sixteen years."

Pete looked a little relieved that he hadn't stirred something best left alone "Why sixteen years?"

"Length of time I've been married to Caroline."

Pete gave me a curious look. *"So ... what exactly is the 'yes and no' about – in terms of Lindie and carrying a torch for her?"*

"Right, I left that in the air didn't I ..." Pause *"What I meant by*—yes and no—*was: I'm not carrying a torch for Lindie – because she's long gone ... but I am in the sense that I found her again*—or rather—*I've found the relationship I*—had—*with Lindie again. Caroline and I admire and respect each other – and we share pretty much everything in life. We don't live in separate compartments. It's something that really hit me quite forcefully writing 'an odd boy'. As I wrote about my life ... I realised that nothing ever really worked out with ladies 'til I found what I had with Lindie again."*

"You've pretty much got yourself a Jane Austen novel there."

"All I need is Pemberley and its fine grounds" I laughed

"And a few of Mr Darcy's costumes" Pete chuckled.

"I've already got the dressing gown."

"You're joking ..." Pete laughed with incredulity.

"Not at all. Had it made last year. Got the riding coat too. Jacket, waistcoat, shirt, and neckscarf are next on the list."

"Guess you're lucky Caroline doesn't mind living on a Merchant Ivory set"[8] Pete cackled. *"So ... can I get back to Lindie Dale's divorce then?"* I nodded assent. *"How'd'you find out about*—that—*then?"*

"Through Susan Wilcox – one of Lindie's three friends. We've kept in contact off and on."

"Really ... any—other—*news come through?"*

---

8   Merchant Ivory – film company specialising in period drama.

an odd boy

"Yes ... Susan told me Sarah Bradley and Daphne Morgan were both fine. Sarah's in the USA—Colorado—and Daphne lives in New Zealand. Both wanted to be remembered to me."

"*That's nice*" said Pete. "*I kind of remember them – but it's a bit hazy. I seem to remember they were all good looking.*"

"*Yes ... I remember that too. They were bright and witty too – I really liked them all.*"

Sarah, Daphne, and Susan weren't hazy to me—I remembered them vividly—and my mind flitted back to that amorphous interlude between school and Art School. I caught a glimpse of *the odd boy* with the three ladies sitting in a candle lit restaurant in London. Fragments of conversation seeped through a fissure in time and wistfulness wafted into a smile.

"*Seems like you liked more than Lindie then*" Pete grinned – noticing the fact that I drifted off somewhere.

"*Certainly ...*" I said – suddenly removed from reverie "*...you remember how I was. I always found ladies ... utterly fascinating.*"

"*Yeah ...*" Pete laughed. "*I remember you were an incurable romantic.*"

"*Still am Pete—still am—haven't changed in that respect.*"

"*So what was wrong with Sarah, Susan, and Daphne then? Did they all have boyfriends or something?*"

"*No ... it was just ... the wrong time. I couldn't look at anyone after Lindie – not for quite a while.*"

"*Right ... it was a bit of a hard time for you. You were cut up about her for a year ... far as I remember.*"

"*One year and ten months.*"

Pete laughed about the exactitude of my memory *"That was an important time for you though, wasn't it – with Savage Cabbage and all that happened."*

"Yes it was Pete ...yes it was."

"That was an amazing time 'cause you were pretty much the high flyer then – being on stage and all that."

"Yes ... for about two years I was all set to vie with the mighty ... and in fact – it felt as if I was already there. I loved being the vocalist for Savage Cabbage – I was in my element there. Being in a band was a dream come true – especially with Ron and Steve. There was no question as to their virtuosity. They were top-flight world-class musicians even at that age – and Ron ... well ... he was in his own category. He could have stood his ground with Jimi Hendrix, Buddy Guy – any of them." Pause *"I was just incredibly lucky ..."*

"Would you like to be back there again?"

"Yes and no ..."

"That's the third time you've answer like that" Pete laughed.

"I can't say 'yes and no' to that can I?" I smiled back *"... but ... y'know ... there are just so many possibilities that seem poised between this and that."*

"Such as?"

"Such as: would you like to be back with Savage Cabbage again? Yes but I wouldn't like to be at School again – or have a stammer again – or have to deal with the mainstream conservatism of that time ... with everything you could mention there's be caveats." Pause *"So ... I'd like to be back there again if I could take Caroline with me."* Pause *"... actually ... no ... maybe not. There's no going back. I'd have to have the mind I had then to enjoy being back in 1968.*

"I have the feeling that being back there with the mind I have now could be ... disappointing. I think the memory of that time is a better experience than I'd get from time travelling. I'm happy to be where I am right now."

"Well yeah – but being younger would be a bonus."

"Too right—in terms of physiology—I'd like the energy I had then and a full head of hair ..." Pause "... but I wouldn't go for being young again – not now."

"Sounds like all those years in the Land of Snows have affected you —'cause you do make the occasional 'holy man' remark—it always puzzled me why you just vanished like that ... just how long were you out there?"

"A decade or more – but I went back and forth y'know. I spent most Summers in Britain working in factories or on building sites to earn money to go out again for the rest of the year ..." Pause "... but it wasn't Tibet – I've never been there. I was just in India, Nepal, and Sikkim. Tibet was too expensive and I had all I needed with the teachers I found there."

"It's sort of amazing that you've ended up here at the Bush Hotel though – looking like ... well looking quite suave – if a little eccentric. I'd have thought you'd have ended up unemployed and unemployable with the direction you took."

"Yes ... that's what I would have thought too – but I didn't ever make any big plan." Pause

"My being a Buddhist teacher now—and travelling round the world teaching—was not something that could ever have been an ambition." Then I laughed "Maybe that's what made this 'impossible dream' possible. It was the only impossible dream I never had ... it just had me."

"I once had a dream or should I say, it once had me?" Pete chuckled misquoting Norwegian Wood.

"Pretty much ... it just happened." Pause *"I won't say it's all been easy – or that my being a Lama doesn't cause irritation here and there."*

"Well you always did cause irritation – but it was mainly the parents of grammar school girls as far as I remember."

"That's true ... although Caroline's a grammar school girl y'know?"

"Really? And her father didn't pepper you with his shotgun?"

"No ... I think society has changed a little ... and maybe I made good in the end." Pause *"I'm glad to have a family. I couldn't have imagined that either."*

"Yeah ... I didn't take that direction. It must be interesting."

"It is. Robert wants to re-build the DEBIL *– and I told him I'd let him attack an old 12 string of mine for the project. We've been reading 'an odd boy' to Robert and Rachel in the evenings. They like the story of my insane youth."*

Pete laughed *"It was insane alright. Not your youth in particular. It was pretty crazy for most of us – but those years were a—lot—of fun."*

"Yeah Pete ... more fun than a—lot—of people have in their—entire—lives."

3

january 2007

born under a glad sign

Good luck and laughter always been my fate / Big Bill Broonzy—yeah— when I was eight / Born under a glad sign – had this smile since I began to crawl, / If it wasn't for good luck – wouldn't've—sung—no Blues at all.
Author's parody—Born Under a Glad Sign—1969

Disassembled diaries: the 27th *of November* – 2007

On an overcast morning—boiling silent with imminent rain—a package arrived. It contained songs I'd written from 1966 to 1972. Thought I'd never see these again – and, suddenly, here they were lying on the dining room table looking like … something from Vic's vault of vague vacuity. There was my teenage handwriting. It hasn't changed that much – but … the colour of the ink and the aged paper lent it an air of something I never thought I'd see. History. The following song 'Amateur Rugby' was based on the Lennon-McCartney song 'Eleanor Rigby'.

Eleanor Rigby's making changes now – she's spent too long feeling floored / Took out her face—you know the one—that she kept in the jar by the door, / She threw it sky high—took careful aim—and shot it with her .44 / Now her mouth hangs up there smiling – and it's grinning from shore to shore / Singing throw down that rice where the wedding was – it ain't no use no more. / Turn a cartwheel for me so we can see the swirls on your tie-dyed drawers. / Father McKenzie wrote a sermon – he'd been making it rhyme for a week / He put it out and commenced to shout 'bout his passion for being a freak / A 1000 came flocking to see the stockings – darned in the darkened street /

an odd boy

They had rainbow ribbons—and I ain't fibbing—shoulda seen 'em on his feet / He's a fast moving priest—got six kids at least—he's advanced and won't retreat / His wife's a real mover with her galactic Hoover she even taught it to speak.

Eleanor gotta new set of clothes, a perfumed rose, and she's singing 3, 6, 9. / She shook out her hair—her feet are bare—and she's having a real good time, / She baked her bread 'till the inkwell fled and headed for the Maginot line / Father McKenzie wrapped his knees round his new trapeze he's really feeling fine / Reading his sermons every day in a curious way juggling bottles of sparkling wine / Both lived happy ever after up in the rafters – they're both really in their prime.
Schubert-Bruce—Amateur Rugby—December 1967

Steve loved this song and wrote a melody for it with Ron – but I have little or no memory of it, as I was never able to play it. It required barré chords …

Disassembled diaries: the 24th *of February* 2007

I went to a Schul [1] in Greenwich Village, New York – to hear Klezmer.[2] The Andy Statman Trio: Andy Statman on clarinet and mandolin, Jim Whitney on bass, and Larry Eagle on percussion. They play most Mondays and Thursdays in a charming informal situation – decorated by paintings of the prophets, executed by children.

The audience helps move classroom tables and set the chairs in position. I muscled in with the assistance of Richard—Mad Dog —Simon (he plays a fine harp).

---

1   Schul – the 'Historic Congregation Derech Amuno' on Charles Street and West 4th Street, New York City.
2   Klezmer – Jewish Jazz.

born under a glad sign

A gracious host offered a glass of Israeli brandy in response to my English voice and ad hoc assortment of Hassidic black: hat, jacquard scarf, and frockcoat … I'm an odd goy.[3]

The feeling was akin to the village hall in Wrecclesham, where Savage Cabbage played their last gig in 1970. At places like these, *anything and everything* can happen: homemade environments with world-class music.

Disassembled diaries: the 26th *of February* 2007

I was sitting in *Heights Coffee*—Prospect Heights, Brooklyn. I'd gone to avail myself of a couple of hot buttered bagels and a duo-octuple espresso for breakfast. I sat down at the far end in an armchair next to a window sill, so I could park my bagel and espresso – there being no vacant table. It hadn't been easy for the barista to understand that I really wanted eight double espressos in one cup. "*Yes please—seriously—eight double espressos.*" Milk? "*No thank you.*" Did I want it watered down? "*No that'll be fine – just as it is please.*" wide-eyed silence. "*I trust you'll excuse me— I'm English.*" As if it wasn't obvious. What wasn't obvious was that the English are not accustomed to drinking inhuman quantities of espresso.

I'd watched Cream the night before with Mad Dog. Their 2005 Albert Hall reunion gig. As I listened, I found myself involved in an age old conjecture. This is the way Blues *could* have moved. Cream really had taken Blues another step along the way to wherever – but when they disbanded the direction was lost and Blues never went that way.

---

3   Goy – a Yiddish word derived from 'goyim' meaning 'non Jewish'.

an odd boy

Most people took a ratchet to the tempo and played everything at either dance-tempo or breakneck speed. Cream had a way of playing a slow Blues interspersed with deliciously complex riffs on bass and lead. That *simultaneous fast-and-slow* made them unique – and almost made Savage Cabbage unique on their demise.

Jack Bruce looked older than I'd anticipated – but then, so was I. Most of my audio-visual attention was with Cream – but *some other sense* floated in a Doppler Effect as memory surged toward the present and fleetingly assimilated my reality. I wasn't daydreaming. I watched intently. It was something like a tactile hallucination. Savage Cabbage haunted the screen as a transparent emotional overlay. I watched Cream viscerally rather than visually – fleetingly searching their expressions and physical movements for signs of the lads. Ron and Steve would have appreciated the radio connections affixed to their guitar straps. I often got snared up – because I was a walker when I wasn't singing. Ron sometimes asked me—jokingly—why I didn't get my exercise like normal people. I'd always reply *"Ain't no normal person Ron—y'should know that by now—I'm a voodoo chile."* I think he used to ask that question just to hear me answer as I did.

The night I was born, Lord I swear the moon turned a fire red.
Jimi Hendrix—Voodoo Chile—Electric Ladyland—1968

We all regarded Ron as the leader of the band – so it came as something of a shock to me when Ron said *"That's how I see you – you're the leader of this band. Wouldn't have happened without you."*

He could see I was puzzled. *"It's not about musical accomplishment. There are plenty of good guitarists out there. I may have an edge ... but I may*—not—*be the best Blues guitarist in the world. Steve gets closer all the time. It's not about your having a voice or writing lyrics or anything.*

"*It's about how you—see—things. It's how you hold us all together*—you —*got the bloody vision of it all.*" Those words stuck with me. I think Ron was right to some degree – because I do have a pronounced sense of loyalty. I still keep the band together posthumously. I even have SAVAGE CABBAGE stencilled on my guitar cases. Cabbage-green paint on black cases is rather sumptuous.

I saw Savage Cabbage as a band of brothers. Could've been sisters – but female players were even thinner on the ground then than they are now. I saw it as important that a band stayed together and grew together. I grew up with the sense of Savage Cabbage as an ongoing venture. That's why it didn't matter that Jack wasn't the best drummer in Britain—or even the best drummer in town—but he was *our* drummer. We'd stand by each other. We were friends. We'd bring each other on. Ron certainly brought us all on.

However much like a *middle-aged Savage Cabbage* Cream might have looked – *the odd boy* wasn't on stage. I found myself, for the very merest fraction of a second, wondering where I was – but I knew exactly where I was. I was watching Cream on a large television screen in Park Slope.

Sitting in *Heights Coffee* I remembered my re-write of 'Born Under a Bad Sign'.

Unending pleasure's been my major trend / Grinnin' Blues ever since I was ten / Born under a glad sign – had this smile since I began to crawl, / If it wasn't for good luck – wouldn't've met with Blues at all.
Author's parody—Born Under a Glad Sign—1969

Ron Larkin roared with laughter "*You*—can't—*do*—that!"

I beamed back at him "*You just watch me.*"

The audience never noticed the changes – and after a while Ron got used to me changing lyrics.

an odd boy

"*Those old Blues players re-wrote songs all the time – so there's no reason why we shouldn't. Blues is a living tradition – which means—we—have to live it.*"

Ron laughed "*No arguing with that Frank—let's go for it then—you gotta sing it.*"

I opened my laptop and downloaded email. There was a letter from my son Robert with a piece of poetry he'd written in school.

Like a flicker – a fire that walks to piers on waves of wood: that moment, / Peace that walks to the sea – as the gong said happily: "Ha—Ha—Ha." / Gongs fall with thud, on ground with thud – as goldfish, with crash bang / Gong on goldfish—red hot ranger, bang ready to roll: deep blue sea on land. / Sea horse trembles, as red hot ranger crash lands to bits.
Robert E Lee Togden—age 10—A Poem of Unbelievable Nonsense—2007

He told me about his piano accomplishments – and guitar lessons. I told him if he could learn to play three songs – we'd get him an electric guitar as a yuletide gift. He's working at it. He wants a FENDER STRATOCASTER. Wouldn't be my choice – but it's what *he* wants.[4] He's a big Jimi Hendrix fan and I cannot fault him for that. He can play two Beatles songs 'Get Back' and 'Good Morning'. He's also started in on Bob Dylan's song 'Idiot Wind'. With his long hair he looks a little like the young John Lennon. I was happy to read Robert's letter – and to hear that Ræchel's big satin spider missed me. My daughter Raechel loves spiders. She's an *odd girl*.

---

4   Robert ended up opting for a vintage reproduction 1959 double cutaway Gibson Les Paul. Robert died of cancer in 2013 at the age of 17. There is a book dedidicated to his life entitled 'The Book of Robert'—Aro Books worldwide—2014. This book was written by his parents and friends and contains many photographs of Robert.

She'll have her first piano lesson and riding lesson this Spring.[5] My wife—Caroline—told me of the first-place rosette she'd won jumping at Liege Manor Equestrian Centre. She told me she was working out the notation for the backward guitar section in 'I'm Only Sleeping' so she could play it with me on violin at the next musical evening we'd organised. She told me that the 'cello maker was getting on well with her second 'cello. It's not a great 'cello. It's cheap—thick and heavily built—so she's experimenting: fitting five resophonic cones inside – on a truss rod that intersects with the sound post. She's also transforming it into a campanola.[6] I'm excited to hear it. I wonder what the Bach 'cello pieces might sound like with an instrument like that.

There was a letter from Michæl Smith in Montreal – a poet and painter I knew in the lost time. He was at Falmouth Art School – and we used to talk poetry late into the night. He'd sent me some of his poetry from that period.

Under fields of drought, / Cambered by the open skies, / they graze through the soot / And under crusted lintels scorched by the sun / These emerald leathers begin their scrawl / like fat enamels / Under old tables / The black flame of a forked tongue / Silently kissing the air: / Blood tongued to a dagger / Slithering oils over the dust.
Michæl Smith—Lizards—1975— Delta Literary Review 56 & 57—1976

'*These emerald leathers begin their scrawl / like fat enamels ...*'
What immense power of language.

---

5   Ræchel now has guitar lessons too and is the proud owner of a pink Telecaster.
6   Campanola – a 'cello with 12 sympathetic strings. Any modern 'cello can be converted into a campanola by simply inserting harpsichord pegs into the base of the neck, and warping the sympathetic strings over the body via a series of small bridges. The strings pass under the main 'cello bridge – through cut-outs in the base of the main bridge. The strings are then secured to button-pegs on either side of the retractable spike.

an odd boy

I've never ceased to be impressed by the way Michæl Smith could be spaciously compressed – and simultaneously as vivid as an etching – teeming with hints. His words seem impressed into the paper – impressed into ideation like sulphuric acid on copper. Someone needs to be reading that stuff aloud in a café somewhere, where people will sit in wonder at words that have such life.

It's always been evident to me, that one's life is *the work of Art* rather than fragmental objects scattered throughout the years. Until we die we can only exhibit or release 'The Work So Far'. That *work*—at any point in time—can be comprised of an assemblage of any number of previous points in time in any medium. Some projects take decades to complete. Sometimes aspects of *the work of Art* have to be put on the back burner for completion at some uncertain future point. Many threads weave in and out of a creative life – occasionally being brought into sharp focus by inspired accidents of time and place.

I'm now inspired—by Missn' Dixie[7]—to compose melodies for the songs *the odd boy* wrote from '68 to '72. Modern technology has made it possible to create at home what Steve and I only dreamed of finding in a recording studio back in 1970. I've no need to replicate Savage Cabbage. That would be impossible without the lads – although I'd still want Blues numbers. For my old Acid Rock numbers however, I'd have a wider variety of instruments: oboe, contrabassoon, resophonic 'cello-campanola, and Bazantar.[8]

---

7   Missn' Dixie – bass player with Terraplane Jane.
8   Bazantar – a five-string double bass, with four drone strings and twenty-nine sympathetic strings. It was invented by Mark Deutsch in San Francisco. The instrument has a range of over five octaves – and its sympathetic range covers four octaves.

born under a glad sign

I'll have friends on the aforementioned instruments and the odd boy on vocals and 12 string guitars: FENDER TELECASTER , GIBSON ES355, and NATIONAL RESOPHONICS. There'd be ladies in the new Savage Cabbage line-up on piano, bull fiddle, and vocals. Album names? *Bellicose Brassica; Surly Kale; Cathartic Chard; Caustic Collards; Rambunctious Rocket; Lettuce Prey*. Still bizarre after three decades ...

I look at my life as a continually varying shift of emphases within a multi-dimensional loom. The fabric weaves itself as the Art of *my* life. The threads of the loom go beyond my private recognition. They're the world and everything it contains. The work of Art that will have been *the odd boy*—after he's dead—will include everyone with whom he's ever spoken. I wouldn't exclude *anyone*. The quality of *all* my relationships is part of *the work of Art*. I recognise the importance of each moment – each connection. I may never speak with those who've inspired me – because they may remain inaccessible. I can't meet John Lennon or Jimi Hendrix because they're *works of Art* who have left the world. They left the world a better place – and I hope, in some small way, to do likewise. I can still hear them, see them, and read them – which means they're still alive. They'll never die as long as people remember them – and remain moved by them.

My wish—in writing *an odd boy*—is that people will feel enthused by the idea that *they* are Artists. Everyone *is* an artist. I say this, not in a slick or trite sense in which *everything is Art* no matter how appalling – but in the sense that effort and refusal to compromise *make* Artists of any of us. Everyone *can* be an Artist if *that* is their desire. As soon as a person follows their appreciative faculties – they put one foot on the road of Art. Further steps are taken when their appreciative faculties begin to make their own demands.

As the demands increase, creativity moves inexorably further – and could even become Art of *worldwide historical renown*. If the intensity of application and self criticality continue to deepen, heighten, and expand – anything is possible.

Everything I've ever done is connected to the senses and to the elements—earth, water, fire, air, and space—which give birth to the senses. They're the tactility, gustatory perception, fragrancing, sonic resonance, and vision of existence.

They're the theatre of sculpture, the theatre of cuisine, perfume, music, poetry, costumery, and the myriad visual and performing arts. They're the vibrancy of the world in which we live. They're the dynamism of *who we are* physically, intellectually, emotionally, and perceptually. This—in my language—is the definition of Vajrayana Buddhism. If you love phenomenal reality – then you love exploring how things come into being. Mathematics, cartography, astronomy, geology – all of the sciences could be Art as far as I am concerned. If you love history, it becomes Art. Then it becomes iconic. Levi Strauss 501 Serge de Nîmes trousers are iconic. I wear my Levis—always—with a British Army officer's Sam Browne belt. A Sam Browne is too wide to wear with Levi 501s – and so I have to remove the belt loops and re-stitch them to accommodate the belt. Someone once observed me carrying out this operation and enquired *"Why not buy a narrower belt?"*

"I like the Sam Browne" I explained.

He looked incredulous *"Why not buy different jeans?"*

"Well … because I like 501*s and … this leaves me no alternative but to remove and re-stitch the belt loops. It's an inconvenience – but … I tend to go out of my way for things I like."*

The gentleman looked confounded – and left me to my sewing.

The moral of this story—if such it can be called—is that *Art is its own meaning*. If you have appreciation – it makes its own demands. An Artist will accept those demands. Bowing to the dictates of ease and convenience are not an option for an Artist.

Living in the theatre of the senses, ideas and threads of connectivity make themselves apparent – *of themselves*. Whatever happens – simply happens. We move *with* what happens – and we're moved *by* what happens. The senses speak of each other in their own languages. We can wordlessly witness that—and in so doing—participate fully in life. In participating, ideas leap to the surface of awareness – and we take cues, *for no reason whatsoever* other than appreciation. We need have no idea of a final outcome –because the process is sufficient unto itself. The universe is self-creating.

'I know that in my own work the best things are the things that just happened ... images that were suddenly caught and that I hadn't anticipated ... I believe in an ordered chaos and in the rules of chance.'
Francis Bacon

Salvador Dali wrote—of his painting—that it was a
'... spontaneous method of irrational knowledge based on the critical and systematic objectification of delirious associations and interpretations.'

I sat looking at my computer screen. My *in box* looked like a juggling act at a Victorian circus where a fellow in evening tails and a top hat—called *professor something-or-other*—keeps a variety of unlikely objects in the air.

For the benefit of Mr. Kite – there will be a show tonight on trampoline, / The Hendersons will all be there – late of Pablo Fanque's Fair, what a scene. Lennon/McCartney—Beatles—Being for the Benefit of Mr Kite—Sgt. Pepper's Lonely Hearts Club Band—1967

an odd boy

There was a letter about my Raven paintings and the preparatory work for presenting them to galleries. The set of 84 slides of 'Speaking With Ravens' turned up after 30 years – in a dusty cracked plastic box that had been in my brother's attic since 1977.

The original paintings had been stored in a garage belonging to the parents of Simon Fenwick – a Fine Art student I once knew in Farnham. They'd agreed to house them for a while – but decided they wanted them moved whilst I was in India. I was in a three month solitary retreat at the time in a place called Triund – which is a four or five hour walk up into the mountains form where the road ends in McLeod Ganj, Himachal Pradesh. There was nothing there but a small stone hut and mountain goats that peered at me with ill-concealed suspicion. Simon sent me a letter asking me what I wanted doing with them – but by the time I returned to McLeod Ganj and had a chance to check the post, the letter was four months old. I replied immediately and apologised for the delay – but his parents had already taken the initiative. They'd taken the entire collection to the local council dump. As it was going to be six months before I came home, my brother Græham went to the dump for me in order to get them back – but by the time my letter got to him there was no trace of the paintings. I hoped people had taken them and were enjoying them. I was not too troubled by that at the time – as I had waved goodbye to my career as a painter, illustrator, and Art School Foundation lecturer. The slides in the box were in bad condition – so I restored them. I scanned them and repaired the damage caused by dust and mould, using PhotoShop. The images are new paintings in some respects – but seem to hold up well.

There was a letter from Willfree —Bluesman from Chicago— about playing harp on his album *Howlin' Wilf*.

The track in question is a Blues number I performed with him in Kila, Montana.

You're always walking around, with your nose in the air, / Wallowing in the spotlight of everybody's stare. / Everywhere you go, you just gotta make a Big-O scene, / Baby who died – and made you Queen?
Craig Donegan—Baby Who Died and Made You Queen?

Willfree is possibly one of the few who regret the passing of the 'sharp clothing Blues era'. Knowing of my penchant for clothing he enquired *"Would you consider designing a '50s style Bluesman costume this piece of po' white trash could wear?"*[9]

I pondered for all of ten seconds *"Green and blue shot silk taffeta evening tailsuit with mother-of-pearl buttons; dark blue collarless shirt; 1950s indigo flared top hat; and, cloven-hoof emerald-green lizard skin Western boots."*

He was a little taken aback but saw the logic behind my suggestion. *"Well ... JB Lenoir wore that fabulous zebra-striped tail coat didn't he?"*[10]

"Mmmm ... but I think I'd go for blue and purple rather than blue and green – and blue manta ray boots. I think we'll cause something of a stir in Whitefish ..."

Craig's fixing me up an old FENDER CUSTOMSHOP 12 string TELECASTER – black with a tortoise-shell pick-guard. I'm having it monogrammed: RON LARKIN XII.

---

9   'Poor white trash' – a term that originated during the 1820s post-revolutionary war reconstruction during which many poor people—white and black—competed for work. Harriet Beecher Stowe (in her book 'A Key to Uncle Tom's Cabin'—1854) entitled a chapter 'Poor White Trash'. She writes that '*slavery produces not only degraded, miserable slaves, but poor whites who are even more degraded and miserable*'.
10 JB Lenoir [1929 – 1967] – a Bluesman guitarist and singer-songwriter who recorded in the '50s and '60s.

an odd boy

I can see the expression on Ron's face on hearing the idea of a 12 string TELECASTER. He'd have said *"That's insane!"* But then he'd have plugged it in—liked it—grown to love it—and played riffs beyond the reach of imagination.

A series of three emails from Dixie betokened extensive finger exercises. I'd asked her if she had any insight into the bass line in Jack Bruce's Blues composition – 'Politician'. The main riff was no problem – but then Jack Bruce proceeds to jump all over the neck. *Back in the day* I'd not have dreamed of attempting this – but life's an adventure. Dixie has a fine assemblage of bass instruments including a French double bass – being a Missouri gal she calls it a bull fiddle. She tells me she just bought a five string FENDER PRECISION bass.

The next letter concerned historical research for my extended poetic narrative about the War Between the States. It follows the lives of two Southern Irregulars—brothers—and their accidental Spanish wives. The two Spanish girls are descended from the children of Basque guerrillas who fought the French in the Napoleonic Wars. They have sympathy for the defeated Southern Irregulars – having themselves been recently orphaned and usurped of their land. I need to take a river crossing lesson —with horse—in order to get the four heroic figures across the Rió Grande in realistic language. I'm awaiting trips to the high desert and the remaining US ghost towns in order to accumulate necessary experiences.[11]

---

11 The final work will appear as a book in English, Spanish, and Basque. A translator has commenced work in both languages.

And it was there the sisters saved what sense was left – a spavined legacy of reckless grace was all we had left: Escutcheon blemished saddlebags— tamped down conscript / Fed'ral coin—primed with collusion, slaked in line. They had run from conspiracy sanctioned debt; with nothing left save overnight wardrobe travel-dress finesse. Alejandrina and Adoracion— father and mother murdered by expedient hands—hogar y tierras pérdida a político / Abducción tormenta—falling fast—the rack conspiring to rein them in. Theirs' was nada, and nothing left to lose – But they were strong – knew their horses, all by name: Él Dorada, Rodrigo, Lucetta, Ignacio, Hernando, Querida – Gitana of the flowing mane – kicking demented dust whorls staining the air with glory, under rampant abriendo sun. Mayhap they'd ride North, begin again—forget the horror—spiked and meshed, fractious in vanity and greed / Drenching through eddies of the Rió Grande – rising out of moonlit turbulence into strange horrísonos blown. The Author—and so we rode down—canto 2—stanza 2—work in progress—2005

I threw some bizarre changes on the cantos set in Mexico by converting occasional Latinate words into Spanish. As always— with my poetry—it's the sound and shapes of the words rather than their direct literal meaning.

Then there's the on-going text: the introduction to my collected poetry 'Ravings of a Mild Mannered Maniac'. I describe conversations with Allen Ginsberg in New York, poetry readings with Nanao Sakaki, and correspondence with the various poets with whom I remain in contact.

I needed to answer an urgent letter from Don Young – President of NATIONAL RESOPHONIC GUITARS. I've had a pleasurable acquaintance and correspondence with Don Young since 2001— we talk about a wide variety of subjects including horses, Blues, Confederate hand guns, and *the lost time*—and today it was a question of the machine-heads on my old 12 String RESOLECTRIC.

an odd boy

The neck had been re-fretted and the action taken down: a general overhaul. My new 12 string RESOLECTRIC was also waiting for me. Don told me that he'd teach me how to '*field-strip my* RESOLECTRIC' so that I could '... *adjust the action on the road – under fire.*' That sounded a fine idea. I need to learn these things. We'd exchanged ideas on building a copper baritone 12 string National Quadracone with 18 sympathetic strings – a long term project.

I'd had an idea about a *jiwari-bridge effect-lever*[12] that Don thought was definitely worth a try – but my idea about fitting a tremolo arm to a 12 string TRICONE seemed doomed. Tremolo arms had been made for acoustic guitars in the 1940s but no one had ever tried it with a 12 string. One manufacturer said "*You'd have to be insane to try that.*" I thought – no ...you'd just have to be *an odd boy*. It's a highly skilled undertaking to make a jiwari bridge – so that will have to be accomplished before we start work on making such a bridge that can be raised and lowered to cause the buzzing effect typical of Indian instruments such as the sitar. Told Don about *Born Under a Glad Sign*.

Red wine and whiskey is what I chase / Red haired woman sitting on my face / Born under a glad sign – had this smile since I began to crawl, / If it wasn't for good luck – wouldn't've met with Blues at all.
Author's parody—Born Under a Glad Sign—1969

Thought it might amuse him. It did. The lyrics were just '*itchin' f 'the switchin'* – like Colin Tozer's '*Born under a Road Sign*'.

Colin Tozer is one of the original English Bluesmen from the Wandle Delta – London.

---

12 Jiwari bridge – made of bone with a cunningly chamfered shelf on which the strings vibrate. Due to the larger oscillations of the heavy gauge strings and the shallower oscillation of the lighter gauge strings the jiwari bridge is more steeply chamfered toward the bass strings.

born under a glad sign

Never knew him back in the day – but hey, it's never too late to meet an old friend for the first time.

I've made several visits to the NATIONAL RESOPHONIC factory in San Louis Obispo – and find it to be a wonderful situation. It's called a factory – but it's not a factory as anyone would normally think of such places. It feels more like Art School. It's housed in a modern warehouse on a small industrial estate – but the *feeling* is there. The folks who work there seem more like art students than employees – and the cordial atmosphere is refreshing and inspiring. Everyone's utterly committed to the guitars they make. The quality of the craftsmanship leaves me wide-eyed and gleeful. They're proud of their work – and with every reason. Maybe *the lost time* is not lost. It exists at NATIONAL RESOPHONIC GUITARS – so maybe it exists elsewhere. Maybe I just have to look further and more closely. Maybe I'll find it hidden in unlikely places everywhere – such as my shoulder bag. Yes—I still carry a shoulder bag—but I designed it. It's made of 200 year old reindeer hide dredged up from Die Frau Metta Catharina von Flensburge which sank off the coast of Cornwall in 1886.[13] It has a compartment for my harp and a central section my poetry notebook. The latest entry was something I'd heard in passing about someone who was '… *in love with the shadow of a dress.*'

---

13 The Danish brigantine, Die Frau Metta Catharina von Flensburge, set sail from Plymouth Harbour, on the 10th of December 1786, and survived ten days of storms. An error of judgment rounding Drake's Island drove her onto the lee shore. The crew escaped with their lives but the cargo of Russian reindeer hides was lost. The ship was discovered in 1973 with the reindeer hides perfectly preserved in estuarial mud. The hides were found baled. They retain the aroma of willow and birch oil from the traditional Russian tanning. See Athene English's website: www.greatenglish.co.uk. The hides became the property of Prince Charles – the Duke of Cornwall. Prince Charles had the hides treated and distributed amongst small-time leather workers in Britain.

Yes ... I knew *that* experience. It was Alice's dress – but that dress was also worn by Anelie, Lindie, Helen, Juliet, Claudette, Rebecca, Penelope, Meryl ... Yes ... I'd been there – but I was the one on that next train leaving town. There'd been many meetings and partings – shadows of many dresses. Each dress was a garment of poetry. There'd been other names—other garments—and other mysteries. They were all intensely real – and yet, far away as Jupiter's sulphur mines.

Well my arrows are made of desire, From far away as Jupiter's sulphur mines. Jimi Hendrix—Voodoo Chile—Electric Ladyland—1968

Intensely real yet far away. I gazed through the window of the magical mystery tour bus on which I've travelled so far in memory. I could have had so many different lives ... I still miss the ladies with whom those names are associated, as far back as Alice – but there's no regret in that missing. Maybe 'missing' is not the right word. Maybe it's a *weird and wonderful wistfulness* which appreciates the poetry of their personalities – the magical efflorescence of the Art they represented in my life. I could still write a song about each lady. I'd only have to dwell on the images that would still arise from contemplating their existences – as they were when I knew them. We're all mortal – but Art is immortal and we're all immortal in the moment of Art.

When was that summer when the skies were blue? / The bright red cardinal flew down from its tree? You tell me. Were we there? Is it true? Was I really there with you? / Let's see – you tell me.
Paul McCartney—You Tell Me—Memory Almost Full—2007

When was that summer when the skies were blue?

It was 1957 – the year this memoir commenced. A cardinal butterfly—a large fritillary—flew down from its sky. Alice and I watched it flittering above our heads as we sat in our golden childhood meadow.

Were we there? Yes.

Is it true? Yes.

Was I really there with you? Yes. I really—*was*—there with you – or with someone in my mind who glows like a siren in a kaleidoscope: images gyrate like the swirling of a dress sewn in helical panels.

Let's see – you tell me. What—*would*—you tell me? Maybe you'd tell me *'I'm here – but I'm someone else now. Now, I'm simply a sense of presence in your imagination.'*

Whenever I look back, I'm also someone else. I'm someone who's lived by never looking back – not in terms of regret at least. I've lived predominantly within *the shine on the passing moment*. The passing moment manifests in a gallery of images whose meaning fluctuates as the present interacts with the past. I could have had so many different lives. If I could programme *the computer of reality* with alternative data – I could have metamorphosed in many different ways according to the many other Artists with whom I have shared time. There could be a version of *the odd boy* who took holidays in Herefordshire with Alice. A version who decided to give up every art-form other than oil-painting and who lived in Scotland with Helen.
A version who went to America and lived in Charleston with Julia. Would any of these versions be writing this book; or would they be reading it – written by someone else?

Reminiscence evokes a subtle sense of wistfulness and aloneness – but, although we each go our own way, we need never feel alone – if we've become Art, through the *Art of life*. The work of Art each person can become—through their lives—can be a wonderful woven world of interconnection that touches every other life.

an odd boy

Sitting there—bagel eaten—espresso dwindling; I gazed at the colour of the room. It was a queer mixture of Victoriana and odd forays into the '40s. I'd left my hat on—the high and wide Montana Pinch—there being no obvious place to set it down. Beside which, it was not exactly warm. I was wearing a collarless shirt and six pocket waistcoat – almost my Savage Cabbage stage appearance. Some pounds heavier—double Albert watch-chain draped to advantage—but the same deal. Penknife on the right —1950s—pitted but smooth from rust removal. Picked it up at the San Francisco gun show for two dollars fifty. Pocket watch on the left – 1890's HAMILTON US Railroad timepiece with large Arabic numerals. That didn't come as cheap.

I peered through espresso machine steam at the falling snow. It was that metropolitan mirage of Iceland again. Steam and snow were a swirling descant behind the hum of voices.

The room was humming harder, as the ceiling flew away, / When we called out for another drink, the waiter brought a tray.
Brooker/Reid/Fisher—Procol Harum—Whiter Shade of Pale—1967

There was no waiter – but, suddenly, the door of the gentleman's facilities swung wide. Out stepped a wiry Black gentleman. Could've been Slim Harpo. He swung round as he caught sight of me. Looked at me square on.

"*D'you riiiiiide?*"

Yes, I rode. Scene from a movie? Highway 61? Juke joint somewhere in Mississippi? No, still in Brooklyn.

"*D'ya—have—a horse?*"

Yes, I had a horse.

He eyed me carefully "*Where you—got—that horse-a-yours?*"

I smiled broadly *"Montana—Promised Land—good riding country. I ride in Wales too."*

"Wales?" he queried.

"Yes" I replied. *"Like Josey—Josey Wales."* He nodded – not sure if he'd understood I continued *"Wales—you know—West of England, East of Ireland. Green valleys. Sheep everywhere you look."*

He smiled *"Yeah ... right ... Wales—like Josey Wales—Wales, England ... Seen that movie twice—Outlaw Josey Wales—good movie. Liked that movie. John Hammond played on that."*

I was considering squaring up to him—same way he'd squared up to me—and asking *'You pack iron?'* but whilst the idea was still twinkling, he said *"I'm from the Federation of Black Cowboys"* and shook me warmly by the hand. *"What you call that—horse-a-yours —in—Montana?"* Told him Quantrelle—quarter horse—sorrel. *"Good name—good name"* he nodded. *"Gotta quarter horse too—name of 'Big Bill' – like Big Bill Broonzy. We got 40 acres – you come out and riiiiide sometime—here's my card. Like yo' hat. Maxwell Jefferson's the name."* He had a wide—wide—wide—grin.

"Much obliged. I'm Doc—Doc Togden. Pleasure to meet you. Always been a—big—fan of Big Bill Broonzy."

He laughed *"Knew you'd be! Just—knew—you'd be! And hey—— fiiiiine——moustache you got there. Y'know ... I tried – but I can't grow—nothing—like that."* Maxwell stroked his chin somewhat regretfully.

"Lord giveth ..." I responded – removing my hat to display the balding pate it concealed *"... Lord taketh away."* He laughed and slapped his leg. We were having big fun.

"You play harp?" I enquired.

He shook his head. *"You?"*

"Got my **G** *harp right there in my bag."*

"I play bass" he said.

Told him I used to play rhythm bass *"But I was mainly a vocalist."*

"Bet you were! Just—bet—you were! You still sing?" Yeah. Still sang. Still blew harp.

"What bass did you play?" Told him GIBSON EB3.

He chuckled *"Jack Bruce—right?"* Right. *"That's what he used to play in Cream."*

"Yeah …"

Asked Maxwell what he played.

*"*HAMER. HAMER 12 *string bass."* He noticed my eyes widen. *"Yeah man—helluva thing—*helluva thing. *Triple strings. Plays just like a 4 – but got 2 octave strings by each."*

Now that sounded serious, I was going to have to mention this to Don Young at NATIONAL to see if he could build a RESOLECTRIC model. *"Can see myself having to investigate that. That'd give an interesting edge to the bass line on Hoochie Coochie Man …"*

Maxwell laughed *"You like Willie Dixon?"*

"Just about my favourite song writer."

Maxwell laughed. *"Ain't it the truth. You're a brother!"* Maybe my bass days weren't over after all. Maxwell looked mischievous for a twinkling of an eye.

"On the seventh hour …" he suddenly sang quietly.

"On the seventh day" I followed softly, glad he'd chosen to sing in my key.

"*On the seventh month*" he sang back louder – stabbing his finger pointedly at my satchel. I took his meaning and pulled my harp out. Maxwell was on the ball – he'd pitched his voice for my **G** harp.

"*The seven doctors say*" I added after wailing on harp—heads turning in our direction—slight consternation from some.

"*He was born for good luck*" he came in impeccably. "*And that you'll see.*" Now we had the whole café looking. Concern turning into smiles as the harp wailed.

"*I got seven hundred*—million—*dollars*" I hollered.

"*Don't you*—mess—*with*—*me!*" he sang—laughing—wagging a mock-cautionary finger at me—and shaking his head with mirth at my change to the lyrics.

Then we both sang together. '*But you know I'm———here, / Everybody knows I'm———here / Well I'm the hoochie coochie man / Everybody knows I am.*'

There was a round of applause and we both chuckled. He sat down on the spare chair—as if it were a horse—leaning his arms on the back.

"*Y'know … that* 12 *string bass of yours …*" I ventured "*…you could*—accompany—*yourself singing on a thing like that.*"

"*Sure could. Sure do. They make fives and sixes too – fifteen'n'eighteen string basses – but my hands ain't big enough.*" I'd talked about an eight string bass along these lines when I was 17 and the consensus of opinion was that I was insane—'*Who'd ever want to play a thing like that?*' And now there was an eighteen string bass. Amazing! Maybe I'm not insane after all …

an odd boy

Maxwell asked, so I told him about Savage Cabbage. Maxwell laughed. "*Liiiiike that name! Savage Cabbage—real funny too—you know that Bessie Smith line? 'When he cooked my cabbage he made it awful hot / and when he put in the bacon, it overflowed the pot.'* "[14]

No—*incredible*—I'd somehow *missed* that Bessie Smith line. It turned out I'd only ever heard *Empty Bed Blues Part* 1 – but there was *Empty Bed Blues Part* 2, because the song was too long to fit on one side of a 78 record. Somehow Part 2 never made it onto the Paul Oliver's 'Blues Women' collection album. *Savage Cabbage* suddenly had Blues implications of which I'd previously been unaware. What a fine name I'd picked! What a name if Savage Cabbage had ever played at the Bush Hotel. What a piece of news for the lads ...

Sure enough, Maxwell wasn't totin' no silver hammer – he had himself a metal-flake silver Hamer. He was a Bluesman and we had a whole bunch in common. Once we'd said our goodbyes and shaken hands again – I sat there grinning.

It took a while for the meaning of the situation to make itself clear – but when it had, I realised that I was back in *the lost time* again. This was *just* what happened then. People would approach you and talk – because you *looked* right. Ideas would flow – just as they did with Don Young. I'd been recognised as a comrade in arms. We weren't hippies or flower children – we were simply *lost time travellers.* We were saddle tramps on the road to glory, in the lost time that is *always there* – when the senses meet the fields of the senses.

If it wasn't for good luck—if it wasn't for real good luck—wouldn't've met with Blues at all. Author's parody—Born Under a Glad Sign—1969

---

14 Bessie Smith—Empty Bed Blues, Part 2—1928

I'd first taken a peek at *the lost time* [15] with Mr Love when I was eight. It looked like Big Bill Bronzy. Now it looked like Maxwell Jefferson—*majoring in everything*—of the Federation of Black Cowboys. These Black guys were somehow *always* in on *the real deal*: Robert Johnson, Bessie Smith, Pharaoh Sanders, Maxwell Jefferson, and everyone who ever made a Resophonic guitar, played Blues, created Art – or rode a horse.

Welcome home.

---

15 Another phase of *the lost time* is recorded in 'wisdom eccentrics' a book by Ngakpa Chögyam—aka Doc Togden—which gives an account of his years in India and Nepal. Wisdom Eccentrics—Ngakpa Chögyam—Aro Books inc— 2011

www.ingramcontent.com/pod-product-compliance
Lightning Source LLC
Chambersburg PA
CBHW021752230426
43669CB00006B/54